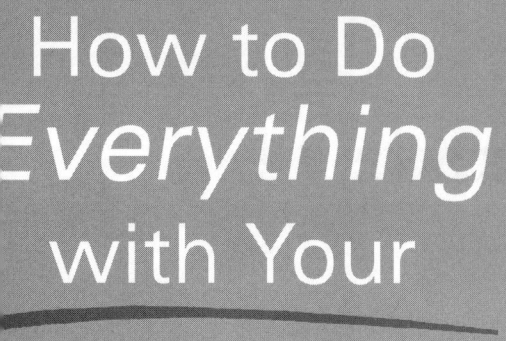

Guy Hart-Davis

McGraw-Hill/Osborne

New York Chicago San Francisco
Lisbon London Madrid Mexico City
Milan New Delhi San Juan
Seoul Singapore Sydney Toronto

The **McGraw·Hill** Companies

McGraw-Hill/Osborne

2100 Powell Street, 10th Floor
Emeryville, California 94608
U.S.A.

To arrange bulk purchase discounts for sales promotions, premiums, or fund-raisers, please contact **McGraw-Hill**/Osborne at the above address. For information on translations or book distributors outside the U.S.A., please see the International Contact Information page immediately following the index of this book.

How To Do Everything with Your iPod™

Copyright © 2003 by The McGraw-Hill Companies. All rights reserved. Printed in the United States of America. Except as permitted under the Copyright Act of 1976, no part of this publication may be reproduced or distributed in any form or by any means, or stored in a database or retrieval system, without the prior written permission of publisher, with the exception that the program listings may be entered, stored, and executed in a computer system, but they may not be reproduced for publication.

234567890 FGR FGR 019876543

ISBN 0-07-222700-1

Publisher:	Brandon A. Nordin
Vice President	
& Associate Publisher:	Scott Rogers
Acquisitions Editor:	Megg Morin
Project Editor:	Julie M. Smith
Acquisitions Coordinator:	Tana Allen
Technical Editor:	Clint Roberts
Copy Editor:	Linda Marousek
Proofreader:	Mike McGee
Indexer:	Valerie Perry
Computer Designers:	George Toma Charbak, Tara A. Davis
Illustrators:	Melinda Moore Lytle, Michael Mueller, Lyssa Wald
Series Design:	Mickey Galicia
Cover Series Design:	Dodie Shoemaker

iPod™ is a trademark of Apple Computer, Inc., registered in the U.S. and other countries.
iPod photo courtesy of Apple Computer, Inc. and Hunter Freeman Photography 2002.

This book was composed with Corel VENTURA™ Publisher.

Information has been obtained by **McGraw-Hill**/Osborne from sources believed to be reliable. However, because of the possibility of human or mechanical error by our sources, **McGraw-Hill**/Osborne, or others, **McGraw-Hill**/Osborne does not guarantee the accuracy, adequacy, or completeness of any information and is not responsible for any errors or omissions or the results obtained from the use of such information.

Dedication

This book is dedicated to the people who gave us MP3 and the iPod.

About the Author

Guy Hart-Davis has written more than 20 critically acclaimed computer books, including Windows XP Professional: The Complete Reference and The XP Files from Osborne, and has contributed to more than a dozen books by other authors. He specializes in MP3, Windows XP (both Professional and Home Edition), Microsoft Office, and Visual Basic for Applications. Guy doubts iPods will ever have enough space to store all the music and data he wants to carry with him, but he will be delighted if Apple proves him wrong.

Contents

	Acknowledgments	xvii
	Introduction	xix
PART I	**Enjoying Audio on Your iPod**	
CHAPTER 1	**Get Up and Running with Your iPod**	**3**
	What Is an iPod?	4
	What Your iPod *Doesn't* Do	5
	You Can't Enter Information Directly on Your iPod	5
	The iPod Isn't the Smallest or Most Skip-Proof Player in Town	5
	Your iPod Supports Only MP3, WAV, and AIFF Audio Formats	6
	Choose the iPod That's Best for You	6
	Understand the Different Models of iPod	8
	What's in the Box?	10
	Set Up Your iPod	11
	Connect Your iPod to Your Computer	12
	Install the iPod Software	13
	Load Your iPod with Music	14
	Load Your iPod on the Mac	14
	Load Your iPod on Windows	14
	Connect Your Headphones or Speakers	15
	Use Your iPod's Controls	16
	Read Your iPod's Display	17
	Use Your iPod's Controls	17
	Browse and Access Your Music	19
	Play Songs	20
	Use the Hold Switch	22
	Attach and Use the Remote Control for Easy Operation . . .	23
	Recharge Your iPod to Keep the Songs Coming	23

		Navigate the Extras Menu	24
		Choose Settings for Your iPod	25
		Check the "About" Information for Your iPod	29
		Set the Backlight Timer	29
CHAPTER 2		**Get Up to Speed with MP3 and Digital Audio**	**31**
		Why Do You Need to Compress the Music?	33
		What Determines Audio Quality?	35
		What Does CD-Quality Audio Mean?	36
		What Is MP3 and Why Should You Use It?	37
		How MP3 Works (The Short Version)	37
		MP3 Patent and Royalty Rates	38
		Understand Other Digital Audio Formats	38
		Understand Ripping, Encoding, and "Copying"	39
		Learn about CDDB and Other Sources of CD Information	41
		Choose an Appropriate Compression Rate	42
		Choose Between Constant Bitrate and Variable Bitrate	43
		Choose Between Normal Stereo and Joint Stereo	43
		Test the Sound Given by Different Bitrates to Find Which Is Best	45
		Load Uncompressed Files on Your iPod for Unbeatable Sound Quality	45
		Copyright Law for Digital Audiophiles	46
		What Copyright Is	46
		When You Can Legally Copy Copyrighted Material, and Why	47
		Burning CDs of Copyrighted Works for Others Is Illegal	48
		Sharing MP3 Files of Copyrighted Material Is Illegal	48
		Circumventing Copy-Protection May Be Illegal	49
		Understand Current Copy-Protection Techniques on the CDs You Buy	50
		Brief and Unapologetic Flashback on the Wonders of the Audio CD	50
		How CD-Protection Solutions Work (in Brief)	52
		If You Can't Play It on Any CD Player, It's Not a CD	52
		How to Recognize Copy-Protected Discs	53
		What Happens When You Try to Use a Copy-Protected Disc on a Computer	53
		Ways to Get Around Copy Protection	55
CHAPTER 3		**Use iTunes to Load Music onto Your Mac iPod**	**57**
		Get Your Mac Ready to Work with Your iPod	59
		Add FireWire if Necessary	59
		Check Your Operating System Version	59

Check Disk Space and Memory	59
Add a CD-R Drive if Necessary	60
Set Up and Configure iTunes on Your Mac	60
Choose Where to Store Your Music Library	62
Choose Whether to Store All Song Files in Your Music Library	63
Choose Whether iTunes Automatically Connects to the Internet	64
Change the Importing Settings in iTunes to Specify Audio Quality	64
Change the Columns Displayed to Show the Information You Need	70
Create, Build, and Manage Your iTunes Music Library	71
Rip and Encode Your CDs	71
Join Tracks Together Without Gaps	74
Add Songs to iTunes to Expand Your Music Library	76
Delete Songs from Your Music Library	76
Consolidate Your Music Library so You Can Always Access All Its Songs	77
Tag Your Songs so iTunes Sorts Them Correctly	78
Apply Ratings to Songs to Tell iTunes Which Music You Like	79
Enjoy Music with iTunes	80
Browse Quickly by Using the Browser Panes	81
Play Back Music with iTunes	81
Use the Graphical Equalizer to Make the Music Sound Great	83
Skip the Boring Intro or Outro on a Song	88
Synchronize Your Music Library with Your iPod	88
Control Synchronization to Get the Music You Want on Your iPod	90
Control Synchronization Manually	91
Return to Automatic Updating from Manual Updating	93
Listen to Audible.com Spoken-Word Files on Your iPod	94
Create Custom Playlists to Enjoy in iTunes or on Your iPod	95
Automatically Create Smart Playlists Based on Your Ratings and Preferences	96

CHAPTER 4 **Use MUSICMATCH Jukebox Plus to Load Music onto Your Windows iPod** **99**

Get Your PC Ready to Work with Your iPod	100
Add a FireWire Card if Necessary	100
Check Your Operating System Version	101

Check Memory and Disk Space	101
Add a CD-R Drive if Necessary	102
Install MUSICMATCH Jukebox Plus on Your PC	102
Configure MUSICMATCH Jukebox Plus for Maximum Effectiveness	106
Choose General Settings to Control MUSICMATCH Jukebox Plus	107
Choose Settings to Create High-Quality MP3 Files	109
Choose Where to Store Your Music Library and How to Name Its Files	112
Choose End-of-Recording Notifications	114
Choose Other Recording Options	114
Use Fades and Offsets to Tweak the Start and End of Tracks	115
Choose CD Lookup Options	115
Configure Your Music Library	118
Keep Your Copy of MUSICMATCH Jukebox Plus Up-to-Date	118
Create, Build, and Manage Your Music Library	118
Rip and Encode Your CDs	119
Add Tracks to Your Music Library	121
Delete Songs from Your Music Library	125
Tag and Super-Tag Your Song Files so They Sort Correctly	126
Use Volume Leveling to Avoid Getting Your Ears Blasted	128
Enjoy Music with MUSICMATCH Jukebox Plus	129
Play Back Music	129
Use the Graphical Equalizer to Improve the Sound	131
Use MUSICMATCH Jukebox Plus as an Alarm	131
Synchronize Your Music Library with Your iPod	132
Connect and Disconnect Your iPod	132
First Connection: Configure Device Setup Options	133
Subsequent Connections	135
Change Synchronization Options for Your iPod	135
Choose Audio Options for Your iPod	136
Add Tracks to Your iPod Manually	137
Choose iPod Options and Rename Your iPod	138
Unmount Your iPod	139
Create Custom Playlists to Enjoy in MUSICMATCH Jukebox Plus or on Your iPod	139
Create a Playlist Manually	139
Use the AutoDJ Feature to Create a Playlist	140

CHAPTER 5	**Create, Edit, and Tag Your MP3 Files**	**141**
	Convert Other File Types to MP3, AIFF, or WAV so You	
	Can Play Them on Your iPod	142
	Windows: GoldWave	143
	Mac: SoundApp	143
	Create MP3 Files from Cassettes or Vinyl Records	144
	Connect the Audio Source to Your Computer	145
	Record on Windows with MUSICMATCH	
	Jukebox Plus	145
	Record Audio on the Mac	147
	Mac: Record Audio with iMovie	148
	Mac: Two Other Options for Recording Audio	150
	Remove Scratches and Hiss from Audio Files	150
	Windows: GoldWave	151
	Mac: Amadeus II	151
	Trim MP3 Files to Get Rid of Intros and Outros You	
	Don't Like	152
	Windows: MP3 TrackMaker	153
	Mac: mEdit	154
	Tag Your MP3 Files with the Correct Information for Sorting ...	154
	Windows: Tag&Rename	155
	Mac: MP3 Rage	155
	Save Audio Streams to Disk so You Can Listen to Them Later ...	157
	Windows: FreeAmp (If You Can Get It)	158
	Windows: TotalRecorder	159
	Mac: StreamRipperX	160
CHAPTER 6	**Download Audio Files from the Internet**	**161**
	Quick Reality Check on the Music Market	162
	What Most Consumers Want	163
	What the Music Industry Wants	163
	What's Happening Between Consumers and the	
	Music Industry	164
	Understand the Darknet and the Light	165
	What Is the Darknet?	166
	How the Darknet Works	166
	How P2P Networks Enlarged the Darknet	166
	Darknet Users: Super-Peers and Free Riders	168
	Efforts to Close Down the Darknet	169
	Dangers of Using the Darknet	170
	Current P2P Networks	172
	Download Music Files from Web Sites	173
	MP3.com	173

	Listen.com	173
	press*play*	174
	Lycos Music	174
	IUMA	174
	Find Music Files in Newsgroups	175
	Share Your Own Music on the Internet	175
CHAPTER 7	**Burn Audio and MP3 CDs with iTunes and MUSICMATCH Jukebox Plus**	**177**
	Understand the Basics of CD Burning	178
	Recordable CDs and Rewritable CDs	178
	Audio CDs, MP3 CDs, and Data CDs	179
	Burn CDs with iTunes	179
	Choose Burning Options	179
	Burn a CD	181
	Burn CDs with MUSICMATCH Jukebox Plus	182
	Choose Burning Settings for MUSICMATCH Burner Plus	182
	Burning a CD	188
	Splitting a Burn List into Two or More CDs	190
	Troubleshoot the Problems You Encounter When Burning CDs	190
	General: Avoid Causing Your Burner Problems	191
	Troubleshoot Burning CDs with iTunes	192
	Troubleshoot Burning CDs with MUSICMATCH Jukebox Plus	195
PART II	**Use Your iPod for Contacts, Calendar, and Other Text**	
CHAPTER 8	**Use Your iPod to Take Your Contacts with You**	**201**
	Understand the Wonders of vCards	203
	A Brief History of vCard	203
	For the Curious Only: A Quick Look Inside a vCard	204
	How Your iPod Handles vCards	205
	Create vCards from Your Contacts	207
	Create vCards on the Mac	207
	Create vCards from Windows	209
	Put Contacts on Your Mac iPod	212
	Use iSync to Put Contacts on Your Mac iPod Automatically	212
	Put Contacts on Your Mac iPod Manually	218
	Put Contacts on Your Windows iPod	220
	View Your Contacts on Your iPod	221

Contents

CHAPTER 9	**Put Your Calendars on Your iPod**	**223**
	What vCalendar and iCalendar Do and What They're For	224
	Where vCalendar and iCalendar Came From	225
	What's Inside a vCalendar/iCalendar File?	225
	Create iCalendar and vCalendar Files from Your Calendars	227
	Create iCalendar Files and vCalendar Files on the Mac	228
	Create vCalendar Files on Windows	230
	Put Your Calendars on Your Mac iPod	231
	Use iSync to Put Your Calendars on Your iPod Automatically from Mac OS X	234
	Put Your Calendars on Your Mac iPod Manually	234
	Put Your Calendars on Your Windows iPod	235
	View Your Calendar on Your iPod	236
CHAPTER 10	**Put Other Information on Your iPod**	**239**
	Limitations to Putting Information on Your iPod	240
	What Text Can You Put on Your iPod?	241
	Mac Utilities for Putting Information on Your iPod	242
	iSpeakIt (Mac OS X)	242
	iPod It (Mac OS X)	242
	PodNews (Mac OS X)	244
	Pod2Go (Mac OS X)	245
	iTeXpod (System 9 and Classic)	245
	Text2iPodX (Mac OS X)	247
	iPodMemo (Mac OS X and System 9)	247
	PodWriter (Mac OS X)	247
	A Windows Utility for Putting (Some) Text on Your iPod	249
	EphPod	249
PART III	**iPod Care, Advanced Topics, and Troubleshooting**	
CHAPTER 11	**Keep Your iPod in Good Working Shape**	**253**
	What You Might Want to Know about Your iPod's Internals	254
	Maximize Your iPod's Battery Life	256
	Don't Let the Battery Discharge Fully	256
	Reduce Demands on the Battery	256
	Understand What Makes Your iPod Unhappy	257
	Disconnecting Your iPod at the Wrong Time	257
	Your iPod Doesn't Like Fire or Water	258
	Your iPod Isn't Indestructible	259
	Keep Your iPod's Operating System Up-to-Date	259
	Update Your Mac iPod	259
	Update Your Windows iPod	263

CHAPTER 12 Use Your iPod as a Hard Drive

Carry and Store Your iPod Safely	266
Clean Your iPod	266
Use Your iPod as a Hard Drive	**267**
Why Use Your iPod as a Hard Drive?	268
Enable FireWire Disk Mode	270
Enable FireWire Disk Mode on the Mac	270
Enable FireWire Disk Mode on the PC	272
Transfer Files to and from Your iPod	273
Start Up Your Mac from Your iPod	274
Install Mac OS X (or System 9) Directly on Your iPod	274
Clone an Existing Operating System onto Your iPod	276
Designate Your iPod as the Startup Disk	277
Back Up Your iPod so You Don't Lose Your Music or Data	279
Optimize Your iPod's Hard Disk to Improve Performance	280
Run the Windows XP Disk Defragmenter	281
Defragment Your Mac iPod (or Windows iPod) the Cheap and Easy Way	283

CHAPTER 13 Enhance Your iPod with Accessories

Enhance Your iPod with Accessories	**285**
Cases	286
Stands, Docks, and Mounting Kits	289
Power Adapters	290
Basic AC Power Adapters	290
Powered FireWire Adapters for Unpowered FireWire Ports	290
Power-Only FireWire Cable for Playing While Charging from a Computer	291
Car Adapters	291
World Travel Adapters	292
Headphones and Enhancers	293
Zip Cord Retractable Earbuds	294
iShare Earbud Splitter	294
Koss eq50 Three-Band Equalizer	294
Weird Stuff	294
Burton Amp Jacket	295
Groove Bag	295
Connect Your iPod to Your Stereo	295
Connect Your iPod to Your Car Stereo	296

CHAPTER 14 Learn Advanced iPod Skills

Learn Advanced iPod Skills	**299**
Convert Your iPod from Mac to Windows—and Back	300
Convert Your Windows iPod to Work with the Mac	301
Convert Your Mac iPod to Work with Windows	301

	Change the Computer to Which Your iPod Is Linked	301
	Change Your Mac iPod's Home Mac	302
	Change Your Windows iPod's Home PC	303
	Synchronize Several iPods with the Same Computer	304
	Load Your iPod from Two or More Computers at Once	306
	Load Your Mac iPod from Two or More Macs	306
	Load Your Windows iPod from Two or More PCs	307
	Transfer Music Files from Your iPod's Music Library to Your Computer	309
	Where—and How—Your iPod Stores Song Files	310
	Transfer Song Files from Your iPod Using the Finder or Windows Explorer	314
	Utilities for Transferring Song Files from Your iPod to Your Computer	315
	Play Songs from Your iPod Through Your Computer	321
CHAPTER 15	**Troubleshoot Any iPod Problems You Encounter**	**323**
	Your Warranty and How to Void It	324
	How to Approach Troubleshooting Your iPod	326
	Learn Troubleshooting Maneuvers	327
	Reset Your iPod	327
	Drain Your iPod's Battery	327
	Restore Your iPod	327
	Run a Disk Scan	333
	Use Your iPod's Diagnostics to Pinpoint Problems	334
	Troubleshoot Specific Problems	336
	Your iPod Won't Respond to Keypresses	336
	Your Remote Control Stops Working	337
	Your Mac or PC Doesn't React When You Plug in Your iPod	338
	Your iPod Says "Do Not Disconnect" Forever When Connected to the Computer	339
	Your iPod Displays a Disk Icon with Magnifying Glass, Arrow, Check Mark, X, or Exclamation Point	340
	Songs in Your Music Library Aren't Transferred to Your iPod	340
	Mac OS X Displays the SBOD and then Fails to Recognize Your iPod	340
	"iTunes Has Detected a Software Update" Message	341
	MUSICMATCH Jukebox Plus Doesn't Recognize Your iPod	341
	"The iPod '*iPod*' Is Linked to Another iTunes Music Library"	342

xiv How to Do Everything with Your iPod

	Letting iTunes Copy All Song Files to Your Music Library Causes You to Run Out of Hard-Disk Space	343
	"Missing theme.ini" Error Message When You First Launch MUSICMATCH Jukebox Plus	345
	"Install Error: Reinstall iPod Plug-In"	346
	MUSICMATCH Portables Plus Synchronizations Are Painfully Slow	348
PART IV	**New iPods, iTunes 4, and the iTunes Music Store**	
CHAPTER 16	**Use the New iPods**	**351**
	Understand How the New iPods Differ from the Earlier iPods	352
	Capacities	353
	Look, Feel, and Heft	353
	Accessories	354
	Software Improvements	354
	Decide Which iPod to Buy	355
	Set Up Your New iPod	356
	Play Music Through the Dock	358
	Use the iPod's Alarm Clock to Wake You Up	358
	Display the Time in the Title Bar	359
	Customize the Main Menu for Quick Access to Items	359
	Queue a List of Songs on Your iPod	360
	Rate Songs on Your iPod	360
	Read Notes on Your iPod	361
	Use iPod Scripts to Create and Manage Text Notes	361
	Put the Script Menu on the Menu Bar	363
CHAPTER 17	**Use iTunes 4**	**365**
	Summary of Changes in iTunes 4	366
	Understand Advanced Audio Coding (AAC)	367
	MPEG-2 AAC and MPEG-4 AAC	367
	AAC's 48 Channels	368
	AAC Licensing	368
	Advantages of AAC	368
	Disadvantages of AAC	369
	Update Your Earlier iPod to iPod Software 1.3	370
	Upgrade from iTunes 3 to iTunes 4	370
	Configure iTunes 4 to Suit Your Needs	372
	Choose Custom MP3 Encoding Settings	372
	Choose Custom AAC Encoding Settings	373
	Use the New CD- and DVD-Burning Features	374

	Share Your Music with Other Users	375
	Access and Play Another Person's Shared Music	377
	Set Your Computer to Look for Shared Music	377
	Access Shared Music on the Same TCP/IP Subnet	377
	Access Shared Music on a Different TCP/IP Subnet	378
	Disconnect a Shared Music Library	379
	Convert a Song from AAC to MP3 (or Vice Versa)	379
	Add Artwork to Songs	380
CHAPTER 18	**Use the iTunes Music Store**	**385**
	Understand What the iTunes Music Store Is	386
	Understand Digital Rights Management (DRM)	387
	What the iTunes Music Store DRM Means to You	389
	What the iTunes Music Store Means for DRM	390
	Set Up an Account with the iTunes Music Store	391
	Understand the Terms of Service	392
	Configure iTunes Music Store Settings	393
	Find the Songs You Want	394
	Preview a Song	395
	Understand A*******s and "Explicit"	395
	Request Music You Can't Find	396
	Buy a Song from the iTunes Music Store	396
	Listen to Songs You've Purchased	396
	Restart a Failed Download	397
	Review What You've Purchased from the iTunes Music Store	397
	(Try to) Fix Problems with Your iTunes Music Store Bill	398
	Authorize and Deauthorize Computers for the iTunes Music Store	398
	Authorize a Computer to Use iTunes Music Store	398
	Deauthorize a Computer from Using iTunes Music Store	399
	Index	**401**

Acknowledgments

I'd like to thank the following people for their help with this book:

- Megg Morin for developing the book and for thinking of me as the author
- Tana Allen for handling the acquisitions end of the book
- Roger Stewart for lurking in the background, pulling strings as required
- Julie Smith for coordinating the editing and production of the book
- Clint Roberts for reviewing the manuscript for technical accuracy and contributing many helpful suggestions
- Linda Marousek for editing the manuscript
- Carie Abrew and Tabi Cagan for their hard work in production
- Mike McGee for proofreading the book
- Valerie Perry for creating the index

Introduction

The iPod is the best portable music player available at this writing. Small enough to fit easily into a hand or a pocket, the iPod can hold the contents of entire CD collection in compressed files and can deliver up 11 hours of music on a single battery charge. You can download a dozen CDs' worth of music from your computer to your iPod in less than a minute, and you can recharge your iPod quickly either from a power outlet or from your computer. And whereas the first iPods worked only with the Mac, the later iPods work with Windows (XP, 2000, and Me) as well.

But the iPod isn't just a portable audio player with terrific sound quality and huge capacity. You can also load it up with your calendars and display your appointments on it. You can also load on your iPod all your contact records and any text that you choose to format as contact data—anything from a shopping list to a book. By using third-party utilities, you can transfer up-to-the-minute headlines, weather reports, stock quotes, driving directions, and other text from the Internet onto your iPod, swiftly and automatically.

So you can use your iPod to carry your essential information with you, and you can check your appointments or display driving directions even while the music keeps thundering. But that's not all. Because the iPod is based around a hard disk and connects to your computer via FireWire, you can transfer to it any files that will fit on the hard disk. So you can use your iPod to carry a backup of your vital documents with you, or even to transfer files from one computer to another. If your computer is a Mac, you can even install Mac OS X or System 9 on your iPod and boot your Mac from the iPod.

Apple keeps improving the iPods and the software that goes with them. The latest improvements (May 2003) include the capability to play music that uses the high-quality Advanced Audio Coding (AAC) format, to use your iPod as an alarm clock, and to buy digital audio from the iTunes Music Store via the Internet. See Chapters 16, 17, and 18 for coverage of these "new" iPods.

What Does This Book Cover?

To help you get the maximum enjoyment and use from your iPod, this book covers just about every iPod topic you can think of and various related topics into the bargain.

NOTE *This book shows you how to make the most of your iPod on Windows XP (on the PC) and Mac OS X on the Mac. If you're using a halfway-recent version of Windows other than Windows XP, you should be able to follow along just fine, but you'll need to choose slightly different commands in the interface at some points. For example, Windows XP's default configuration is to use a different Start menu layout than earlier versions of Windows did—so if you're using an earlier version of Windows, you'll need to make different Start menu choices.*

Chapter 1, "Get Up and Running with Your iPod," explains what an iPod is (okay, you know this), how to choose the iPod that's best for you, and how to set up your iPod. This chapter runs you briefly through the steps of connecting your iPod to your computer, installing the iPod software on your Mac or PC, and loading your iPod with music. It also shows you how to connect your speakers or headphones to your iPod and how to use your iPod's controls.

Chapter 2, "Get Up to Speed with MP3 and Digital Audio," tells you what you need to know about audio quality and compression. This chapter explains what CD-quality audio is and why it sounds good, why MP3 sounds almost as good as CD-quality audio and what MP3's advantages are, and how to get the best possible results when creating MP3 files from CDs or other audio sources. This chapter also briefs you on the basics of copyright law regarding MP3 and digital audio, and explains the copy-protection techniques the record companies are using to prevent people from copying CDs.

Chapter 3, "Use iTunes to Load Music onto Your Mac iPod," shows you how to master iTunes, the software Apple provides for enjoying digital audio on Mac OS and for managing your iPod. You'll learn how to set up and configure iTunes, choose suitable settings for ripping and encoding MP3 files and other file types, and create a music library that you synchronize with your iPod. You'll also learn to use the graphical equalizer to improve the sound of music both on iTunes and on your iPod.

Chapter 4, "Use MUSICMATCH Jukebox Plus to Load Music onto Your Windows iPod," brings you up to speed with MUSICMATCH Jukebox Plus, the software Apple supplies for working with digital audio on Windows and for managing your iPod. Among other things, this chapter shows you how to upgrade your PC to get it ready for your iPod, set up and configure MUSICMATCH Jukebox Plus, and create a music library for synchronizing with your iPod.

Chapter 5, "Create, Edit, and Tag Your MP3 Files," shows you how to work with MP3 files in ways that iTunes and MUSICMATCH Jukebox Plus can't manage, by using various Windows and Mac audio utilities. This chapter starts by telling you how to convert other audio file types to MP3, WAV, or AIFF so you can play them on your iPod. The chapter then discusses how to create MP3 files from cassettes or vinyl records and how to remove scratches and hiss from audio files created from sources such as these. It also shows you how to trim MP3 files to remove intros or outros you don't like; how to tag your MP3 files with accurate data so iTunes, MUSICMATCH Jukebox Plus, and your iPod can sort the MP3 files correctly; and how to save audio streams to disk so you can listen to them later.

Chapter 6, "Download Audio Files from the Internet," discusses the various sources of audio files on the Internet and makes sure you understand the dangers of downloading unauthorized copies of copyrighted works. This chapter explores the tension between the music industry and music consumers, explains what the "darknet" is and how P2P networks greatly enlarged it, and shows you sites where you can find authorized, legitimate audio files. Finally, the chapter mentions ways in which you may want to promote your own music on the net.

Chapter 7, "Burn Audio and MP3 CDs with iTunes and MUSICMATCH Jukebox Plus," shows you how to use the features built into iTunes and MUSICMATCH Jukebox Plus to burn audio CDs and MP3 CDs. You'll learn the basics of CD burning and the differences between audio CDs, data CDs, and MP3 CDs; learn to configure iTunes and MUSICMATCH Jukebox Plus for burning CDs; and learn how to troubleshoot problems you encounter when burning CDs.

Chapter 8, "Use Your iPod to Take Your Contacts with You," covers how to put your contact information on your iPod. This chapter explains the vCard format, which is the key to putting contact information—or other text—onto the iPod, and shows you how to create vCards using several widely used applications on both Windows and the Mac. The chapter then tells you how to put contacts on your iPod and how to view them on it.

Chapter 9, "Put Your Calendars on Your iPod," explains how to transfer your calendar information from your Mac or PC to your iPod and view it there. The key to putting calendar information on your iPod is the vCalendar format.

Chapter 10, "Put Other Information on Your iPod," shows you how to put text other than contacts and calendar information on your iPod. This chapter starts by discussing the limitations of the iPod as a text-display device and mentioning types of text best suited to the iPod. It then covers a variety of Mac utilities, and a single Windows utility, for putting text on your iPod.

Chapter 11, "Keep Your iPod in Good Working Shape," covers how to keep your iPod in good working shape. The chapter starts by discussing the components that make up your iPod, then moves along to tell you how to maximize battery life. From there, this chapter walks you through things that make your iPod unhappy; how to keep your iPod's operating system up to date; and how to carry, store, and clean your iPod.

Chapter 12, "Use Your iPod As a Hard Drive," shows you how to use your iPod as a hard drive for backup and portable storage. If your computer is a Mac, you can even boot from your iPod for security or to recover from disaster. Along the way, you'll learn how to enable FireWire disk mode on your iPod, transfer files to and from your iPod, and optimize your iPod's hard disk to improve performance if necessary.

Chapter 13, "Enhance Your iPod with Accessories," discusses the various types of accessories available for the iPod, from mainstream accessories (such as cases and stands) to more esoteric accessories (wait and see). This chapter also discusses how to connect your iPod to your home stereo or car stereo.

Chapter 14, "Learn Advanced iPod Skills," shows you how to perform a variety of advanced maneuvers with your iPod. The chapter starts by walking you through the processes of converting a Mac iPod to a Windows iPod and a Windows iPod to a Mac iPod. It then shows you how to change the computer to which your iPod is linked—a useful skill when you upgrade your computer. The chapter explains how to synchronize several iPods with the same computer and shows you how to load your iPod from multiple Macs or multiple PCs (but not a mixture of the two). You'll also learn how to transfer song files from your iPod's music library to your computer and how to use your computer to play songs directly from your iPod.

Chapter 15, "Troubleshoot Any iPod Problems You Encounter," shows you how to work your way through troubleshooting your iPod when normal service is interrupted. You'll learn how to avoid voiding your warranty; approach the troubleshooting process in the right way; learn key troubleshooting maneuvers; and use your iPod's built-in diagnostic tools to identify suspected problems.

Chapter 16, "Using the New iPods," describes the new features included in the iPod models released in May 2003. You'll learn how the new iPods differ from the old iPods and how to use compelling new features such as the Alarm Clock, the On-the-Go playlist, and the customizable main menu. You'll also learn how to rate songs on your iPod and how to quickly transfer text files to notes you can read in the iPods' new Notes feature.

Chapter 17, "Using iTunes 4," covers the new features introduced in iTunes 4: support for Advanced Audio Coding (AAC), the ability to share your Mac's music library with other users and play music from music libraries they're sharing, converting tracks from AAC to MP3 (or from MP3 to AAC), and adding artwork to songs. Use this chapter to supplement the discussion of iTunes in Chapter 3.

Chapter 18, "Using the iTunes Music Store," explains what the iTunes Music Store is, how to set up an account, how to find music by browsing and searching, and how to buy and download music. The chapter also explains what digital rights management (DRM) is, what its implications are, and why you should think about them even when using the iTunes Music Store. At the end of the chapter, you'll learn how to authorize and "deauthorize" computers for using the iTunes Music Store.

Part I: Enjoying Audio on Your iPod

Chapter 1

Get Up and Running with Your iPod

How to...

- Choose the right iPod for your needs
- Identify the different components included with your iPod
- Set up your iPod, connect it to your computer, and install the software
- Load music onto your iPod
- Connect your speakers or headphones to your iPod
- Use your iPod's controls
- Navigate through your iPod's screens
- Customize the settings on your iPod

This chapter shows you how to get started using your iPod. It covers a lot of ground, but most of that ground is flat and smooth, so we can move quickly. To keep things rolling, I'll also refer you to discussions in other chapters if you need to get up to speed on certain topics.

If you're reading this book, chances are you've got an iPod already and you've at least torn apart the packaging to gaze upon it with starry-eyed delight. But if you haven't got an iPod, this chapter tells you what an iPod is, what it does, and what choices you'll need to make when buying one. And if you've got an iPod but haven't unpacked it, this chapter explains briefly the items you should find in the box and what they're for.

After that, this chapter runs you through how to attach your iPod to your computer, how to install the software that lets the computer talk to your iPod, and how to get music loaded onto your iPod. The chapter then takes you on a tour of the iPod's interface, getting you up to speed with the controls and the navigation screens quickly and easily.

 *For coverage of the new features introduced in the 10GB, 15GB, and 30GB "new" iPods, see Chapter 16.*

What Is an iPod?

An iPod is a portable music player that can also display your contacts and calendar, enabling you to carry all your music and your vital information around with you. By using other software, you can also put other information on your iPod so you can carry that information with you and view it on the iPod screen.

If music, contacts, and calendaring aren't enough for you, you can use your iPod as an external hard disk for your Mac or PC. Your iPod provides an easy and convenient means of backing up your files, storing files, and transporting files from one computer to another. And because your iPod is ultra-portable, you can take those files with you wherever you go.

Your iPod weighs about 7 ounces and measures around 4"×2.4"×0.8". The exact weight and measurements depend on the hard drive installed in your iPod. The 20GB iPods are a fraction bigger and heavier than the 5GB iPods, which in turn are a fraction bigger and heavier than the 10GB iPods, because the drives are different physical sizes. Subsequent models of iPod may have different sizes yet—even smaller, if we're lucky.

Your iPod contains a rechargeable battery that powers it. Depending on how you use your iPod and its backlight, you may be able to get up to 10 hours of music from a full battery charge.

Your iPod contains a relatively small operating system (OS) that lets it function on its own—for example, for playing back music, displaying contact information, and so on. The OS also lets your iPod know when it's been connected to a computer, at which point the OS hands over control to the computer so you can manage it from there.

What Your iPod *Doesn't* Do

So much for what your iPod does and what it consists of. This section discusses some of the things your iPod *doesn't* do and what its limitations are. Some parts of this are less obvious than others, so stay with me.

You Can't Enter Information Directly on Your iPod

Your iPod is strictly a play-and-display device: you can't enter information directly on it. All the information your iPod contains must come from a computer (a Mac or a PC) across a FireWire cable.

The iPod Isn't the Smallest or Most Skip-Proof Player in Town

Because your iPod is based around a hard drive, it's far larger than the smallest digital audio players around. Some of the smallest players are about the size of a cigarette lighter, while your iPod is more the size of a packet of cigarettes.

Your iPod is also less resistant to skips than solid-state players (such as the Creative Labs Nomad MuVo or the SONICblue Rio S35S Sport players) that store data on flash memory rather than on a hard disk. But as you'll see in the section "What You Might Want to Know About Your iPod's Internals" in Chapter 14, Apple has done some clever engineering to reduce skipping caused by the hard drive being knocked around. That said, if you need a super-lightweight, super-tough, or wholly skip-proof digital audio player, you should probably look beyond the iPod.

One solution is to use your iPod for most of your music and buy an inexpensive, low-capacity digital audio player for your higher-energy or higher-impact pursuits. That way, if you wipe out while trying to set a new speed record on your street luge, you won't need to buy a new iPod, just a titanium ultraportable player, a pair of Kevlar shorts, and a pack of Moleskin.

Your iPod Supports Only MP3, WAV, and AIFF Audio Formats

At this writing, your iPod supports only a limited range of audio formats: MP3, WAV, and AIFF (Mac iPods only) and Audible (Mac iPods only). Your iPod doesn't support major formats such as the following:

- Windows Media Audio (WMA), Microsoft's proprietary format
- RealAudio, the RealNetworks format in which much audio is streamed across the Internet and other networks
- Ogg Vorbis, the new open-source audio format intended to provide royalty-free competition to MP3

This limitation isn't too painful because you can convert audio files from one format to another, and because the MP3 format is very widely used. But if your entire music library is in, say, WMA or Ogg format, you'll have to do some work before you can use it on your iPod.

Choose the iPod That's Best for You

If you don't already have an iPod, here's what you need to know to choose the one that best suits you. The choices are so simple you'll kick yourself if you get them wrong.

There are two essential differences among the iPods currently on sale:

- Some iPods are designed for use with the Mac, while other iPods are designed for use with Windows PCs. Mac iPods (sometimes called *MiPods*) and Windows iPods (*WiPods*) differ both in their formatting and the software they come with. Mac iPods include Apple's iTunes software, whereas Windows iPods include MUSICMATCH Jukebox Plus. You can convert an iPod from Mac format to Windows format, and vice versa, so if your favorite relative gave you the wrong format of iPod for your birthday, all isn't lost. (See the section "Convert Your iPod from Mac to Windows—and Back" in Chapter 14 for details on how to convert an iPod from one format to another.)

- iPods have different capacities. At this writing, you can get 5GB iPods, 10GB iPods, and 20GB iPods. Given the iPod's popularity, Apple's pretty much guaranteed to release higher-capacity models in the future as hard-drive technology continues to improve. As you'd imagine, the greater the capacity, the more the iPod costs and the more you regret dropping it.

NOTE *Unfortunately, the hard-drive capacities on iPods are "marketing gigabytes" rather than real gigabytes. A real gigabyte is 1024 megabytes; a megabyte is 1024 kilobytes; and a kilobyte is 1024 bytes. That makes 1,073,741,824 bytes in a real gigabyte. By contrast, a marketing gigabyte has 1,000,000,000 bytes—a difference of 7.4 percent. So your iPod will actually hold 7.4 percent less data than its listed drive size suggests. You can see why marketing folks ("marketeers," as some call themselves) choose to use marketing megabytes and gigabytes rather than real megabytes and gigabytes—the numbers are more impressive. But customers tend to be disappointed when they discover that the real capacity of a device is substantially less than the device's packaging and literature promised. Beyond this discrepancy between marketing gigabytes and real gigabytes, you also lose some hard-disk space to the iPod's OS and the file allocation table that records which file is stored where on the disk.*

Table 1-1 shows you how much music you can fit onto the different models of iPod at widely used compression ratios for music. For spoken audio (such as audio books, plays, or talk radio), you can use lower compression ratios (such as 64 Kbps or even 32 Kbps) and still get acceptable sound with much smaller file sizes. The table assumes a "song" to be about four minutes long and rounds the figures to the nearest sensible point. The table doesn't show less widely used compression ratios such as 224 Kbps or 256 Kbps. (For 256 Kbps, halve the 128 Kbps numbers.)

How to Do Everything with Your iPod

iPod Nominal Capacity	iPod Real Capacity	128 Kbps		160 Kbps		192 Kbps		320 Kbps	
		Hours	Songs	Hours	Songs	Hours	Songs	Hours	Songs
5GB	4.66GB	83	1,250	67	1,000	56	835	33	500
10GB	9.31GB	166	2,500	134	2,000	110	1,670	67	1,000
20GB	18.62GB	332	5,000	268	4,000	220	3350	134	2,000

TABLE 1-1 iPod Capacities at Typical Compression Ratios

The iPod refers to tracks as "songs," so this book does the same. Even if the tracks you're listening to aren't music, the iPod considers them to be songs. Similarly, the iPod and this book refer to "artists" rather than "singers," "bands," or other terms.

To decide which model to buy, you'll probably want to ask yourself the following questions:

- How much music do I want to put on my iPod, and at what quality? (Usually the answer to the first part of the question is "as much music as possible," and the answer to the second part is "high enough quality that it sounds great on my headphones and speakers.")
- What other items do I want to put on my iPod, and how much space will they need?
- How much can I afford to spend?
- Will I use my iPod with a Mac, a PC, or both?

If money is no object, buy the largest-capacity iPod available: between your music and the other items you'll probably want to use the iPod for, you'll very likely take up most of its capacity soon enough. But if money is tight, you may need to sacrifice iPod capacity for solvency. Never mind—you may be richer next year, or at least iPod prices will probably have come down.

Understand the Different Models of iPod

All three models of iPod released at this writing—the 5GB, 10GB, and 20GB iPods, each of which is available in a Mac model and a Windows model—look essentially

CHAPTER 1: Get Up and Running with Your iPod

the same. As mentioned earlier, the different-capacity iPods have different sizes but share the same design. So unless you have two iPods with different capacities side by side for comparison, chances are you won't notice the difference.

If you're not sure which capacity iPod you have, turn the iPod over and read the box near the bottom of the back. It'll say "5GB", "10GB", or "20GB"—or, if you're either lucky or this book has dropped through a wormhole in the space-time continuum, a much larger capacity.

> **NOTE** *You can also check your iPod's capacity through iTunes or MUSICMATCH Jukebox Plus. When your iPod is connected to the Mac, the status bar in iTunes displays a readout of the amount of space on your iPod, dividing it into Used and Free categories: for example, Used: 11.03GB, Free: 7.57GB. Add those two figures together, round them up to the nearest multiple of five to account for marketing megabytes, and you'll know the capacity of your iPod. When your iPod is selected in the MUSICMATCH Portables Plus window, the status bar shows the Total Space and Free Space on your iPod. Round the Total Space figure up to the nearest multiple of five.*

Apart from capacity, the main differences among the various iPod models have been in their system software. Apart from patching holes and fixing bugs, Apple has added various features to the iPod, such as the following:

- Contact-management storage that lets you add your contacts to your iPod and view them on the screen
- A graphical equalizer you can use for changing the sound of the music to suit your tastes
- A Shuffle feature that lets you shuffle playback not only by songs but also by albums
- A feature called *scrubbing* that lets you wind forward or backward through the song you're playing so you can find the part you want to hear
- A Calendar application that can synchronize with calendaring software
- A Clock application

If your iPod is not as new as it might be, check if you can update its operating system with any features that Apple has released more recently. See the section "Keep Your iPod's Operating System Up-to-Date" in Chapter 12 for details on how to download and install updates.

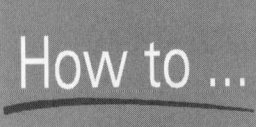 **How to Check the iPod Software Version**

To check which version of software is installed on your iPod, follow these steps:

1. Scroll down to the About item on the main menu.
2. Select the About item and view the version number displayed at the bottom of the screen.

What's in the Box?

Your iPod's box should include the following components:

- Your iPod.
- A case for your iPod (not included with the 5GB iPod). This case has a sturdy belt clip and grips your iPod firmly but provides no direct access to your iPod's controls. Various other iPod cases are available from third parties; some cases are for general use, and some are for more specialized use. See the section "Cases" in Chapter 13 for a discussion of some of the more interesting types of cases you can get.
- A pair of ear-bud headphones.
- A wired remote control (not included with the 5GB iPod) that lets you control the music while your iPod is stowed in its case or your pocket.
- A FireWire cable for attaching your iPod to your Mac, your PC, or your iPod power adapter.
- A power adapter for the occasions when you want to recharge your iPod from a wall socket. (As you'll see in Chapters 3 and 4, you can also recharge your iPod directly from the FireWire port on your Mac or the FireWire port on some PCs.) Depending on the country in which you buy your iPod, the power adapter probably has retractable prongs (to avoid damaging anything else you're carrying it with—or stabbing backwards into you from your pocket). It may also have removable prongs you can change to use the adapter in a variety of sockets. The power adapter is built to accept 100 to 240 volts AC, so with the right prongs (or adapters), you can use it to power your iPod most of the way around the world.

 *The Apple Store (**store.apple.com**) sells a World Travel Kit Adapter for the iPod. You can also get clumsier but less expensive adapters at RadioShack or any competent electrical store.*

- A CD containing software (iTunes or MUSICMATCH Jukebox Plus) and several booklets of instructions, the license agreement for the iPod, and so on.

Set Up Your iPod

After you've unpacked your iPod, turn it on and choose the display language it should use for communicating with you. (Depending on where you bought your iPod, it may be set to display a different language at first than the language you want.) Your choices range from English, German, French, Italian, and Spanish through Norwegian and Finnish to Japanese, Korean, and Simplified and Traditional Chinese.

To turn on your iPod, press any button. Your iPod displays the Apple logo for a few seconds and then shows the Language Settings screen. Use the Scroll wheel to scroll to the language you want to use, and then press the Select button.

To turn off your iPod, press and hold the Play/Pause button for a couple of seconds until the display goes blank.

If you don't turn your iPod off, and it's not playing any music, it automatically goes to sleep after a few minutes if you don't press any buttons.

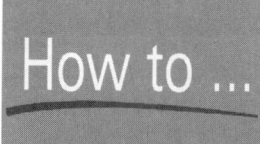 ## How to Reset the iPod to Recover from the Wrong Language

If you choose the wrong language on your iPod, or a helpful friend changes the language for you, you may find it difficult to navigate the menus to change the language back to your usual language. You can recover by resetting all settings. This option isn't as drastic as it sounds: it turns off Repeat, Shuffle, EQ, Sleep Timer, and Backlight Timer; it puts Startup Volume and Contrast to their midpoints; and it sets the language to its local default. For example, if you bought your iPod in the United States, resetting all settings should return the language to English.

To reset all settings, follow these steps:

1. Press the Menu button as many times as is necessary to return to the main screen. (Five times is the most you should need to press the Menu button to get back to the main screen, even from the deepest recesses of the menus.) You'll see the iPod text at the top of the menu, no matter which language your iPod is using.

2. Scroll down three clicks to select the fourth item on the main menu. This is the Settings item, but you may not be able to recognize the name in another language.

3. Press the Select button to display that menu.

4. Scroll down to the last item on the menu, the Reset All Settings item. This item appears in English, no matter which language your iPod is currently using.

5. Press the Select button.

6. Scroll down to the second item. This is the Reset item; again, it appears in English, no matter which language your iPod is using.

7. Press the Select button. Your iPod displays the Language selection menu startup screen.

8. Choose your preferred language.

Connect Your iPod to Your Computer

Your iPod connects to your computer (Mac or PC) via a FireWire cable supplied with the iPod. Once your iPod is connected to your computer, the iPod acts as a hard drive controlled by the computer.

FireWire is Apple's name for the Institute of Electrical and Electronics Engineers (IEEE) standard 1394 (IEEE 1394). The name *FireWire* is widespread for IEEE 1394, but you'll also see devices described as "IEEE 1394" rather than "FireWire." Sony uses the trademarked term "i.Link" for IEEE 1394, so if you have a Sony computer, look for i.Link.

When Apple introduced the iPod, FireWire was by far the best technology for loading large amounts of data onto a portable device. At that time, the USB 2.0 standard hadn't yet been implemented, and FireWire blew USB 1 out of the water. Now, USB 2.0 is giving FireWire direct competition.

FireWire delivers speeds of up to 400 megabits per second (Mbps—about 50MB of data per second), compared to USB 1's 12 Mbps (about 1.5MB of data per second). USB 2 provides speeds of up to 480 Mbps, so USB 2 devices can be faster than FireWire devices. Some of the Windows-based competitors to the iPod, such as the Archos MP3 Jukebox and some of the Creative Nomad models, use USB 2.0 for data transfer. However, FireWire has a couple of other tricks up its sleeve, as you'll see in Chapter 12 and Chapter 14.

FireWire ports and cables come in two basic types: four-pin and six-pin. Four-pin cables are more compact than six-pin cables. Six-pin cables supply power to the FireWire devices via the cable, whereas four-pin cables don't supply power. Most of Sony's VAIO notebooks have four-pin FireWire/i.Link ports. Six-pin cables can recharge your iPod, whereas four-pin cables cannot.

All current Macs—iMacs, eMacs, iBooks, PowerBooks, and Power Macs—include at least one or two FireWire ports: Apple has made FireWire a standard for Macs. You'll need to add a FireWire port only if you have an older Mac or a Mac clone. For example, if you have a PowerBook G3, you may need to add a FireWire PC Card.

Many current PCs include FireWire ports, but because the PC makers have standardized on USB more than on FireWire, some current PCs don't have FireWire ports. You can add one or more FireWire ports to your PC by installing a PCI card (in a desktop PC) or a PC Card (in a notebook PC). See the section "Get Your Mac Ready for Working with Your iPod" in Chapter 3 or the section "Get Your PC Ready for Working with Your iPod" in Chapter 4, as appropriate, for details on how to add FireWire to your Mac or PC.

To connect your iPod to your computer, plug one end of the FireWire cable into the FireWire port on the top of your iPod and the other end into a FireWire port on your computer. If you're using a FireWire cable with six pins on each plug, it doesn't matter which end goes into the computer and which goes into the iPod. If you're using a six-pin–to–four-pin FireWire cable, the four-pin end goes into the PC and the six-pin end goes into the iPod.

Install the iPod Software

The next step to getting going with your iPod is to install the iPod software—if you need to:

- ■ If you have a Mac with Mac OS X or System 9 on it, you probably have a version of iTunes you can use with your iPod. You may choose to update iTunes to the latest version in any case. If you have an older Mac without a viable version of iTunes installed, you'll need to install iTunes to get started with your iPod. To install iTunes, follow the instructions in the section "Set Up iTunes on Your Mac" in Chapter 3.

- If you have a PC, install MUSICMATCH Jukebox Plus as described in the section "Install MUSICMATCH Jukebox Plus on Your PC" in Chapter 4. If you already have MUSICMATCH Jukebox Plus (the paid version of the MUSICMATCH software) installed on your computer, you need only install the iPod software. If you have MUSICMATCH Jukebox (the free version of the MUSICMATCH software) installed, you'll need to upgrade to MUSICMATCH Jukebox Plus.

Load Your iPod with Music

This section provides a brief introduction to how you load your iPod with music using either the Mac (discussed first) or the PC (discussed second). For full details on using iTunes to create MP3 files and load them on your iPod, see Chapter 3. For full details on using MUSICMATCH Jukebox Plus to create MP3 files and load them on your iPod, see Chapter 4.

Load Your iPod on the Mac

If you have iTunes installed on your Mac, iTunes automatically synchronizes your music library with your iPod as soon as you connect your iPod to your Mac.

Even though FireWire is one of the fastest connection technologies available to consumers, your first-ever synchronization may take as long as 20 or 30 minutes if your music library contains a large number of songs. This is because iTunes copies each song and playlist to the iPod. Subsequent synchronizations will be much quicker, as iTunes will need only to transfer new songs and playlists you've added to your music library, remove songs and playlists you've deleted, and update the data on songs whose tags you've changed. (A *tag* is a container on an MP3 file that has slots for information such as the song's name and the artist's name.)

Load Your iPod on Windows

By default, MUSICMATCH Jukebox Plus automatically launches its MUSICMATCH Portables Plus component when you connect your iPod to your PC. If you accepted the default settings of synchronizing automatically on connection, MUSICMATCH Portables Plus synchronizes your iPod with your music library.

> **NOTE** *The first time you connect your iPod to your PC, MUSICMATCH Portables Plus displays the Device Setup dialog box so you can name and configure your iPod. See "First Connection: Configure Device Setup Options" in Chapter 4 for details.*

As with the Mac, your first-ever synchronization with MUSICMATCH Portables Plus will take a while—perhaps 20 to 30 minutes—if your music library is large, because MUSICMATCH Portables Plus has to copy each song and playlist to your iPod. Subsequent synchronizations will be faster, but synchronizations with MUSICMATCH Portables Plus tend to take substantially longer than synchronizations with iTunes.

Connect Your Headphones or Speakers

As you learned earlier in this chapter, your iPod comes with a pair of ear-bud headphones—the kind that fit in your ear rather than sit on your ear (*supra-aural headphones*) or over your ear (*circumaural headphones*). The headphones come with foam covers that fulfill the dual purposes of softening the impact of the headphones on your ears and cleaning from your ears any wax and debris you missed with your latest Q-Tip.

Ear buds are the most discreet type of headphones and could probably be used by long-haired monks without being detected as long as they didn't start rocking out during their devotions. Most ear buds wedge in your ears like the iPod's ear buds do, but others sit on a headband and poke in sideways.

There's nothing magical about the iPod's headphones—they're designed to look good with the iPod, and they're quality headphones with a wide frequency range, but otherwise they're normal headphones. I find they deliver pretty good sound and are tolerably comfortable for short or moderate periods of listening. For extended listening, I prefer circumaural headphones, such as Sennheiser Ovations. In a noisy environment, noise-canceling circumaural headphones such as Bose's QuietComfort headphones are hard to beat. (Like all Bose products, the QuietComfort headphones are so expensive—about as much as a 5GB iPod, since you ask—that Bose doesn't advertise the price but rather the installment plan they offer.)

If you don't like the sound your iPod's headphones deliver, or if you just don't find them comfortable, use another pair of headphones with your iPod. Any headphones with a standard jack will work; if your headphones have a quarter-inch jack, get a good-quality miniplug converter. You can get better ear buds than the iPod's headphones (but you'll pay for the privilege) or use another type of headphones. Whichever type of headphones you choose to use, don't turn the volume up high enough to cause hearing damage.

TIP *Given that I've just suggested you refrain from deafening yourself with headphones, this next suggestion may come as a surprise: if you use your iPod often with a high-end pair of headphones, get a headphone amplifier to improve the sound. A headphone amplifier plugs in between the sound source (in this case, your iPod) and your headphones to boost and condition the signal. You don't necessarily have to listen to music louder through a headphone amplifier—the amplifier can also improve the sound at a lower volume.*

Instead of using headphones, you can also connect your iPod to a pair of powered speakers, a receiver or an amplifier, or your car stereo. To make such a connection, use a standard cable with a stereo miniplug connector at the iPod end and the appropriate type of connector at the other end. For example, to connect your iPod to a conventional amplifier, you need two phono plugs on the other end of the cable.

NOTE *Powered speakers are speakers that contain an amplifier so you don't need to use an external amplifier. Many speaker sets designed for use with portable CD players, MP3 players, and computers are powered speakers. Usually only one of the speakers contains an amplifier, making one speaker far heavier than the other. Sometimes the amplifier is hidden in the subwoofer, which lets you put the weight on the floor rather than on the furniture.*

The iPod headphone jack delivers up to 60 milliwatts (mW) altogether—30 mW per channel. Turn the volume down when connecting your iPod to a different pair of headphones, powered speakers, or an amplifier. Make the connection, set the volume to low on the speakers or amplifier, and then start playing the audio. Turn the volume up as necessary. That way, you won't deafen yourself, blast your neighbors, or blow the speakers or amplifier.

Use Your iPod's Controls

This section shows you how to use your iPod's controls. Apple has reduced the number of controls to a minimum by making each control fulfill more than one purpose. You'll get the hang of the controls' basic functions easily, but you also need to know how to use the controls' secondary functions to get the most out of your iPod—so keep reading.

Read Your iPod's Display

Your iPod has an LCD display (Figure 1-1) that shows up to six lines of text and multiple icons.

The title bar at the top of the display shows the title of the screen currently displayed—for example, iPod for the main menu (the top-level menu) or Artists when you're viewing the list of artists—or the month or date you're viewing in the Calendar.

To turn on the display's backlight, hold down the Menu button for a few seconds. The backlight uses far more power than the LCD screen, so don't use the backlight unnecessarily when you're trying to extract the maximum amount of playing time from a single battery charge. As you'll see in "Set the Backlight Timer," later in this chapter, you can configure how long your iPod keeps the backlight on after you press a button.

Use Your iPod's Controls

Below the iPod's display are the six main controls for accessing songs (and data) and playing them back. These controls are arranged as a ring of four buttons around the scroll wheel and the Select button (Figure 1-2).

- Press any button (but not the Scroll wheel) to switch on your iPod.

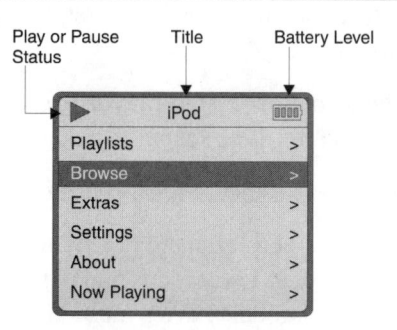

FIGURE 1-1 Your iPod's LCD display contains six lines of text and key icons.

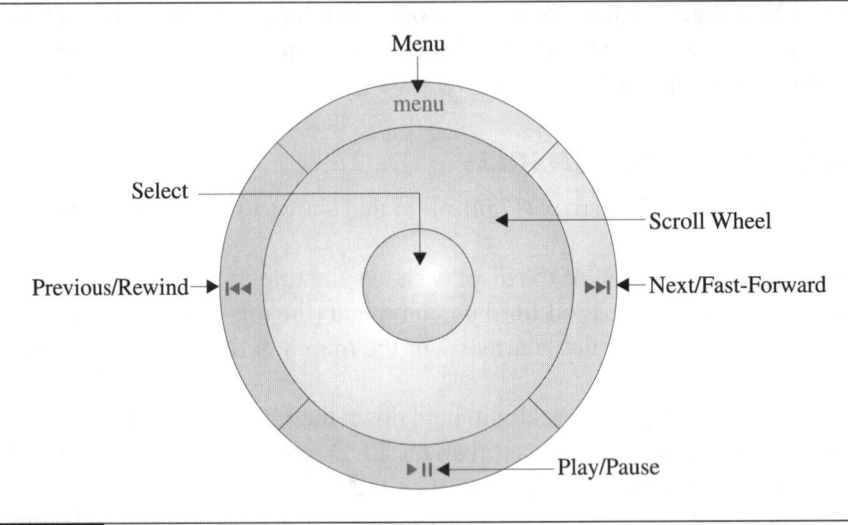

FIGURE 1-2 Your iPod's six controls

- Press the Menu button to move up to the next level of menus. Hold down the Menu button for a second to turn the backlight on or off.

- Press the Previous/Rewind button and the Next/Fast-Forward button to navigate from one song to another and to rewind or fast-forward the playing song. Press one of these buttons once (and release it immediately) to issue the Previous command or the Next command. Hold the button down to issue the Rewind command or the Fast-Forward command. Your iPod rewinds or fast-forwards slowly at first, but then speeds up if you keep holding the button down.

- Press the Play/Pause button to start playback or to pause it. Hold down the Play/Pause button for three seconds or so to switch off your iPod.

- Press the Select button to select the current menu item.

- Use the Scroll wheel to scroll up and down menus, change the volume, or change the place in a song. Early iPods had a moving Scroll wheel mounted on ball bearings. Later models have a more durable solid-state Scroll wheel that's touch-sensitive. By default, your iPod plays a clicking sound as you move the Scroll wheel to give you feedback. You can turn off this clicking sound if you don't like it.

NOTE *The Scroll wheel adjusts the scrolling speed in response to your finger movements on the scroll wheel and the length of time you scroll for: when you're scrolling a long list, it speeds up the scrolling as you continue the scroll, then slows down as you ease back on the scroll. This behavior makes scrolling even long lists (such as the Songs list, which lists every song on your iPod) swift and comfortable.*

Browse and Access Your Music

The iPod's menu-driven interface makes browsing and accessing your music as easy as possible on the device's diminutive display.

Once you've accessed a list of songs—be it a playlist, an album, or a listing of all songs by an artist or composer, you can press the Play button to play the list from the start. Alternatively, scroll down to another song, and then press the Play button to start playing from that song.

Play a Playlist

To access your playlists, scroll to the Playlists item on the main menu (it's the top item, so it may be selected by default), and then press the Select button. On the resulting screen, scroll down to the playlist you want to play, and then press the Select button.

Browse Your Music

To browse your music, select the Browse item on the main menu. Your iPod displays the Browse menu, which contains entries for Artists, Albums, Songs, Genres, and Composers. Press the Select button for the browse category you want to use.

The Artists category displays an alphabetical list of all the music on your iPod sorted by artist. The first entry, All, displays an alphabetical list of all the albums on your iPod. Otherwise, scroll down to the artist and press the Select button to display a list of the albums by the artist. This menu also has a first entry called All. This entry displays an alphabetical list of all songs by the artist.

NOTE *The data for the artist, album, song title, genre, composer, and so on comes from the tag information for an MP3 file. An album shows up in the Artists category, the Albums category, the Genre category, or the Composers category because one or more MP3 files on your iPod has that album entered in the Album field on its tag. So the entry for an album doesn't necessarily mean that you have that entire album on your iPod—you may only have one song from that album. (Or you may have no songs at all from the album, if another song has that album's name incorrectly entered in its tag.)*

- The Albums category displays an alphabetical list of all the albums on your iPod. Scroll down to the album you want and press the Select button to display its songs.

- The Songs category displays an alphabetical list of every song on your iPod. Scroll down to the song you want to play—it may take a while to scroll that far—and then press the Select button to start playing the song.

- The Genre category displays a list of the genres you've assigned to the music on your iPod. (Your iPod builds the list of genres from the Genre field in the tags in MP3 files.) Scroll to a genre and press the Select button to display the artists whose songs are tagged with that genre. You can then navigate to albums and songs by an artist.

- The Composers category displays a list of the composers listed for the songs on your iPod. (Your iPod builds the list of composers from the Composer field in the tags in MP3 files.) Scroll to a composer and press the Select button to display a list of the songs by that composer.

Play Songs

Playing songs on your iPod could hardly be easier. The following subsections discuss what you may well have figured out already.

Start and Pause Play

To start playing a song, take either of the following actions:

- Navigate to the song and press the Play/Pause button or the Select button.

- Navigate to a playlist or an album and press the Play/Pause button or the Select button.

To pause play, press the Play/Pause button.

Change the Volume

To change the volume, scroll counterclockwise (to reduce the volume) or clockwise (to increase it) from the Now Playing screen. Figure 1-3 shows the volume control on the Now Playing screen.

Change the Place in a Song

As well as fast-forwarding through a song by using the Fast-Forward button, or rewinding through a song by using the Rewind button, you can *scrub* through a song to quickly change the location.

```
           ┌─────────────────────┐
           │ ▶      Car 1    ▮▮▮ │
           │ 8 of 33             │
           │                     │
           │ Julian Cope is Dead │
           │    Bill Drummond    │
           │       The Man       │
           │                     │
           │ ◀))▬▬▬▬▬▬▬▬▬  ◀))) │
           └─────────────────────┘
```

FIGURE 1-3 From the Now Playing screen, scroll counterclockwise to reduce the volume or clockwise to increase the volume.

Scrubbing can be easier than fast-forwarding or rewinding because your iPod displays a readout of how far through the song the playing location currently is.

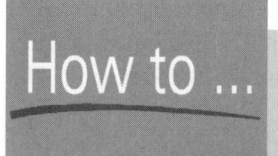

How to ... How to Use the Composers Category Effectively to Find Music

The Composers category is primarily useful for classical music, because these songs may be tagged with the name of the recording artist rather than that of the composer. For example, an album of The Fargo Philharmonic playing Beethoven's Ninth Symphony might list The Fargo Philharmonic as the artist and Beethoven as the composer. By using the Composers category, you can access the works by composer: Bach, Beethoven, Brahms, and so on.

But there's no reason why you shouldn't use the Composers category to access nonclassical songs as well. For example, you could use the Composers category to quickly access all your Nick Drake cover versions as well as Drake's own recordings of his songs. The only disadvantage to doing so is that the tags for many MP3 files don't include an entry in the Composer field, so you'll need to add this information if you want to use it. In this case, you may be better off using iTunes or MUSICMATCH Jukebox Plus to create a playlist that contains the tracks you want in the order you prefer.

There's also no reason why you should confine the contents of the Composers field to information about composers. By editing the tags manually, you can add to the Composer field any information by which you want to be able to sort songs on your iPod.

Scrubbing is also more peaceful, because while Fast Forward and Rewind play blips of the parts of the song you're passing through (to help you locate the passage you want), scrubbing keeps the song playing until you indicate you've reached the part you're interested in.

To scrub through a song, follow these steps:

1. Display the Now Playing screen.
2. Press the Select button to display the scroll bar (Figure 1-4).
3. Scroll counterclockwise to move backward through the song or clockwise to move forward through the song.
4. Press the Select button to cancel the display of the scroll bar, or wait a few seconds for your iPod to cancel its display automatically.

Use the Hold Switch

The Hold switch, located on the top of your iPod, locks your iPod controls in their current configuration. The Hold switch is intended to protect your iPod controls against being bumped in active environments—for example, when you're exercising at the gym or barging your way onto a packed bus or subway train. When the Hold switch is pushed to the left so the red underlay shows, your iPod is on Hold.

The Hold switch is equally useful for keeping music playing without unintended interruptions and for keeping your iPod locked in the Off position, which prevents the battery from being drained by the iPod being switched on accidentally when you're carrying it.

If your iPod seems to stop responding to its other controls, check first that the Hold switch isn't on.

FIGURE 1-4 From the Now Playing screen, you can change the place in the song by pressing the Select button, and then scrolling counterclockwise (to move backward) or clockwise (to move forward).

Attach and Use the Remote Control for Easy Operation

The 10GB and 20GB iPod models include a remote-control unit that plugs into the headphone port so you can secrete the iPod around your person and control the music without continually having to detach the iPod from your belt or disentangle it from your pocket. Your headphones (or speakers) then plug into the socket on the cable of the remote-control unit.

The remote control could hardly be simpler to use. It contains a volume control, a Play/Pause button, Fast-Forward and Rewind buttons, and a Hold switch (on the side). The only point worth mentioning is that you need to push the jack of the remote-control unit firmly into its socket for it to engage. If the remote control seems to stop working, check first that it's properly plugged in, and second that the Hold switch hasn't become engaged without your knowing it.

Recharge Your iPod to Keep the Songs Coming

The battery icon on your iPod's display shows you how your iPod is doing for battery power. Four bars is a full charge; one bar means the gas tank is nearing empty.

You can recharge your iPod by plugging it into your computer (if you're using a Mac or a PC with a six-pin FireWire connector) or by plugging in the iPod AC adapter.

- The advantage to using the computer is that you don't need to lug the AC adapter around with you; the disadvantage is that if your computer is a portable, you'll need to lug around the computer's AC adapter, because the iPod draws power from the computer's battery when the computer is running on the battery. Another disadvantage is that the hard drive on some iPods can get stuck spinning (so it doesn't stop spinning when it should) when recharging from the computer via FireWire. (If this happens to your iPod, see the section "iPod Says 'Do Not Disconnect' for Ages When Connected to the Computer" in Chapter 15 for advice on how to fix the problem.)

- The advantage to using the AC adapter is that you can run the iPod from the adapter even while the battery is charging.

Your iPod battery is designed to recharge in about three hours. After about an hour of recharging, the battery should be at about 80 percent of its charge capacity—enough for you to use the iPod for a while.

When recharging from a computer, your iPod displays each of the four bars in the battery icon in sequence. When your iPod displays all four bars together, the charging is complete.

When recharging from the AC adapter, your iPod flashes a large battery icon and displays the word *Charging* at the top of the screen. When charging is complete, your iPod displays the battery icon without flashing it and with the word *Charged* at the top of the screen.

> **NOTE** *See the section "Maximize Your iPod's Battery Life" in Chapter 14 for advice on how to get the longest life possible from your iPod's battery.*

Navigate the Extras Menu

The Extras menu provides access to your iPod's Contacts, Calendar, Clock, and Game.

- To access a contact, scroll to the Contacts item on the Extras menu, and then press the Select button. On the Contacts screen, scroll to the contact, and then press the Select button. See Chapter 8 for a discussion of how to put contacts onto your iPod.

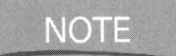

> **NOTE** *The original 5GB iPod didn't include the Contacts feature, which was added in the 10GB iPod. If you have one of the original 5GB iPods, you can use the iPod Software Updater to add the Contacts feature to your iPod.*

- To use Calendar, scroll to the Calendar item on the Extras menu, and then press the Select button. Calendar displays the current month. Use the Scroll wheel to access the day you're interested in, and then press the Select button to display the events listed for that day. The one-month display shows empty squares for days that have no events scheduled and dots for days that have one or more events. If the day contains more appointments than will fit on the iPod display, use the Scroll wheel to scroll up and down. See Chapter 9 for a discussion of how to transfer your schedule to the iPod.

- To use Clock, scroll to the Clock item on the Extras menu, and then press the Select button.

- To play the Breakout game included with the iPod, scroll to the Game item on the Extras menu, and then press the Select button. Start the game by pressing the Select button again, and then use the Scroll wheel to control the paddle. You get three balls per game. Press the Select button again to start a new game.

Choose Settings for Your iPod

To choose settings for your iPod, scroll to the Settings item on the main menu, and then press the Select button. The resulting menu offers the following choices: Info, Shuffle, Repeat, Sound Check, EQ, Backlight Timer, Contrast, Alarms, Sleep Timer, Date & Time, Contacts, Clicker, Language, Legal, and Reset All Settings. The following subsections discuss what you need to know about these items, spending time only where it's required.

Apply Shuffle Settings to Randomize Songs or Albums

Instead of playing the songs in the current list in their usual order, you can have your iPod shuffle them into a randomized order by changing the Shuffle setting to Songs. (For technical reasons, the order is actually pseudo-random rather than truly random, but you'd have a monumentally hard time predicting what the order would be.) Similarly, you can have your iPod shuffle the albums by a particular artist or composer into a (pseudo-)random order by changing the Shuffle setting to Albums.

To apply a Shuffle setting, scroll up to the Shuffle item on the Settings menu and press the Select button to apply the Shuffle setting you want. The settings are Off (the default), Songs, and Albums.

Repeat One Track or All Tracks

The Repeat item on the Settings menu lets you choose between repeating the current song (choose the One setting), all the songs in the current list (the All setting), or not repeating any songs (Off, the default setting). Scroll to the Repeat item, and then press the Select button to change the setting.

Use Sound Check to Standardize the Volume

Your iPod's Sound Check feature doesn't involve beefy roadies muttering "Check Two! Check. Check!" into the microphones as the audience crushes plastic beer glasses underfoot and grows sweaty with anticipation (or with the suffocating stuffiness of the venue). Sound Check on the iPod is a feature for normalizing the volume of different songs so you don't have to crank up the volume to hear a song encoded at a low volume and then suffer ear damage because the next song was recorded at a far higher volume. At this writing, Sound Check works only with iTunes, not with MUSICMATCH Jukebox Plus.

> **NOTE** *For Sound Check to work on your iPod, you need to turn on the Sound Check feature in iTunes. Press COMMAND-Y or choose iTunes | Preferences to display the Preferences dialog box. Click the Effects button to display the Effects sheet. Select the Sound Check check box, and then click the OK button to close the dialog box.*

Choose Equalizations to Make Your Music Sound Better

Your iPod contains a graphical equalizer—a device that alters the sound of music by changing the level of different frequency bands. For example, a typical equalization for rock music boosts the lowest bass frequencies and most of the treble frequencies, while reducing some of the midrange frequencies. This arrangement typically punches up the drums, bass, and vocals, making the music sound more dynamic. A typical equalization for classical music leaves the bass frequencies and midrange frequencies at their normal levels while reducing the treble frequencies. This arrangement should provide a less shrill and mellower effect than steel strings being scraped by horsehair bows or woodwind reeds being blasted by powerful lungs might otherwise produce.

Generally speaking, graphical equalizers are intended to make music sound better, but you can use a graphical equalizer to make music sound bad or odd if you prefer. Graphical equalizers also have more specialized uses. For example, the air crash–analysis teams use complex graphical equalizers to eliminate as much machine noise as possible from cockpit voice recorders so they can identify what the pilots and engineer were yelling when things went wrong.

Your iPod should include the following equalizations (Apple may have increased the selection): Acoustic, Bass Booster, Bass Reducer, Classical, Dance, Deep, Electronic, Flat, Hip Hop, Jazz, Latin, Lounge, Piano, Pop, R & B, Rock, Small Speakers, Spoken Word, Treble Booster, Treble Reducer, and Vocal Booster. (You might long for a Vocal Reducer setting for some artists or for karaoke, but the iPod doesn't provide one.)

Most of these equalizations are clearly named, but Flat and Small Speakers aren't entirely obvious:

- *Flat* is an equalization with all the sliders at their midpoints—an equalization that applies no filtering to any of the frequency bands. If you don't normally use an equalization, there's no point in applying Flat to a song, because it's essentially the same as not using an equalization. But if you *do* use an equalization for most of your tracks, you can apply Flat to individual tracks to turn off the equalization while they play.

- *Small Speakers*, as you'd guess, is for use with small loudspeakers, not for audio by small orators. This equalization boosts the frequency bands typically lost by smaller loudspeakers. If you listen to your iPod through portable speakers, you may want to try this equalization for general listening.

To apply an equalization, scroll to the EQ item on the Settings menu. The EQ item shows the current equalization—for example, EQ – Rock. To change the equalization, press the Select button. On the EQ screen, scroll to the equalization you want, and then press the Select button to apply it.

If you're using your iPod with a Mac, you can apply equalization to music in two ways:

- On the iPod, choose the equalization you want to use for all music. You can change from one equalization to another as often as you want.

- In iTunes on your Mac, specify the equalization to use for any particular song. Your iPod then applies this equalization when you play back the track on the iPod. The equalization also applies when you play the track in iTunes.

If you're using your iPod with a Windows computer, you can't associate an equalization with a song: you can only choose an equalization on the iPod.

> **TIP** *Don't take the names of the equalizations too literally, because which of them you find best will depend on your ears, your earphones or speakers, and the type of music you listen to. For example, if you find (say) thrash sounds best played with the Classical equalization, don't scorn the Classical equalization because of its name. (Alternatively, create a custom equalization that duplicates the Classical equalization, but assign it a more suitable name.)*

Change the Contrast to Make the Screen Readable

To change the contrast to make the screen more readable under the prevailing light conditions, scroll to the Contrast item, and then press the Select button to access the Contrast screen. Scroll clockwise to darken the screen, counterclockwise to lighten it.

You can change the contrast both when you're using the backlight and when you're not using it.

Turn Alarms On and Off

You can't use your iPod as an alarm clock, but it can remind you of appointments in your Calendar when their times arrive. Choose the On setting for Alarms to receive a beep and a message on the screen. Choose the Silent setting to receive only the message. Choose the Off setting to receive neither the beep nor the message.

Use the Sleep Timer to Lull You to Sleep

The Sleep Timer on your iPod is like the Sleep button on a clock radio or boom box: it lets you tell your iPod how long to continue playing music, presumably to lull you to sleep. You can set values of 15, 30, 60, 90, or 120 minutes.

Your iPod displays a clock icon and the number of minutes remaining on the Now Playing screen so you can see the Sleep Timer is running. To turn the Sleep Timer off, access the Sleep screen again and select the Off setting.

Set the Date and Time

Use the Set Time Zone item on the Date & Time screen to access the Time Zone screen, on which you can set the time zone (for example, US Mountain). Use the Set Date & Time item on the Date & Time screen to access the Date & Time screen, which presents a simple interface for setting the time and date. Use the Scroll wheel to adjust each value in turn. Press the Select button to move to the next value.

Choose How to Sort and Display Your Contacts

To specify how your iPod should sort your contacts names and display them on the screen, scroll to the Contacts item on the Settings screen, and then press the Select button to display the Contacts screen.

To change the sort order, scroll (if necessary) to the Sort item, and then press the Select button to toggle between the First Last setting (for example, *Joe Public*) and the Last, First setting (for example, *Public, Joe*).

To change the display format, scroll (if necessary) to the Display item, and then press the Select button to toggle between the First Last setting and the Last, First setting.

Most people find using the same sort order and display format best, but you may prefer otherwise. For example, you might sort by Last, First but display by First Last.

Turn the Clicker On or Off

The Clicker item on the Settings screen toggles the clicking sound your iPod plays when you use the Scroll wheel. Press the Select button to toggle the setting between On and Off. (The default setting is On.)

Check the "About" Information for Your iPod

From the main menu, you can scroll down to the About item and press the Select button to display the following information about your iPod:

- Your iPod's name and serial number
- Your iPod's hard disk capacity and the amount of space free right now
- The version number of the software installed on your iPod

NOTE *In most cases, it's worth updating your software to the latest version available. This book assumes you're running version 1.2 of the iPod software. See the section "Keep Your iPod's Operating System Up-to-Date" in Chapter 11 for details on how to update your iPod.*

Set the Backlight Timer

To customize the length of time that the display backlight stays on after you press one of the iPod's controls, scroll to the Backlight Timer option and press the Select button. You can then choose from the following settings:

- Choose the Off setting to keep the backlight off until you turn it on manually by holding down the Menu button for a couple of seconds. You can then let the backlight go off automatically after the set delay or hold down the Menu button again for a couple of seconds to turn it off.

- Specify the number of seconds (between 1 and 10) for the backlight to stay on after your press a control.

- Choose the Always On setting to keep the backlight on until you choose a new setting from this screen. (Even holding down the Menu button doesn't turn the backlight off when you choose Always On.) This setting is useful when you're using your iPod as a sound source in a place that's too dark to see the display without the backlight and when you need to change the music frequently.

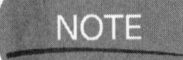

NOTE *When you use the Always On setting, it's best to have your iPod running on main power. Try not to use the Always On setting when running on battery power, because doing so chews through the battery surprisingly quickly. In a pinch, you can use the Always On setting to light your way with the iPod—for example, if you have a power outage at night, or if you happen to get stuck in a cave. But unless you're strapped for light, you'll find your iPod makes a poor substitute for a flashlight, because the light isn't focused into a beam.*

Chapter 2

Get Up to Speed with MP3 and Digital Audio

How to...

- Understand why music needs compression
- Understand lossless and lossy compression
- Learn what MP3 is and how it works
- Learn about other key digital audio formats
- Understand ripping, encoding, and "copying"
- Choose an appropriate compression rate for MP3 files you create
- Load uncompressed WAV and AIFF files on your iPod
- Understand the basics of copyright law as regards MP3
- Understand copy-protection techniques for CDs

You'll almost certainly want to use your iPod extensively for carrying your music and listening to it. That means putting as much music on your iPod as possible, probably in MP3 format—and keeping the quality as high as you need for all types of playback you perform. (I'll explain what MP3 means in the section "What Is MP3 and Why Should You Use It?," a little later in this chapter.)

This chapter discusses the background you need to understand in order to make the most of digital audio on your iPod. I understand your focus is on results rather than theory, but to get the right results with MP3, you need to understand a little theory about what MP3 is and why it works.

In particular, if your music collection is extensive, you'll need to balance music quality against quantity. You can store pure CD-quality audio on your iPod, but you can't store very much of it. You can store a huge quantity of highly-compressed audio on your iPod, but the audio won't sound too great. Or you can settle for a happier medium that delivers high-enough audio quality but lets you take all your essential music with you.

This chapter shows you how to do so. It starts by explaining why music files are so big that they need compressing.

NOTE *The new iPods can play back files encoded in the high-quality Advanced Audio Coding (AAC) format as well as the MP3 format. See "Understand Advanced Audio Coding (AAC)" in Chapter 17 for a discussion of AAC and how to use it with the new iPods.*

Why Do You Need to Compress the Music?

The brief answer is that you need to compress music files because they're huge. For music files to sound passable, they need to contain a lot of data. For them to sound perfect to the human ear, they need to contain a *huge* amount of data. (More on what such perfection entails and on the precise quantities of data later in this chapter.)

As you'll know if you've surfed the Web using a slow Internet connection, different types of content require different amounts of data to represent them. Text typically requires the smallest amount because of the (relatively) minuscule number of possible characters in the Western European character set: letters (in uppercase and lowercase), letters with modifications signs (such as å and ÿ), numbers, punctuation, symbols, and so on.

So to represent text, you need to represent only the sequence of letters and any necessary formatting information. For text, basic ASCII uses seven bits of data for each character, giving 128 different permutations (2×2×2×2×2×2×2). Extended ASCII uses eight bits of data for each character, giving 256 different permutations (2×2×2×2×2×2×2×2)—enough for the vast majority of Western languages. (By comparison, Chinese and Japanese—each of which has many thousand characters—require larger numbers of bits. But Unicode takes care of them by using a relatively extravagant 64 bits of data for each character.) You then need to represent the font name, size, and so on, but this information can be represented in text as well, so it doesn't require much more data.

Graphics, audio, and video require far more data than text because they contain so many more variables. A text character can be any of the (say) 256 in the extended ASCII character set, but a graphic can show anything visible, a moment of audio can represent any sound, and a moment of video can represent a combination of the two.

Some of this data is more compressible than others. For example, high-resolution graphics contain a huge amount of data, but they can be highly compressible. To give a crude example, a compressed graphics format (or a compression program, such as WinZip), can give an instruction such as "use blue of the hue 0,64,192 for the next 2,000 pixels" instead of saying "blue of the hue 0,64,192" 2,000 times in succession. (Actually, the file just says "0,64,192" because it knows it's talking about colors using Red, Green, Blue [RGB] data—but you get the idea.) The program that opens the compressed file then restores the compressed information to its former state, essentially recreating the full picture. This is called *lossless* compression—the compressed file contains the information necessary to recreate the complete original file.

But audio is much harder to compress than graphics, because it's less static. (Video is even worse, but we won't go there in this book.) You can perform some audio compression by reducing repeated information to a set of instructions for repeating it—hold this sound for three seconds, and so on. But to significantly reduce the amount of data needed to represent audio, you usually need to discard some of the data. This is called *lossy* compression because the data discarded is lost. As you'd think, to make the compressed audio sound as good as possible, the compression format must discard the data that's least important to the listener. Hold that thought; we'll get back to how MP3 does this in a page or two.

In the meantime, there *is* one means of stripping down music to a minimal set of information—a means other than writing it down as a score on paper. That way is called MIDI (Musical Instrument Digital Interface), a music format for representing music as a set of computer instructions. MIDI essentially assumes that each particular instrument sounds a given way, and provides a set of instructions for how each of the instruments in the song should play.

For example, you can tell a MIDI file to play a piano note for a given time, with a given attack (how hard the note is struck), given sustain (how long the note is held), and so on. In this way, a minimal amount of data can produce a full-sounding track. Depending on the set of instruments used, the MIDI track will sound different on different equipment—but so will the same score played by the same pianist on a different Steinway, the same Beethoven symphony played by different orchestras (leaving the conductors out of the equation), or the same Beatles instrumental standard covered by different substandard tribute bands.

That all works well enough for music that can use generic or genericized instrument sounds—for example, a grand piano, a distorted electric guitar, or a regulation snare drum. But it doesn't work for vocals, because you can't effectively synthesize a voice. Even if you could, you couldn't synthesize the right voice. And even if you could synthesize the right voice, you would need to describe the tone, expression, and delivery. You can't exactly say "use the tortured tone of Ozzy Osbourne wailing 'Sabbath, Bloody Sabbath' for one second" or "Mariah Carey a shade off a breathy high note" and expect a computer to deliver it.

So compression for music needs to take a subtler approach—knocking out the less important parts of the music while preserving as much as possible.

But we're getting ahead of ourselves here. First, let's consider what audio quality is and what data is required to deliver it.

What Determines Audio Quality?

Having high audio quality essentially means having enough data for your audio equipment to deliver playback that not only sounds similar to the original but also good.

That much is pretty obvious once you think about it. But to get high-quality audio playback, you need to get several different things in balance:

- You need a high-quality audio signal—for example, an uncompressed audio file (such as a CD track, a WAV file, or an AIFF file) or a compressed audio file (such as an MP3 file, a WMA file, or an Ogg Vorbis file). (WAV is a Windows Audio format for uncompressed audio. AIFF—Audio Interchange File Format—is a Mac format for uncompressed audio. WMA stands for Windows Media Audio, a Windows file format for compressed audio. Ogg Vorbis is another file format for compressed audio.)

- You need a high-quality playback device. Your iPod can be that playback device.

- You need good speakers or earphones. With speakers, you also need an amplifier, either built into the speakers or separate.

- Your ears need to be in tolerable condition. If you've lost hearing in some parts of the audio spectrum, you may need your audio equipment to compensate in order to make the music sound good to you. Even if you have perfect hearing, you still need to get music of a quality you like.

The first two items—the audio signal and the playback device—aren't subjective: most people can agree whether an audio signal is high quality or not, because audio quality is measured by the amount of data conveyed rather than by whether you like the audio or not, and you can objectively compare the playback quality of different audio devices.

But the last two items—the speakers or headphones, and your ears—are highly subjective. If you like Limp Bizkit, you probably won't get good mileage out of a system designed to deliver quality Liszt. If you prefer Beethoven, you'll need speakers that can deliver the subtleties and the thunder of classical music rather than speakers designed to churn out country and western. If acoustic folk music is what brings light into your life, speakers or headphones designed to deliver stomach-churning bass and explosions in action games won't do you much good.

You get the idea. Enough of that for now. We'll consider all these variables later in this chapter.

What Does CD-Quality Audio Mean?

As you probably know, the human ear is an imperfect audio instrument, capable of detecting (and conveying to the brain) a limited set of audio frequencies that spans the range of experiences that humans evolved (or were designed, depending on your point of view) to know about.

Sound frequency is measured in hertz (Hz) and kilohertz (kHz). 1Hz is one cycle per second; 1kHz is a thousand cycles per second. The typical human ear (let's assume it's yours, even if you know you've been listening to loud music more than you should have) can detect sound waves from about 20Hz to 20kHz. Not surprisingly, most music made by, and for, humans concentrates on these frequencies, with some (usually unnoticed) overlap at each end. Low-frequency sounds below 20Hz are called *infrasound* and high-frequency sounds above 20kHz are called *ultrasound*. (The ultrasound devices used for physical therapy emit very high- frequency waves to subtly rearrange your tissues. If you hear these waves, you're in trouble.)

> **NOTE** *Animals' hearing overlaps human hearing at both ends of the scale. Dogs' hearing typically ranges from 50Hz to about 45kHz, which is why they can hear dog whistles that most people can't. Bats' ears can hear up to 120kHz, which is why they can navigate without bothering humans or dogs. Dolphins can hear up to 200kHz, so bats might be able to annoy them in certain limited circumstances. Elephants can hear infrasound frequencies down to about 5Hz, so bats don't bother them but earth tremors may.*

CD-quality audio is digital audio that includes the full range of frequencies that humans can hear (again, with some overlap at the high and low ends for the gifted and to annoy susceptible animals). The digital audio is created by using a process called *sampling*—taking snapshots of the audio stream to determine how a particular moment sounds.

CD-quality audio samples audio 44,100 times per second (a sampling rate of 44.1kHz) to provide coverage with no gaps. Each sample contains 16 bits (2 bytes) of data, which is enough information to convey the full range of frequencies. There are two tracks (for stereo), doubling the amount of data. The data on audio CDs is stored in *pulse code modulation* (*PCM*), a standard format for uncompressed audio.

CD-quality audio consumes around 10MB (megabytes) of storage space per minute of audio—a huge amount of data even in these days of 250+GB hard drives. So you can see why you need compression to make a large amount of music fit on a device like your iPod.

What Is MP3 and Why Should You Use It?

For music enthusiasts, MP3 is one of the most exciting developments since the sound card, amplifier-inside speakers, or noise-canceling headphones. This is because MP3 allows you to carry a large amount of high-quality audio with you on a small device and enjoy it at the cost of nothing but battery power and time. But in the real world, MP3 is merely a file format—or perhaps we should say *another* file format—for compressed audio.

The MP3 name comes from the Motion Picture Experts Group (MPEG; **mpeg .telecomitalialab.com**—not **www.mpeg.org**, which you might expect it to be), which oversaw the development of the MP3 format. MP3 is both the extension used by the files and the name commonly used for them. More correctly, MP3 is the file format for MPEG-1 Layer 3—but most people who listen to MP3 files neither know that nor care to know such details.

MP3 can deliver high-quality music in files that take up as little as a tenth as much space as uncompressed CD-quality files. For speech, which typically requires less fidelity than music, you can create even smaller files that still sound good, enabling you to pack that much more audio in the same amount of disk space.

How MP3 Works (The Short Version)

As mentioned at the beginning of this chapter, digital audio data tends to be difficult to compress using lossless compression because it contains so much rapidly changing information. So, most methods of compressing digital audio data tend to use lossy compression, discarding the least important parts of the audio while trying to keep everything vital for the sound.

As you'd imagine, the first part of this reduction is getting rid of data on any frequencies that fall outside the hearing range of most humans. There's no point in including any frequency that the vast majority of listeners won't even be able to hear.

But MP3 gets more subtle than that. Besides taking into account the limitations of the human ear, it uses *psychoacoustics*, the science of how the human brain processes sound, to select which data to keep and which to discard. As a crude example, when one part of the sound is masked by another part of the sound, the encoder discards the masked part, because you wouldn't hear it.

How much data the encoder keeps depends on a setting called the *bitrate*. Most MP3 encoders can encode either at a *constant bitrate* (CBR) or a *variable bitrate* (VBR). I'll discuss the pros and cons of CBR and VBR in the section "Choose Between Constant Bitrate and Variable Bitrate," later in this chapter.

MP3 Patent and Royalty Rates

There's a widespread perception that MP3 is an open standard that anyone can use, but the reality is a bit different. Although MPEG oversaw the development of MP3, most of the work was done by a German company called Fraunhofer IIS-A.

Fraunhofer IIS-A and Thomson Corporation (which describes itself as providing "information workflow solutions that help business and professional customers work more productively") hold patent rights over MP3 audio compression. Anyone who wants to create an MP3 encoder or decoder, whether hardware or software, needs to pay a per-unit royalty to Fraunhofer and Thomson. For example, if you choose to create a hardware MP3 decoder, you need to pay 75¢ per unit; if you create a hardware encoder, the fee is $5.00 per unit.

You don't need a license to *use* MP3 hardware or software, as long as the hardware or software is licensed. You're also free to stream MP3 audio for "private, non-commercial activities" such as home entertainment. But you do need a license to stream MP3 audio for commercial purposes—for example, if you're using MP3 for webcasting. (See www.mp3licensing.com for details.) For commercial MP3 software, licensing isn't an issue—whoever developed the software will have paid the licensing fee (and you'll probably have paid them for the software). But for MP3 freeware, licensing is potentially an issue—although the developers of such software are much more likely to be the targets of patent enforcement than users of the software because the developers are easier and juicier targets.

Understand Other Digital Audio Formats

This section briefly discusses other important formats for digital audio.

For your iPod, the only two formats of any interest apart from MP3 are WAV, AIFF (Mac iPods only), and Audible (Mac iPods only). Both WAV files and AIFF files are uncompressed PCM audio. WAV files are PCM audio files with a header that identifies them as WAV files; AIFF files are PCM (pulse code modulation) audio files with an AIFF header. AIFF tends to be more widely used on the Mac than on Windows, which favors WAV. The section "Load Uncompressed Files on Your iPod for Unbeatable Sound Quality," later in this chapter, discusses the pros and cons of using WAV and AIFF on your iPod. (Quick preview: perfect sound but few songs.) Audible files are compressed audio files that can include navigation markers.

For you as a digital-audio enthusiast, other formats that may be of interest include the following:

- Windows Media Audio (WMA) is an audio format developed by Microsoft. As you'd imagine, WMA is the preferred format of Windows Media Player, the Microsoft audio and video player included with all desktop versions of Windows.

- mp3PRO is designed to be a successor to MP3, as its name implies. mp3PRO delivers higher audio quality than MP3 at the same bitrates. For example, mp3PRO files encoded at the 64 Kbps bitrate are similar in quality to MP3 files encoded at the 128 Kbps bitrate. Like MP3, mp3PRO requires hardware and software manufacturers to pay royalties to Fraunhofer IIS-A and Thomson Corporation.

- Ogg Vorbis is an open-source format that's patent free. Ogg Vorbis is relatively new and has yet to catch the public's attention. You can get an Ogg Vorbis plug-in for iTunes. MUSICMATCH Jukebox and MUSICMATCH Jukebox Plus don't yet offer Ogg Vorbis support.

- MP4 is the audio file format for the MPEG-4 encoding scheme, designed as a successor to MP3.

Understand Ripping, Encoding, and "Copying"

Audio CDs store data in a format different to that of data CDs (for example, a CD containing software or your favorite spreadsheets). Most audio CDs use a format called Red Book and contain only audio data. Other CDs use a format called CD Extra that lets the creator include a data track as well as the audio tracks. This data track can contain any kind of data—for example, videos, pictures, or text.

Audio CDs store the data for their songs in a format that file-management programs on Windows (for example, Windows Explorer) and System 9 (for example, the Finder) can't access directly. If you put an audio CD in your CD drive and open a Windows Explorer window or a System 9 Finder window, you'll see only minuscule CDA (CD Audio) files rather than the huge uncompressed files that contain the songs. The CDA files are pointers to the song files. These pointers are called *handles*. You can use Windows Explorer or the Finder to copy the handles from the CD to your hard disk, but copying them won't do you much good, because the audio will still be on the CD.

By contrast, Mac OS X can access the data on an audio CD seamlessly. As you can see in the top screen in Figure 2-1, Mac OS X shows the true file sizes of the audio data referenced by the handles rather than the handles themselves. If your Mac has an Internet connection, as the Mac in the top screen does, Mac OS X can also download the CD information automatically for you. By contrast, System 9 (the middle screen in Figure 2-1) and Windows XP (the bottom screen) show only the handles.

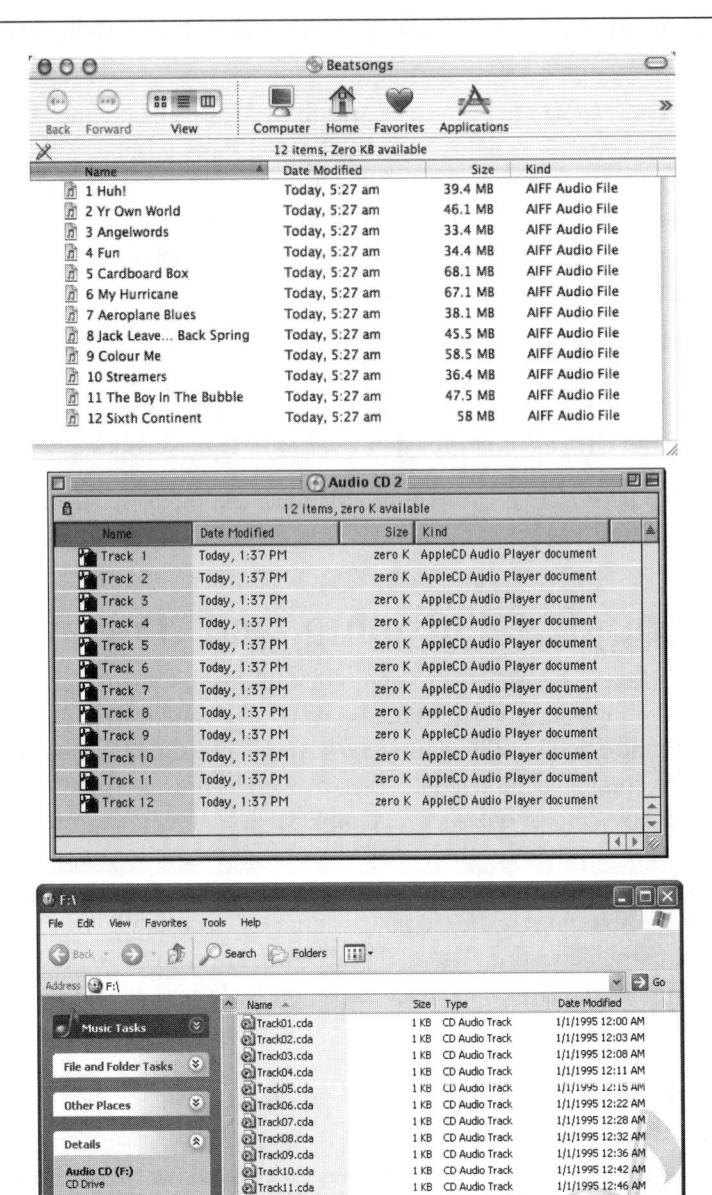

FIGURE 2-1 Audio CDs contain "handles" (pointers to the audio data) rather than actual files. Mac OS X (top) is smart enough to read the handles, give you direct access to the data, and download the track names from the Internet. System 9 (middle) and Windows XP (bottom) show you only the handles.

To get the audio off the CD, you need to perform a process called *ripping*. Ripping sounds vigorous but simply means using a program to extract the audio from the CD (by using the handle to access the audio data). You can rip audio to uncompressed files—typically WAV files or AIFF files—or immediately encode it to a compressed file format such as MP3 or WMA.

> **TIP** *In Mac OS X, you can rip a song to an AIFF file by performing a Copy operation from the CD using the Finder. For example, drag the song from a Finder window to the desktop to rip it to an AIFF file there. However, in most cases, it makes more sense to use iTunes to rip songs and encode them to MP3 files. See Chapter 3 for a discussion of how to rip and encode using iTunes.*

In Windows Media Player, Microsoft uses the term "copying" for ripping and encoding a CD to WMA files or MP3 files using Windows Media Player. "Copying" is an interesting term, because it's both accurate and inaccurate, clarifying and misleading, at the same time. "Copying" is accurate because ripping and encoding a WMA file or MP3 file of a song on a CD does create a copy of it, with all the copyright implications involved.

"Copying" is inaccurate because in the computer sense, a Copy operation almost always creates a perfect copy of the file involved, not a lower-quality version in a substantially different format. (For example, if you copy a Word document, you expect the copy to be a Word document with the same contents, not a WordPad document with a minimal amount of formatting and some of the less interesting parts of the text—as judged by the computer—missing.) But for users who don't understand how audio is stored on CDs and how compression works, the term "copying" implies creating a perfect copy of the CD audio on the computer's hard disk. And that's not the case.

Learn about CDDB and Other Sources of CD Information

iTunes, MUSICMATCH Jukebox, and many other ripping and encoding programs download CD information from the CD Database (CDDB; **www.cddb.com**). CDDB is a collaborative project that allows anyone who can connect to the Internet to access its data.

You can look up information manually by using the CDDB interface, but in most cases audio programs look up CD information automatically for you, either when you insert a CD or when you instruct the program to look up the current CD.

Anyone can submit entries to CDDB for CDs it doesn't currently cover. The section "Submit CD Information to CDDB Using iTunes" in Chapter 3 and the section "Submit CD Information to CDDB Using MUSICMATCH Jukebox Plus" in Chapter 4 show you how to use the iTunes and MUSICMATCH Jukebox Plus's features (respectively) for submitting information to CDDB.

Choose an Appropriate Compression Rate

This section discusses how to choose an appropriate compression rate for the audio files you encode. It doesn't *show* you how to set the compression rate—you'll learn how to do that in the chapter on iTunes and the chapter on MUSICMATCH Jukebox Plus.

The iTunes default settings are to rip and encode CDs to MP3 files at the 160 Kbps bitrate using CBR (constant bitrate; see the next subsection). The MUSICMATCH Jukebox Plus default settings use 128 Kbps and CBR.

iTunes offers the following settings for encoding MP3 files:

- Good Quality (128 Kbps)
- Better Quality (160 Kbps)
- High Quality (192 Kbps)
- Custom. You can choose bitrates from 8 Kbps to 320 Kbps—the full range available for most MP3 encoders and players. You can also choose between CBR and VBR.

iTunes can also rip to WAV files and AIFF files. Chapter 3 shows you how to do this.

MUSICMATCH Jukebox Plus offers the following settings for encoding MP3 files:

- CD Quality (128 Kbps)
- Near CD Quality (96 Kbps)
- FM Radio Quality (64 Kbps)
- Custom Quality. As with iTunes, you can choose constant bitrates from 8 Kbps to 320 Kbps.
- Custom Quality (VBR). You can specify the percentage of the file to save, from 1 percent to 100 percent. The more data you save, the higher the quality.

MUSICMATCH Jukebox Plus can also rip to WAV files and rip and encode to mp3PRO and WMA files. MUSICMATCH Jukebox Plus can't rip to AIFF files. Chapter 4 shows you how to rip and encode with MUSICMATCH Jukebox Plus.

Choose Between Constant Bitrate and Variable Bitrate

As you saw in the previous section, both iTunes and MUSICMATCH Jukebox Plus let you encode MP3 files using either constant bitrate (CBR) or variable bitrate (VBR).

Constant bitrate simply records each part of the file at the specified bitrate. CBR files can sound great, particularly at higher bitrates, but VBR generally delivers better quality than CBR. This is because VBR can allocate space more intelligently as the audio needs it. For example, a complex passage of a song will require more data to represent it accurately than will a simple passage, which in turn will require more data than the two seconds of silence before the massed guitars come crashing back in.

The disadvantage to VBR, and the reason most MP3 encoders are set to use CBR by default, is that many older decoders and hardware devices can't play them. If you're using iTunes or MUSICMATCH Jukebox Plus and an iPod, you won't need to worry about this. But if you're using an older decoder or hardware device, you may need to.

Choose Between Normal Stereo and Joint Stereo

As you'll know if you've browsed through ancient vinyl records, early recordings used *mono*—a single channel that didn't deliver any separation among the sounds. On a song recorded in mono, all the instruments sound as though they're located in the same place. Many mono recordings sound pretty good, but the effect is different than listening to a live band playing. In most cases, you'll want to stick with stereo. But if your sound source is mono (for example, a live recording with a single microphone), stick with mono when encoding the audio.

Once you've decided to use stereo, you next have to choose between normal stereo and joint stereo. This section explains the difference so you understand which type of stereo to choose when. If you haven't met these terms before, don't worry: the last few conventional forms of consumer audio—LPs, cassette tapes (including digital audio tapes, DAT), and CDs—essentially removed this choice, so you didn't need to worry about it. But computer audio (and specifically MP3) has re-equipped you with this choice. So it's a good idea to understand your options and use them as necessary—even if that means simply choosing the best setting for your needs and sticking with it through thick and thin.

Stereo delivers two channels: a left channel and a right channel. These two channels provide positional audio, enabling recording and mixing engineers to separate the audio so different sounds appear to be coming from different places. For example, the engineer can make one guitar sound as though it's positioned on the left and another guitar sound as though it's positioned on the right. Or the engineer might fade a sound from left to right so it appears to travel in front of the listener.

> **NOTE** Surround sound goes much further than stereo, enabling the sound engineer to make sounds seem like they're behind you, moving through your mouth from molar to incisor, and so on. MP3 doesn't support surround sound, but the Advanced Audio Coding (AAC) used in the MPEG-4 audio specification does.

Normal stereo (sometimes called *plain stereo*) uses two tracks: one for the left stereo channel and another for the right stereo channel. As its name suggests, normal stereo is the normal form of stereo. For example, if you buy a CD recorded in stereo and play it back through your boom box, you're using normal stereo.

Joint stereo (sometimes called *mid/side stereo*) divides the channel data differently to make better use of a small amount of space. The encoder averages out the two original channels (assuming the sound source is normal stereo) to a mid channel. The encoder then encodes this channel, devoting to it the bulk of the available space assigned by the bitrate. One channel contains the data that's the same on both channels. The second channel contains the data that's different on one of the channels. By reducing the channel data to the common data (which takes the bulk of the available space) and the data that's different on one of the channels (which takes much less space), joint stereo can deliver higher audio quality at the same bitrate as normal stereo.

> **TIP** Use joint stereo to produce better-sounding audio when encoding at lower bitrates. Use normal stereo for all your recordings at your preferred bitrate. Where the threshold for lower-bitrate recording falls depends on you. Many people recommend using normal stereo for encoding at bitrates of 160 Kbps and above, and using joint stereo for lower bitrates (128 Kbps and below). Others recommend not using normal stereo below 192 Kbps. Experiment to establish what works for you.

The results you get with joint stereo depend on the quality of the MP3 encoder you use. Some of the less capable MP3 encoders produce joint-stereo tracks that sound more like mono tracks than normal-stereo tracks. Better encoders produce joint-stereo tracks that sound very close to normal-stereo tracks. Both MUSICMATCH Jukebox Plus and iTunes produce pretty good joint-stereo tracks.

Using the same MP3 encoder, normal stereo delivers better sound quality than joint stereo—at high bitrates. At lower bitrates, joint stereo delivers better sound quality than normal stereo, because joint stereo can retain more data about the basic sound (in the mid channel) than normal stereo can retain about the sound in its two separate channels. However, joint stereo provides less separation between the left and right channels than normal stereo provides. (The lack of separation is what produces the mono-like effect.)

Test the Sound Given by Different Bitrates to Find Which Is Best

Choosing a compression rate for your music collection shouldn't be a snap decision, because making the wrong decision can cost you disk space (if you record at too high a bitrate), audio quality (too low a bitrate), and also the time it takes to rip your entire collection again at the bitrate you should have chosen in the first place.

Ideally, you should rip a representative selection of the types of music you plan to listen to using your computer and your iPod. Encode several copies of each test track at different bitrates, and then listen to them over a period of several days to see which provides the best balance between file size and audio quality.

Make sure some of the songs test the different aspects of music that are important to you. For example, if your musical tastes lean to female vocalists, listen to plenty of those. If you prefer bass-heavy, bludgeoning rock, listen to that. If you go for classical music as well, add that to the mix.

This probably all sounds obvious enough—and it should be. But plenty of people don't take the time to find out which bitrate is best for them and their music. Then they complain about the results.

Load Uncompressed Files on Your iPod for Unbeatable Sound Quality

To get the ultimate music quality, you can load uncompressed audio files—either WAV files (on Windows or the Mac) or AIFF files (on the Mac only)—on your iPod. If you rip these audio files directly from the CD at full quality, you'll have truly CD-quality files. (You can also create lower-quality WAV files or AIFF files if you choose.) Such files provide the equivalent of carrying your CDs with you on your iPod.

The disadvantages to loading uncompressed files on your iPod are as follows:

- You can't fit as much music on your iPod. You'll be able to fit only about 30 full-length CDs on a 20GB iPod.

■ You'll wear out your iPod's battery much more quickly. This is because the uncompressed files will be too large for your iPod's memory to cache effectively, so the hard disk will be used much more often than if you're playing smaller files.

Copyright Law for Digital Audiophiles

Unless you've created an original work yourself and needed to protect it, you may well never have needed to bother yourself with copyright law. But if you're listening to digital audio on your iPod, knowing the basics of copyright law is a good idea, for two reasons. First, you can make sure you don't take any actions that breach copyright law (or that, if you do take such actions, you do so wittingly rather than otherwise). Second, you can be an empowered consumer and defend your rights against companies (and lobbyists, and lobbied governments) that want to take them away from you for commercial reasons. (More on this in a moment.)

NOTE *This section discusses U.S. law. If you live in another country, check the laws to make sure your actions with copyrighted works stay within them.*

What Copyright Is

Copyright consists of a set of laws designed to encourage authors to produce original works by preventing other people from copying those works without permission. Copyright protection acts as an incentive for authors to put time into creating works in the hope of receiving money from the sales of those works.

For example, say you write the ultimate truck-driving anthem. Copyright ensures Garth Brooks can't make a hit of it and rake in millions of dollars without your granting him (or his record company) the right to record and distribute the song. In exchange for granting those rights, you'll typically receive money. Without copyright, you might receive nothing.

Copyright applies to almost all original works. There are some limitations, of which the key one is that you can't copyright an idea, only the expression of an idea. For example, you can't copyright the idea of your truck-driving anthem— you have to go ahead and write the anthem. Once you've stored the anthem in a tangible form (for example, by writing it on paper or as a computer file, or by recording it), you have a copyrighted work. You don't even have to register the copyright with the Copyright Office, but doing so is a good idea because it makes dealing with copyright infringements much easier. For works created since January 1, 1978, copyright lasts until 70 years after the death of the author or last surviving coauthor.

When You Can Legally Copy Copyrighted Material, and Why

Copyright law is sweeping. Basically, it says you need permission from the copyright holder to copy any copyrighted work. But there are various specific exceptions and some gray areas, of which some directly affect copying audio CDs and creating MP3 files from them.

The following subsections run through the key elements in the puzzle.

What Time-Shifting and Place-Shifting Are

The Betamax Decision of 1984, sometimes also called the "Sony Decision" because Sony created the Betamax video form, allows you to time-shift or place-shift a copyrighted work. This decision, handed down by the Supreme Court, established that home taping of broadcasts didn't infringe copyright.

You're allowed to copy a copyrighted broadcast work to *time-shift* it for personal use so you can experience it later. For example, you may record a radio show so you can listen to it the next day. Similarly, you may *place-shift* a copyrighted work for personal use so you can listen to it somewhere else on different equipment. For example, you may create MP3 files from a copyrighted CD so you can listen to them on your iPod while skiing.

What Personal Use Allows You to Do

The Audio Home Recording Act (AHRA) of 1992 includes a provision called *personal use* that allows you to use what the AHRA terms a "digital audio recording device" to copy a copyrighted work onto a different medium so you can listen to it. For example, you can transfer a CD to a MiniDisc so you can listen to it on your MiniDisc player.

Personal use seems to perfectly cover ripping and extracting CDs—except that the AHRA considers computers "multipurpose devices" rather than "digital audio recording devices." The digital audio recording devices the AHRA covers were digital tapes such as DAT and Digital Compact Cassette (DCC, a short-lived competitor to DAT).

Fair Use and Why It Doesn't Apply to MP3

Fair use is a copyright provision that causes huge amounts of confusion. Fair use allows you to reproduce part of a copyrighted work without permission but without infringing copyright in limited circumstances. For example, if you're reviewing a book, you might be able to fairly use short quotes from it to illustrate the points you're making. When criticizing a movie, you might be able to fairly reproduce a picture from it. When teaching, you might be able to make multiple copies of a couple of pages from a book so each member of the class could read them.

All those examples say "might" because fair use is judged according to four very fluid factors (which we won't get into here). One person's understanding of fair use may be very different from another's, and fair use issues are frequently taken to court.

What you need to know about fair use is this: fair use is seldom, if ever, relevant to copying audio CDs or creating MP3 files. But you'll often hear people using the phrase as justification for illegal copying they've performed.

Burning CDs of Copyrighted Works for Others Is Illegal

Burning CDs of copyrighted works for others without permission is illegal, no matter how easy it is to do or how many people seem to be doing it. Burning backup CDs of copyrighted works for yourself may be legal—but it's seldom entirely clear. For example, you'll see notices on many software CDs that say things like "Do not make illegal copies of this disc," suggesting that making *legal* copies (for backup) is acceptable. By contrast, many audio CDs bear notices such as "Unauthorized copying, reproduction, hiring, lending, public performance, and broadcasting prohibited."

Sharing MP3 Files of Copyrighted Material Is Illegal

Sharing files containing other people's copyrighted material without permission is illegal. For example, many of the MP3 files shared on peer-to-peer file-sharing services (such as the pioneering but now-defunct Napster and successors including Gnutella, Kazaa, and Aimster) are shared illegally.

That said, some artists encourage you to distribute their works freely. For example, artists who choose to make tracks available on web music sites such as **www.mp3.com** generally allow those tracks to be downloaded for free to generate publicity. Most of those artists encourage those who download the tracks to pass them on to other people to spread their music further, in the hopes of increasing their audience or selling CDs of their other music.

Even some CDs encourage you to distribute the copyrighted works they contain. For example, if you're one of the (apparently few) people who has an original copy (so to speak) of the album Igneous Rock by the Tempe, Arizona band Sledville, you'll find that the CD insert card states "Unauthorized duplication is encouraged. Distribute freely."

Circumventing Copy-Protection May Be Illegal

Copying CDs for others and sharing MP3 files with others are clearly illegal. But now we come to a strange item: as a result of Title I of the Digital Millennium Copyright Act (DMCA), which was passed in 1998, it's illegal to circumvent "effective technological measures" protecting a copyrighted work. There are various ifs and buts (for example, you can circumvent such measures to make another program interoperate with a copyrighted work), but essentially Title I says if someone has protected a copyrighted work with a technological measure that could be argued to be "effective" (whatever that means), it's illegal to crack that measure. There are heavy penalties if you do so deliberately and for "commercial advantage" or private gain: fines of up to $500,000 and five years' imprisonment for a first offense, and double those for a second offense.

How the DMCA will pan out in the real world is still very much open to question. Here are three examples for you to chew on:

- In December 2002, the Russian software company Elcomsoft was acquitted of breaking the law by creating a program that enabled people to read Adobe eBook files that used technological protection. As the judge saw it, the crux of the question was whether Elcomsoft had *intended* the software to be used to violate copyright, not whether the software *could* be used to violate copyright. (Much software *can* be used to violate copyright, in much the same way that many consumer items—from, say, contact lenses to Hummers—*can* be used for battery but normally aren't.)

- In January 2003, a Norwegian hacker was acquitted of breaking the law by creating a software decoder to play back DVDs on Linux. No Linux DVD decoder was available, so the hacker took advantage of some unprotected code in a commercial DVD player to create his own DVD decoder. In a decision that was widely seen as sensible, the Norwegian judges ruled that because the hacker owned the DVDs in question, he hadn't broken into them. The Oslo City Court ruling said "The court finds that someone who buys a DVD film that has been legally produced has legal access to the film"—a finding most consumers can easily understand.

- A major retailer has used the DMCA to claim that its price lists constitute trade secrets. (Most people have a hard time accepting this one.)

Understand Current Copy-Protection Techniques on the CDs You Buy

To prevent customers from ripping or burning copies of the CDs they buy, record companies have turned to a variety of copy-protection solutions. High-profile copy-protection solutions include Cactus-200 Data Shield (developed by the Israel-based company Midbar Tech Ltd.; www.midbartech.com) and key2audio (from Sony DADC; www.key2audio.com). Midbar Tech was acquired by Macrovision Corporation. You'll probably recognize the name Macrovision from their video-protection products.

Midbar Tech claims Cactus-200 Data Shield is the leading copy-protection solution; and as of January 2003, more than 30 million discs using key2audio protection had been sold; so altogether there are plenty of these discs out there in the wild. Anecdotal evidence suggests that most of these protected audio discs have been sold in Europe, with smaller numbers having been sold in the U.S.

This section outlines how those two copy-protection solutions work, the effects you'll see when you encounter such protected discs, ways some users have found of using protected discs on computers—and why it may be illegal to do so. But first, I'd like to make sure you're aware of why the CD has been such a success, and why the record companies are so worried about piracy.

Brief and Unapologetic Flashback on the Wonders of the Audio CD

You've probably never bothered to contemplate the wonders of the common or garden audio CD. But if you have, you may have realized that the CD is pretty wonderful—not for the sound quality, although that was a great improvement on the cassette tapes and the vinyl LPs that preceded it; nor for its capacity, because other storage technologies (such as DVDs and magneto-optical disks) have far exceeded that; but for its standards-based universality.

You can buy a CD in just about any country on the planet, buy a CD player or CD drive in just about any other country, insert the CD, and play it. Depending on the quality of the CD player and the playback system, the audio should sound more or less as the artist and producer intended it to. As a result of this universality, CDs became widespread in the 1980s and remain the most popular medium for music distribution.

At first, record companies loved CDs more than consumers did, because CDs allowed them to sell to consumers the same music for a second or even a third time: the consumers had bought the music on LP; some of them had bought it on cassette tapes to play in their Walkmans; and now they could buy it once again on CD to play in their CD players. Better yet, because the CD was a newer, more faithful, and ostensibly more expensive-to-produce medium, the record companies could charge around twice as much for CDs as for LPs or cassette tapes. Since then, CD prices have come down a bit, but they remain far more profitable for the record companies than LPs or cassette tapes.

But soon, despite the prices, consumers began to love CDs as well, because CDs began to deliver on their promise of combining portability and acceptable durability with high-quality sound. And as you know, by 2003 CDs had almost entirely replaced vinyl as the medium on which people buy their music.

As discussed in the previous section, starting in late 1999, and taking effect in 2000, Napster put a severe crimp in the dominance of the CD as the primary means of distributing music. Other file-sharing services followed. Around the same time, CD recording became easier and recordable (and rewritable) CD media became very affordable. So consumers could easily share compressed digital audio files with friends and strangers alike on file-sharing services, or burn perfect copies of CDs to give to people they knew in the physical world.

CD sales fell by five percent in 2001, by seven percent in the first half of 2002, and by 9.3 percent in the whole of 2002. The Recording Industry Association of America (RIAA), which represents the record companies, has claimed that "illegal music downloading was the main culprit in the drop in sales" and has also put part of the blame on recordable CDs, even though it acknowledges that "the decline in consumer spending [has] played a role."

Other commentators argue other factors have almost certainly reduced CD sales as well. For example, the record industry released approximately 27,000 CDs in 2001 compared to nearly 39,000 CDs in 1999. Less choice, less appealing music: it makes sense that consumers would buy fewer CDs, especially if they have substantially less disposable income to spend on music thanks to the recession— I'm sorry, I mean the *economic downturn*.

In August 2002, the analysts at Forrester Research argued the decline in CD sales was mostly attributable to the economic downturn. Forrester also argued MP3 had been *good* for the music business, because people who download MP3 files still tend to buy CDs. In effect, MP3 lets people preview music they might not otherwise have heard. If they like the music, they may well buy the CDs.

How CD-Protection Solutions Work (in Brief)

In brief, and at the risk of generalizing wildly, CD-protection solutions work by corrupting the data on audio discs so the data can still be read by audio CD players but can't be read by computer CD drives. Some high-end audio players, such as car CD players and DVD players, also have trouble reading some copy-protected audio discs.

key2audio uses a hidden signature on the disc to prevent playback on computers. Sony DADC claims the "audio part" of discs protected with key2audio fully complies with the Red Book standard because "no uncorrectable errors are used to protect the audio data." However, because key2audio discs by design don't work with Red Book–compliant CD drives and DVD drives, the discs themselves clearly aren't Red Book–compliant. This might seem like a fine point, but it's not—if the disc won't play back on a CD drive, it's not a CD.

According to Midbar Technologies, Cactus-200 Data Shield is an "engineering solution" (rather than a software solution) that "slightly alters the information on the CD [sic] in several ways while maintaining perfect audio quality."

Consumer advocates put it differently: Cactus introduces errors in the data on the audio disc that require the error-correction mechanisms on the player to compensate. Using the error-correction mechanism on the player like this makes the disc less resistant to damage (for example, scratches), because the player will be unable to correct many damage-related errors on top of the deliberate copy-protection errors. The discs may also degrade more quickly than unprotected CDs. Some consumer advocates claim copy-protection solutions may also lead older or more delicate CD players to fail sooner than they would otherwise have done because they make the players work harder than unprotected CDs do, much as driving at full-speed over rough roads will wear out your car's suspension much more quickly than driving at the same speed on freeways will.

If You Can't Play It on Any CD Player, It's Not a CD

As you learned in "Understand Ripping, Encoding, and 'Copying'" earlier in this chapter, most audio CDs use the Red Book format, while others use the CD Extra format (a subset of Red Book) to put non-audio data on the CD as well.

Red Book was defined by Philips and Sony in 1980. (The standard was published in a red binder—hence the name. Subsequent standards include Orange Book and Yellow Book—three guesses why.) Red Book ensures the disc will work with all drives that bear the Compact Disc logo and entitles the disc to bear the Compact Disc Digital Audio logo.

How to Recognize Copy-Protected Discs

Copy-protected discs won't play on all CD drives and so are technically and legally *not* CDs. You should be able to recognize them as follows:

- The discs shouldn't bear the Compact Disc Digital Audio logo (because they're not CDs). But some do. And in any case, many Red Book CDs don't bear this logo, usually for reasons of label design or laziness.

- The disc may carry a disclaimer, warning, or notice such as "Will *not* play on PC or Mac," "This CD [*sic*] cannot be played on a PC/Mac," "Copy Control," or "Copy Protected."

- The disc won't play on your computer, or will play but won't rip.

What Happens When You Try to Use a Copy-Protected Disc on a Computer

When you try to use a copy-protected disc on a computer, any of the following may happen:

- The disc may play back without problems. You may even be able to rip it by using a conventional audio program such as iTunes or MUSICMATCH Jukebox Plus or a specialized, heavy-duty ripper (such as Exact Audio Copy). If you can rip the disc, the copy-protection has failed (or your drive has defeated it). You may be liable for five years' imprisonment and a half-million-dollar fine.

- The disc may not play at all.

- The disc may cause your computer's operating system to hang.

- You may be unable to eject the disc on some PCs and many Macs. (See the sidebar "How to Eject Stuck Audio Discs.")

> **TIP** *If your Mac has a SuperDrive, download the Apple SuperDrive Update from **www.apple.com/hardware/superdrive/** before attempting to use any copy-protected audio discs in the drive. Once you've installed this update, you'll be able to eject copy-protected audio discs from the drive.*

How to ... How to Eject Stuck Audio Discs

If you insert a non-CD audio disc into your CD drive, and your PC or Mac can't handle it, you may be unable to eject the disc. The PC or Mac may hang. If your computer is a Mac, and you restart it with the disc in the CD drive, your Mac may start up to a gray screen.

On PCs and some Macs, you can use the manual eject hole on the CD drive to eject the disc. Straighten one end of a sturdy paperclip and push it into the hole to eject the disc.

G4 Cubes, some Power Mac G4s, and flat-panel iMacs don't have a manual eject hole, so don't go prodding the wrong hole. Instead, follow as many of these steps as necessary to fix the problem:

1. Restart your Mac. If it's too hung to restart by conventional means, press the Reset button or press COMMAND-CONTROL-POWER. At the system startup sound, hold down the mouse button until your Mac finishes booting. This action may eject the disc.

2. If you're using System 9 and have Mac OS X installed, restart your Mac and boot Mac OS X. Again, if your Mac is too hung to restart by conventional means, press the Reset button or press COMMAND-CONTROL-POWER. At the system startup sound, hold down X to boot Mac OS X. Open iTunes from the dock or the Applications folder, and then click the Eject button.

3. Restart your Mac. Once again, if it's too hung to restart by conventional means, press the Reset button or press COMMAND-CONTROL-POWER. At the system startup sound, hold down COMMAND-OPTION-O-F to boot the Open Firmware mode. You'll see a prompt screen that contains something like the text shown in Figure 2-2 (the exact text varies depending on the model of Mac). Type **eject cd** and press RETURN. If all is well, the CD drive will open. If not, you may see the message "read of block0 failed. can't OPEN the EJECT device". Either way, type **mac-boot** and press RETURN to reboot your Mac.

If Open Firmware mode won't fix the problem, you'll need to take your Mac to a service shop.

```
Apple PowerBook3, 5 4.5.3f2 BootROM built on 10/25/02 at 10:31:30
Copyright 1994-2002 Apple Computer, Inc.
All Rights Reserved

Welcome to Open Firmware, the system time and date is:  10:27:06 02/03/2003

To continue booting, type "mac-boot" and press return.
To shut down, type "shut-down" and press return.

 ok
 0> _
```

FIGURE 2-2 Try using the Open Firmware mode on your Mac to eject a copy-protected disc if conventional means of ejection fail.

Ways to Get Around Copy Protection

Customers annoyed by copy-protected audio discs quickly found ways to circumvent the copy protection.

In many cases, the most effective solution is to experiment with different drives. Some drives can play audio discs protected with some technologies; others can't.

TIP *Many DVD drives are better at playing copy-protected discs than many plain CD-ROM drives. This is because the DVD drives are designed to work with multiple types of discs—DVDs, CDs, recordable CD (CD-R) discs, rewritable CD (CD-RW) discs, and even various types of recordable DVDs, depending on the capabilities of the drive.*

If you don't have multiple CD or DVD drives to experiment with, you might be interested to hear of two crude solutions that have proved successful with some copy-protected audio discs:

- Stick a strip of tape on the disc to mask the outermost track. This track contains extra information intended to confuse computer CD drives. By masking the track, people have managed to obviate the confusion.

- Use a marker to color the outermost track on the disc dark so the laser of the drive won't read it.

Both these techniques require a steady hand—and both constitute willful circumvention of the copy protection, possibly exposing those performing them to retribution under the DMCA.

Chapter 3

Use iTunes to Load Music onto Your Mac iPod

How to...

- Upgrade your Mac to get it iPod-ready
- Set up and configure iTunes
- Choose suitable settings for ripping and encoding MP3, AIFF, and WAV files
- Create, build, and manage your music library
- Play back music with iTunes
- Use the graphical equalizer to improve the sound of music
- Synchronize your music library with your iPod automatically or manually
- Create custom playlists containing only the tracks you like
- Use the Smart Playlist feature to create playlists based on your preferences

This chapter discusses how to master iTunes, the software Apple provides for enjoying digital audio on Mac OS and for managing your iPod. iTunes provides a graphical interface for ripping and encoding songs on CDs to digital audio files you can store and manipulate on your Mac, allowing fast and easy synchronization with your iPod.

This chapter assumes you're using iTunes 3.0.1 or later. iTunes 3.0.1 runs on Mac OS X 10.1.4 or later. If you're using System 9, you'll have to use iTunes 2; if you're using a version of Mac OS X earlier than 10.1.4, you'll have to use iTunes 3.0 or an earlier version. These earlier versions of iTunes lack features such as ratings, equalization, and smart playlists.

iTunes contains a fair number of configuration options. Rather than lumping all the configuration options together into a heavy-going section you'll refuse to read, this chapter presents the configuration options as needed to accomplish particular tasks you're likely to want to undertake.

NOTE *The new iPods require iTunes 4, which offers several significant improvements over iTune 3. See Chapter 17 for coverage of the differences in iTunes 4.*

Get Your Mac Ready to Work with Your iPod

If you bought your Mac in 2002 or later, chances are it's already all set for working with your iPod: it has one or more FireWire ports, System 9 or Mac OS X with iTunes, plenty of disk space and memory, and a recordable CD drive as well. But if you have an earlier Mac, or if your recent Mac came with a plain CD-ROM drive rather than a recordable CD drive, you may need to bring one or more of these areas up to date. The following subsections briefly discuss what you need.

Add FireWire if Necessary

To use an iPod at all, your Mac must have a FireWire port. Because Apple has been plugging FireWire assiduously for several years now, almost all currently usable Macs do have FireWire. If yours doesn't, you can add one or more FireWire ports easily enough to most Macs that lack FireWire by using a PCI card (for a desktop Mac) or a PC Card (for a PowerBook).

You need to make sure the card is compatible with the version of Mac OS you're using. You then need to install the card and any drivers needed to make it work. But that's about as difficult as adding FireWire to a fireless Mac gets.

Check Your Operating System Version

Make sure your version of Mac OS is advanced enough to work with your iPod. You need Mac OS X 10.1.4 or later or System 9.2.1 or later. Upgrade if necessary.

NOTE *This chapter uses Mac OS X for its examples.*

Check Disk Space and Memory

Make sure your Mac has enough disk space and memory to serve your iPod adequately.

In most cases, memory shouldn't be an issue: if your Mac can run System 9 or Mac OS X and conventional applications at a speed you can tolerate without sedation, it should be able to handle your iPod. Disk space is more likely to be an issue because of the vast amount of space you're likely to want to dedicate to your music library.

The best situation is to have enough space on your hard drive to contain your entire music library, both at its current size and at whatever size you expect it to grow to in the foreseeable future (or within the lifetime of your Mac). That way, you can easily synchronize your entire music library with your iPod (if your music library fits on your iPod) or just whichever part of your music library you want to take around with you for the time being. For example, to fill a 20GB iPod with music, you'll need 20GB of hard-disk space to devote to your music library. Recent desktop Macs have hard disks large enough to spare 20GB without serious hardship, but if you have an older Mac, a PowerBook, or an iBook, space problems may be looming in your horoscope. For example, the G3 800MHz iBook comes with a 30GB hard disk—so to fill your 20GB iPod, you'd need to use two-thirds of your hard disk for your music library.

If you have a desktop Mac, you should be able to add another hard drive without undue effort. The least expensive option will typically be to add another EIDE hard drive or SCSI drive (depending on the configuration of your Mac) to the inside of your Mac. Alternatively, you can go for an external FireWire, USB, or SCSI drive (again, that's if your Mac has SCSI).

If you have a PowerBook or an iBook, your best bet is probably to add an external FireWire or USB hard drive. Upgrading the internal hard drive on a laptop tends to be prohibitively expensive—and of course you have to transfer or reinstall the operating system, your applications, and all your data after the upgrade.

Add a CD-R Drive if Necessary

If your Mac doesn't have a CD recorder, you may want to add one so you can burn CDs from iTunes and other applications.

For a desktop Mac that has a full-size drive bay free, an internal CD-R drive is the least expensive option. Alternatively, turn to something else that suits both desktop Macs and portables: external FireWire, USB, or SCSI recordable CD drives.

TIP *iTunes doesn't work flawlessly with all CD recorders. Before buying, check* **www.apple.com/itunes/compatibility** *to make sure the drive you're coveting will work with iTunes.*

Set Up and Configure iTunes on Your Mac

If you haven't already set up iTunes on your Mac, do so now by following these steps:

1. Click the iTunes icon in the Dock or run iTunes from the iTunes icon in your Applications folder. The first time you run iTunes, the OS launches the iTunes Setup Assistant.

2. On the Welcome to iTunes! page, click the Next button to display the Internet Audio page.

CHAPTER 3: Use iTunes to Load Music onto Your Mac iPod   61

3. Choose whether or not to let iTunes connect to the Internet automatically to download information about CDs you insert in your CD drive or information about streaming broadcasts.

4. Click the Next button to display the Find MP3 Files page.

5. If you want to have iTunes scan your hard disk for any MP3 files it contains and add them to your music library, select the Yes, Find Any MP3 Files I Have on My Hard Disk option button. If not, select the No, I'll Add Them Myself Later option button.

6. Click the Done button. iTunes searches your disk for MP3 files if you chose to let it, and then adds them to your music library.

Figure 3-1 shows the iTunes interface.

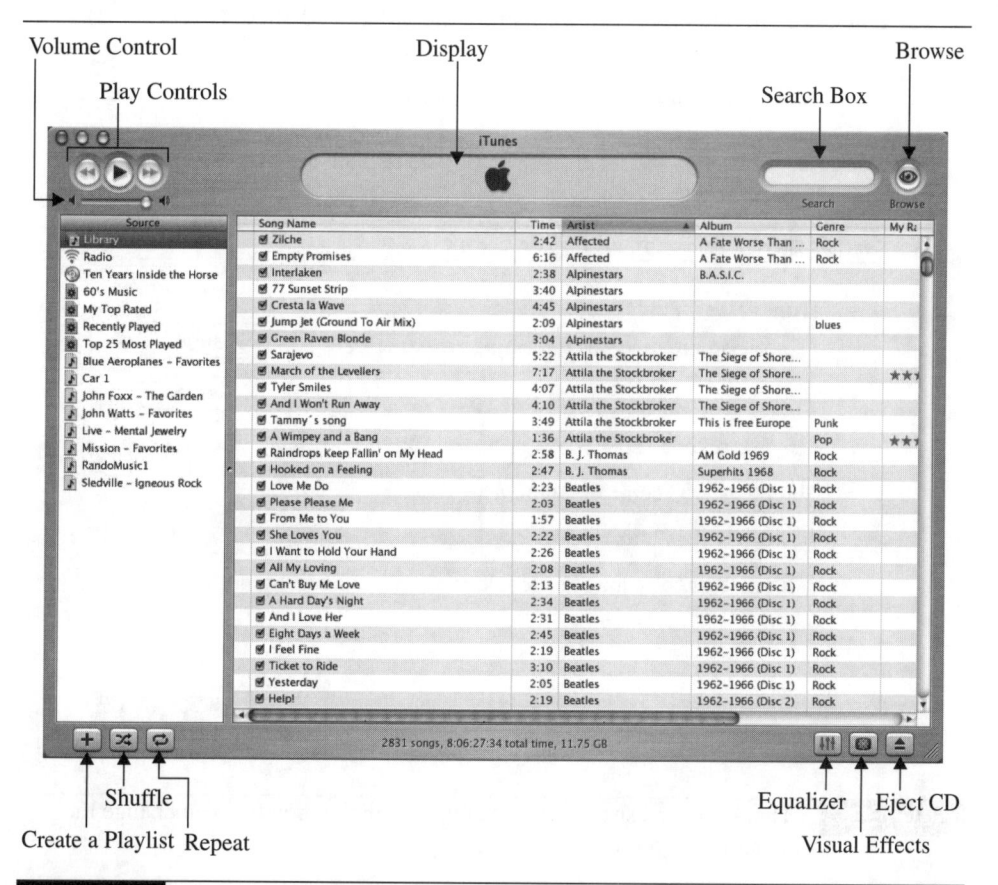

FIGURE 3-1   iTunes's streamlined interface gives you direct access to your music.

Choose Where to Store Your Music Library

Because your music library can contain dozens—or even hundreds—of gigabytes of music files, storing it in a suitable location is important.

As you'll see in the next section, you don't have to actually store all your music files in your music library—instead, you can store the music library references to where the files are located in other folders. Doing so enables you to keep down the size of your music library. But for maximum flexibility and to make sure you can access all the tracks in your music library all the time, keeping all your music files in your music library folder is best—if you can do so.

To change the location of your music library, follow these steps:

1. Press COMMAND-Y or choose iTunes | Preferences to display the Preferences dialog box.

2. Click the Advanced button to display the Advanced sheet (Figure 3-2).

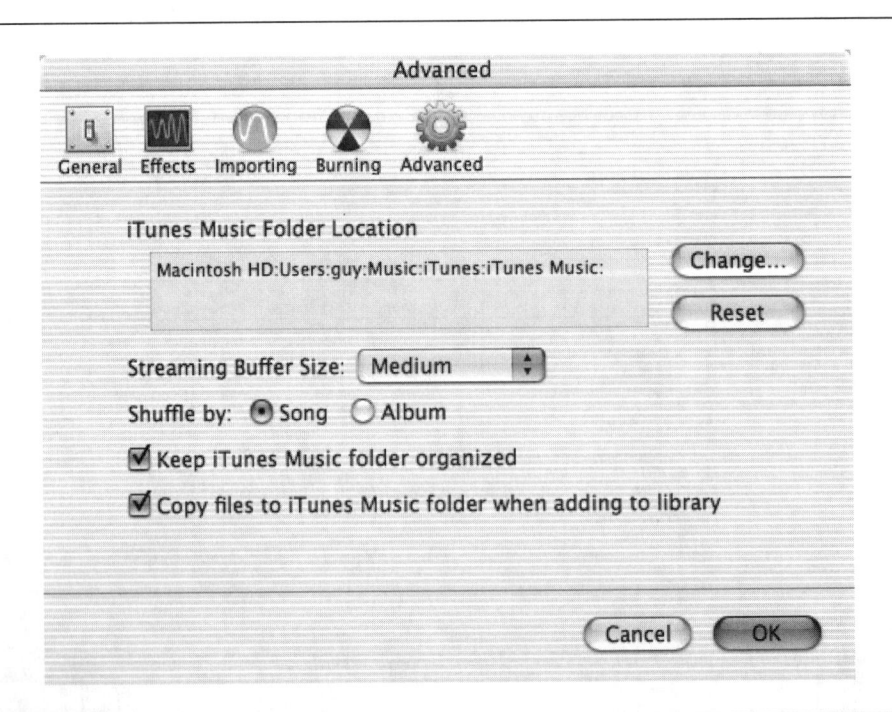

FIGURE 3-2   The Advanced sheet of the Preferences dialog box lets you change the location of your music library.

3. Click the Change button to display the Change Music Folder Location dialog box.

4. Navigate to the folder that will contain your music library, select the folder, and then click the Choose button. iTunes closes the Change Music Folder Location and returns you to the Advanced sheet of the Preferences dialog box.

5. Click the OK button to close the Preferences dialog box. iTunes displays the dialog box shown in the following image, asking if you want iTunes "to organize the music files that are already in your library to match your new preferences"—in other words, whether you want iTunes to move your existing music library files to the folder you specified.

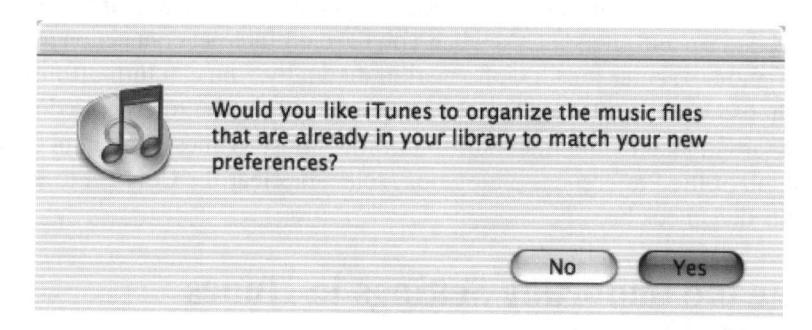

6. If you want to keep all your music library files together in the new location, click the Yes button. You'll see the Organizing Files dialog box as iTunes organizes the files into the new location. If you want to keep your existing music library files in their current locations but put any new files in the new location, click the No button.

NOTE *To reset your music library folder to its default location (the iTunes:iTunes Music folder), click the Reset button on the Advanced sheet of the Preferences dialog box. Again, iTunes asks if you want to move your existing files to the new location.*

Choose Whether to Store All Song Files in Your Music Library

As mentioned in the previous section, iTunes can store references to where song files are located in folders other than your music library folder instead of creating a copy of each file in the music library folder. To make iTunes store references, clear the Copy Files to iTunes Music Folder When Adding to Library check box on the Advanced sheet of the Preferences dialog box (Figure 3-2).

CAUTION *Before allowing iTunes to copy each song file to your music library, make sure you have plenty of hard-disk space first. iTunes doesn't check that there's enough extra space to hold the copies of the song files, so using this option could run you out of hard-disk space and leave you with only some song files copied to your music library.*

Choose Whether iTunes Automatically Connects to the Internet

iTunes can automatically download CD information from the CDDB site on the Web. This saves you a large amount of typing and is great if you have a permanent Internet connection or an Internet connection you can establish at any time. But if you'll need to rip and encode CDs when you have no Internet connection available, or if you prefer to enter the CD information manually, you can turn off this feature.

To choose whether iTunes automatically connects to the Internet to download CD data (artist, album, and track information), choose iTunes | Preferences. On the General tab of the Preferences dialog box, select or clear the Connect to Internet When Needed check box.

Change the Importing Settings in iTunes to Specify Audio Quality

Before you rip any CDs using iTunes, check that the settings are suitable for your needs. As discussed in Chapter 2, iTunes's default settings are a fair choice for defaults, but you may well want to change them. It's worth investing a little time in choosing the right settings for ripping and encoding, because ripping tracks more than once quickly becomes a severe waste of time.

Several variables are involved in getting a high-quality MP3 file:

- Reading the CD accurately (assuming the source is a CD).

- Using an encoder capable of creating high-quality MP3 encodings. The Fraunhofer encoder iTunes uses is high quality.

- Choosing a suitable compression rate to save the right amount of data.

- Making sure the data saved is as accurate as possible.

To check or change the importing settings, follow these steps:

1. Choose iTunes | Preferences or press OPTION-Y to display the Preferences dialog box.

CHAPTER 3: Use iTunes to Load Music onto Your Mac iPod 65

2. Click the Importing tab to display the Importing sheet (Figure 3-3).

3. In the Import Using drop-down list, specify the file format you want to use by choosing the appropriate encoder. The default setting is MP3 Encoder, which creates MP3 files. MP3 files are the type of files you'll probably want to create most often, because they offer the best combination of audio quality and compact file size. If you want to create AIFF files, choose AIFF Encoder. If you want to create WAV files, choose WAV Encoder.

4. In the Configuration drop-down list, choose the setting you want to use:

   - For the MP3 Encoder, the Configuration drop-down list offers the settings Good Quality (128 Kbps), Better Quality (160 Kbps), High Quality (192 Kbps), and Custom. When you select the Custom item, iTunes displays the MP3 Encoder dialog box so you can specify custom settings. See "Choose Custom MP3 Encoding Settings," next, for a discussion of these options.

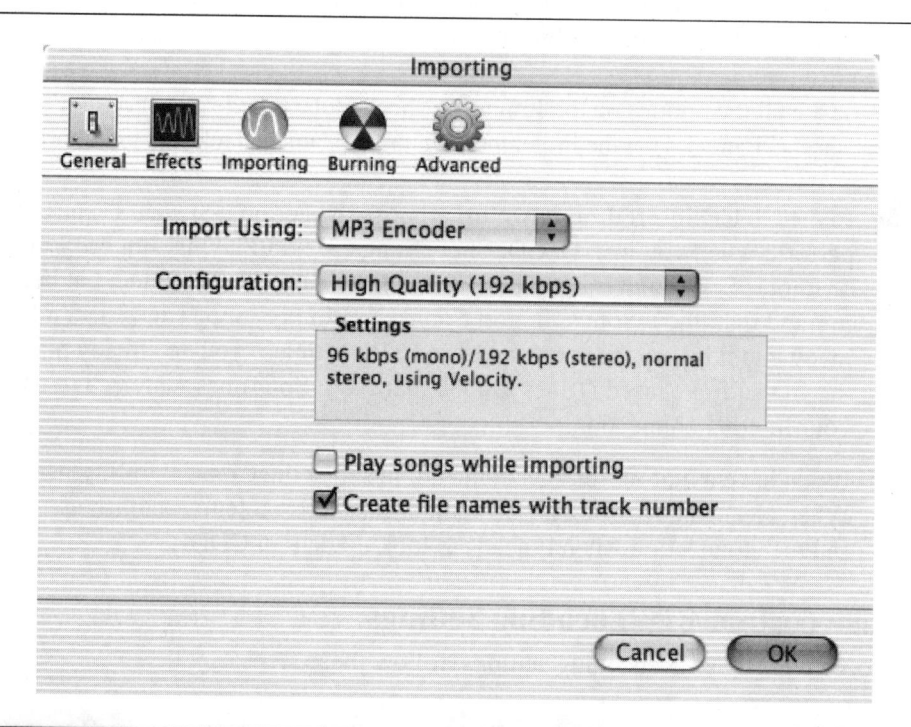

FIGURE 3-3 Choose the appropriate file format and compression settings on the Importing sheet of the Preferences dialog box.

- For the AIFF Encoder and the WAV Encoder, the Configuration drop-down list offers the settings Automatic and Custom. When you select the Custom item, iTunes displays the AIFF Encoder dialog box or the WAV Encoder dialog box (as appropriate) so you can specify custom settings. See "Choose Custom AIFF and WAV Encoding Settings," later in this chapter, for a discussion of these options.

5. If you want iTunes to play each CD as you import it, leave the Play Songs While Importing check box selected (it's selected by default). Listening to the CD slows down the rate of ripping and encoding, so you may prefer not to use this option.

6. If you want iTunes to include track numbers in song names (creating names such as *01 Cortez the Killer* instead of *Cortez the Killer*, leave the Create File Names with Track Number check box selected (it's selected by default). Including the track numbers in the filenames lets you sort the songs in the Finder and may make it easier for you to recover songs from your iPod if your computer's hard disk fails. (Some utilities for downloading songs from an iPod can sort the song files by their tag information, as iTunes does.)

Those are all the options on the Importing sheet. But a couple of options on the General sheet (Figure 3-4) of the Preferences dialog box are also relevant to importing:

- In the On CD Insert drop-down list, choose the action you want iTunes to perform when you insert a CD: Show Songs, Begin Playing, Import Songs, or Import Songs and Eject. These settings are easy to understand, but bear in mind that Show Songs, Import Songs, and Import Songs and Eject all involve looking up the song names in CDDB (unless you've already played the CD and so caused iTunes to look them up). So iTunes will need to use your Internet connection.

- If you have a dial-up Internet connection, select the Connect to Internet When Needed check box if you want iTunes to be able to establish an Internet connection when it needs to look up data in CDDB.

Choose Custom MP3 Encoding Settings

To choose custom MP3 encoding settings, follow these steps:

1. On the Importing sheet of the Preferences dialog box, choose the Custom item in the Configuration drop-down list to display the MP3 Encoder dialog box (Figure 3-5).

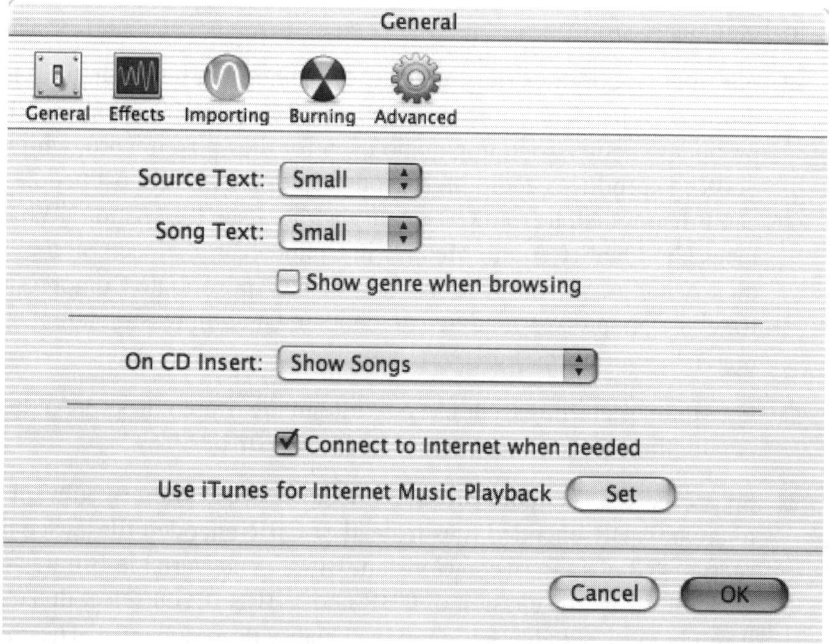

CHAPTER 3: Use iTunes to Load Music onto Your Mac iPod   67

FIGURE 3-4   On the General sheet of the Preferences dialog box, specify what iTunes should do when you insert a CD.

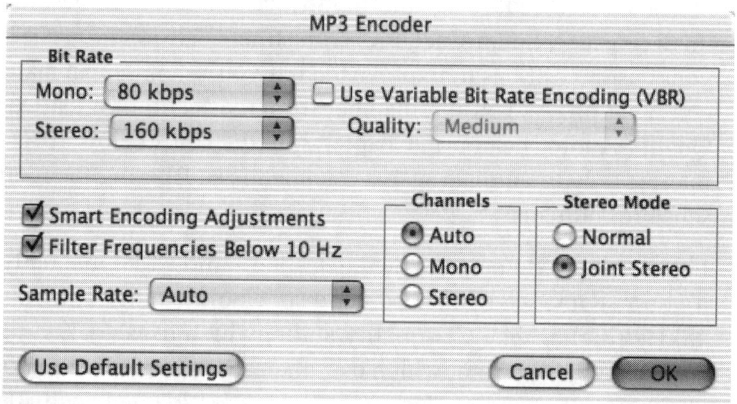

FIGURE 3-5   You can use the MP3 Encoder dialog box to specify custom settings for the MP3 files you create using iTunes.

2. Use the controls in the Bit Rate group box to specify the bitrates for mono and stereo encoding:

- For mono recordings (if you make any), choose a bitrate in the Mono drop-down list. The choices range from 8 Kbps to 320 Kbps. 8 Kbps produces shoddy-sounding audio even for the spoken word, while 320Kbps produces audio high enough in quality that most people can't distinguish it from CD-quality audio. (See the section "What Does CD-Quality Audio Mean?" in Chapter 2 for a discussion of CD-quality audio. See the section "Choose an Appropriate Compression Rate" in Chapter 2 for advice on choosing a compression rate that matches your needs.)

- For stereo recordings, choose a bitrate in the Stereo drop-down list. Again, the choices range from 8Kbps to 320Kbps.

- Select the Use Variable Bit Rate Encoding check box if you want to create VBR-encoded files instead of CBR-encoded files. (See the section "Choose Between Constant Bitrate and Variable Bitrate" in Chapter 2 for a discussion of CBR and VBR.) If you select this check box, choose a suitable setting in the Quality drop-down list. The choices are Lowest, Low, Medium Low, Medium, Medium High, High, and Highest. For VBR encoding, iTunes uses the bitrates specified in the Mono and Stereo drop-down lists as the guaranteed minimum bitrates.

- Select or clear the Smart Encoding Adjustments check box and the Filter Frequencies Below 10Hz check box as appropriate. These check boxes are selected by default. In most cases, you'll do best to leave them selected. Smart Encoding Adjustments allows iTunes to tweak your custom settings to improve them if you've chosen an inappropriate combination. As you'll remember from the section "What Does CD-Quality Audio Mean?" in Chapter 2, frequencies below 10Hz are of interest only to animals such as elephants, so filtering them out makes sense for humans.

- In the Sample Rate drop-down list, set a sample rate manually only if you're convinced you need to do so. Choices range from 8kHz to 48kHz (higher than CD-quality audio, which uses 44.1kHz). The default setting is Auto, which uses the same sample rate as does the music you're encoding. Using the same sample rate usually delivers optimal results.

- In the Channels group box, you can select the Auto option button, the Mono option button, or the Stereo option button. The default setting is Auto, which uses mono for encoding mono sources and stereo for stereo sources.

- In the Stereo Mode group box, you can choose between normal stereo and joint stereo. See the section "Choose Between Normal Stereo and Joint Stereo" in Chapter 2 for a discussion of the difference between normal stereo and joint stereo. If you select the Mono option button in the Channels group box, the Stereo Mode group box becomes unavailable because its options don't apply to mono.

NOTE *To restore iTunes to using its default settings for encoding MP3 files, click the Use Default Settings button in the MP3 Encoder dialog box.*

3. Click the OK button to close the MP3 Encoder dialog box.
4. Click the OK button to close the Importing sheet of the Preferences dialog box.

Choose Custom AIFF and WAV Encoding Settings

Other than creating different file formats, the AIFF Encoder dialog box (shown on the left in Figure 3-6) and the WAV Encoder dialog box (shown on the right in Figure 3-6) offer the same settings. This isn't surprising, because AIFFs and WAVs are essentially the same apart from the file header, which distinguishes the file formats from each other.

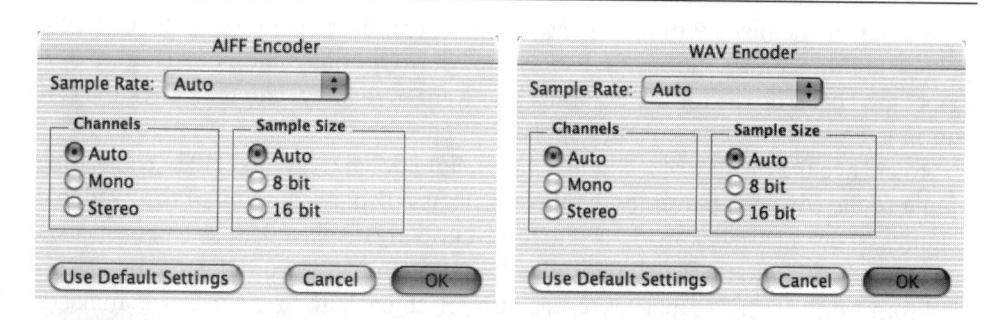

FIGURE 3-6 If you choose to encode to AIFF or WAV files, you can set encoding options in the AIFF Encoder dialog box (left) or the WAV Encoder dialog box (right).

In either of these dialog boxes, you can choose the following settings:

- **Sample Rate**   Choose Auto (the default setting) to encode at the same sample rate as the original you're ripping. Otherwise, choose a value from the range available (8kHz to 48kHz).
- **Channels**   Select the Auto option button (the default setting) to encode mono files from mono sources and stereo files from stereo sources. Otherwise, select the Mono option button or the Stereo option button as appropriate.
- **Sample Size**   Select the Auto option button to have iTunes automatically match the sample size to that of the source. Otherwise, select the 8 bit option button or the 16 bit option button as appropriate. PCM audio uses 16 bits, so if you're encoding files from CDs, iTunes automatically uses a 16-bit sample size.

Change the Columns Displayed to Show the Information You Need

By default, iTunes displays the following columns: Song Name, Time, Artist, Album, Genre, My Rating, Play Count, and Last Played. (The Play Count item stores the number of times you've played the song in iTunes. iTunes uses this information to determine your favorite tracks—for example, to decide which tracks Smart Playlist should add to a playlist. You can also use this information yourself if you so choose. The other items are self-explanatory.)

You can change the columns displayed for the current item (for example, your music library or a playlist) by using either of two techniques.

To change the display of multiple columns in the same operation, press OPTION-J or choose Edit | View Options to display the View Options dialog box (Figure 3-7). Select the check boxes for the columns you want to display, and then click the OK button to close the dialog box and apply your choices.

To change the display of a single column, hold down CTRL and click the heading of one of the columns currently displayed. iTunes displays a menu of the available columns, showing a check mark next to those currently displayed. Select an unchecked column to display it. Select a checked column to remove it from the display.

From the CTRL-CLICK menu, you can also select the Auto Size Column command to automatically resize the column whose heading you clicked so the column's width best fits its contents. Select the Auto Size All Columns command to automatically resize all columns so their widths best fit their contents.

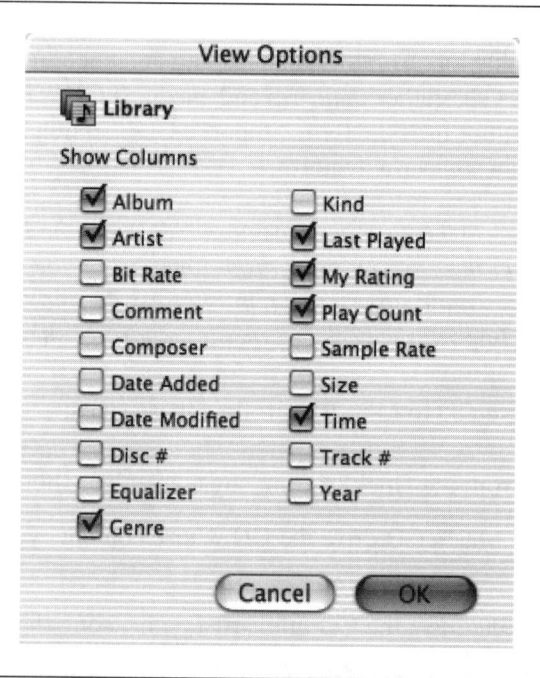

CHAPTER 3: Use iTunes to Load Music onto Your Mac iPod   71

FIGURE 3-7 Use the View Options dialog box to choose which columns iTunes displays.

TIP *You can also change the column width by dragging a column heading to the left or right.*

Create, Build, and Manage Your iTunes Music Library

Before you can load music onto your iPod, you need to create your music library in iTunes. This section discusses how to do so. Most likely, you'll start by ripping some of your CDs and encoding them to MP3 files. You may also need to add to your music library any songs you already have on your Mac, consolidate your music library (putting the whole library in one folder), and change the tags on some MP3 files so iTunes and your iPod list them correctly.

Rip and Encode Your CDs

As discussed in Chapter 2, there are two steps to getting the audio off a CD and into a digital audio file your computer can use: ripping the audio from the CD, and encoding it to the file (for example, an MP3 file). But because most people speak simply of "ripping" a CD rather than ripping and encoding it, this book also uses the phrase "rip a CD" rather than "rip and encode a CD." To make things even more complicated, iTunes uses the term "import a CD," so this book uses that term when referring to iTunes-specific features.

> **TIP** *To rip a stack of CDs as quickly as possible, select the Import Songs and Eject option in the On CD Insert drop-down list on the General sheet of the Preferences dialog box (shown in Figure 3-4), and clear the Play Songs While Importing check box on the Importing sheet.*

To rip and encode a CD to MP3 files, follow these steps:

1. Start iTunes from the Dock or from any convenient shortcut.

2. Insert in your Mac's CD drive the CD whose contents you want to rip and encode.

3. Enter the CD details—the CD title, artist name, song titles, and genre:

   - The easiest way to enter the details is to let iTunes connect automatically to the Internet to download the CD details automatically and enter them in the appropriate fields. (See "Choose Whether iTunes Automatically Connects to the Internet," earlier in this chapter, for details on how to control whether iTunes connects automatically.)

   - Alternatively, choose Advanced | Get CD Track Names to force iTunes to search CDDB for the information.

   - If you don't have an Internet connection, enter the data manually. The easiest way to do so is to choose Advanced | Submit CD Track Names to display the CD Info dialog box. Enter the information in this dialog box. Make sure your Internet connection isn't connected and that iTunes won't establish it automatically. Then click the OK button. iTunes displays an error because it can't access CDDB, but it enters the information in the appropriate fields much more quickly than you could do manually.

4. Click the Import button to start the importing process. iTunes displays its progress (Figure 3-8). If you need to stop the import process, click the Import button again.

CHAPTER 3: Use iTunes to Load Music onto Your Mac iPod 73

FIGURE 3-8 iTunes shows you its progress as it rips songs from a CD and encodes them to MP3 files.

How to ... How to Submit CD Information to CDDB Using iTunes

If a CD you want to rip turns out not to have an entry in CDDB, you can submit an entry yourself. Many of the entries in CDDB for older or less widely known CDs have been added by users submitting entries like this. Mainstream entries are submitted by the record companies themselves: the record companies submit a listing to CDDB (and other online CD-information services, such as **WindowsMedia.com**) as a matter of course when they release a new CD.

At this writing, CDDB contains entries for an enormous number of CDs—so unless you have an unusual CD, chances are any CD you want to rip already has an entry in CDDB. You may find that your CD is listed under a slightly different title or artist name than you're expecting—for example, the artist might be listed as *Sixpack, Joe* rather than *Joe Sixpack*. Check carefully for any close matches before submitting an entry so you don't waste your time.

NOTE *You may also find CDDB contains two or more entries for the same CD. This can happen when two or more people simultaneously submit information for a CD that doesn't have an entry, or someone submits information for a previously existing selection. The people who run CDDB routinely discard duplicate entries when they find them, but given how many CDs CDDB contains entries for, it's not surprising that they're unable to catch all duplicates. When you run into a duplicate, you need to guess from the names shown which entry matches your CD.*

When submitting an entry to CDDB, type the CD title, artist name, and song titles carefully using standard capitalization, and double-check all the information before you submit it. Otherwise, if your entry is accepted and entered in CDDB, anyone who looks up that CD will get the misspellings or wrong information you entered.

To submit an entry to CDDB, follow these steps:

1. Insert the CD in your CD drive and check that CDDB doesn't already have an entry for it.
2. Enter the song names in the Song Name column.
3. Choose Advanced | Submit CD Track Names to display the CD Info dialog box (Figure 3-9).
4. Enter as much information as possible in the Artist text box, the Composer text box, the Album text box, the Disc Number text boxes, the Genre drop-down list, and the Year text box. Select the Compilation CD check box if the CD is a compilation rather than a work by an individual artist.
5. Establish an Internet connection if you need to do so manually.
6. Click the OK button. iTunes connects to CDDB and submits the information. iTunes also enters the information in the appropriate columns for the CD.

Join Tracks Together Without Gaps

The default settings in iTunes create a separate file (MP3, AIFF, or WAV, depending on your preferences) from each song on CDs you rip. For most CDs, this works

CHAPTER 3: Use iTunes to Load Music onto Your Mac iPod   **75**

FIGURE 3-10   If CDDB doesn't contain an entry for a CD you're ripping, use the CD Info dialog box to submit an entry for it.

well. But sometimes you'll want to rip multiple tracks from a CD into a single file so they play back without a break. For example, some CDs are produced so one song runs into the next.

To rip two or more tracks from a CD into a single file, select the tracks, and then choose Advanced | Join CD Tracks. iTunes brackets the tracks, as shown in Figure 3-10. These tracks then rip to a single file.

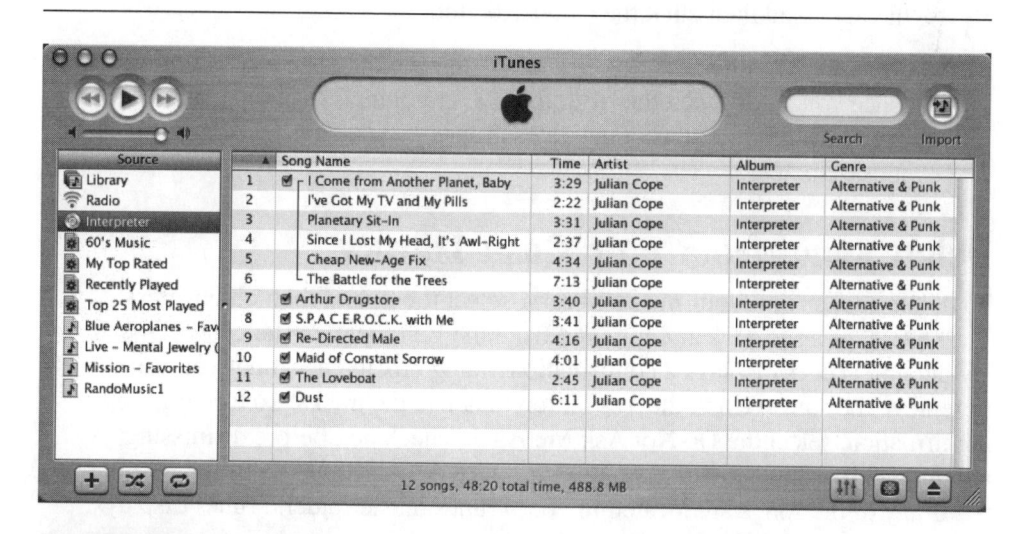

FIGURE 3-9   Use the Join CD Tracks command to rip two or more tracks to a single file.

NOTE *If you made a mistake with the junction, select one or more of the joined tracks, and then choose Advanced | Unjoin CD Tracks to separate the tracks again.*

Add Songs to iTunes to Expand Your Music Library

You can add songs to iTunes in any of the following ways:

- Import the songs from a CD as described earlier in this chapter. Alternatively, import the songs from another sound source.

- Drag one or more song files, folders, or volumes and drop them in the iTunes main window.

NOTE *If you left the Copy Files to iTunes Music Folder When Adding to Library check box (on the Advanced sheet of the Preferences dialog box in Figure 3-2) selected, iTunes copies the song files to your music library. If you cleared this check box, iTunes displays a dialog box that tells you iTunes will add a reference to the files but won't move or copy them to your music library. This dialog box also warns you that, if you move the files from the location to which the reference points, iTunes will no longer be able to play them.*

- Choose File | Add to Library and use the Add to Library dialog box to specify the file or the folder or volume of songs you want to add. Select the item, and then click the Choose button.

- Drag one or more files, folders, or volumes to the iTunes icon in the Dock. Once you've dropped the files, folders, or volumes on a representation of iTunes, Mac OS opens or activates iTunes, which adds the song files to the music library.

Delete Songs from Your Music Library

To delete songs from your music library, select them, and then either press BACKSPACE or issue a Clear command from the Edit menu or the context menu. By default, iTunes displays a confirmation dialog box to check that you want to remove the songs. Click the Yes button to delete the tracks. To turn off the confirmation, select the Do Not Ask Me Again check box before dismissing the dialog box.

If any of the songs are located in your iTunes music folder, iTunes displays the dialog box shown in the following image to tell you so and ask if you want to move these files to the Trash. Select the Yes button, the No button, or the Cancel button as appropriate.

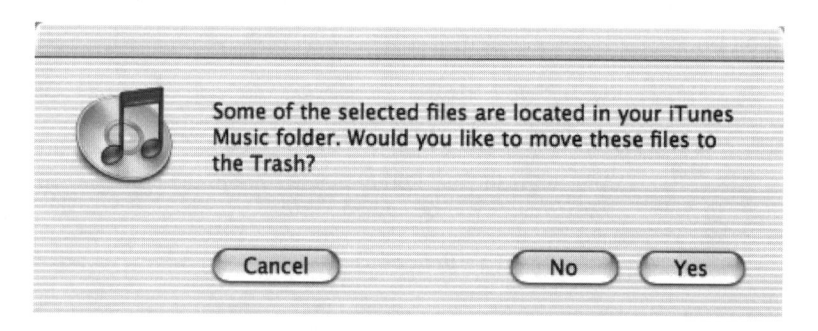

> Some of the selected files are located in your iTunes Music folder. Would you like to move these files to the Trash?
>
> Cancel   No   Yes

Consolidate Your Music Library so You Can Always Access All Its Songs

As you saw in "Choose Whether to Store All Song Files in Your Music Library," earlier in this chapter, if you clear the Copy Files to iTunes Music Folder when Adding to Library check box on the Advanced sheet of the iTunes Preferences dialog box, iTunes places in the music library only a pointer to the file. When your external drives, network drives, or removable media aren't available (for example, when you grab your iBook and head over to a friend's house for a night of gaming), the songs stored on those drives or media won't be available.

To make sure you can play the music you want wherever you want, you can *consolidate* your music library, making iTunes copy all the files currently outside your iTunes music folder to the music folder. Consolidation is new in iTunes 3.

Don't rush into consolidating your music library without understanding its implications:

- Consolidation can take a long time, depending on the number of files to be copied and the speed of the network connection you're using. Don't consolidate your library just as the airport shuttle is about to arrive.

- The drive that holds your music library must have enough space free to hold all your songs. If lack of space was the reason you didn't copy the songs to your music library in the first place, you probably don't want to consolidate your library.

- Songs on removable media such as CDs or Zip disks won't be copied unless the medium is in the drive at the time.

To consolidate your music library, follow these steps:

1. Choose Advanced | Consolidate Library. iTunes displays the following dialog box:

   > Any songs in your library that are not in the iTunes Music folder will be copied there.
   >
   > This cannot be undone.
   >
   > Cancel   OK

2. Click the OK button. iTunes displays the Copying Files dialog box as it copies the files to your music library.

Tag Your Songs so iTunes Sorts Them Correctly

Each MP3 file contains a *tag*—a container with a number of slots for different types of information, from the song name, artist name, and album name to the year and the genre. iTunes displays some of this information by default in its Artist, Album, and Genre columns, but it can handle MP3 files without tag information. Your iPod, on the other hand, requires the artist, song, and album information to be supplied so it can add a song to its database and allow you to access it.

As you saw earlier in this chapter, the easiest way to add tag information to an MP3 file is by downloading the information from CDDB when you rip the CD. But sometimes you'll need to enter (or change) tag information manually to make iTunes sort the MP3 files correctly.

NOTE *MP3 files distributed illegally on the Internet often lack tag information or include incorrect tags.*

To edit the tag information for a single song, select it and issue a Get Info command (press COMMAND-I or choose File | Get Info), and then work on the Tags tab of the Song Information dialog box (Figure 3-11).

To edit the tag information for multiple songs at once, select the songs by SHIFT-clicking or COMMAND-clicking (as appropriate), and then press COMMAND-I

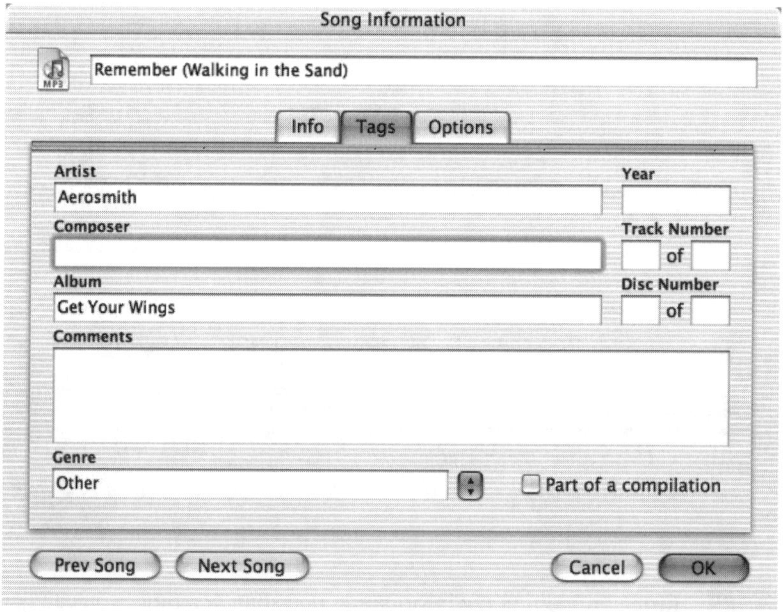

FIGURE 3-11 Use the Tags tab of the Song Information dialog box to edit the tag information for a single song.

or choose File | Get Info. In the Multiple Song Information dialog box (Figure 3-12), enter the information common to the songs you selected.

NOTE *By default, when you issue a Get Info command with multiple songs selected, iTunes displays a dialog box to check that you want to edit the information for multiple songs. Click the Yes button to proceed; click the Cancel button to cancel. If you're less adept with the Mac interface, this double-check may help prevent you from entering the wrong tag information for multiple songs. But if you frequently want to edit tag information for multiple songs, select the Do Not Ask Me Again check box in the confirmation dialog box to turn off confirmations in the future.*

Apply Ratings to Songs to Tell iTunes Which Music You Like

iTunes's My Rating feature (added in iTunes 3.0.1) lets you assign a rating of one star to five stars to each song in your music library. You can then sort the songs by rating or tell Smart Playlist to add only songs of a certain ranking or better

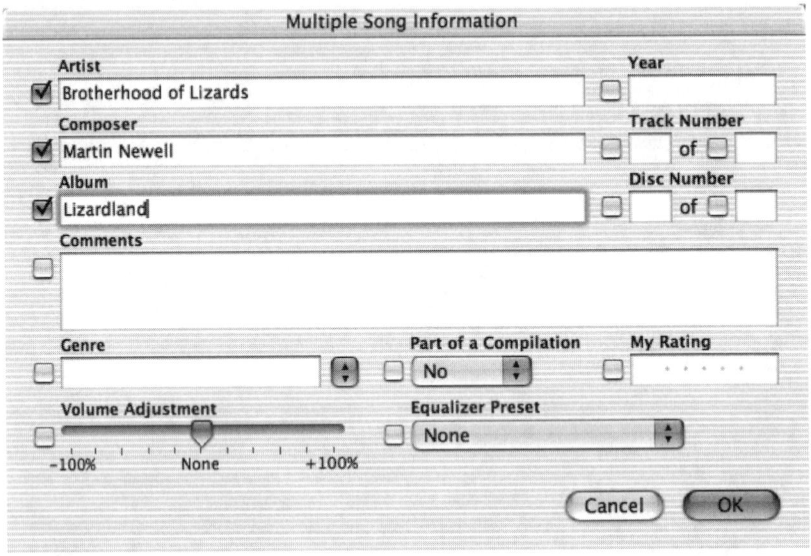

FIGURE 3-12 Instead of editing tag information one song at a time, you can edit tag information for multiple songs at once by using the Multiple Song Information dialog box.

to a playlist. (See the section "Automatically Create Smart Playlists Based on Your Ratings and Preferences," later in this chapter, for a discussion of Smart Playlist.)

You can apply a rating in either of two ways:

- Right-click (or CTRL-click) a song, choose My Rating from the context menu, and select the appropriate number of stars from the submenu.

- Use the My Rating box on the Options tab of the Song Information dialog box (COMMAND-I or File | Get Info) to specify the number of stars.

Enjoy Music with iTunes

This section shows you what you need to know to enjoy music on your Mac with iTunes: how to browse by using the Browser panes; how to play back music, how to use the graphical equalizer to improve the sound of the music, and how to fade one track into another track.

CHAPTER 3: Use iTunes to Load Music onto Your Mac iPod 81

Browse Quickly by Using the Browser Panes

Use the Browser panes to browse quickly by artist or album. Display the Browser panes (Figure 3-13) by clicking the Browse button, pressing COMMAND-B, or choosing Edit | Show Browser. Click an item in the Artist column to display the albums by that artist in the Album column, and then click an item in the Albums column to display that album in the lower pane. To hide the Browser panes, click the Browse button or press COMMAND-B again, or choose Edit | Hide Browser.

Play Back Music with iTunes

Playing back music with iTunes is so simple it barely deserves comment. Here's what you need to know:

- Navigate to the album, playlist, or song you want to play, select it, and then click the Play button.

FIGURE 3-13 To browse quickly through your music library by artist or album, display the Browser panes.

- Drag the diamond on the progress bar in the display to scroll forward or backward through the current track.

- Use the Shuffle button to shuffle the order of the tracks in the current album or playlist. (To change whether iTunes shuffles by song or by album, select the Song option button or the Album option button on the Advanced sheet of the Preferences dialog box.)

- Use the Repeat button to repeat the current song or the current playlist.

- To enjoy visualizations with your music, set a size by choosing Visuals | Small, Visuals | Medium, or Visuals | Large. To start a visualization of that size, press COMMAND-T or choose Visuals | Turn Visual On. To turn a windowed visualization off, press COMMAND-T or choose Visuals | Turn Visual Off. To launch full-screen visualizations, press COMMAND-F or choose Visuals | Full Screen. To stop full-screen visualizations, click your mouse button anywhere or press ESC.

> **TIP** *You can change the information shown in the display window by clicking the items in it. Click the top line to move among the song title, the artist's name, and the album title. Click the Play icon at the left of the display window to toggle between the track information and the equalization graph. Click the time readout to move among Elapsed Time, Remaining Time, and Total Time.*

The Effects sheet of the Preferences dialog box (Figure 3-14) offers options for crossfading playback and changing the Sound Enhancer.

- The Crossfade Playback check box, which is selected by default, makes iTunes fade in the start of the next track as the current track is about to end. This option lets you eliminate gaps between songs the way most DJs do. Drag the slider to increase or decrease the length of time that's crossfaded. Turn off crossfading if you don't like it.

- The Sound Enhancer check box, which is selected by default, applies sound enhancement to the music being played back. Experiment with different settings on the Low–High scale by dragging the slider to see which setting sounds best to you—or turn off sound enhancement if you don't like it.

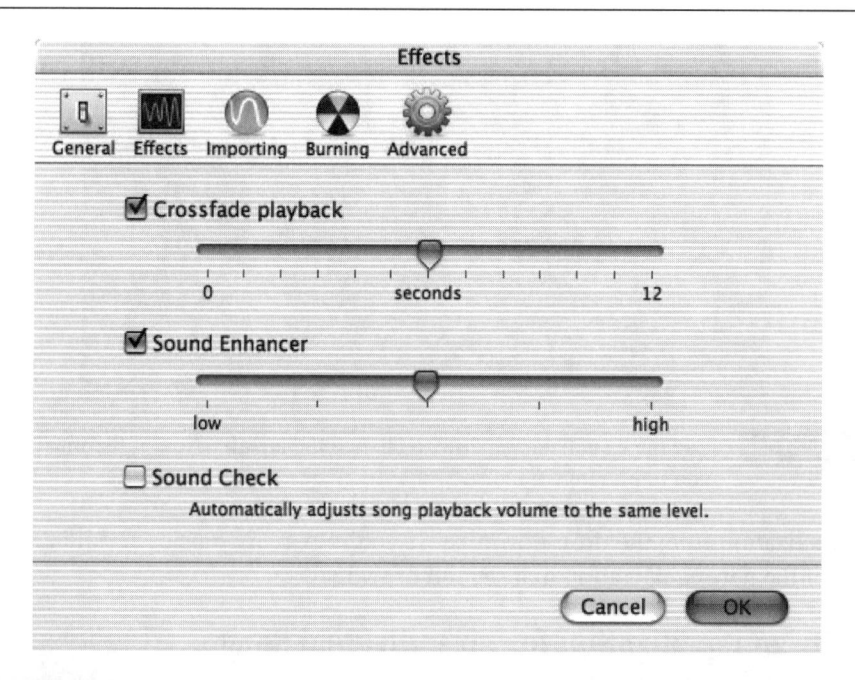

CHAPTER 3: Use iTunes to Load Music onto Your Mac iPod   83

FIGURE 3-14   Choose playback options on the Effects sheet of the Preferences dialog box.

Use the Graphical Equalizer to Make the Music Sound Great

iTunes includes a graphical equalizer that you can use to change the sound of the music (or other audio) you're playing. You can apply an equalization directly to the playlist you're currently playing, much as you would apply an equalization manually to a physical amplifier or receiver. But you can also apply a specific equalization to each song in your iTunes music library. Once you've done this, iTunes always uses that equalization when playing that song, no matter which equalization is currently applied to iTunes itself. After playing a song that has an equalization specified, iTunes switches back to the previous equalization for the next song that doesn't have an equalization specified.

Apply an Equalization to the Current Playlist

To apply an equalization to the current playlist, display the Equalizer window (Figure 3-15) by choosing Window | Equalizer or pressing COMMAND-2. Select

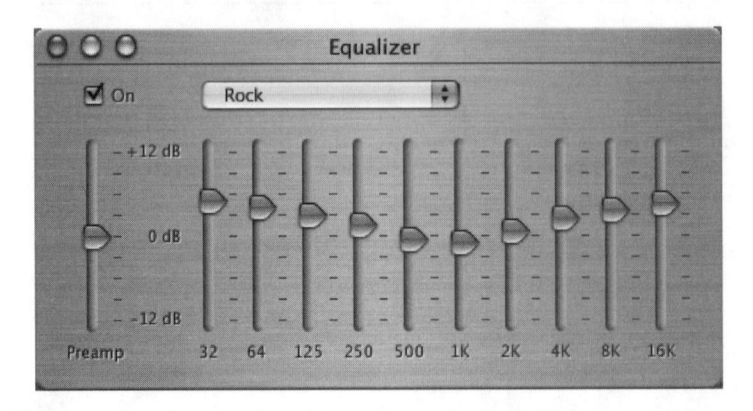

FIGURE 3-15 Use the Equalizer window to change the equalization of the music you're playing.

the equalization from the drop-down list. If you're playing music, you'll hear the effect of the new equalization in a second or two.

Specify an Equalization for an Individual Song

To specify the equalization iTunes should use for a particular song, follow these steps:

1. Select the song in your music library or in a playlist.

NOTE *It doesn't matter whether you apply the equalization to the song in the music library or in a playlist, because applying the equalization even in a playlist affects the song in the music library. So if you can access a song more easily through a playlist than through your music library, start from the playlist.*

2. Press COMMAND-I or choose File | Get Info to display the Song Information dialog box.
3. Click the Options tab to display the Options tab (Figure 3-16).
4. Select the equalization for the song in the Equalizer Preset drop-down list.
5. Choose other options as necessary, and then click the OK button to close the Song Information dialog box. Alternatively, click the Prev Song button or the Next Song button to display the information for the previous song or next song in the Song Information dialog box.

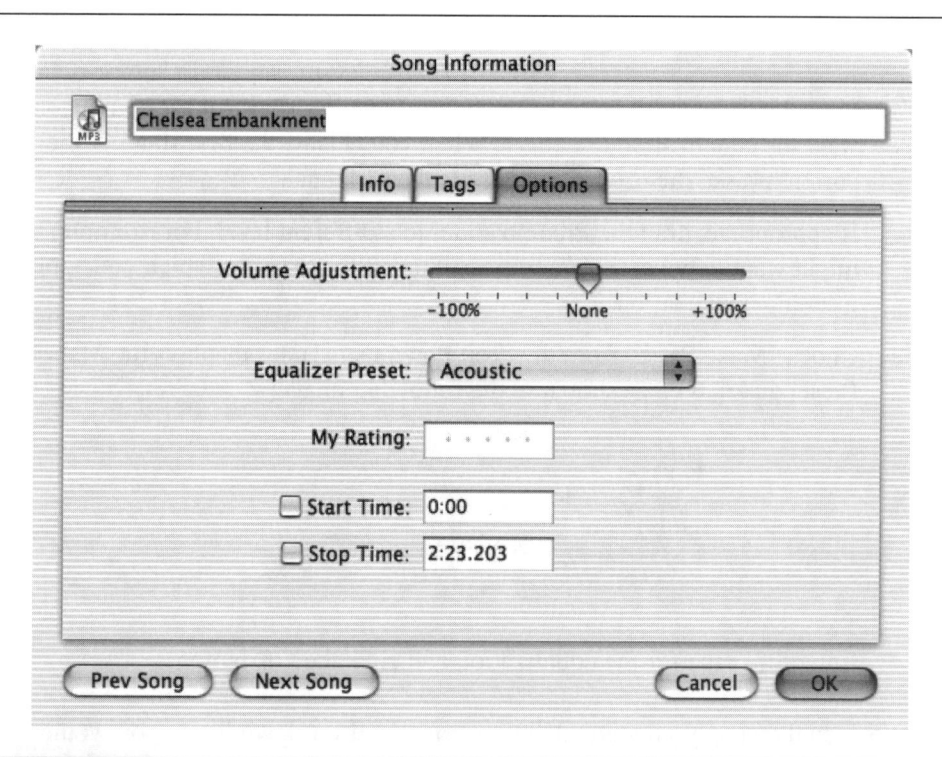

CHAPTER 3:   Use iTunes to Load Music onto Your Mac iPod   **85**

FIGURE 3-16   You can apply an equalization to a song on the Options tab of the Song Information dialog box.

NOTE   *If the equalization you apply to a song is one of the equalizations built into your iPod, your iPod also automatically uses the equalization for playing back the track. But if the equalization is a custom one your iPod doesn't have, your iPod can't use it. Custom equalizations you create aren't added to your iPod.*

Create a Custom Equalization that Sounds Good to You

The preset equalizations in iTunes span a wide range of musical types—but even if there's one named after the type of music you're currently listening to, you may not like the effects it produces. When this happens, try all the other equalizations—however unsuitable their names may make them seem—to see if any of them just happens to sound great with this type of music. (For example, some people swear the Classical equalization is perfect for many Grateful Dead tracks.) If none of them suits you, create a custom equalization that delivers the goods.

To create a new custom equalization, follow these steps:

1. Drag the frequency sliders to the appropriate positions for the sound you want the equalization to deliver. When you change the first slider in the current preset, the drop-down list displays Manual.

2. If appropriate, drag the Preamp slider to a different level. For example, you might want to boost the preamp level on all the songs to which you apply a certain equalization.

3. Choose Make Preset from the drop-down list. iTunes displays the Make Preset dialog box, as shown in the following image.

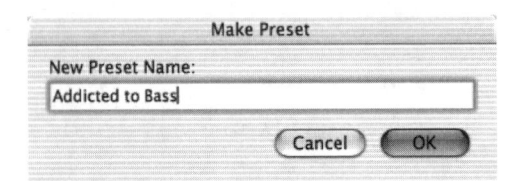

4. Enter the name for the equalization and click the OK button.

You can then apply your equalization from the drop-down list as you would any other preset equalization.

Delete and Rename Preset Equalizations

If you don't like a preset equalization, you can delete it. If you find an equalization's name unsuitable, you can rename it. To delete or rename an equalization, follow these steps:

1. Select the Edit Presets item from the drop-down list in the Equalizer window. iTunes displays the Edit Presets dialog box (Figure 3-17).

2. Select the preset equalization you want to affect.

3. To rename the equalization, follow these steps:
   - Click the Rename button. iTunes displays the Rename dialog box.
   - Type the new name in the New Preset Name text box.

CHAPTER 3: Use iTunes to Load Music onto Your Mac iPod   87

- Click the OK button. iTunes displays a dialog box like that shown in the following image, asking whether you want to change all songs currently set to use this equalization under its current name to use the equalization under the new name you've just specified.

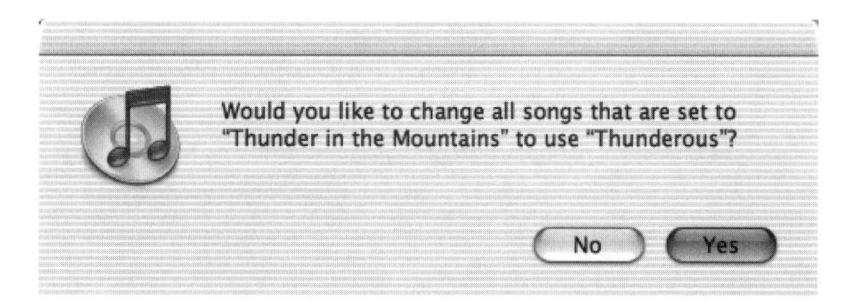

> Would you like to change all songs that are set to "Thunder in the Mountains" to use "Thunderous"?
>
> No   Yes

- Choose the Yes button or the No button as appropriate.

4. To delete a preset equalization, click the Delete button. iTunes displays a dialog box like that in the following image, asking you to confirm the deletion. Click the Yes button or the No button as appropriate. To stop

FIGURE 3-17 From the Edit Presets dialog box, you can rename or delete a preset equalization.

iTunes from confirming the deletion of preset equalizations, select the Do Not Warn Me Again check box before clicking the Yes button or the No button.

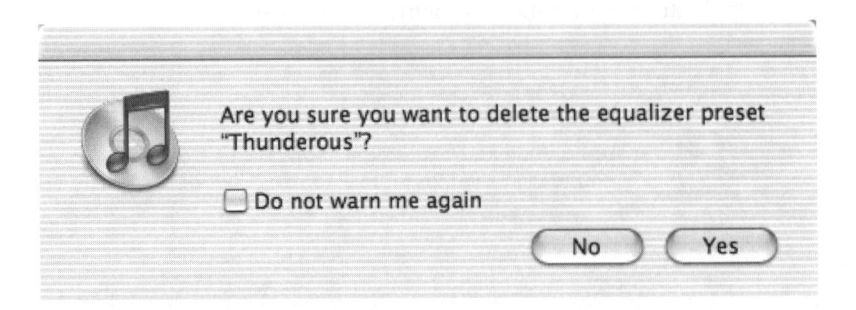

Skip the Boring Intro or Outro on a Song

If you disagree with the producer of a song about when the song should begin or end, use the Start Time and Stop Time controls on the Options page of the Song Information dialog box to specify how much of the track to lop off. This trimming works both in iTunes and on your iPod.

To trim the intro, enter in the Start Time text box the point at which you want the song to start. For example, enter **1:15** to skip the first minute and a quarter of a song. When you start typing in the Start Time text box, iTunes selects the Start Time check box for you, so you don't need to select it manually.

Similarly, you can change the value in the Stop Time text box to stop the song playing before its end. By default, the Stop Time text box contains a time showing when the song ends, down to thousandths of a second—for example, 4:56:769. When you reduce this time, iTunes automatically selects the Stop Time check box.

Synchronize Your Music Library with Your iPod

By default, iTunes synchronizes all the changes you make to your music library with your iPod. When you buy a couple of CDs and rip them to your music library, iTunes adds them to your iPod the next time you synchronize. If you build a new playlist, iTunes adds it to your iPod. And if you delete your playlists in iTunes in a fit of pique, they'll disappear from your iPod at its next synchronization.

CHAPTER 3: Use iTunes to Load Music onto Your Mac iPod   89

These default settings work well provided your iPod has enough free disk space to contain your entire music library. If not, you may want to control synchronization manually, as described in this section.

To synchronize, connect one end of your iPod's FireWire cable to a FireWire port on your Mac, and then connect the other end to the port in the top of your iPod. When iTunes detects your iPod, it displays an entry for it in the Source pane. When this entry is selected, as in Figure 3-18, the lower-right corner of iTunes displays a Display Options for Player button and an Eject iPod button. Your desktop also displays an icon for your iPod. You can eject your iPod by dragging this icon to the trash.

> **TIP** *If you make changes to your music library after iTunes has automatically updated your iPod but before you've unplugged your iPod, you can force an update by choosing File | Update Songs on NNNN iPod, where NNNN is the name assigned to your iPod.*

FIGURE 3-18 iTunes displays your iPod in the Source pane, together with buttons for manipulating it.

Control Synchronization to Get the Music You Want on Your iPod

If your iPod's default synchronization settings don't agree with you, change them. To do so, follow these steps:

1. Connect your iPod to your Mac.
2. Select the iPod icon in the Source pane.
3. Click the iPod Preferences icon in the lower-right corner of the iTunes window to display the iPod Preferences dialog box (see Figure 3-19).
4. Choose the appropriate option button:

   - **Automatically Update All Songs and Playlists option button** Select this option button to have iTunes automatically synchronize all your changes with your iPod. This is the default setting.

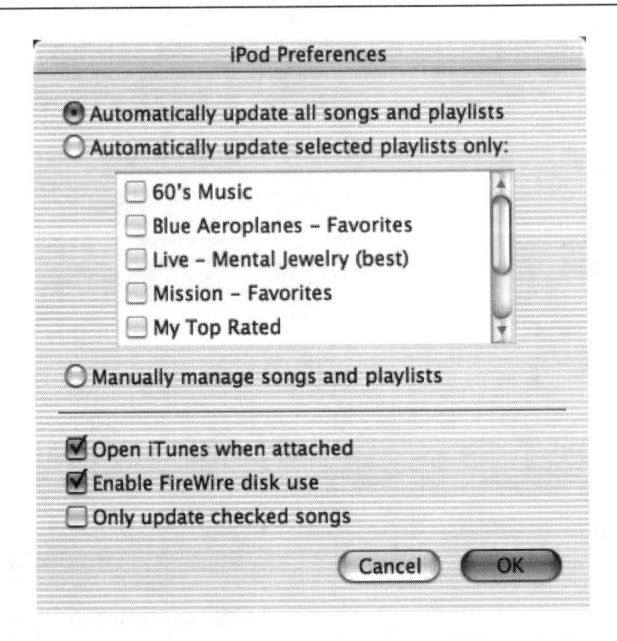

FIGURE 3-19 Use the iPod Preferences dialog box to configure how iTunes updates your iPod.

CHAPTER 3:   Use iTunes to Load Music onto Your Mac iPod   **91**

- **Automatically Update Selected Playlists Only option button**   Select this option button if you want to be able to limit iTunes to updating only specific playlists. This option allows you to keep different playlists in iTunes than on your iPod. This option is useful when your iPod doesn't have enough free space for your entire iTunes music library, and you've gotten onto your iPod most of the tracks you want to have on it.

- **Manually Manage Songs and Playlists option button**   Select this option button to take manual control of synchronization. This option is useful both when you need to choose which parts of your colossal music library to pack onto your iPod's comparatively puny amount of storage space, and when you want to add more music to your iPod than will fit onto your Mac. See the section "Load More Music on Your iPod than Will Fit on Your Mac," later in this chapter, for a discussion of how to do this.

5. Click the OK button to close the iPod Preferences dialog box. If you selected the Manually Manage Songs and Playlists option button, iTunes displays the dialog box shown in the following image warning you that you'll need to manually unmount the iPod before disconnecting it.

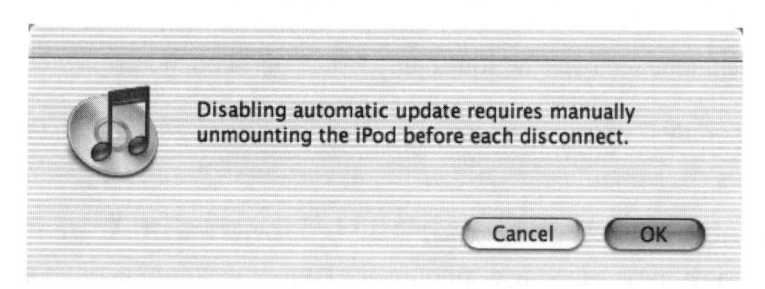

> Disabling automatic update requires manually unmounting the iPod before each disconnect.
>
> Cancel   OK

6. Click the OK button if you're sure you want to proceed. Otherwise, click the Cancel button to return to the iPod Preferences dialog box, and then select one of the automatic-updating options.

Control Synchronization Manually

If you chose the Manually Manage Songs and Playlists option button in the iPod Preferences dialog box, you can control synchronization manually as follows:

1. Select your iPod's icon in the Source pane to display your iPod's contents.

2. Select the songs you want to copy to your iPod, either in your iTunes music library or in a Finder window.

3. Drag the songs to the iPod's icon or to the appropriate playlist. If you're dragging from a Finder window and you have the iPod's contents displayed in the main iTunes pane, you can drop the tracks there.

Remove Songs from Your iPod

The other half of the battle is removing songs from your iPod so you can put other songs on it.

To remove songs, follow these steps:

1. Select your iPod's icon in the Source pane to display your iPod's contents.

2. Select the songs you want to remove.

3. Drag the songs to the Trash. (Alternatively, press DELETE.) iTunes displays a confirmation dialog box.

4. Click the Yes button. Select the Do Not Ask Me Again check box first if you don't want iTunes to confirm each deletion with you in the future.

This technique removes the songs only from your iPod, not from your Mac.

CAUTION *Use only iTunes to remove songs from your iPod—don't use the Finder.*

Synchronize Only Part of Your Music Library with Your iPod

If your music library is too big to fit on your iPod (or that portion of your iPod capacity you're using for music), you can specify which songs and playlists to synchronize with your iPod in either of two ways:

- Select the Automatically Update Selected Playlists Only option button in the iPod Preferences dialog box. Then, in the list box in the iPod Preferences dialog box, select the check boxes for the playlists you want to synchronize. This technique works only for songs included in playlists.

- Control all synchronization manually, as described in "Control Synchronization Manually," earlier in this chapter.

Load More Music on Your iPod than Will Fit on Your Mac

If you have a newish iPod and an older Mac, the boot may be on the other foot: your Mac may not have enough free disk space to hold all the songs you want to load on your iPod.

To get around this problem, follow these steps:

1. Turn on manual synchronization in the iPod Preferences dialog box. (See "Control Synchronization to Get the Music You Want on Your iPod," earlier in this chapter.)

2. Synchronize your iPod manually, as described in "Control Synchronization Manually," earlier in this chapter.

If your Mac is connected to a network on which it can access drives, you can get around the lack of disk space on your Mac in two other ways:

- Keep a significant part of your music library on a network drive to supplement that part you can fit on your hard drive. To prevent iTunes from copying files to your hard drive, clear the Copy Files to iTunes Music Folder when Adding to Library check box on the Advanced sheet of the Preferences dialog box.

- Keep your entire music library on a network drive. In this case, you don't need to clear the Copy Files to iTunes Music Folder When Adding to Library check box.

In either case, if you use automatic updating, you'll need to make sure the network drive is available whenever you synchronize your iPod. If it's not, you'll be unable to synchronize any of the tracks on that drive.

Return to Automatic Updating from Manual Updating

If you read the preceding sections, you'll realize that returning your iPod to automatic updating is as simple as selecting one of the automatic-updating options in the iPod Preferences dialog box. But there's a complication: automatic updating will overwrite your manually-managed iPod library with either the complete iTunes music library or with the playlists you specify (depending on which automatic-updating option you choose).

So before you return to automatic updating, make sure your library will fit on your iPod and that you won't lose any tracks stored only on your iPod and not in your music library.

When you select either of the automatic-updating options in the iPod Preferences dialog box, iTunes displays the following dialog box to warn you of what will happen. Click the OK button if you're comfortable with this.

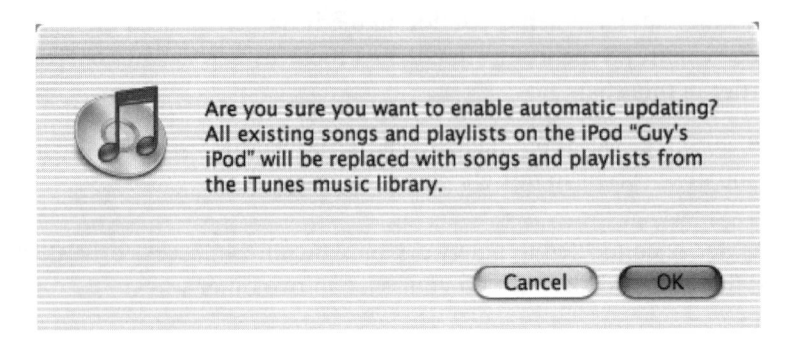

Listen to Audible.com Spoken-Word Files on Your iPod

Even if your iPod is laden nearly to the gunwales with songs, you may be able to cram on a goodly amount of spoken-word audio. This is because spoken-word audio can sound great at much lower bitrates than music.

Audible.com provides a wide variety of content, such as audio books, magazines, and plays, in a selection of different subscription types and accounts. To get started, go to the Audible.com web site (**www.audible.com**) and set up an account. You can then download files to up to three different computers for that account. The first time you download Audible.com content to a particular computer, you need to enter your Audible.com account information on it. After that, you can simply drag an Audible file to the iTunes window to add it to your music library.

If you need to transfer one of the three manifestations of your Audible.com account from one Mac to another, choose Advanced | Remove Audible Account in iTunes, and then use the Remove Audible Account dialog box to specify the account to remove.

CHAPTER 3: Use iTunes to Load Music onto Your Mac iPod 95

Create Custom Playlists to Enjoy in iTunes or on Your iPod

iTunes automatically transfers to your iPod all the playlists you create in iTunes. As you saw in Chapter 1, your iPod's top-level menu contains a Playlists item, which gives you direct access to your playlists. So by creating playlists in iTunes, you can access your music more easily on the iPod. And you can use the playlists in iTunes, of course.

> **TIP** *To force iTunes to copy to your iPod MP3 files that lack the tag information your iPod normally requires, add the tracks to a playlist. Doing so can save you time over retagging many files manually and can be useful in a pinch. (In the long term, you'll probably want to make sure all your MP3 files are tagged properly.)*

To create a playlist in iTunes, follow these steps:

1. Click the + button in the Source pane, choose File | New Playlist, or press COMMAND-N. iTunes adds a new playlist to the source pane, names it **untitled playlist** (or the next available name, such as **untitled playlist 2**), and displays an edit box around it.

2. Type the name for the playlist, and then press RETURN or click elsewhere to apply the name.

3. Select the Library item in the Source pane to display your songs. If you want to work by artist and album, press OPTION-B or choose Edit | Show Browser to display the Browser pane.

4. Select the songs you want to add to the playlist, and then drag them to the playlist's name. You can drag one song at a time or multiple songs—whatever you find easiest.

5. Click the playlist's name in the source pane to display the playlist.

6. Drag the tracks into the order in which you want them to play.

> **NOTE** *For you to be able to drag the tracks about in the playlist, the playlist must be sorted by the track-number column. If any other column heading is selected, you won't be able to rearrange the order of the tracks in the playlist.*

Automatically Create Smart Playlists Based on Your Ratings and Preferences

The Smart Playlist feature lets you instruct iTunes about how to build a list of songs automatically for you. You can tell Smart Playlist to build playlists by artist, composer, or genre; to select up to a specific number of songs at random, by artist, by most played, by last played, or by song name; and to automatically update a playlist as you add tracks to your music library or remove tracks from it. For example, if you tell Smart Playlist to make you a playlist of songs by Shakira, Smart Playlist can update the list with new Shakira tracks after you import them into your music library.

By using Smart Playlist's advanced features, you can even specify multiple conditions. For example, you might choose to include songs tagged with the genre Gothic Rock but exclude certain artists by name, such as The Fields of the Nephilim.

NOTE *Smart Playlist maintains playlists such as the My Top Rated playlist, the Recently Played playlist, and the Top 25 Most Played playlist, that iTunes creates by default.*

To create a playlist using the Smart Playlist feature, follow these steps:

1. Press COMMAND-ALT-N or choose File | New Smart Playlist to display the Smart Playlist dialog box. Figure 3-20 shows the Simple tab (above) and Advanced tab (below) of the Smart Playlist dialog box.

2. To create a simple playlist, work with the controls on the Simple tab.

    - Select the top check box.
    - Choose Artist, Composer, or Genre in the top drop-down list.
    - Enter the item to match in the Contains text box. For example, you might choose Artist Contains Springsteen to create a Smart Playlist of tracks by Bruce Springsteen.
    - To limit the playlist to a maximum number of tracks, time, or disk space, select the second check box and use the controls to specify the limit and how iTunes should select the songs. For example, you could specify Limit to 30 Songs Selected by Last Played or Limit to 100 Minutes Selected by Random.

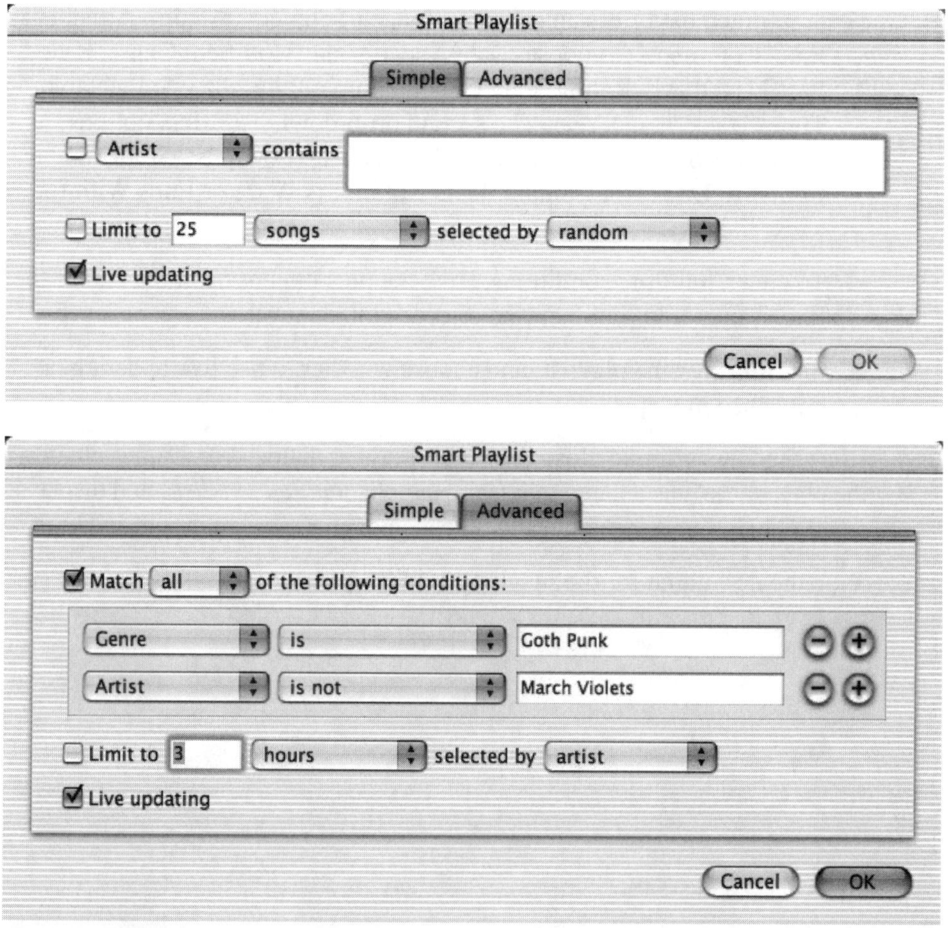

CHAPTER 3: Use iTunes to Load Music onto Your Mac iPod   97

FIGURE 3-20   Use the Simple tab (above) and Advanced tab (below) of the Smart Playlist dialog box to create a new Smart Playlist based on your listening preferences.

- Select or clear the Live Updating check box to specify whether iTunes should periodically update the playlist according to your listening patterns.

3. To create an advanced playlist, work with the controls on the Advanced tab.

- Select the Match the Following Condition check box. If you create multiple conditions, this check box offers the choices Match All of the Following Conditions and Match Any of the Following Conditions. Choose the appropriate one.

- Use the controls in the first line to specify the first condition. The first drop-down list offers an extensive range of choices: Album, Artist, Bit Rate, Comment, Compose, Date Added, Date Modified, Genre, Kind, Last Played, My Rating, Play Count, Sample Rate, Size, Song Name, Time, Track #, and Year. The second drop-down list offers options suitable to the item you chose in the first drop-down list—for example, Contains, Does Not Contain, Is, Is Not, Starts With, or Ends With for a text field.
- To create multiple conditions, click the plus (+) button at the end of the line. iTunes adds another line of condition controls.
- Set limits for the playlist, and choose whether to use live updating, as described in step 2.

4. Click the OK button to close the Smart Playlist dialog box. iTunes creates the playlist, assigns a name to it (for example, *untitled playlist*), and displays an edit box around the name so you can change it.

5. Type the new name for the playlist, and then press RETURN.

Chapter 4

Use MUSICMATCH Jukebox Plus to Load Music onto Your Windows iPod

How to...

- Upgrade your PC to get it iPod-ready
- Set up and configure MUSICMATCH Jukebox Plus
- Choose suitable settings for ripping and encoding MP3 files
- Create, build, and manage your music library
- Play music back with MUSICMATCH Jukebox Plus
- Synchronize your music library with your iPod automatically or manually
- Create custom playlists for MUSICMATCH Jukebox Plus and your iPod

Get Your PC Ready to Work with Your iPod

If you bought your PC in 2002 or later, and it considers itself a power-user model, there's a fair chance it'll have everything you need to start using your iPod: one or more FireWire ports; Windows XP (either Home Edition or Professional), Windows 2000 (either Professional or Server), or Windows Me; a 300MHz or faster processor; 128MB RAM (for Windows XP) or 96MB RAM for Windows Me or Windows 2000; enough disk space to contain your music library; and a CD recorder (optional but recommended).

If your PC can't meet those specifications, read the following subsections for a discussion of possible upgrades.

Add a FireWire Card if Necessary

Many high-end PCs include one or more FireWire ports—but most low-end PCs don't. This is because adding FireWire ports costs money and because FireWire hasn't yet—and may never—become part of the basic PC specification.

FireWire and USB essentially compete for the same area of computer functionality—a fast bus for connecting peripheral equipment to the computer. Apple helped develop and popularize FireWire, so all modern Macs include FireWire ports. PC makers went with USB instead, with the exception of Sony, which chose four-pin FireWire as the connection for its digital camcorders. So almost all recent PCs include USB ports, but only high-end PCs and Sony multimedia PCs include FireWire ports.

CHAPTER 4:   Use MUSICMATCH Jukebox Plus to Load Music onto Your Windows iPod

The reason high-end PCs include FireWire ports is that FireWire used to be much faster than USB until recently. USB 1.*x* managed speeds of 12 Mbps compared to FireWire's 400 Mbps. (These are both maximum speeds.) So any PC that needed a high-speed connection for bandwidth-hungry technologies, such as video transfer, needed to use FireWire rather than USB. But now that USB 2 equipment is available, USB is faster than FireWire: USB 2 can manage 480 Mbps to FireWire's 400 Mbps. The latest iPods can use a USB connection instead of FireWire. See "Connect a New iPod to a PC via USB" in Chapter 16.

If you're a current PC owner looking to upgrade from USB 1.*x*, choosing between USB 2 and FireWire can be tough, particularly if you don't have a clear picture of all the peripherals you're likely to want to connect to your PC during the rest of its lifetime. Your best choice may be to add both USB 2 and FireWire to your PC. Various companies make PCI cards that include both USB 2 and FireWire ports, so you need sacrifice only a single slot on a desktop PC. On a portable PC, you'll probably need separate PC Card devices for USB 2 and FireWire.

> **TIP**   *If you're adding a FireWire card to your PC, choose a card that has a six-pin socket rather than one with a four-pin socket. Six-pin sockets can transfer power across the cable (for example, for recharging your iPod), whereas four-pin sockets can't.*

Check Your Operating System Version

Make sure your PC is running Windows XP, Windows 2000, or Windows Me. If you're in doubt about which of the many versions of Windows your computer is running, display the System Properties dialog box (press WINDOWS KEY–BREAK or choose Start | Control Panel | System) and check the readout on the General tab. If you don't have one of these versions of Windows, upgrade to one of them—preferably to Windows XP.

Check Memory and Disk Space

If you don't know how much memory your computer has, check it. The easiest place to check is the General tab of the System Properties dialog box (Start | Control Panel | System).

To check disk space, open a Windows Explorer window to display all the drives on your computer. Right-click the drive in question and choose Properties from the shortcut menu to display the Properties dialog box for the drive. The General tab of this dialog box shows the amount of free space and used space on the drive.

Add a CD-R Drive if Necessary

If you want to be able to burn audio CDs from MUSICMATCH Jukebox Plus, add a recordable CD drive to your computer. Which drive technology is most appropriate depends on your computer type and configuration:

- For a desktop PC that has an open 5.25" bay and a spare connector on an EIDE channel, an internal EIDE CD drive is easiest. (If your desktop PC has SCSI, use SCSI instead, because SCSI requires fewer processor cycles than EIDE.)

- For a desktop PC that has no open 5.25" bay or no spare EIDE connector, or for a portable PC, consider either a FireWire CD drive or a USB 2 CD drive.

NOTE *Because USB 1.x is relatively slow, USB 1.x CD recorders can manage only 4× burning speeds. So you'll probably want to use USB 1.x only when you must—for example, because you have a USB 1.x drive available and can't afford anything better.*

Install MUSICMATCH Jukebox Plus on Your PC

Before connecting your iPod to your PC, you need to install the iPod plug-in and MUSICMATCH Jukebox Plus on your PC. If you already have a full copy of MUSICMATCH Jukebox Plus installed on your PC, you need only to download the iPod plug-in from the Apple website (**www.apple.com/ipod/**) or install it from the CD that came with your iPod.

CAUTION *The version of MUSICMATCH Jukebox Plus that comes with your iPod may not be the latest version available. This chapter covers MUSICMATCH Jukebox Plus 7.10.4060Apple, the version shipping with Windows iPods at this writing—but you can already download version 7.5 from the MUSICMATCH web site. If you have a later version of MUSICMATCHII Jukebox Plus, you may see substantial differences in the interface and configuration screens, but you should find most of the options are the same as those discussed here.*

TIP *To keep your Windows iPod up to date, check for the latest updates on the AppleCare Support site (**www.apple.com/support**). Enter "iPod Windows updater" in the Search text box and choose Downloads in the drop-down list.*

CHAPTER 4: Use MUSICMATCH Jukebox Plus to Load Music onto Your Windows iPod

Installing the iPod plug-in and MUSICMATCH Jukebox Plus is straightforward but contains plenty of detail you'll want to get right the first time. The following are the main points of interest:

- Insert the CD that came with your iPod. If AutoPlay on the computer CD drive is configured to run for software CDs, the installation routine starts automatically. If not, press WINDOWS KEY–R or choose Start | Run to display the Run dialog box, enter *cd*:\setup.exe (where *cd* is the letter assigned to your CD drive), and click the OK button to start the installation routine.

- In the iPod for Windows dialog box (which shows an attractive graphic of an iPod), click the Install button.

- On the iPod Serial Number page, enter the serial number from the back of your iPod. You might need a magnifying glass to read it.

- On the License Agreement page, accept the agreement if you want to proceed.

- On the Select Country or Region page, specify your country or region. If your country hasn't made the shortlist this page displays, select the Show All check box to display the full list of countries.

NOTE *The choice you make on the Select Country or Region page controls the address format shown on the Registration Information page. Because registration is mandatory, there's no point in specifying the wrong country unless you also intend to supply an address in that country as well.*

- Apple demands two pages of registration information. The first page requires your name, address, e-mail address, and phone number. The second page demands to know where you'll primarily use your iPod, what school or employment field you're in, and whether you want to receive Apple news and promotional e-mail messages.

NOTE *If you want to know why Apple demands your details, click the Privacy button on the Registration Information page to open a web browser window to the Apple Customer Privacy Statement page. To change your Apple contact information so Apple and its partners don't send you promotional e-mail messages, follow the link to **www.apple.com/contact/myinfo** and use the resulting form. If you don't have an Apple ID, you'll need to create one.*

- On the Choose Destination Location page, check the folder in which the installation routine is proposing to install the iPod software. If necessary, click the Browse button and use the resulting Choose Folder dialog box to specify a better folder. The default location is a folder named iPod located in your Program Files folder. This location is fine for most installations of the iPod software. (What's more important is to put your music folder in a suitable location that has plenty of space for all your song files.)

- After installing the iPod software, the installation routine automatically launches the MUSICMATCH Jukebox Plus setup routine.

- On the Software License Agreement page, read the end-user license agreement. Click the Yes button if you want to proceed.

- In the MUSICMATCH Jukebox Plus User Registration dialog box (shown on the left in Figure 4-1), you must enter your "Year of Birth" (a valid two-digit number assumed to start with *19*). If the year you enter makes your age 13 or older, MUSICMATCH Jukebox Plus activates the Name, E-mail, and Country/Region controls so you can specify this information (which is required for people 13 or over but cannot legally be collected from anyone younger). Specify this information. Enter your ZIP code or Postal code and gender if you want MUSICMATCH to know them. (There's no reason to enter this information.) The Register Electronically check box is selected by default. Clear this check box if you don't want to register electronically during setup. Likewise, the Send Me Music-Related News and Special Offers check box is selected by default for the over-13s. Clear this check box if you don't want to receive these messages. This check box isn't available for under-13s because they're not allowed to register an e-mail address. It's not available if you choose not to register electronically.

- In the Personal Music Recommendations dialog box (shown on the right in Figure 4-1), choose whether or not to use the MUSICMATCH Jukebox Plus personal music recommendations service. Signing up for this option essentially commits you to buying "free" music by paying with information about your listening habits. If you think this is a fair exchange (I don't), select the Yes (Recommended) option button. To preserve your privacy, select the No option button. MUSICMATCH guarantees that your personal music preferences "will never be sold or shared." However, many people prefer not to allow the collection of such information.

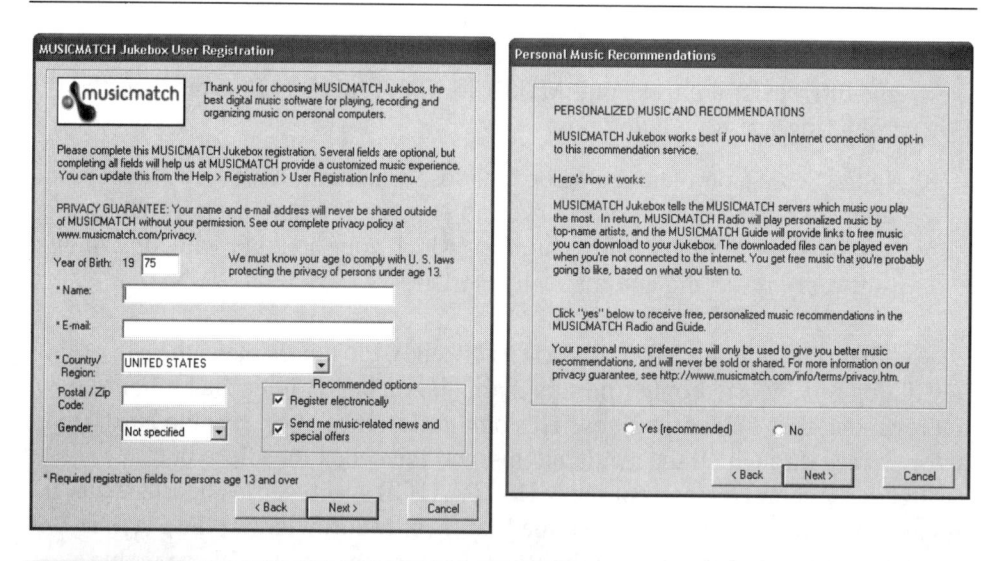

CHAPTER 4: Use MUSICMATCH Jukebox Plus to Load Music onto Your Windows iPod   **105**

FIGURE 4-1 Like the iPod software, MUSICMATCH Jukebox Plus requires you to register (left). You can choose whether or not to receive personalized music and recommendations (right).

- On the Installations Options page, choose between the Express installation and a Custom installation. The Express installation uses the default setting shown in Table 4-1. The Custom installation displays a page for you to make each of these choices manually.

Item	Description
Installation Folder	Program Files\MUSICMATCH\MUSICMATCH JUKEBOX
Music Library Folder	My Documents\My Music
Active Radio Buffering Disk Cache	On
Start Menu Folder	MUSICMATCH
Shortcuts	Desktop, Quick Launch toolbar, notification area
MUSICMATCH Jukebox Plus default player for	Windows Media (WMA) files, MP3 files, M3U (playlist) files, SHOUTcast (streaming audio), audio CDs (CDA files), WAV files, secure music files

TABLE 4-1 MUSICMATCH Jukebox Plus Express Installation Settings

- On the Enter Upgrade Key page, enter the key on the sleeve of your iPod for Windows sleeve. MUSICMATCH Jukebox Plus validates the key over the Internet. If it checks out, MUSICMATCH Jukebox Plus displays the New Upgrade Key dialog box.

- In the Setup Complete dialog box, choose whether to let Setup restart your computer automatically now or restart it yourself manually later. Unless you have something sensitive running (which you shouldn't while installing software), restarting automatically is easiest.

The first time you run MUSICMATCH Jukebox Plus, it displays the Tip of the Day dialog box. Most people find this dialog box a bane rather than a boon. If you're among them, clear the Show Tips on StartUp check box, use the Next Tip button to race through all the available tips, and then click the Close button.

Figure 4-2 shows the parts of the MUSICMATCH Jukebox Plus interface you'll probably have displayed most often: the Player (or Main) window, the Playlist window, the Library window, and the Recorder window. (As you'll see in due course, MUSICMATCH Jukebox Plus contains various other interface elements that it displays as necessary.)

Configure MUSICMATCH Jukebox Plus for Maximum Effectiveness

Like most complex applications, MUSICMATCH Jukebox Plus offers many configuration options. You can access most of these options through the Settings dialog box (Options | Settings or CTRL-SHIFT-S).

> **TIP** *For speed, you can also change many of the settings from the submenus on the Options menu without displaying the Settings dialog box. For example, to change the CD drive or other input (such as the Line In socket) you're recording from, choose Options | Recorder | Source, and then select the source from the resulting submenu.*

This section discusses the key options for ripping and encoding tracks with MUSICMATCH Jukebox Plus, playing them back, and synchronizing them with your iPod.

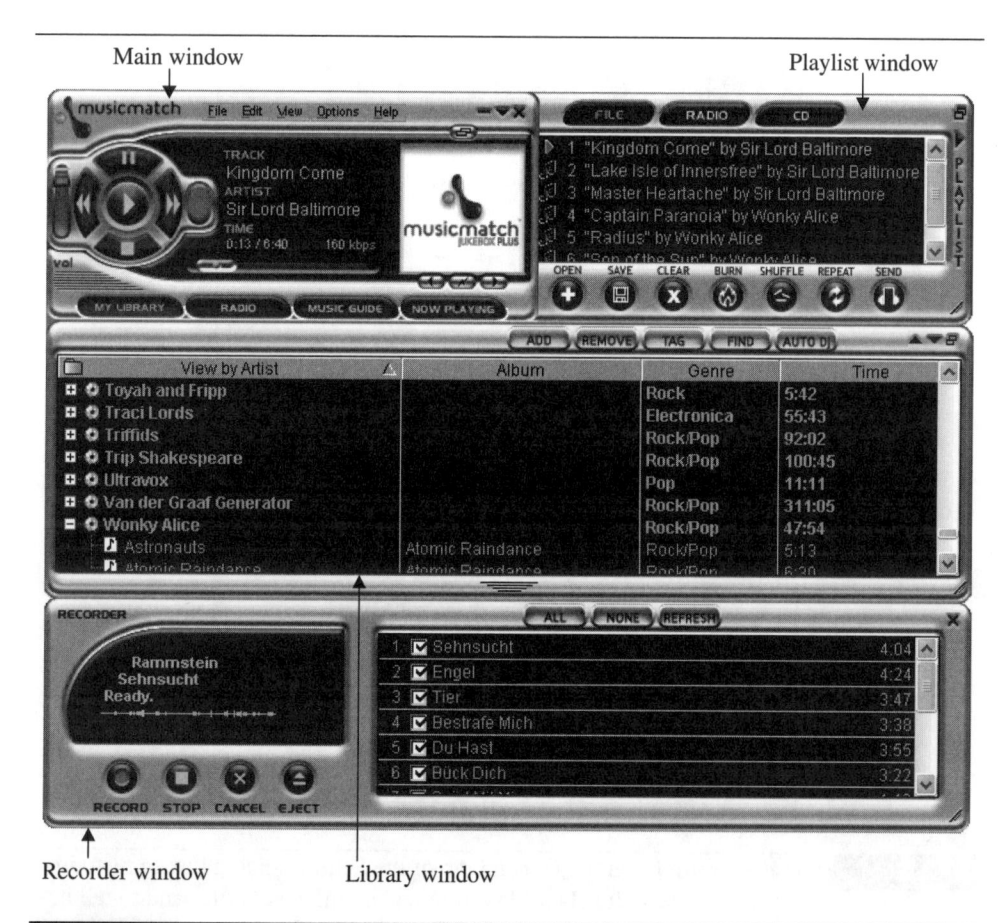

CHAPTER 4: Use MUSICMATCH Jukebox Plus to Load Music onto Your Windows iPod 107

FIGURE 4-2   MUSICMATCH Jukebox Plus in a typical configuration. Main window, Playlist window, Library window, and Recorder window

Choose General Settings to Control MUSICMATCH Jukebox Plus

The General tab of the Settings dialog box (Figure 4-3) contains vital settings that control how MUSICMATCH Jukebox Plus behaves:

- **Use MUSICMATCH Jukebox Plus As the Default Player For group box**   Select the check boxes for the file types you want to associate with MUSICMATCH Jukebox Plus. The association means that when you double-click one of these files, Windows uses MUSICMATCH Jukebox Plus to handle the file. If you use MUSICMATCH Jukebox Plus for audio playback, you'll probably want to select all the check boxes.

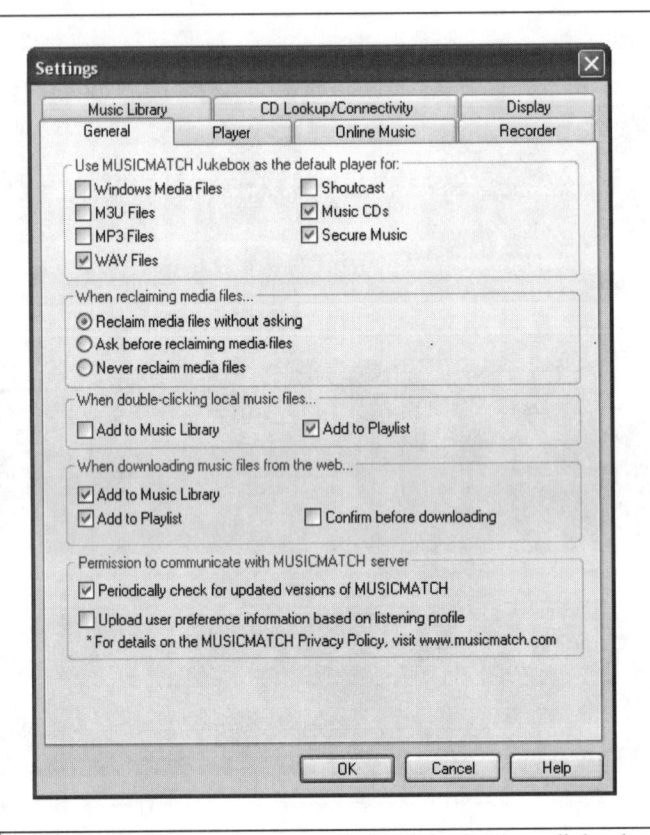

FIGURE 4-3 Use the settings on the General tab of the Settings dialog box to restrain MUSICMATCH Jukebox Plus from reclaiming media files and to tell it how to treat local music files and files you download.

- **When Reclaiming Media Files group box** Select the appropriate option button to specify whether MUSICMATCH Jukebox Plus may reclaim those file types you associated with it after other applications have grabbed them. Your options are the Reclaim Media Files Without Asking option button, the Ask Before Reclaiming Media Files option button, or the Never Reclaim Media Files option button.

- **When Double-Clicking Local Music Files group box** Select or clear the Add to Music Library check box and the Add to Playlist check box to specify what MUSICMATCH Jukebox Plus should do when you double-click a file on a local drive.

CHAPTER 4: Use MUSICMATCH Jukebox Plus to Load Music onto Your Windows iPod 109

- **When Downloading Music Files from the Web group box** Select or clear the Add to Music Library check box, the Add to Playlist check box, and the Confirm Before Downloading check box to specify what MUSICMATCH Jukebox Plus should do when you download a music file from the Web.

- **Permission to Communicate with MUSICMATCH Server group box** Select or clear the check boxes to specify whether MUSICMATCH Jukebox Plus may automatically check for updates and upload the information it has collected about your listening preferences.

Choose Settings to Create High-Quality MP3 Files

This section discusses the settings you need to set in MUSICMATCH Jukebox Plus to create high-quality MP3 files. As you'll see, there are more than a handful of settings, each of which needs explanation—so be patient. This is for your own good, even if you don't enjoy it.

Creating high-quality MP3 files costs you time and processor cycles. You may find there are occasions when getting the tracks ripped quickly is more important than getting them ripped at the highest quality possible. For example, you might find yourself with only a couple of hours to (illegally) rip as much as possible of a friend's CD collection and make a getaway before the Digital Millennium Copyright Act (DMCA) can land on you with a half-million-dollar fine and five years' free accommodation. Or (more charitably) you might need to rip a handful of your own CDs to your laptop as quickly as possible before heading for work.

But in general, ripping tracks at a low quality is a waste of time and energy. If you like the music enough to devote hard disk space to it (on your computer, your iPod, or both), you might as well expend the time and effort to rip the music at a high-enough quality for it to be worth keeping. That way, you'll need to rip each track only once ever. If you buy even a dozen new CDs every week, you should have little trouble finding enough time to rip them at high quality.

Several variables are involved in getting a high-quality MP3 file:

- Reading the CD accurately (assuming the source is a CD).

- Using an encoder capable of creating high-quality MP3 encodings. The Fraunhofer encoder that MUSICMATCH Jukebox Plus uses is high quality.

- Choosing a suitable compression rate to save the right amount of data.

- Making sure the data saved is as accurate as possible.

To choose settings for creating high-quality MP3 files, follow these steps:

1. Display the Recorder tab of the Settings dialog box. The left screen in Figure 4-4 shows this tab.

2. In the Recording Source drop-down list on the left screen, select the CD drive from which you want to record. If you have multiple CD drives, choose the most reliable one (perhaps the newest).

NOTE *In newer versions of MUSICMATCH Jukebox Plus, the Recorder options are laid out differently. In the Recording Format drop-down list, select the file format to use: MP3, WAV, mp3PRO, or Windows Media Audio (WMA). Of these, your iPod can handle only MP3 and WAV; so, because WAV is uncompressed, you're most likely to stick with MP3 (the default). Then select the option button for the quality you want to use.*

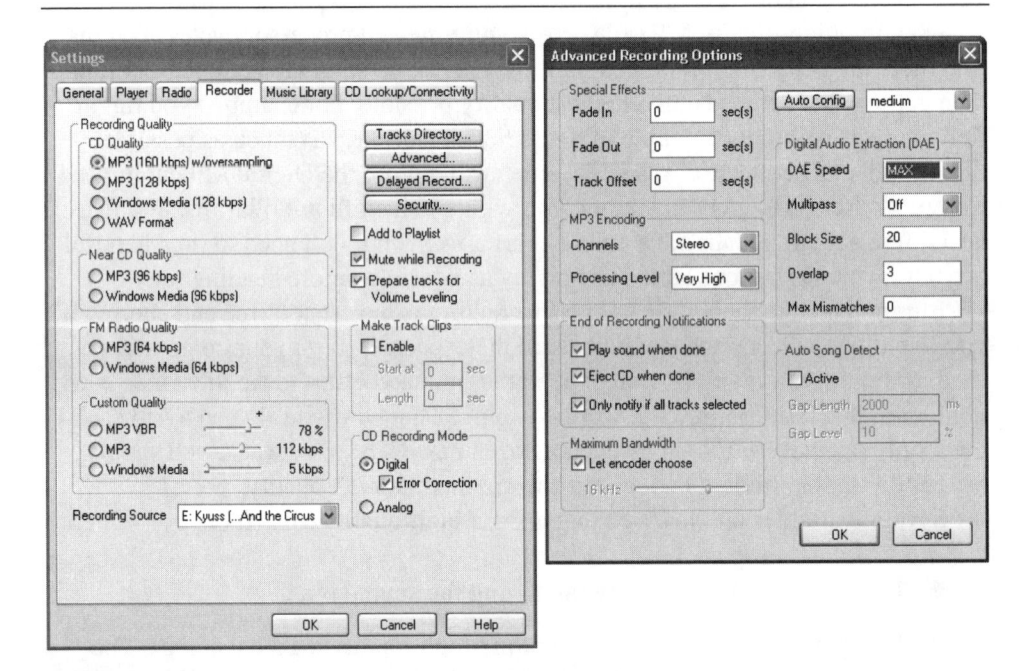

FIGURE 4-4 Choose MP3-encoding settings on the Recorder tab of the Settings dialog box (left). In the Advanced Recording Options dialog box (right), specify the number of Channels, the Processing Level, and the Maximum Bandwidth to use.

CHAPTER 4: Use MUSICMATCH Jukebox Plus to Load Music onto Your Windows iPod

3. In the Recording Quality group box on the left screen, select the option button for the format and quality you want. For audio that you're ripping from CDs for use with your iPod, you'll typically want to choose among the MP3 (160 Kbps) w/ Oversampling option button, the MP3 (128 Kbps) option button, the MP3 VBR option button (choose a percentage that suits your ears), or the MP3 option button (set a bitrate of 192 Kbps, 224 Kbps, 256 Kbps, or 320 Kbps). Lower bitrates produce results that most music-lovers find disappointing.

> **TIP** *See the section "Choose an Appropriate Compression Rate" in Chapter 2 for a discussion of how to decide which compression rate is best for your needs.*

4. In the CD Recording Mode group box on the left screen, make sure the Digital option button is selected rather than the Analog option button.

   ■ Don't use analog recording from CDs unless digital recording isn't available. The conversion from the CD's digital audio to analog, and the conversion back to digital, loses audio quality. Analog recording is also slower than digital recording. However, some CD drives can't provide satisfactory digital audio. For such drives, MUSICMATCH Jukebox Plus configures itself to use analog recording.

   ■ For digital recording, you may need to select the Error Correction check box to avoid getting jitter or clicks and pops in the audio. Either experiment with several CDs to see if you need error correction, or simply turn it on anyway. The only disadvantage to using error correction all the time is that ripping will take longer than it otherwise would.

5. Click the Advanced button to display the Advanced Recording Options dialog box (shown on the right in Figure 4-4).

6. In the Channels drop-down list, select Stereo or Mono as appropriate. Usually, you'll want stereo if the source is stereo, mono if the source is mono.

7. In the Processing Level drop-down list, select the processing level to use a Normal (the default), High, or Very High.

   ■ Choosing High or Very High improves the sound of your MP3 files but makes encoding take longer.

- How much longer depends on the compression rate and the speed of your computer processor. On a modest computer, and using high compression, Very High can take ten times longer than Normal. If you can afford the time, use the Very High setting.

- The size of the resulting MP3 files remains the same no matter which processing setting you use, but the quality of the file contents varies.

8. In the Maximum Bandwidth group box, you can change the range of frequencies the encoder uses in the file.

    - The MUSICMATCH Jukebox Plus default setting is to have the Let Encoder Choose check box selected, which cuts off frequencies above 16kHz—the point above which most people's ears can't hear.

    - If you can hear above 16kHz, you'll notice the higher frequencies seem to be missing. In this case, clear the Let Encoder Choose check box and drag the slider all the way to the right, to its 22kHz setting.

    - Alternatively, set a maximum frequency between 16kHz and 22kHz—but for most people with good ears, jumping straight to 22kHz is best.

NOTE *Classical music tends to hit the high frequencies more than other types of music, but rock and other types can get up there too.*

9. Close the Advanced Recording Options dialog box and the Settings dialog box.

TIP *When ripping and encoding with MUSICMATCH Jukebox Plus, run as few other applications as possible so MUSICMATCH Jukebox Plus can grab as many processor cycles as it needs. If possible, leave MUSICMATCH Jukebox Plus as the foreground application while ripping, because Windows XP and Windows 2000 Professional (by default) allocate more processor cycles to the foreground application than to other applications. If this sounds as though you should leave your PC strictly alone while MUSICMATCH Jukebox Plus is ripping—then yes, doing that will help you get high-quality MP3 files.*

Choose Where to Store Your Music Library and How to Name Its Files

The default location for your MUSICMATCH Jukebox Plus music library is your My Music folder. For Windows, this is a good location, because it keeps your music out of the way of any other users of your PC. But you may want to move your music library to a folder on a drive that has more space.

To move your music library, click the Tracks Directory button on the Recorder tab of the Settings dialog box. In the New Tracks Directory Options dialog box (Figure 4-5), click the ... button, use the resulting Browse for Folder dialog box to identify the folder, and then click the OK button. The Directory Information shows how much free space is available on that drive.

The other controls in the New Tracks Directory Options dialog box let you specify how MUSICMATCH Jukebox Plus should name the music files it creates and where it should put them.

- **Make Sub-Path Using group box**   Select or clear the Artist check box and the Album check box to tell MUSICMATCH Jukebox Plus whether to use them for the folder path. The default arrangement is to create a subfolder for the artist with a subfolder for each album under it. For example, if you ripped Shakira's *Laundry Service*, MUSICMATCH Jukebox Plus would create the folder Shakira\Laundry Service and put the music files in it.

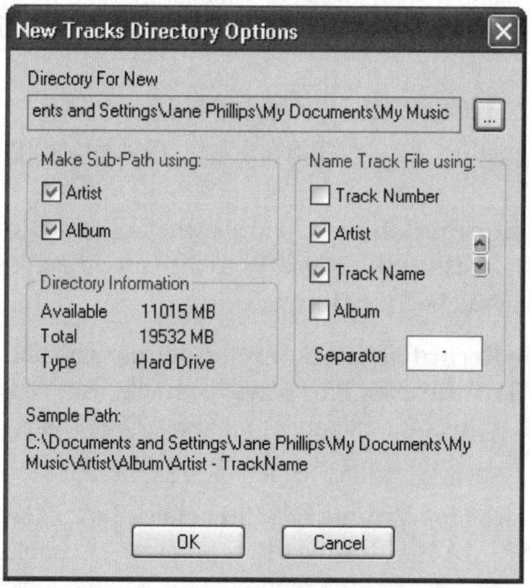

FIGURE 4-5   In the New Tracks Directory Options dialog box, specify the music folder and the naming convention to use.

- **Name Track File Using group box** Select or clear the Track Number check box, the Artist check box, the Track Name check box, and the Album check box to specify which items to include in the file name. Use the Up and Down buttons to shuffle the items you use into the right order. In the Separator text box, enter the character or sequence of characters to use for separating the different items. Watch the Sample Path to see the effects of your changes. As you can see in Figure 4-5, the separator is a space, a hyphen, and another space.

Choose End-of-Recording Notifications

The options in the End of Recording Notifications group box in the Advanced Recording Options dialog box let you specify whether and how MUSICMATCH Jukebox Plus should notify you when it has finished ripping a CD or some tracks from a CD.

Choose whether MUSICMATCH Jukebox Plus should play a sound when it has finished ripping the tracks, whether it should play a sound only after ripping an entire CD (as opposed to just some tracks), and whether it should eject the CD. Ejection tends to be useful on desktop computers, on which the CD drive typically has space to open unannounced, but dangerous on portables, where anything from your body to your gear may be blocking the CD drive at the critical moment.

Choose Other Recording Options

The Recorder tab of the Settings dialog box also offers the following options:

- **Add to Playlist check box** Controls whether or not MUSICMATCH Jukebox Plus adds the ripped tracks to the current playlist. You decide whether this is a good idea for you.

- **Mute While Recording check box** Controls whether or not MUSICMATCH Jukebox Plus plays the tracks as it's ripping the CD. This feature is great for listening to a new CD as you rip it, but you may prefer to turn it off for heavy-duty ripping sessions.

- **Prepare Tracks for Volume Leveling check box** Controls whether or not MUSICMATCH Jukebox Plus prepares the tracks for having their volumes normalized. See the section "Use Volume Leveling to Avoid Getting Your Ears Blasted" later in this chapter, for details.

- **Make Track Clips group box** Contains controls for making short clips from tracks. Clips can be useful for providing samples—for example, of your own music—on a web site, or for creating small sample files to send to a friend to get them to identify a mystery track. Creating short clips of other people's copyrighted tracks without permission is arguably fair use in some cases. Creating long clips of other people's copyrighted tracks without permission is almost invariably a copyright infringement.

Use Fades and Offsets to Tweak the Start and End of Tracks

The Special Effects group box in the Advanced Recording Options dialog box contains options for tweaking the start and end of tracks.

- Use the Fade In text box and Fade Out text box to fade in or fade out a number of seconds on the track. Most professionally produced tracks have all the fading they need (or their producers think they need), but you might want to use this option on recordings you've produced.

- Use the Offset text box to apply an offset to a track. For example, if the tracks on a CD all seem to start with three seconds of silence, use an offset of three seconds to cut out that silence.

Choose CD Lookup Options

The CD Lookup/Connectivity tab of the Settings dialog box (Figure 4-6) lets you specify whether MUSICMATCH Jukebox Plus should automatically download CD information from CDDB.

- **Enable CD Lookup check box**   This check box controls whether MUSICMATCH Jukebox Plus looks up CDs in CDDB. Increase the number of seconds in the Timeout Limit text box if you have a slow connection or CDDB is too busy to respond within the current timeout.

- **Enable Deferred CD Lookup check box**   Select this check box if you don't have an Internet connection available when you're ripping. This check box makes MUSICMATCH Jukebox Plus track the MP3 files you rip. MUSICMATCH Jukebox Plus then looks up the CDs when an Internet connection is available and applies tag information to the files. This check box is available only when the Enable CD Lookup check box is selected.

- **Prompt to Submit CD Information when Not Found check box**   This check box controls whether MUSICMATCH Jukebox Plus prompts you to submit CD information to CDDB when a CD lookup attempt comes up dry.

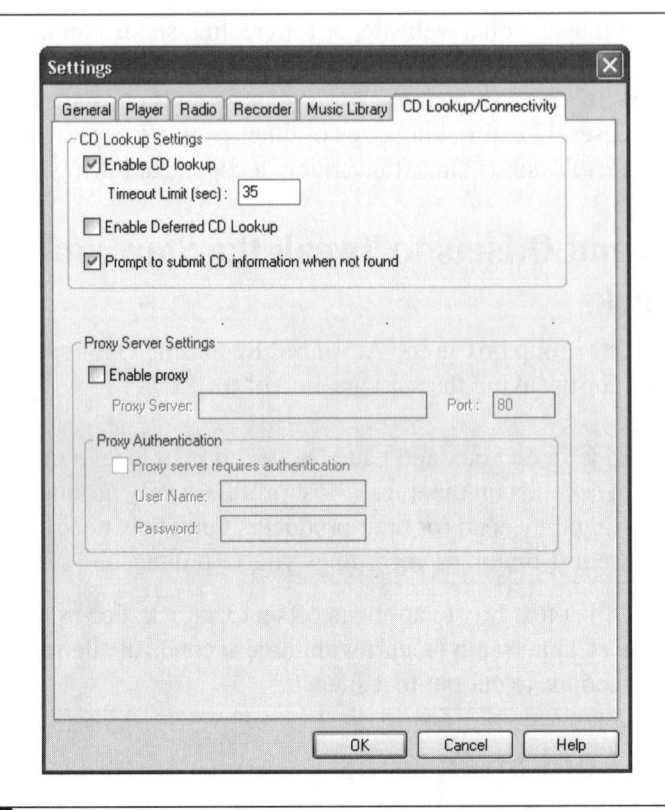

FIGURE 4-6 On the CD Lookup/Connectivity tab of the Settings dialog box, choose whether MUSICMATCH Jukebox Plus should automatically look up CDs in CDDB.

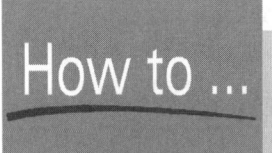

How to... How to Troubleshoot Ripping Problems

If the CD drive you're using is old or wobbly; or if the CD drive is disagreeing with Windows or MUSICMATCH Jukebox Plus in some way; *or* if the CD is disagreeing with the drive, Windows, or MUSICMATCH Jukebox Plus—if any or all of these is the case, your MP3 files may suffer from *jitter* (drive-seeking errors) or pops. Jitter typically makes audio sound as though it's being played too fast, too slow, or jerkily, like a tightly or loosely wound cassette tape. Pops you won't have any trouble identifying—your MP3 file will sound as though someone spilled Rice Krispies in it.

CHAPTER 4: Use MUSICMATCH Jukebox Plus to Load Music onto Your Windows iPod

To troubleshoot these problems, turn to the five options in the Digital Audio Extraction (DAE) group box in the Advanced Recording Options dialog box.

- **DAE Speed drop-down list**   Select a lower speed than MAX if your MP3 files seem to be playing too fast. Be prepared to use the speed 1 if necessary. As you'd imagine, a lower speed takes longer to rip the same track.

- **Multipass drop-down list**   If your tracks suffer from jitter, select On instead of Off. Multipass makes MUSICMATCH Jukebox Plus read each track more than once to get an accurate reading. The disadvantage—you guessed it—is that multipass takes longer.

- **Block Size text box**   To cure jitter, you can also increase this value from its default (20) to a value of up to 100.

- **Overlap text box**   To cure pops, clicks, or jitter, increase this value from its default (3) to a value of up to 10. A larger overlap makes MUSICMATCH Jukebox Plus check each block of data more carefully.

- **Max Mismatches text box**   To enable MUSICMATCH Jukebox Plus to deal with bad blocks of data on a CD, increase this value from its default (0) to up to 255. Increase the value gradually and see what results you get. Increasing the number of mismatches increases your chance of being able to record a track at all, but it also increases the likelihood of the track having corruption in it. So proceed delicately.

NOTE   *About this point, you're probably wondering about the Delayed Record button and the Security button on the Recorder tab of the Settings dialog box. The Delayed Record button and Delayed Recording dialog box let you set MUSICMATCH Jukebox Plus up to record an audio program later—for example, a radio broadcast. The Security button displays the Digital Rights Management dialog box, which works with WMA files but not with MP3 files.*

NOTE   *The CD Lookup/Connectivity tab of the Settings dialog box also contains options for connecting to the Internet through a proxy server. Most home Internet connections, even shared Internet connections, don't use a proxy server. If your computer is connected to a network that uses a proxy server, consult the network administrator for details of the settings to use.*

Configure Your Music Library

The Music Library tab of the Settings dialog box (Figure 4-7) lets you configure the following aspects of your music library:

- **Music Library Display Settings group box** In the View By drop-down list, select the category of data by which to sort the music library. Use the Column 2 through Column 7 check boxes and drop-down lists to specify how many columns to display and what the contents of each should be.

- **If ID3V1 Tag Doesn't Match ID3V2 Tag group box** Choose what MUSICMATCH Jukebox Plus should do if the ID3 version 1 tag on an MP3 file doesn't match the ID3 version 2 tag: use the ID3 version 1 tag info, use the ID3 version 2 tag info, or prompt you to choose between them.

- **Update Tags group box** Select the Convert Tags when Adding Tracks with Old Format Tags check box if you want MUSICMATCH Jukebox Plus to update tags in old formats.

- **Library Auto-Load group box** Click the Browse button and use the resulting Browse for Folder dialog box to designate a folder that MUSICMATCH Jukebox Plus should check for audio files. You can then add files to this folder and have MUSICMATCH Jukebox Plus add them automatically to your music library.

Keep Your Copy of MUSICMATCH Jukebox Plus Up-to-Date

MUSICMATCH Jukebox Plus includes an auto-update feature that periodically checks the MUSICMATCH web site for updates. If you disable this option, or if you want to make sure MUSICMATCH Jukebox Plus is up-to-date right now, choose Options | Update Software, and then click the Continue button in the Software Update dialog box. MUSICMATCH Jukebox Plus displays the Software Update Status dialog box to show you its progress as it downloads the updates.

Create, Build, and Manage Your Music Library

Before you can load music onto your iPod, you need to create your MUSICMATCH Jukebox Plus music library. Your first step should be to rip some (or all) of your CDs to MP3 files. Then, if you already have other MP3 files on your computer,

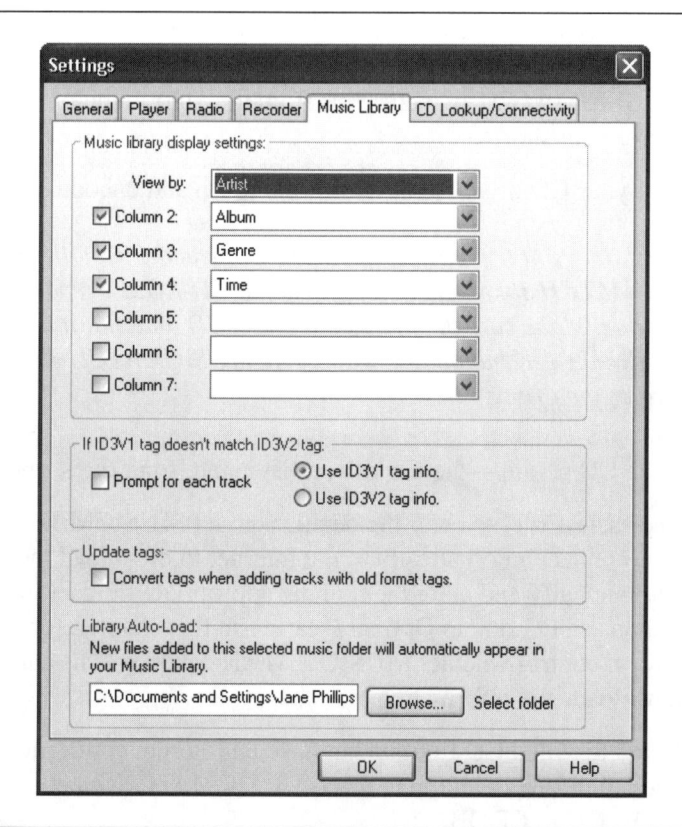

CHAPTER 4: Use MUSICMATCH Jukebox Plus to Load Music onto Your Windows iPod   **119**

FIGURE 4-7   Choose configuration settings for your music library on the Music Library tab of the Settings dialog box.

add those to your music library as well. You may also need to tag (or re-tag) some MP3 files so MUSICMATCH Jukebox Plus lists them correctly and your iPod can add them to its database.

Rip and Encode Your CDs

As discussed in Chapter 2, there are two steps to getting the audio off a CD and into a digital audio file that your computer can use: ripping the audio from the CD, and encoding it to the file (for example, an MP3 file). But because most people speak simply of "ripping" a CD rather than ripping and encoding it, this book also uses the phrase "rip a CD" rather than "rip and encode a CD." Complicating matters further, MUSICMATCH Jukebox Plus talks of "recording" a CD rather than "ripping" it, so don't be put off by any references to "recording."

To rip and encode a CD to MP3 files, follow these steps:

1. Start MUSICMATCH Jukebox Plus from the Start menu or from any convenient shortcut.

2. Insert in your CD drive the CD you want to rip and encode.

   NOTE *The first time you try to rip a CD using a particular CD drive, MUSICMATCH Jukebox Plus displays the CD-ROM Preparation dialog box. Make sure the drive contains a CD and that it isn't playing. Then click the OK button and wait while MUSICMATCH Jukebox Plus calibrates the drive.*

3. Enter the CD details—the CD title, artist name, song titles, and genre:

   - The easiest way to enter the details is to let MUSICMATCH Jukebox Plus connect automatically to the Internet to download the CD details automatically and enter them in the appropriate fields. (See the section "Choose CD Lookup Options," earlier in this chapter, for details on how to control whether MUSICMATCH Jukebox Plus automatically downloads the information.)

   - If you disabled CD Lookup but have an Internet connection available, click the Refresh button to force MUSICMATCH Jukebox Plus to look up the CD in CDDB.

   - If you don't have an Internet connection available, either use Deferred CD Lookup (again, see the section "Choose CD Lookup Options," earlier in this chapter) to rip the tracks and then tag them later or enter the information manually. Set the artist name and album name by clicking the Artist item and Album item in the Recorder window and typing the names. Then enter the name of each track you plan to rip (Figure 4-8). Press TAB to move from one track name to the next.

4. Select the check boxes for the tracks you want to rip. By default, MUSICMATCH Jukebox Plus selects all the check boxes. Click the None button to clear all the check boxes. Click the All button to restore them.

CHAPTER 4: Use MUSICMATCH Jukebox Plus to Load Music onto Your Windows iPod　　**121**

FIGURE 4-8　If you don't have an Internet connection and don't want to use Deferred CD Lookup, enter the CD information manually in the Recorder window.

5. Click the Record button to start ripping the tracks. The Recorder window displays its progress, as shown in the following image:

NOTE　*To stop ripping the current track and skip to ripping the next track, click the Stop button. To cancel ripping the current track and all the other tracks, click the Cancel button.*

6. By default, MUSICMATCH Jukebox Plus plays a sound and ejects the CD when it has finished ripping it. Load the next CD, rinse, and repeat.

Add Tracks to Your Music Library

Besides ripping CDs, you can add tracks to your music library in any of several ways.

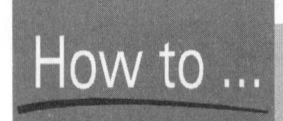

How to... Submit CD Information to CDDB Using MUSICMATCH Jukebox Plus

Like iTunes, MUSICMATCH Jukebox Plus lets you submit CD data to CDDB for CDs that don't have entries in them. As discussed in the section "Choose CD Lookup Options," earlier in this chapter, the default setting is to prompt you to submit CD information when CDDB doesn't provide a match. First, though, MUSICMATCH Jukebox Plus displays the Advanced Search dialog box (Figure 4-9) to let you search manually.

Enter the artist and album information in the Artist text box and Album text box, and then click the Search button. MUSICMATCH Jukebox Plus searches for the data you've entered, and then returns a list of possible matches.

If one of the results is correct, select it, and then click the Select button. If none of the results is correct, click the Not Found button to display the CD Lookup – Submit CD Information dialog box (shown in Figure 4-10 with some information entered).

Type the Artist name in the Artist text box. If you don't want to apply the artist's name to all tracks, clear the Apply Artist to All Tracks check box, which is selected by default. For example, if you're entering the information for a compilation album, clear this check box, and then type the artist names in the Artist column. Otherwise, when you move the focus from the Artist text box, MUSICMATCH Jukebox Plus automatically enters the artist name in each field in the Artist column.

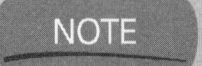

> **NOTE** *Clear the Prompt to Submit CD Information when Not Found check box if you don't want MUSICMATCH Jukebox Plus to prompt you like this.*

Enter the album title in the Album text box. Select the nearest genre in the Genre drop-down list. Then click the OK button to close the CD Lookup – Submit CD Information dialog box and submit the information. If you don't have an Internet connection established, MUSICMATCH Jukebox Plus will attempt to establish one.

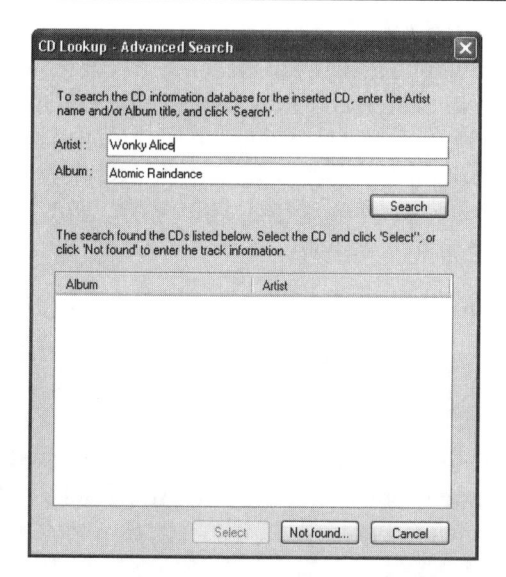

CHAPTER 4: Use MUSICMATCH Jukebox Plus to Load Music onto Your Windows iPod 123

FIGURE 4-9 If MUSICMATCH Jukebox Plus can't find the CD in CDDB automatically, enter the artist and album information in the Advanced Search dialog box.

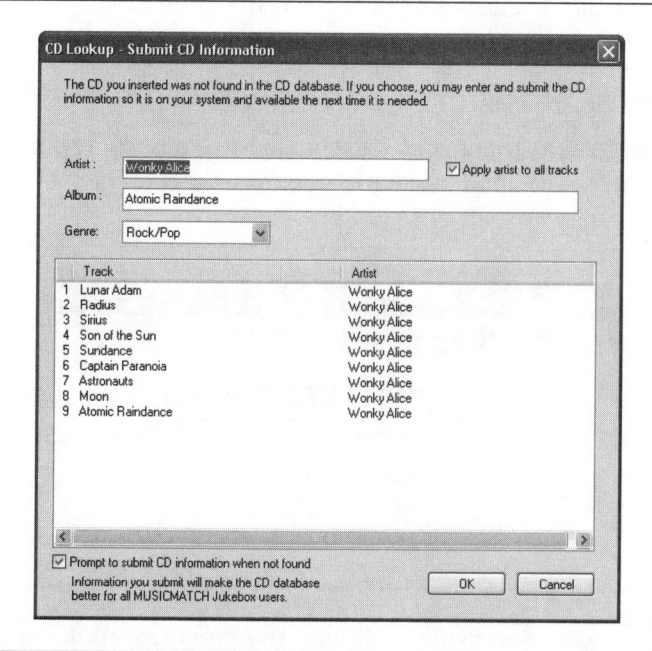

FIGURE 4-10 Use the CD Lookup – Submit CD Information dialog box to submit CD information to CDDB.

Search Your Computer for Tracks

In most cases, the best way to add any tracks on your computer is to choose Options | Music Library | Search and Add Songs from All Drives. In the Search for Music dialog box (Figure 4-11), specify the locations to search and the types of file to find. Then click the OK button to start the search running. Allow a few minutes for the search to complete—longer if you have many hefty drives to search through and many files to find on them.

Add Specific Folders or Tracks to Your Music Library

You can also specify particular folders—or even particular tracks—to add to your music library. To do so, follow these steps:

1. Click the Add button in the Library window or choose File | Add New Track(s) to Music Library to display the Add Tracks to Music Library dialog box (shown in Figure 4-12 with a track selected).

2. Use the Directory list box to navigate to the folder that contains the files or subfolders you want to add.

3. If you navigated to a folder that contains files, use the Files list box to select the file or files to add. Click the Select All button to select all the files.

4. If you navigated to a folder that contains subfolders holding the files you want to add, select the Also Add Tracks from Subfolders check box.

5. If you need to restrict the files to certain file types (for example, MP3 files), choose the appropriate file type from the drop-down list.

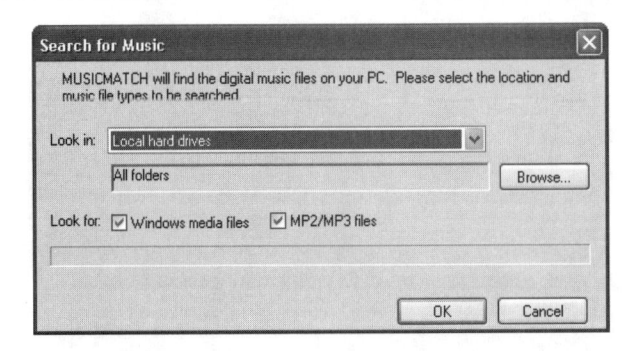

FIGURE 4-11 Use the Search for Music dialog box to add any tracks on your computer to your music library.

6. Click the Add button to add the files to your music library. MUSICMATCH Jukebox Plus displays a dialog box as it adds the files.

7. Add further files from other folders, and then click the Exit button to close the Add Tracks to Music Library dialog box.

> **NOTE** *You can also add tracks to your music library by placing them in the folder specified in the Library Auto-Load text box on the Music Library tab of the Settings dialog box.*

Delete Songs from Your Music Library

To delete one or more selected tracks from your music library, right-click the selection, and then choose Remove Track(s) from the shortcut menu. MUSICMATCH Jukebox Plus displays the dialog box shown in the following image. Click the Yes button to remove the track or tracks from your music library. Select the Also Delete the Selected File(s) from My Computer check box before clicking the Yes button

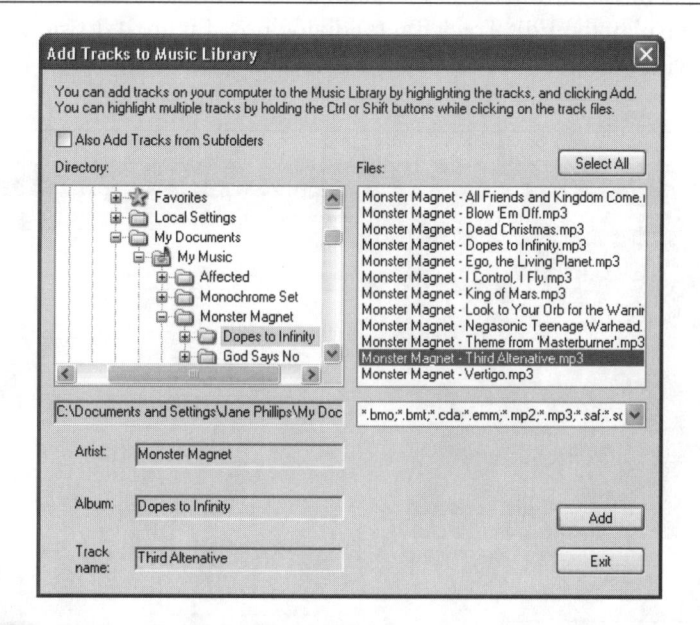

FIGURE 4-12 Use the Add Tracks to Music Library dialog box to add tracks.

if you want to get rid of the files as well. If not, the files remain in their current location even though the reference to them in your music library has gone.

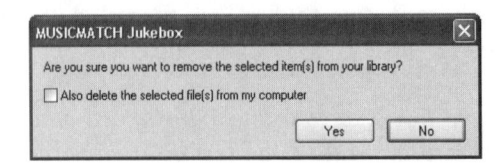

Tag and Super-Tag Your Song Files so They Sort Correctly

The folks who built MUSICMATCH Jukebox Plus recognize both how vital tags are and how much effort they require to edit manually. MUSICMATCH Jukebox Plus includes powerful tagging features that can work either with individual tracks or multiple tracks at once. This section introduces you to the tagging features.

To start editing the tags for one or more files, select the file or files in your music library. Then click the Tag button in the Library window or issue an Edit Track Tag(s) command from either the shortcut menu or the Options | Music Library submenu to display the Edit Track Tag(s) dialog box. Figure 4-13 shows the Edit Track Tags with multiple files loaded and selected.

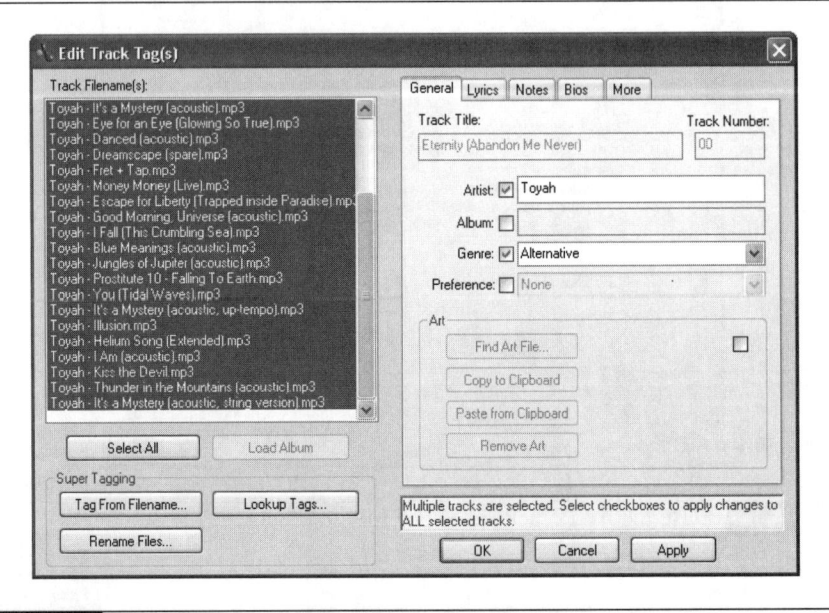

FIGURE 4-13   You can use the Edit Track Tag(s) dialog box to edit the tags for multiple MP3 files at the same time.

CHAPTER 4: Use MUSICMATCH Jukebox Plus to Load Music onto Your Windows iPod

Most of the tagging options are straightforward: you select the tracks you want to affect in the Track Filename(s) list box, fill in the appropriate fields, and then click the Apply button to apply the information to the files. But the following items deserve comment:

- For MP3 files that have filenames but no tags, click the Tag from Filename button in the Super Tagging group box to display the Tag from Filename dialog box (Figure 4-14). MUSICMATCH Jukebox Plus automatically parses each MP3 file name into parts that can be used for tags. If necessary, correct the entries in the Tag Separator text box and the Field 1 through Field 4 list boxes to produce the correct information. Double-click a particular cell of new information to edit it manually. Then click the OK button to assign the tags to the files. You'll still need to click the Apply button in the Edit Track Tag(s) dialog box (Figure 4-13) to write the tag information to the files.

- For MP3 files that have tags but mangled filenames, click the Rename Files button, and then use the Create Filename from Tags dialog box to specify the format of the filename to create.

- Click the Lookup Tags button to look up tag information for the selected file or files in the MUSICMATCH Jukebox Plus database. Check the results in the Tag Lookup Results dialog box, and then click the Accept Selected Tags button once you've got the information straight.

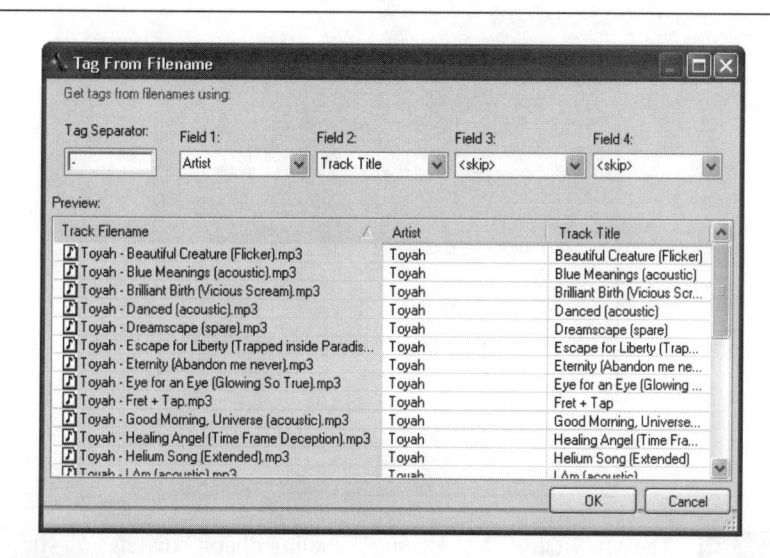

FIGURE 4-14 The Tag from Filename feature derives tags from the naming convention applied to the file.

Use Volume Leveling to Avoid Getting Your Ears Blasted

To help you avoid getting your ears blasted by tracks that are recorded at higher volume levels than other tracks, MUSICMATCH Jukebox Plus includes a feature called Volume Leveling.

To turn Volume Leveling on and off, choose Options | Player | Volume Leveling. In the MUSICMATCH Volume Leveling dialog box (Figure 4-15), select the Turn on Volume Leveling but Don't Prepare Any Tracks option button, and then click the OK button.

Before you can use Volume Leveling when playing back a track, you need to "process" the track—in other words, let MUSICMATCH Jukebox Plus find the track's loudest point to use as a reference point in setting the volume in the future.

The easiest way to process a track is while you rip it. To do so, select the Prepare Tracks for Volume Leveling check box on the Recorder tab of the Settings dialog box. But if you didn't process a track while ripping it, or you received the track from another source, you can process it later. To do so, select the track or tracks, right-click, and choose Prepare Tracks for Volume Leveling from the shortcut menu.

Alternatively, choose Options | Player | Volume Leveling to display the MUSICMATCH Volume Leveling dialog box; choose the Prepare All Tracks in Music Library for Volume Leveling option button, the Prepare Selected Tracks in Music Library for Volume Leveling option button, or the Prepare Tracks in

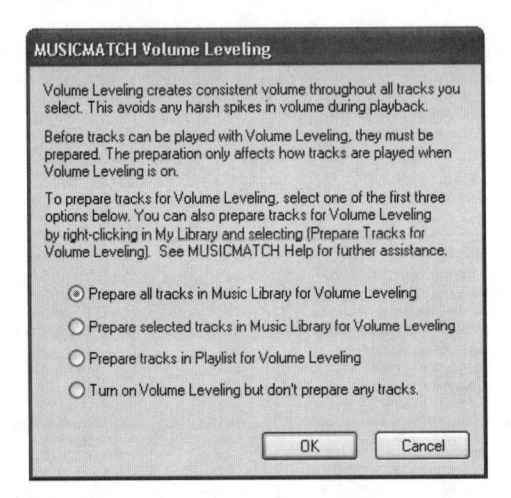

FIGURE 4-15 The MUSICMATCH Volume Leveling dialog box lets you simply turn on Volume Leveling or prepare certain tracks for Volume Leveling.

Playlist for Volume Leveling option button, as appropriate; and then click the OK button. Bear in mind that preparing a large number of tracks for Volume Leveling will take a long time—for example, overnight.

You'll see the Building the Volume Leveling Curve on Source Files dialog box while MUSICMATCH Jukebox Plus processes the track. Once the track has been processed for Volume Leveling, MUSICMATCH Jukebox Plus displays a green note beside it in the music library instead of the crimson note.

The best thing to do is try Volume Leveling on a few dozen tracks and see whether you like its effect. If you do, apply it to all the tracks in your music library—preferable when you're about to leave your computer alone for a while, such as when heading off to work or to bed (or both, if you're lucky).

If you don't like the effect Volume Leveling has, you can remove it. To do so, select the Not Prepared option button in the Volume Leveling group box on the More tab of the Edit Track Tag(s) dialog box for the track.

Enjoy Music with MUSICMATCH Jukebox Plus

This section runs through what you need to know to enjoy music on your PC with MUSICMATCH Jukebox Plus: how to play music back, how to use the graphical equalizer to improve the sound of the music, and even how to use MUSICMATCH Jukebox Plus as an alarm clock.

Play Back Music

Playing back music with MUSICMATCH Jukebox Plus is straightforward. The following paragraphs outline the key points:

- To start a track in the playlist, select the track, and then click the Play button.

- To save a playlist, click the Save button, and then use the resulting Save Playlist dialog box. To open a saved playlist, click the Open button, and then use the Open Music dialog box to select the playlist.

- Double-click a track in the music library to add it to the playlist.

- You can navigate through the My Library pane by scrolling with the mouse. But you can also navigate more quickly by using the keyboard: put the focus in the My Library pane, and then type the first few letters of the artist name you want to reach.

- Click a column heading to sort your music library alphabetically by that column. Click again to reverse the order of the sort.

TIP *You can right-click many elements in the MUSICMATCH Jukebox Plus interface to display a context menu of commands related to that element.*

- Use the Find in Music Library dialog box (CTRL-F) to search your music library for songs matching a string of text.

- MUSICMATCH Jukebox Plus comes with various skins you can apply to change its looks. Choose View | Change Skin to display the Change Skin dialog box, select a skin, and then click the Apply button. Click the OK button to close the dialog box when you've found a skin you like. You can download further skins by choosing View | Download Skins.

TIP *To change skins quickly, SHIFT-click the Previous Visualization button or the Next Visualization button.*

- If you're at a loose end, right-click anywhere in the My Library pane and choose Play My Library from the shortcut menu. MUSICMATCH Jukebox Plus plays random tracks until it exhausts your patience or your library.

- Click the Now Playing tab in the Player window to search the MUSICMATCH Guide for information on the current song.

- Use the options on the View | Visualizations menu to configure, start, and stop visualizations.

How to ... How to Keep MUSICMATCH Jukebox Plus Always at Hand

With its huge windows, MUSICMATCH Jukebox Plus tends to dominate even respectable-size screens. But it also has a Small Player view, which you can access by choosing View | Small Player View or pressing ALT-PAGEDOWN.

With the Small Player view, you may also want to keep MUSICMATCH Jukebox Plus on top of all other windows; to do so, right-click the left end of the player and choose Always on Top from the shortcut menu, or press ALT-T. Issue the command again when you want to stop MUSICMATCH Jukebox Plus being on top.

To restore MUSICMATCH Jukebox Plus to full size, right-click the left end of the player and choose Full Player View from the shortcut menu, or press ALT-PAGEUP.

CHAPTER 4: Use MUSICMATCH Jukebox Plus to Load Music onto Your Windows iPod   131

Use the Graphical Equalizer to Improve the Sound

To improve the sound, use the graphical equalizer. Choose Options | Player | Equalizer to display the MUSICMATCH Jukebox Equalizer window (Figure 4-16).

Select the Enable EQ check box to turn on equalization, and then choose an equalization from the drop-down list. You can also create custom equalizations by dragging the frequency sliders to suitable positions, entering a name in the text box (on the drop-down list), and then clicking the Save button.

Click the Close button to close the MUSICMATCH Jukebox Equalizer window when you've finished working in it.

Use MUSICMATCH Jukebox Plus as an Alarm

One of the nicer features of MUSICMATCH Jukebox Plus is its ability to act as a musical alarm clock. You can set up to five different alarms—for example, a different alarm for each working day.

To set an alarm, follow these steps:

1. Right-click the MUSICMATCH Jukebox Plus icon in the notification area and choose Alarm Settings to display the MUSICMATCH Jukebox Plus Alarm Settings dialog box (Figure 4-17).

2. Select the Alarm On check box, and then use the controls in the Alarm Time group box and the Alarm Frequency group box to specify when the alarm should go off.

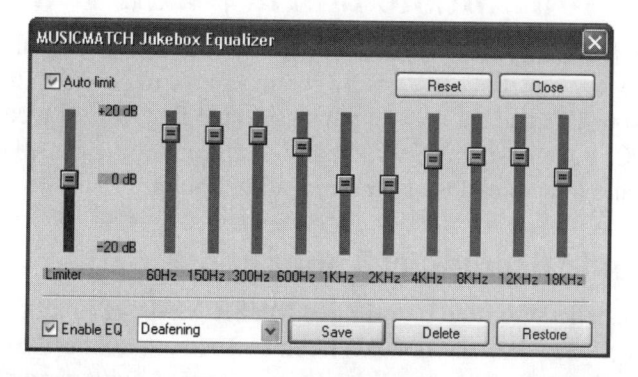

FIGURE 4-16   Use the MUSICMATCH Jukebox Equalizer to improve the sound of music.

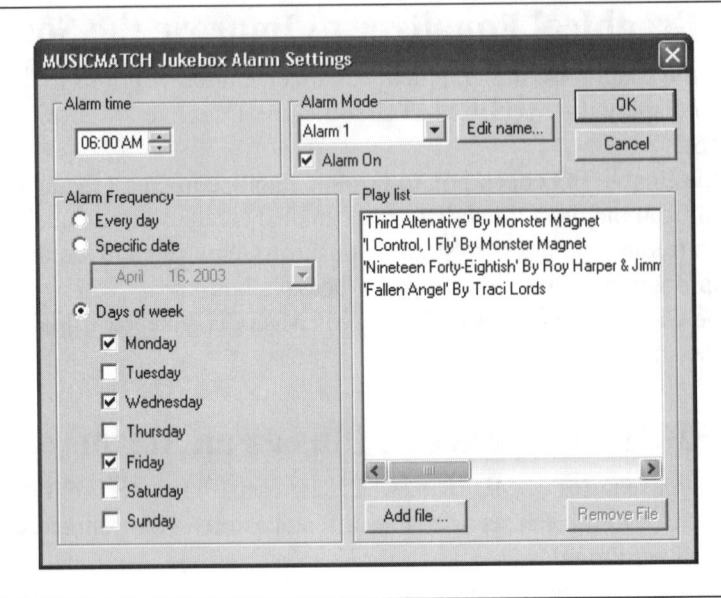

FIGURE 4-17 MUSICMATCH Jukebox Plus can even wake you up in the mornings.

3. Use the Add File button (and if necessary, the Remove File button) to add the appropriate files to the Play List box.

4. Set the volume to a suitable whisper or blast, depending on your sleeping patterns.

Synchronize Your Music Library with Your iPod

This section discusses how to synchronize your MUSICMATCH Jukebox Plus music library with your iPod. It starts by covering how to connect and disconnect your iPod to your PC, and shows you what to do the first time you connect your iPod to your PC. It then explains how to configure iPod settings in MUSICMATCH Jukebox Plus and how to choose synchronization options.

Connect and Disconnect Your iPod

Once you've installed the iPod plug-in and MUSICMATCH Jukebox Plus, you're ready to connect your iPod to your PC. Even before your connect your iPod, Windows displays an iPod icon in the notification area—with a red ✕ to indicate that your iPod isn't connected.

CHAPTER 4: Use MUSICMATCH Jukebox Plus to Load Music onto Your Windows iPod

Connect your iPod to the FireWire cable. Wait for a few seconds while Windows registers your iPod's presence. The red × then disappears from the iPod icon in the notification area, and Windows automatically launches MUSICMATCH Jukebox Plus (if it's not already running) or activates it (if it is running).

First Connection: Configure Device Setup Options

The first time you connect your iPod to a PC (or when you reconnect it after performing a Restore operation, which reformats the hard disk), MUSICMATCH Jukebox Plus displays the Device Setup dialog box (Figure 4-18).

To perform basic configuration of your iPod, follow these steps:

1. Your iPod's default name is *iPod*. If you feel you can improve on this, enter the new name in the Device Name text box. The name can be up to 11 characters long.

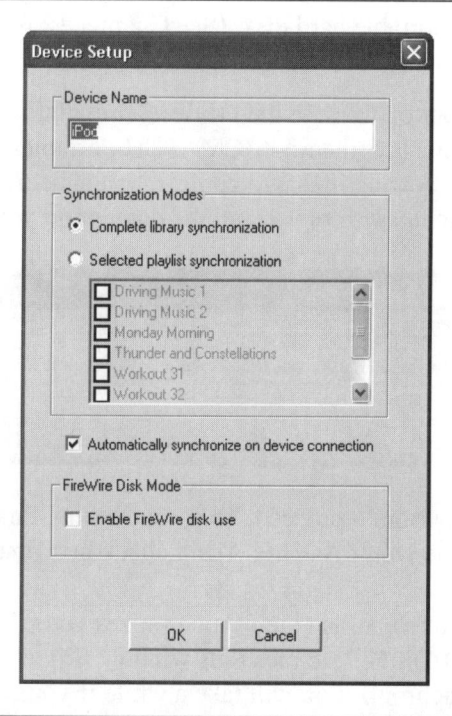

FIGURE 4-18 MUSICMATCH Jukebox Plus displays the Device Setup dialog box when you first connect your iPod to your PC. Choose basic configuration parameters for your iPod.

134 How to Do Everything with Your iPod

2. Choose how to synchronize your iPod with your music library:
   - The MUSICMATCH Jukebox Plus default is to synchronize the complete library automatically when you connect your iPod to your PC. To use this option, leave the Complete Library Synchronization option button and the Automatically Synchronize on Device Connection check box selected.
   - To prevent automatic synchronization, clear the Automatically Synchronize on Device Connection check box. You can then force synchronization at your convenience by clicking the Sync button in the MUSICMATCH Portables Plus window.
   - To synchronize only some playlists, choose the Selected Playlist Synchronization option button in the Synchronization Modes group box, and then select the appropriate playlists in the list box.

3. Select the Enable FireWire Disk Use check box only if you want to use your iPod as a portable hard disk. (See Chapter 12 for a discussion of this topic—preferably before you select this check box.)

4. Click the OK button to close the Device Setup dialog box. MUSICMATCH Jukebox Plus displays the MUSICMATCH Portables Plus dialog box shown in the following image to confirm that synchronizing your iPod with your computer will replace all the content on your iPod.

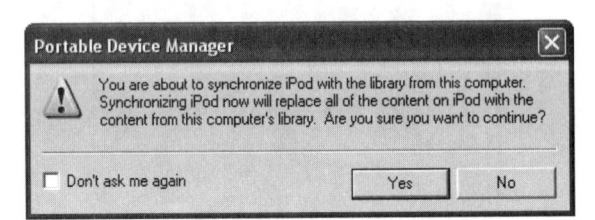

5. Click the Yes button to proceed. To escape seeing this warning in the future, select the Don't Ask Me Again check box first.

MUSICMATCH Jukebox Plus then synchronizes your iPod with your music library. The MUSICMATCH Portables Plus window (Figure 4-19) shows its progress. The first synchronization will take a while if your music library contains many tracks, so be patient.

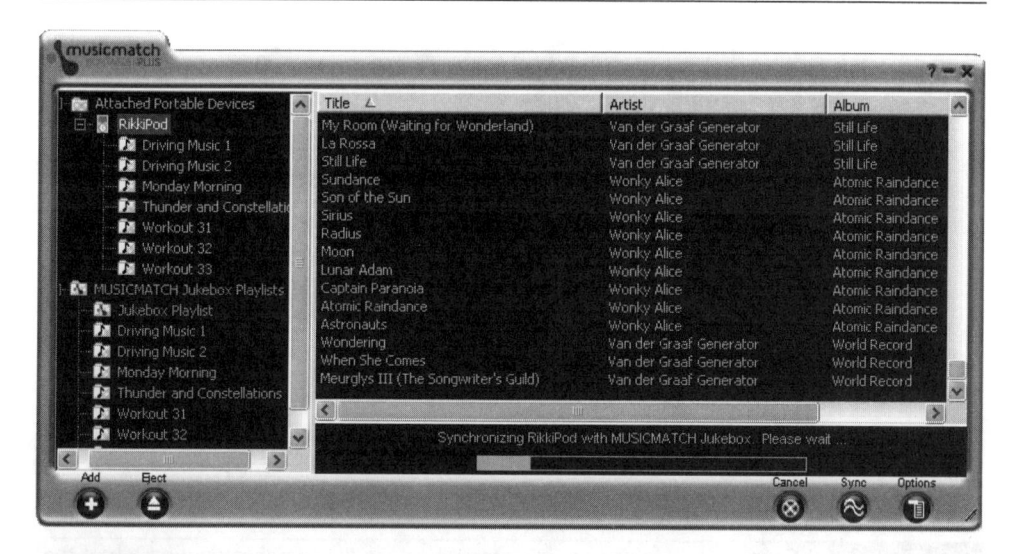

CHAPTER 4:   Use MUSICMATCH Jukebox Plus to Load Music onto Your Windows iPod   **135**

FIGURE 4-19   The MUSICMATCH Portables Plus window provides access to your iPod. Here, initial synchronization is taking place.

Subsequent Connections

Subsequent connections are far simpler than the first. When you connect your iPod, MUSICMATCH Jukebox Plus displays the MUSICMATCH Portables Plus window. If you chose to use automatic synchronization, MUSICMATCH Jukebox Plus synchronizes your iPod on connection. If not, MUSICMATCH Jukebox Plus waits for you to take an action.

Change Synchronization Options for Your iPod

The default setting for MUSICMATCH Jukebox Plus is to automatically synchronize your iPod when you connect it to your PC. To change synchronization settings, select your iPod in the Portable Device Manager window, and then click the Options button to display the Options dialog box. Then choose synchronization options on the Synchronization tab (Figure 4-20) as follows:

- To prevent automatic synchronization, clear the Automatically Synchronize on Device Connection check box. You can then force synchronization at your convenience by clicking the Sync button in the MUSICMATCH Portables Plus window.

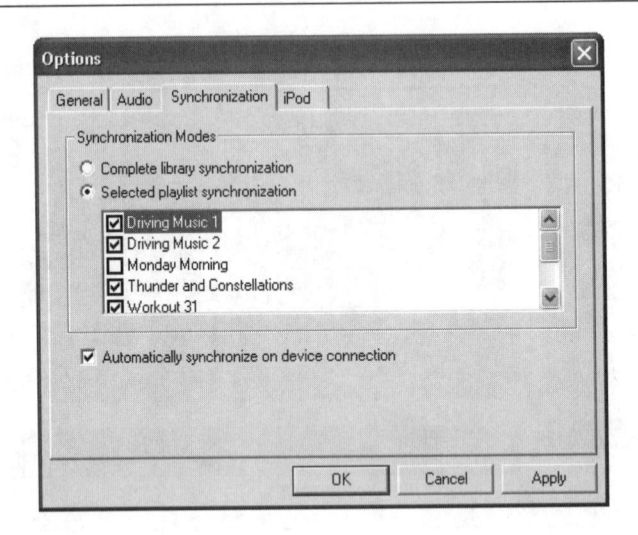

FIGURE 4-20 Configure synchronization preferences on the Synchronization tab of the Options dialog box.

- To synchronize your whole music library, select the Complete Library Synchronization option button. (This option button is selected by default.)

- To synchronize only some playlists, choose the Selected Playlist Synchronization option button in the Synchronization Modes group box, and then select the appropriate playlists in the list box.

Choose Audio Options for Your iPod

When setting up your iPod to work with MUSICMATCH Jukebox Plus, you should also consider applying some of the settings on the Audio tab of the Options dialog box (Figure 4-21):

- **Apply Current Digital Sound Enhancements check box** If you have the DFX digital-effects plug-in (which you can get from **www.musicmatch.com**) installed for MUSICMATCH Jukebox Plus, you can select this check box to use the effects on your iPod as well.

- **Apply Volume Leveling check box** Select this check box to have the MUSICMATCH Jukebox Plus Volume Leveling feature carry through to your iPod. (See the section "Use Volume Leveling to Avoid Getting Your Ears Blasted," earlier in this chapter, for a discussion of Volume Leveling.)

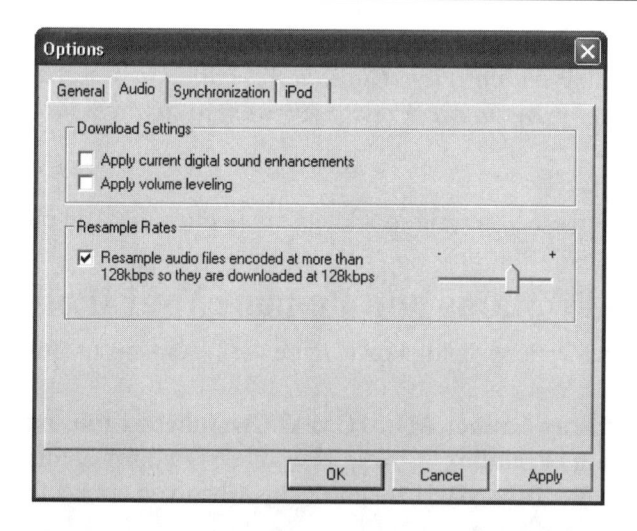

CHAPTER 4:   Use MUSICMATCH Jukebox Plus to Load Music onto Your Windows iPod   **137**

FIGURE 4-21   The Audio tab of the Options dialog box lets you apply digital sound enhancements and Volume Leveling to your iPod. It also lets you resample tracks to reduce their size.

- **Resample Rates group box**   To squeeze more audio onto your iPod, you can have MUSICMATCH Jukebox Plus resample (or, more accurately, downsample) any tracks in your music library that are encoded above a certain bitrate. Select the Resample Audio Files check box to activate this feature, and then drag the slider to set a suitable bitrate. The default setting is 64 Kbps, which most people find too low for comfort. Try resampling at 128 Kbps and see whether the sound quality is high enough for you. This feature lets you use a high bitrate (for example, 320 Kbps) on your PC and a lower bitrate (for example, 128 Kbps) on your iPod.

Add Tracks to Your iPod Manually

If you turn off automatic synchronization, you can add tracks to your iPod manually. To do so, follow these steps:

1. In the MUSICMATCH Portables Plus window, select your iPod.

2. Click the Add button in the MUSICMATCH Portables Plus window or issue an Add Track(s) to Player command from the shortcut menu to display the Open Music dialog box.

NOTE *If your iPod is configured for automatic synchronization, MUSICMATCH Jukebox Plus displays a dialog box to warn you that you're turning off automatic synchronization. Click the Yes button to proceed. Select the Don't Ask Me Again check box if you want to suppress this warning in the future.*

3. Select the tracks you want to add, and then click the Add button.

Choose iPod Options and Rename Your iPod

The iPod tab of the Options dialog box (Figure 4-22) contains the following options:

- **Automatically Launch MUSICMATCH Jukebox Plus on Device Connection check box** Controls whether Windows automatically launches MUSICMATCH Jukebox Plus when you connect your iPod to the FireWire cable.

NOTE *Launching MUSICMATCH Jukebox Plus doesn't trigger synchronization if you turned off the Automatically Synchronize on Device Connection check box on the Synchronization tab of the Options dialog box.*

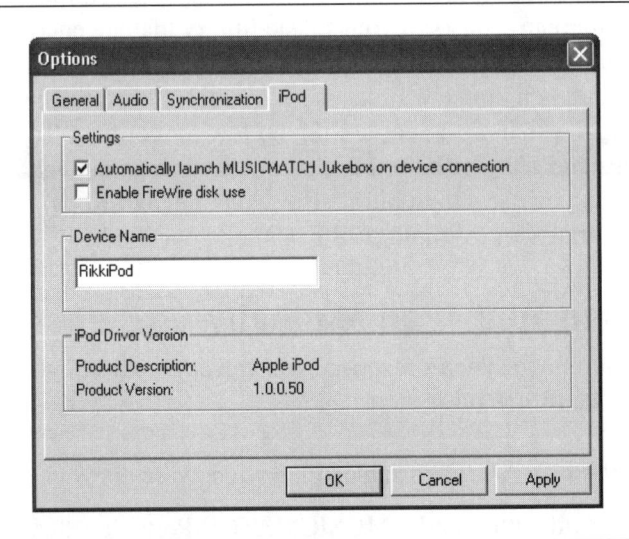

FIGURE 4-22 On the iPod tab of the Options dialog box, you can automatically launch MUSICMATCH Jukebox Plus, enable FireWire disk use, and rename your iPod.

- **Enable FireWire Disk Use check box** Controls whether you can use your iPod as a FireWire disk (for example, to store document files). See Chapter 12 for a discussion of how to use your iPod like this.

- **Device Name text box** To rename your iPod, enter the new name in this text box. iPod names can be up to 11 characters long. Be creative.

Unmount Your iPod

After synchronization, you'll see the message "Unmounting *iPod*. Please wait." followed by the message "It is now safe to disconnect *iPod*." (Again, *iPod* here represents the name assigned to your iPod.)

To unmount your iPod manually, click the Eject button in the MUSICMATCH Portables Plus window, and then click the Yes button in the confirmation dialog box. (You can prevent MUSICMATCH Jukebox Plus from displaying this confirmation dialog box in the future by selecting the Don't Ask Me Again check box.) Wait until MUSICMATCH Jukebox Plus displays the message "It is safe to disconnect *iPod*" before disconnecting your iPod from the FireWire cable.

Create Custom Playlists to Enjoy in MUSICMATCH Jukebox Plus or on Your iPod

MUSICMATCH Jukebox Plus lets you create playlists either manually or by using its AutoDJ feature. You can then play back these playlists either on MUSICMATCH Jukebox Plus or on your iPod.

Create a Playlist Manually

To create a playlist manually, you add the tracks to the Playlist window by double-clicking them in the music library. Before creating a playlist, remove the existing tracks from the Playlist window by clicking the Clear button (unless you want to have these tracks in your playlist).

To save a playlist, click the Save button, enter the name in the Save Playlist dialog box, and then click the Save button.

To open a saved playlist, follow these steps:

1. Click the Open button to display the Open Music dialog box.
2. Click the Playlists button in the Places bar (on the left of the dialog box) to display your playlists.
3. Select the playlist in the list box, and then click the Play button.

Use the AutoDJ Feature to Create a Playlist

The AutoDJ feature creates playlists automatically according to criteria you specify. To use AutoDJ, click the AutoDJ button in the Music Library window, use the controls in the AutoDJ dialog box (Figure 4-23) to specify the criteria, and then click the Get Tracks button to create the playlist. If you like the result, you can save it for reuse as you would any other playlist.

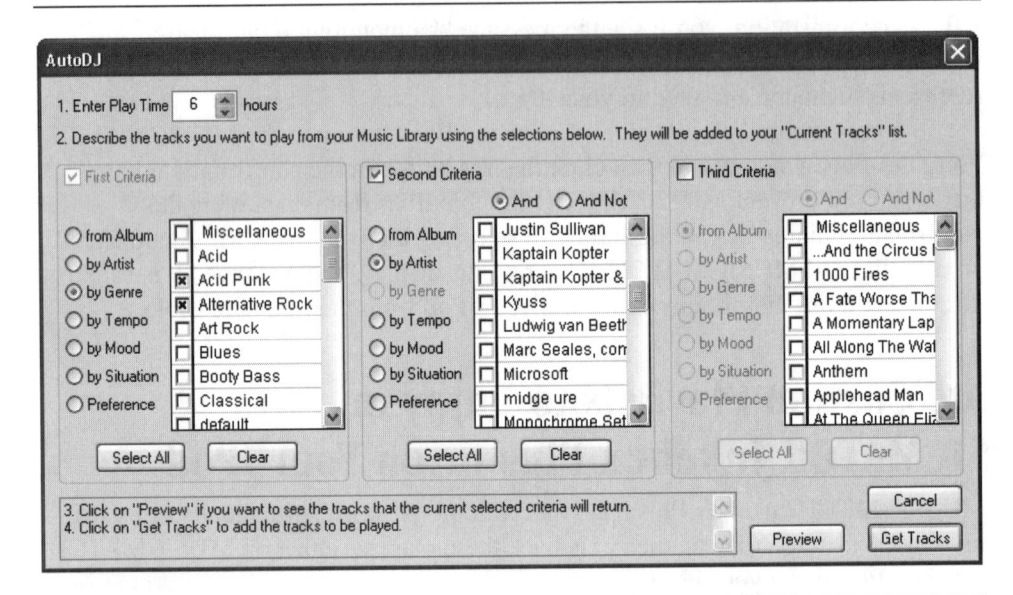

FIGURE 4-23 Use the AutoDJ feature to create playlists automatically.

Chapter 5

Create, Edit, and Tag Your MP3 Files

How to...

- Convert audio files from other audio formats to MP3
- Create MP3 files from cassettes, vinyl, or other sources
- Remove scratches, hiss, and hum from audio files
- Trim, sever, and otherwise abbreviate MP3 files
- Rename MP3 files efficiently
- Save audio streams to disk

As you saw in Chapter 3, iTunes offers great features for creating MP3 files from CDs, organizing them into playlists, playing them back, synchronizing with your iPod, and more. And as you saw in Chapter 4, MUSICMATCH Jukebox Plus offers similar (though not as extensive) features for creating MP3 files, playing them, and working with your iPod on Windows.

But sometimes you'll want to take actions with MP3 files that iTunes and MUSICMATCH Jukebox Plus don't support. For example, you may receive (or acquire) files in formats your iPod can't handle, so you'll need to convert the files before you can use them on your iPod. You may want to create MP3 files from cassettes, LPs, or other media you own, and you may need to remove clicks, pops, and other extraneous noises from such recordings you make. You may want to trim intros or outros off MP3 files, split MP3 files into smaller files, or retag batches of files in ways iTunes and MUSICMATCH Jukebox Plus can't handle. Last, you may want to record streaming audio to your hard disk.

> **NOTE** *Where many applications offer similar functionality, I've preferred freeware applications and applications that offer functional evaluation versions over applications that insist you buy them outright without giving you a chance to try them.*

Convert Other File Types to MP3, AIFF, or WAV so You Can Play Them on Your iPod

Your iPod can play MP3 files, AIFF files (Mac iPods only), and WAV files—three of the most common digital-audio formats. (Mac iPods can also play files in the

> **Did you know?**
>
> ## What Happens When You Convert a File from One Compressed Format to Another?
>
> Before we get started, here's a point that's essential to grasp: when you convert audio from one compressed format to another, audio quality is liable to suffer even further. So the results may not sound too great.
>
> For example, say you have a WMA file. The audio is already compressed with lossy compression, so some parts of the audio have been lost. When you convert this file to an MP3 file, the conversion utility has to expand the compressed WMA audio to uncompressed audio—essentially, to a PCM file (such as WAV or AIFF)— and then recompress it to the MP3 format, again using lossy compression.
>
> The uncompressed audio contains a faithful rendering of all the defects in the WMA file. The MP3 file will contain as faithful a rendering of this defective audio as the MP3 encoder can provide at that compression rate—plus any defects the MP3 encoding introduces.

specialized Audible format.) But if you receive files from friends (or PR firms), or download audio from the Internet (as described in Chapter 6), you'll encounter many other digital-audio formats. This section describes a couple of utilities for converting files from one format to another—preferably to a format your iPod can use, or from which you can encode an MP3 file.

Windows: GoldWave

GoldWave from GoldWave Inc. (**www.goldwave.com**) is a powerful audio editor that lets you convert files from various audio formats to other formats. GoldWave's Batch Conversion feature (File | Batch Conversion) is great for converting a slew of files at once. Figure 5-1 shows the Batch Conversion dialog box.

You can download a 15-day evaluation version of GoldWave from the GoldWave Inc. web site or from various Internet locations, including ClNet's **Download.com**. The registered version of GoldWave costs $40.

Mac: SoundApp

You can get various audio conversion utilities for the Mac. Most of them cost you money, but one of the best is free. That utility is called SoundApp, and you can

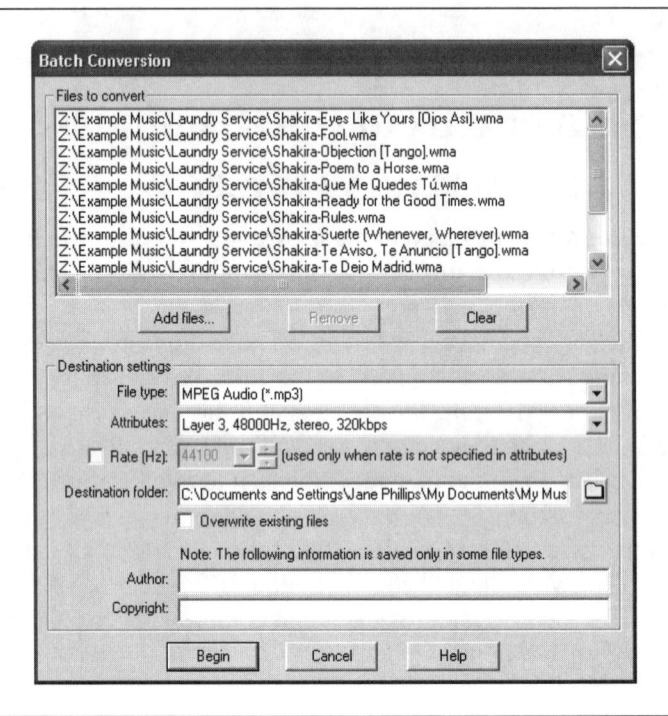

FIGURE 5-1 GoldWave's Batch Conversion dialog box lets you quickly convert many files at once from one format to another.

download it from **www.spies.com/~franke/SoundApp** (and many Internet archives). At this writing, the current version has a minimalist interface and runs in Classic (if you're using Mac OS X), but it works fine.

Create MP3 Files from Cassettes or Vinyl Records

If you have audio on analog media such as cassette tapes, vinyl records, or other waning technologies (8-Track, anyone?), you may want to transfer that audio to your computer so you can listen to it on your iPod. Dust off your gramophone, cassette deck, or other audio source, and then work your way through the following subsections.

Before you start, however, remember the legalities of creating MP3 files. (See Chapter 2 for a discussion of this topic.) If you hold the copyright to the audio, you can copy it as much as you want. If not, you need specific permission to copy it, unless it falls under a specific copyright exemption. For example, the Audio Home Recording Act's personal use provision lets you copy a copyrighted work (for example, an LP) onto a different medium so you can listen to it—provided that you use a "digital audio recording device," a term that doesn't cover computers.

Connect the Audio Source to Your Computer

Start by connecting the audio source to your computer with a suitable type of cable. Obviously, "suitable" depends on the connectors on the audio source and on your sound card. For example, to connect a typical cassette player to a typical sound card, you'll need a cable with two RCA plugs at the cassette player's end (or at the receiver's end) and a male-end stereo miniplug at the other end to plug into your sound card.

NOTE *Because record players produce a low volume of sound, you'll almost always need to put a record player's output through the Phono input of an amplifier before you can record it on your computer.*

If your sound card has a Line In port and a Mic port, use the Line In port. If your sound card has only a Mic port, turn the source volume down to a minimum for the initial connection, because Mic ports tend to be sensitive.

Record on Windows with MUSICMATCH Jukebox Plus

Next, to record audio on Windows using MUSICMATCH Jukebox Plus, work through the steps in the following subsections.

Specify the Source

To set Windows to accept input from the source so you can record from it, follow these steps:

1. If the notification area includes a Volume icon, double-click this icon to display the Volume Control window. Otherwise, choose Start | Control Panel to display the Control Panel and display the Volume Control window from there. For example, in Windows XP, click the Advanced button in the Device Volume group box on the Volume tab of the Sounds and Audio Devices Properties dialog box.

NOTE *The Volume Control window may have a different name (for example, Play Control) depending on your audio hardware and its drivers.*

2. Choose Options | Properties to display the Properties dialog box, then select the Recording option button to display the list of devices for recording (as opposed to the devices for playback). The left screen in Figure 5-2 shows this list.

3. Select the check box for the input device you want to use—for example, select the Line-In check box or the Microphone check box, depending on which you're using.

4. Click the OK button to close the Properties dialog box. Windows displays the Record Control window, an example of which is shown on the right in Figure 5-2. (Like the Volume Control window, this window may have a different name—for example, Recording Control.)

5. Choose the Select check box for the source you want to use.

Leave the Record Control window open for the time being so you can adjust the input volume on the device if necessary.

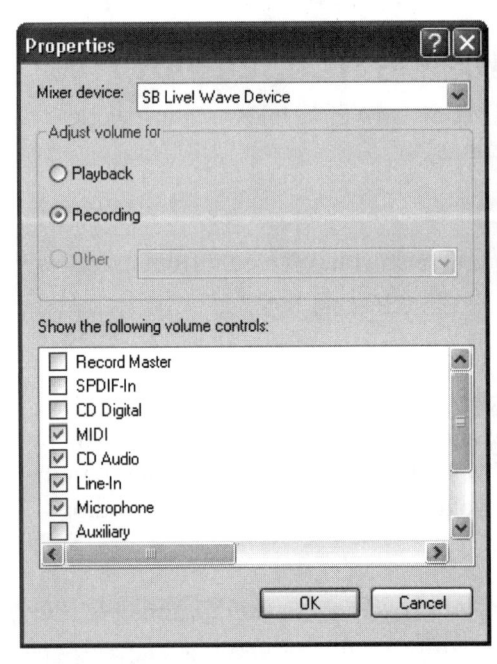

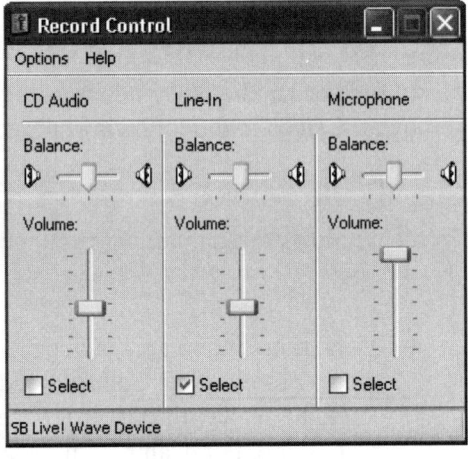

FIGURE 5-2 Select the Recording option button in the Properties dialog box (left) to display the Record Control window (right) instead of the Volume Control.

Set MUSICMATCH Jukebox Plus to Record from the Source

Next, set MUSICMATCH Jukebox Plus to accept input from the same device. Choose Options | Recorder | Source | Line In or Options | Recorder | Source | Mic In as appropriate. Alternatively, display the Recorder tab of the Settings dialog box and select Line In or Mic in the Recording Source drop-down list.

> **TIP** *If you're recording several tracks of material from an external source, consider using the Auto Song Detect feature. To use it, select the Active check box in the Advanced Recorder Options dialog box, and then use the Gap Length text box and Gap Level text box to specify the amount and level of silence that represent a break between tracks. The default is 2000 ms (two seconds) at 10 percent volume.*

Start Recording

To start recording in MUSICMATCH Jukebox Plus, follow these steps:

1. Get the sound source ready to roll.
2. In the Recorder window, enter the artist name, album name, and track name. (Otherwise, MUSICMATCH Jukebox Plus uses the default data: Artist, Album, and "line in track *NN*"—so if you're using the default naming convention, you'll find the tracks in the Artist\Album folder.)
3. Click the Record button in the Recorder window in MUSICMATCH Jukebox Plus to start recording from the source.
4. Click the Stop button to stop recording the current track. MUSICMATCH Jukebox Plus adds the track to your music library and sets you up to record another track.

Record Audio on the Mac

To record audio on the Mac, work through the first subsection, and then choose which of the following subsections to work through.

Specify the Source

To specify the source on the Mac, follow these steps:

1. Choose Apple | System Preferences to display the System Preferences window.

2. Click the Sound item to display the Sound preferences sheet.

3. Click the Input tab to display it (Figure 5-3).

4. In the Choose a Device for Sound Input list box, select the device to use (for example, Line In).

5. Watch the Input Level readout as you drag the Input Volume slider to a suitable level.

Mac: Record Audio with iMovie

iMovie, one of Apple's iApps included with Mac OS X (and part of the iLife suite of applications), lets you record audio files as well as create your own videos.

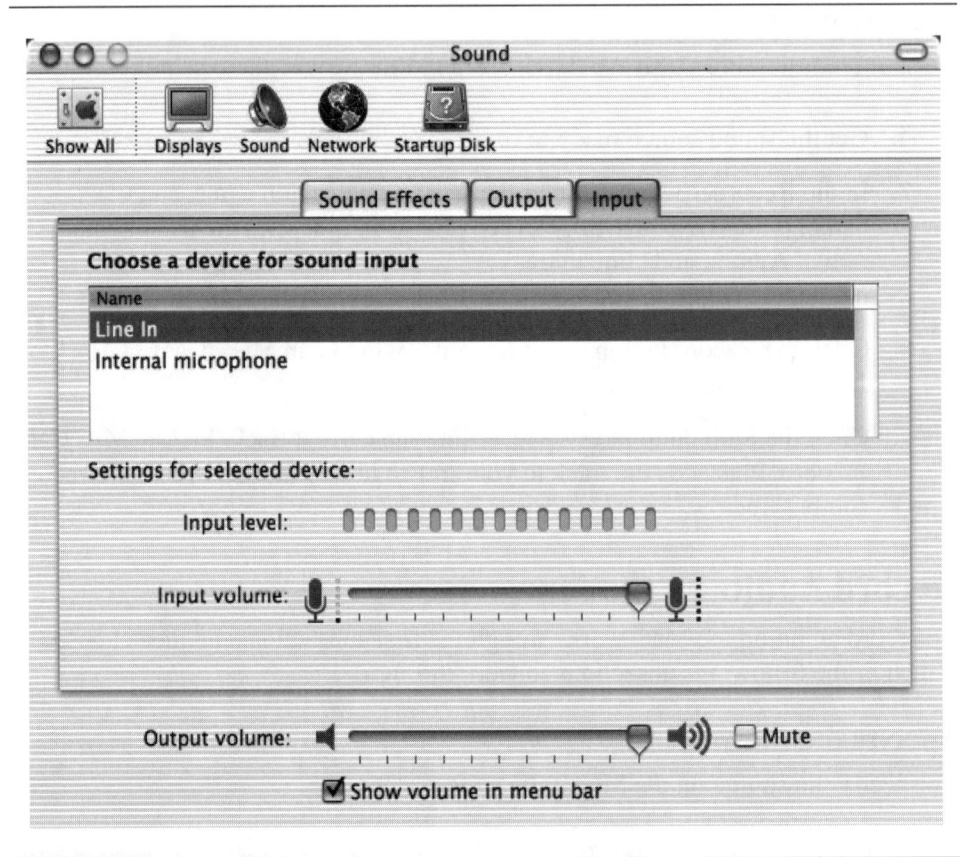

FIGURE 5-3   On the Mac, choose the source on the Input tab of the Sound preferences sheet.

CHAPTER 5: Create, Edit, and Tag Your MP3 Files 149

But the process and results are so clumsy you're unlikely to want to use iMovie for recording sound alone. Still, in case you do, here's a summary of the main steps:

1. Launch iMovie from the icon in the Applications folder (Go | Applications).
2. Click the New Project button in the opening dialog box.
3. In the Create New Project dialog box, enter the name for the file, choose where to save it, and then click the Create button.
4. In the rectangular window, click the Audio button to display the audio controls.
5. Check the input level shown above the Record Voice button. Boost it if necessary.
6. Click the Record Voice button to start recording the audio. (It doesn't matter if the audio is music rather than voice.) iMovie displays the progress of the audio in the first audio track on the timeline window.
7. Click the Stop button (which replaces the Record Voice button) to stop recording the audio.
8. Fade the audio if necessary by double-clicking its track on the timeline window and working in the resulting Clip Info dialog box.
9. Choose File | Export Movie to display the Export Movie dialog box.
10. In the Export drop-down list, select the To QuickTime item.
11. In the Formats drop-down list, select the Expert item to display the Expert QuickTime Settings dialog box.
12. Check the settings in the Audio Settings group box. If necessary, click the Settings button to display the Sound Settings dialog box and use its controls to apply suitable settings. (For example, you might choose 44.100kHz, 16 bit, and Stereo.)
13. Click the OK button to close the Expert QuickTime Settings dialog box.
14. Click the Export button in the Export Movie dialog box.
15. In the Export QuickTime Movie dialog box, specify the name and location for the movie file, and then click the Save button.
16. Open the movie in SoundApp, and then convert it to a usable format (for example, AIFF).

Mac: Two Other Options for Recording Audio

As you saw if you read the previous subsection, the sound-recording capabilities in iMovie are workable only for those determined not to spend extra money on sound-recording applications. If you can spare the equivalent of a week's lunch money, you can have sound-recording and -editing software that's much easier to use and that offers far greater capabilities.

Two such applications you may want to try are Amadeus II and Sound Studio for OS X.

Amadeus II

Amadeus II from HairerSoft (**www.hairersoft.com/Amadeus.html**) is a powerful application for recording and editing audio. You can download a 15-day trial version of Amadeus II. The full version costs $25 for a single-user license.

> **TIP** *Amadeus II includes repair functions you can use to eliminate hiss and crackles from recordings.*

Sound Studio for OS X

Sound Studio for OS X from Felt Tip Software (**www.felttip.com**) is a digital audio editor with a wide range of features. You can download an evaluation version of the software from the Felt Tip Software web site. The full version costs $49.99. Figure 5-4 shows Sound Studio for OS X recording audio.

> **TIP** *Sound Studio for OS X also includes repair features for eliminating noise from recordings.*

Remove Scratches and Hiss from Audio Files

If you record tracks from vinyl records, audio cassettes, or other analog sources, you may well get some clicks or pops, hiss, or background humming in the file. Scratches on a record can cause clicks and pops, audio cassettes tend to hiss (even with noise-reduction such as Dolby), and record players or other machinery can add hum.

All these noises—very much part of the analog audio experience, and actually appreciated as such by some enthusiasts—tend to annoy people accustomed to digital audio. The good news is that you can remove many such noises by using the right software.

CHAPTER 5: Create, Edit, and Tag Your MP3 Files **151**

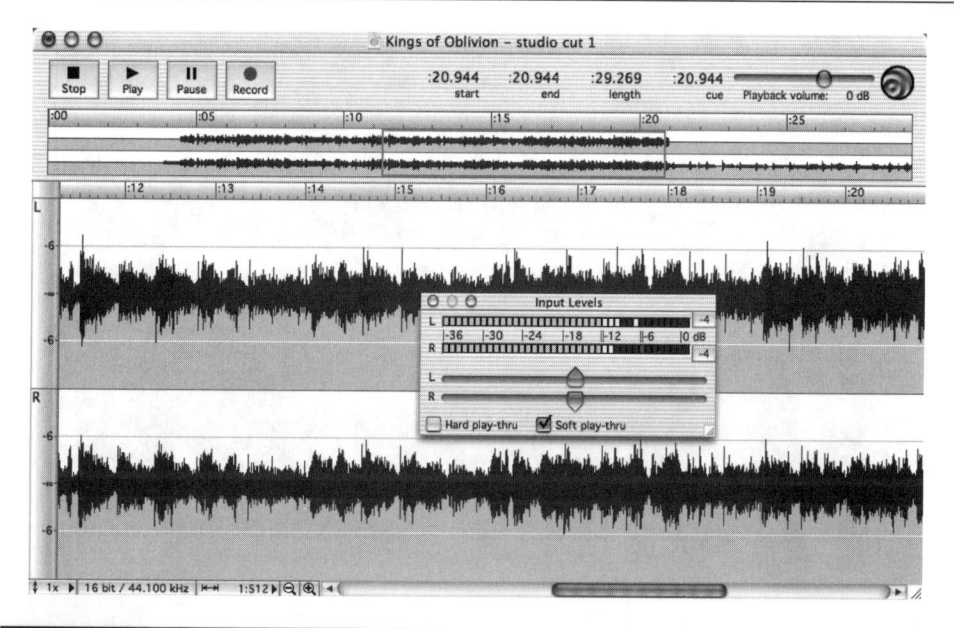

FIGURE 5-4 Recording audio with Sound Studio for OS X

> **NOTE** *Another Windows application for cleaning up audio files is Sound Forge Studio from Sonic Foundry (**www.soundforge.com**). Sound Forge Studio costs about $70 and is a stripped-down version of Sound Forge, which costs $300 or so.*

Windows: GoldWave

Earlier in this chapter, you met GoldWave, an audio editor you can use to convert audio files from one format to another. GoldWave also includes features for filtering audio and eliminating unwanted sounds. Figure 5-5 shows GoldWave working on eliminating the pops and clicks from a WAV file.

Mac: Amadeus II

Amadeus II (introduced earlier in this chapter) offers the following strong features for cleaning up audio files:

- Use the Repair Centre (Effects | Sound Repair | Open Repair Centre) to hunt down and eliminate clicks and pops in a sound.

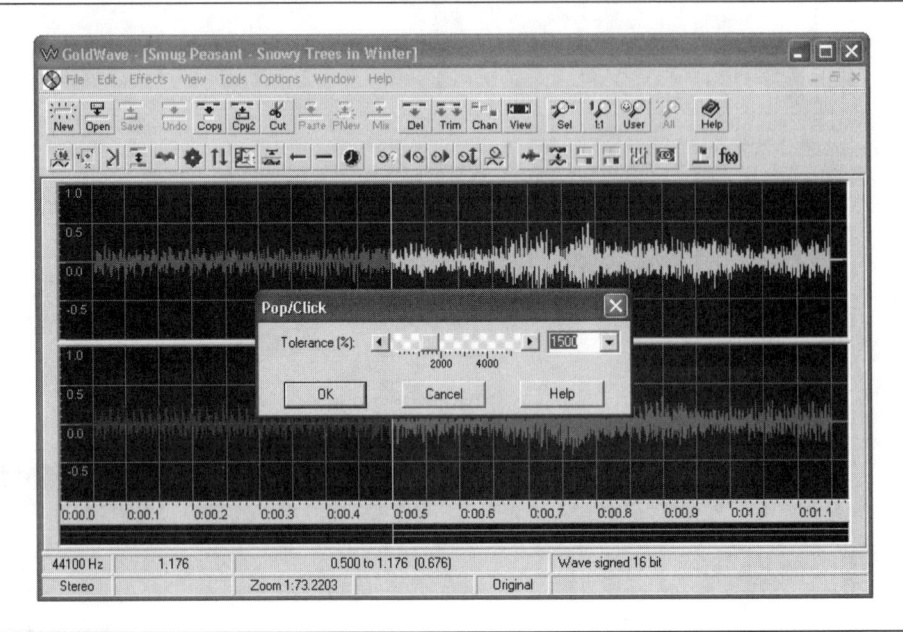

FIGURE 5-5 GoldWave can also remove pops and clicks from an audio file.

- The Effects | Denoising submenu contains options for suppressing various types of noise (for example, white noise).
- The Filter window (Effects | Filter) lets you apply specific filtering to a channel.

Trim MP3 Files to Get Rid of Intros and Outros You Don't Like

As you saw in Chapter 3, the Start Time and Stop Time features in iTunes let you suppress the beginning or end of an MP3 file if you don't want to hear them. But you may want to go further and remove the introduction or the end of the file—or you may want to split an MP3 file into two or more separate files.

This section presents a Windows utility and a Mac utility for doing that.

Windows: MP3 TrackMaker

MP3 TrackMaker from Heathco Software (**www.heathcosoft.com**) is a small utility for dividing MP3 files into smaller files and for joining two or more MP3 files into a single MP3 file. You can download an almost fully functional demo version (it's limited to joining three tracks or splitting a file into three tracks) or pay $13 for the full version.

MP3 TrackMaker needs little explanation. Use the controls on its Split tab (shown on the left in Figure 5-6) to divide an MP3 file into smaller files. Use the controls on its Join tab (shown on the right in Figure 5-6) to join two or more MP3 files into a single MP3 file.

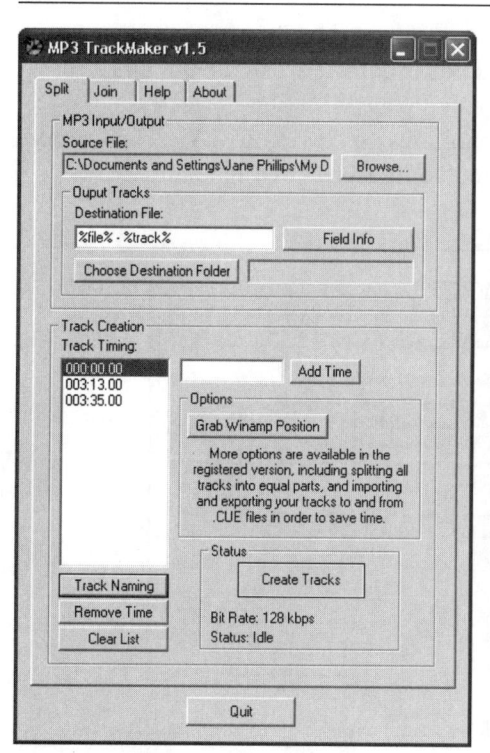

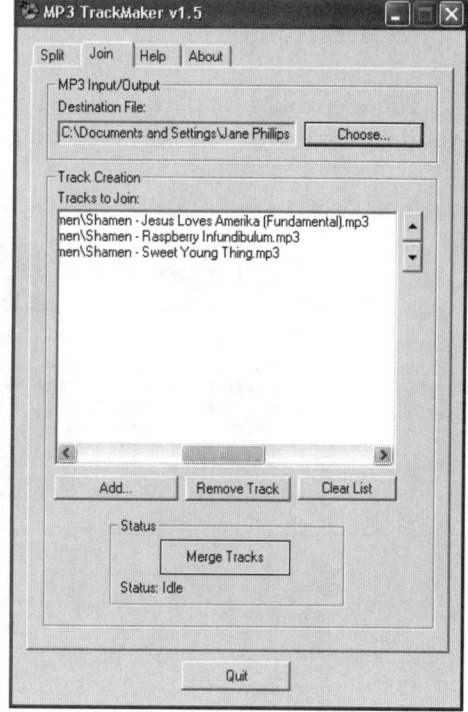

FIGURE 5-6 Use MP3 TrackMaker to divide MP3 files into smaller MP3 files or to join multiple MP3 files into a single MP3 file.

Mac: mEdit

mEdit is a freeware tool for cropping MP3 files on the Mac. You can download it from **www.mcode.de/edit/** or from various software archives on the Internet.

mEdit (Figure 5-7) is straightforward to use. You open the file you want to crop, specify cropping options, execute the crop, and then save the file. You can also use mEdit to cut a section out of the middle of a file. By cropping the same source file twice (or more times) to different destination files, you can effectively use mEdit to split MP3 tracks into multiple files as well.

Tag Your MP3 Files with the Correct Information for Sorting

As you saw in Chapters 3 and 4, your iPod needs correct artist, album, and track name information in tags to be able to organize your MP3 files correctly.

iTunes provides simple tag-editing capabilities, and MUSICMATCH Jukebox Plus provides more powerful tag editing, including its Smart Tag feature.

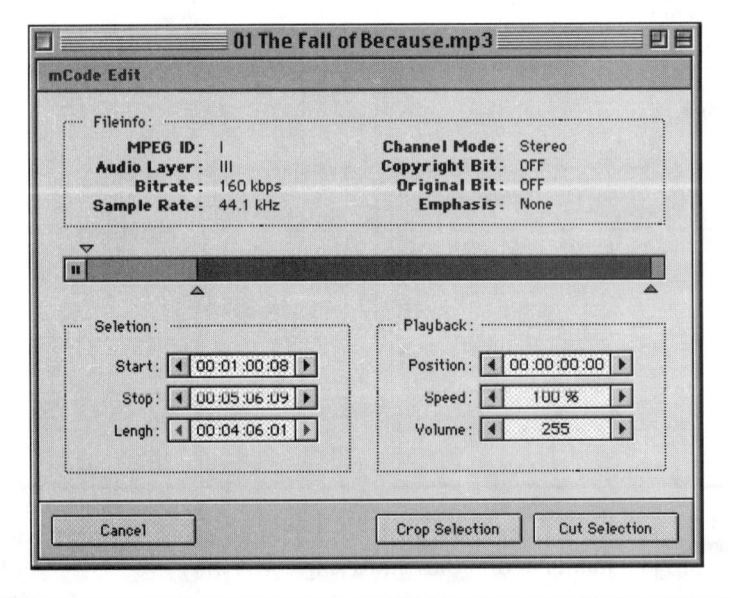

FIGURE 5-7   Use mEdit to trim the ends off an MP3 file or to a cut a section out of it.

But if your music library contains many untagged or mistagged files, you may need a heavier-duty application. The following subsections present two such applications—one for Windows, and one for the Mac.

Windows: Tag&Rename

Tag&Rename from SOFTPOINTER Ltd. is a terrific tag-editing application. But you neither have to take my word for it nor pay any money to prove me wrong, because you can download a free 30-day evaluation version from **www.softpointer.com/tr.htm**.

In Chapter 4, you saw how MUSICMATCH Jukebox Plus can derive tag information by breaking down an MP3 file's name into its constituents. For example, if you have the file Shakira – Laundry Service – 01 – Objection (Tango).mp3 and sic Super Tag on it, Super Tag can derive the artist name (Shakira), the album name (Laundry Service), the track number (01), and the track name (Objection [Tango]) from it. If you have this file, Sony Music is likely to be annoyed, because they copy protected Laundry Service in several markets to prevent people from ripping it...but I digress.

Tag&Rename can perform this filename-dicing as well, but it goes to 11: Tag&Rename can also derive tag information from the folder structure that contains an MP3 file that needs tagging. For example, if you have the file 01 – Objection (Tango).mp3 stored in the folder Shakira\Laundry Service, Sony will be mad—I mean, Tag&Rename will be able to tag the file with the artist name, album name, track name, and track number.

Figure 5-8 shows Tag&Rename in action working on the ID3 tags of some MP3 files.

Mac: MP3 Rage

MP3 Rage from Chaotic Software (**www.chaoticsoftware.com**) is an impressive bundle of utilities for tagging, organizing, and improving your MP3 files. The tagging features in MP3 Rage include deriving tag information from filenames and folder paths (see the left screen in Figure 5-9) and changing the tags on multiple files at once (see the right screen in Figure 5-9).

You can download a fully functional evaluation version of MP3 Rage from the Chaotic Software web site. The registered version of MP3 Rage costs $24.95.

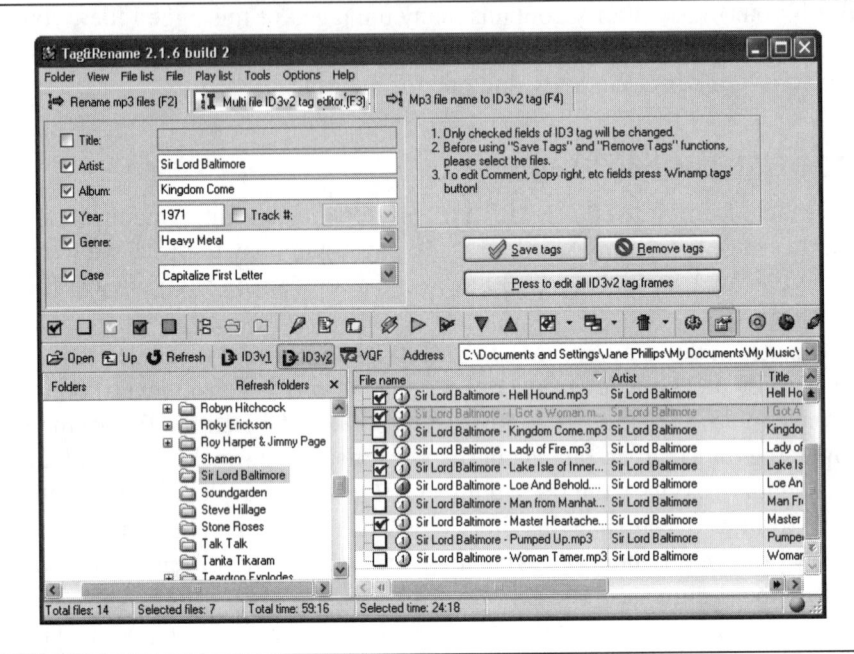

FIGURE 5-8 Tag&Rename can edit multiple ID3 tags at once.

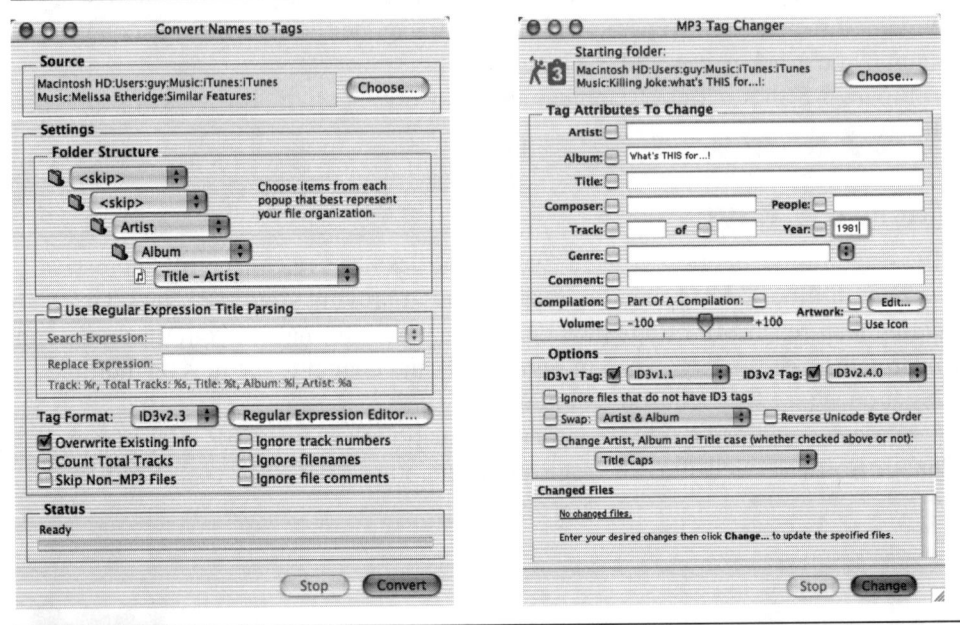

FIGURE 5-9 MP3 Rage includes powerful tagging—among many other features.

Save Audio Streams to Disk so You Can Listen to Them Later

Something you may well want to do with your iPod is listen to streaming audio on it. For example, you might want to record a webcast of an Internet radio show so you can listen to it later on your iPod. Most Internet radio broadcasts are much lower quality than CD audio, so you can pack a huge amount of webcast onto your iPod if you choose to do so.

There are a couple of problems with recording streaming audio like this:

- First, recording streaming audio is usually a breach of copyright law, so it's illegal. Chances are you won't be caught doing it, because to the streaming server, you appear simply to be streaming the audio so you can listen to it. Even so, you probably won't want to advertise the fact that you record streaming audio.

- Second, because recording streaming audio is so often illegal, many streaming programs don't provide any features for recording the streams. For example, RealNetworks' various programs (such as RealPlayer and RealOne) have a large chunk of the streaming client market, but if you want to record the audio you receive, you need to look elsewhere.

So to record streaming audio, you must either resort to hardware subterfuge or use one of the few programs that allows recording. The following subsections discuss two applications for recording MP3 streams (FreeAmp for Windows, and StreamRipperX for Mac) and one application for recording other types of streaming audio (TotalRecorder for Windows).

The easiest form of hardware solution is to use a standard audio cable to pipe the output from your sound card to your computer's Line In socket. You can then record the audio stream as you would any other external input, as discussed earlier in this chapter. For example, on Windows, you could use MUSICMATCH Jukebox Plus to record the audio stream. On the Mac, you could use Amadeus II, Sound Studio for OS X, or another application.

The only problem with using a standard audio cable is that you won't be able to hear the audio stream you're recording via external speakers. To solve this problem, get a stereo Y-connector. Connect one of the outputs to your external speakers and the other to your Line In socket.

Windows: FreeAmp (If You Can Get It)

For Windows, the easiest option for recording MP3 streams is FreeAmp, a freeware open-source MP3 player. The FreeAmp web site (**www.freeamp.org**) appears to have gone dark, but you can still find FreeAmp in various freeware software archives.

To record MP3 streams with FreeAmp (shown on the left in Figure 5-10), follow these steps:

1. Click the Options button to display the FreeAmp Preferences dialog box (shown on the right in Figure 5-10).

2. Click the Streaming tab to display it.

3. Select the Save SHOUTcast/icecast Streams Locally check box.

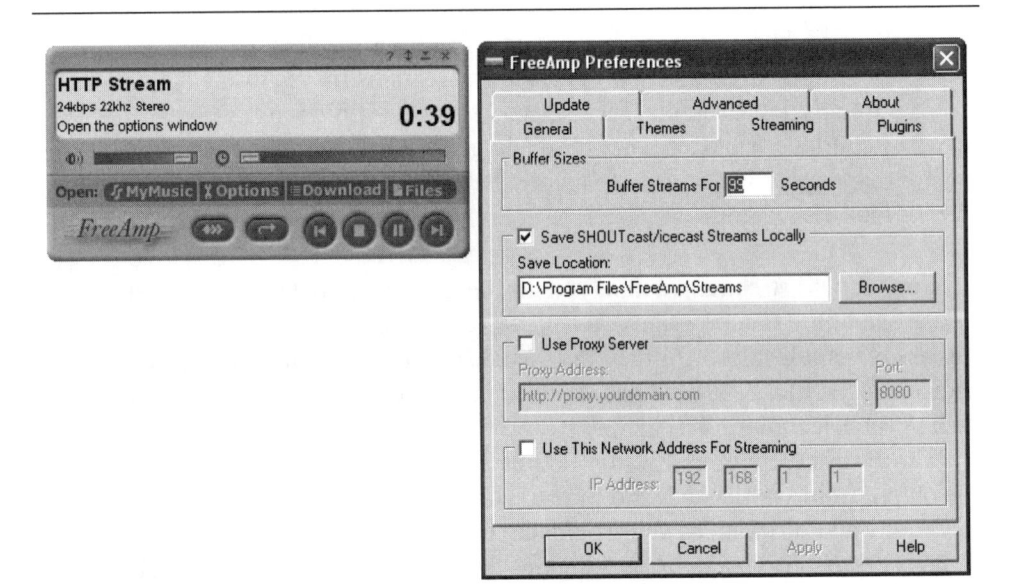

FIGURE 5-10 To record streaming audio with FreeAmp, select the Save SHOUTcast/icecast Streams Locally check box on the Streaming tab of the FreeAmp Preferences dialog box.

CHAPTER 5: Create, Edit, and Tag Your MP3 Files

4. Use the Browse button and the resulting Browse for Folder dialog box to specify the folder in which to save the streamed files. Make sure the drive on which the folder is located contains plenty of free space.

5. Click the OK button to close the FreeAmp Preferences dialog box.

6. Tune into the audio stream. FreeAmp records the stream automatically under an autonamed file.

Windows: TotalRecorder

If you can't get FreeAmp, or if you want to record other types of streams than MP3 streams, you may want to try TotalRecorder from High Criteria Inc. (**www.highcriteria.com**).

TotalRecorder comes in a Standard Edition ($11.95 for a license), a Professional Edition ($35.95), and a Developer Edition ($64, but you won't want it unless you're developing software). Both Standard and Professional can save MP3 streams. High Criteria provides trial versions of TotalRecorder, but they're so thoroughly crippled you'll need to open your wallet to actually get anything done with TotalRecorder.

Figure 5-11 shows TotalRecorder Standard Edition recording streaming audio.

FIGURE 5-11 TotalRecorder can record MP3 streams and other types of streaming audio.

Mac: StreamRipperX

For the Mac, the best option (at this writing) for recording MP3 streams is StreamRipperX from VersionTracker.com (**www.versiontracker.com**). StreamRipperX features an intuitive three-tab interface, as shown in Figure 5-12.

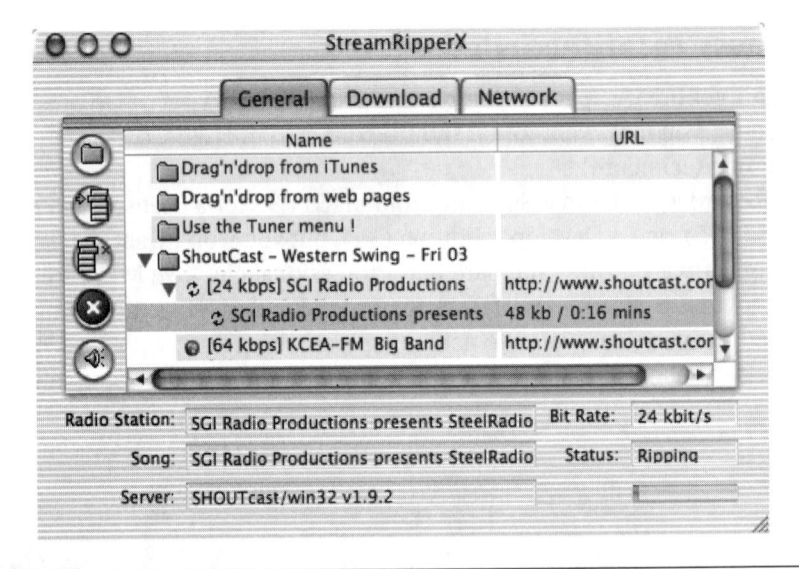

FIGURE 5-12 StreamRipperX can rip MP3 streams to MP3 files.

Chapter 6
Download Audio Files from the Internet

How to...

- Understand the conflict between consumers and the music industry
- Know what's happening on the darknet—and what the dangers are
- Understand the basics of P2P networks
- Find legal audio online
- Make your own music available online

Ripping your own CDs, tapes, and LPs can produce an impressive library of MP3 files, but in the process it's likely to make you wonder if you couldn't just get the MP3 files directly without needing to mess with the physical media. And of course you can, by downloading them via the Internet—in an entertaining variety of ways.

How you actually download a file from the Internet depends on the technologies used, but most of those currently in circulation make downloading very simple—in most cases, as easy as clicking a button or a link. So this chapter concentrates not on the process of downloading but on the more difficult issues involved, such as the legalities involved in downloading audio and how to tell which audio files are aboveboard and which are stolen.

> **NOTE** *With iTunes 4 on the Mac, you can buy and download songs from the iTunes music store. See Chapter 18 for details.*

Quick Reality Check on the Music Market

In pretty much every marketplace, there's a tension between the supply side and the demand side, between the suppliers (the sellers or producers) and the consumers. Usually, the tension is straightforward: the consumers want only products that appeal to them, and are prepared to pay only a certain amount for them; the suppliers want consumers to buy various products and, in general, pay as much as possible for them.

Usually, the tension between supply and demand creates a balance between the suppliers and the consumers. For example, if your nearest clothing store tried to charge $100 for a basic pair of jeans, you'd probably go elsewhere. So the clothing store will offer the jeans for a good price but hope to "upsell" you to a shirt, belt, or complete outfit when you come in for the jeans.

The tension in the music market between the music industry and the consumers is extreme at present. This is partly because of the way people regard music and partly because music is almost ideal for digital distribution. But it's mostly because digital distribution of music has endangered the market for traditional media—records (singles, EPs, and LPs), cassettes, and CDs—and the music industry hasn't yet worked out how to cope. Also, many artists have entered the fray instead of allowing the music industry to represent them. For example, many artists make some of their music available on the Internet in the hope of enlarging their fan base and their sales.

What Most Consumers Want

What most consumers want (as you probably don't need telling) is high-quality music they can acquire easily and inexpensively and with which they can do what they please. These wishes explain why MP3 has been such a screaming success. These wishes also explain why Microsoft has expended huge amounts of effort into trying to take mind-share and market-share from MP3 with its proprietary audio format, Windows Media Audio (WMA), which it can control.

For example, as a consumer, you may well want to do the following:

- Download music from the Internet—either for free or at an acceptable cost.
- Rip and encode digital files of your music so you can listen to it on any of your computers, on your iPod, or on another portable player.
- Put the music on that computer or portable player and play the music on it.
- Send music to friends so they can listen to it.
- Have friends send music to you so you can listen to it.
- Burn custom CDs containing the tracks you want to listen to.

Computers and the Internet enable you to do all of the preceding. But what the music industry wants is quite different…

What the Music Industry Wants

The music industry has been based on selling music on physical media—records, cassettes, and CDs—and is struggling to come to terms with digital distribution. The problem is that digital media enables consumers to copy music and distribute it worldwide with minimal effort and cost. For example, in theory, only one person needs to buy the next Christina Aguilera CD. They can then copy it and distribute it instantly on the Internet or on physical media (such as recordable CDs).

NOTE *The music industry isn't alone in struggling with digital distribution—publishing is struggling too. The Internet enables publishers to distribute digital content easily, and software such as Adobe eBook Reader and Microsoft Reader enables publishers to protect digital content (to some extent), but here you are with a physical book in your hand...*

From a consumer's point of view, looking at the various unsatisfactory copyright-protection schemes that have so far appeared, the music industry appears to want an unreasonable degree of control over its products. For example, some copyright-protection schemes for digital audio files permanently lock a file to a particular computer. If you upgrade your computer, or if your operating system blows a gasket and you need to reinstall it, you lose the files permanently. Similarly, for CDs protected with anti-copy technologies, record companies have offered to sell consumers digital audio files separately from the CDs. So you'd need to buy a CD to use on your CD player and then buy MP3 files to use on your MP3 player.

For the music industry, the ultimate sales goal would be pay-per-use, so not only would they know how often any consumer had played a particular track, but they'd also receive a micropayment for each use. Consumers are likely to give the music industry a hard time on pay-per-use.

What's Happening Between Consumers and the Music Industry

The tension between consumers and the music industry has been playing out for several years now and most likely will continue to play out as you read this. Here's a summary of what's happened so far:

- Many consumers have taken to ripping their music collections to formats such as MP3, WMA, and Ogg Vorbis so they can place-shift the music more easily (and enjoy it in a variety of places), manage the music using their computers, and share the music with their friends.

- Many consumers have embraced the unauthorized distribution of copyrighted content, some in ignorance of the law but many in open defiance of it. Popular distribution mechanisms have included physical media (such as recordable CDs), e-mail, newsgroups, instant messaging, and custom P2P file-sharing technologies such as Napster, Aimster/Madster, Kazaa, and Freenet.

- To prevent people from ripping the audio discs they buy, the music industry has started introducing assorted copyright-protection mechanisms, such as the copy-protection on some recent audio discs (see the section "Understand Current Copy-Protection Techniques on the CDs You Buy" in Chapter 2).

- To prevent people from sharing music, the music industry (led by the RIAA—the Recording Industry Association of America) has pushed for restrictive legislation. (Other interested parties, such as the Motion Picture Association of America and the movie studios, are also pushing for legislation to protect their copyrighted content and their interests, but we'll concentrate on the music side here.) As a result, some ill-thought-out and strongly anti-consumer legislation has been passed, and more is being put forward at this writing. For example, as you saw in Chapter 2, the DMCA (Digital Millennium Copyright Act) makes it illegal to circumvent anti-copying measures on works.

- Computer hardware and software manufacturers are exploring the possibility of including digital-rights management (DRM) hardware and software in computer components and operating systems. For example, some Creative Labs sound cards already won't output digital audio from audio discs marked with copyright-protection systems; they'll output only analog audio, preventing you from making perfect digital copies via the sound card. Further out, Microsoft is working on an operating-system component, at first codenamed Palladium and subsequently tagged the "next-generation secure computing base," that will work with hardware developed by the Trusted Computing Platform Alliance (TCPA) to secure transactions. In this sense, a "transaction" can be anything from playing back a protected song or movie to something that actually involves money changing hands.

Understand the Darknet and the Light

(So to speak. The light is relative here—as it is always. Only darkness can be absolute.)

You can find a huge amount of music on the Internet. Depending on where you go for the files and the tools you use, the files may be entirely aboveboard and legitimate or wholly illegal. As discussed in Chapter 2, sharing digital files of other people's copyrighted content without permission is illegal. So is receiving such illegal files. The No Electronic Theft Act (NET Act) of 1997 and the Digital Millennium Copyright Act (DMCA) of 1998 provide savage penalties for people caught distributing copyrighted materials illegally. So before you start searching for and downloading music from the Internet, it's a good idea to know who you're dealing with and whether the files are legal or illegal.

What Is the Darknet?

The *darknet* is an umbrella term some observers use for the unauthorized distribution of copyrighted digital content via computers. At present, the darknet uses the Internet extensively, because the Internet provides an easy and efficient distribution mechanism. But the darknet can also use many other types of networks, some of which are networks only in the loosest sense of the word. For example, Sneakernet can also be part of the darknet. Using Sneakernet (a pun on the networking technology called Ethernet) involves transferring files by physically carrying a disk from one computer to another.

How the Darknet Works

So far, the darknet has used various forms of distribution, including e-mail attachments, newsgroup attachments, web sites and FTP sites, custom P2P software (more on this in a moment), direct connections, and Sneakernet with physical media.

The key point about the darknet is that, like most aspects of any underground economy, it mutates to circumvent any restrictions placed upon it. For example, if the music industry (or any other body) is successful in preventing the distribution of music or other copyrighted content across the Internet, the darknet will turn to non-Internet methods of distributing the content, such as direct connections, local networks, or Sneakernet.

The darknet has been around since the early days of the Internet, but it assumed significant proportions only in the late 1990s. The growth of the darknet in the late 1990s was spurred largely by the widespread adoption of the Internet (including broadband connections such as cable and DSL) and the incorporation of multimedia features in computers, which meant that even relatively modest computers could be used for enjoying high-quality audio and acceptable video.

At the same time, hardware and software for creating digital content became widely available and affordable. With rippers and audio-compression technologies (notably MP3 encoders), users could add music from CDs or other sources to the darknet. With scanners, they could add pictures and text from books and magazines. With video-capture boards, they could capture video from a variety of sources. With an Internet connection, they could share those files with others and partake of the files others were sharing. With a broadband Internet connection, they could share even large files quickly.

How P2P Networks Enlarged the Darknet

The key to the explosion of the darknet was the rapid development of peer-to-peer (P2P) networks in 1999 and 2000. This development was spearheaded by Napster, the company, eponymous service, and eponymous application that made music-swapping a household pursuit. Napster was followed by a slew of similar services that exploited the power, flexibility, and legal uncertainty of P2P networks.

In a P2P network, instead of the shared files being stored on centralized file servers and controlled by the network's host, the files are stored on the computers of the individual users who connect to the network. When connecting to the network, each user supplies a list of the files they're sharing, together with other relevant information such as their IP address and the speed of their Internet connection. The list of files and their associated information is added to the central database, which all users of the network can then search by various criteria. For example, a user could search for MP3 files by a certain artist that include a particular word in their title, or that have a specific bitrate or higher bitrate. (When a user logs out of the P2P network, their files become unavailable.)

When a user has found a file they want to download, the P2P service puts the user in direct communication with the host offering the file. The user then downloads the file from the host (as opposed to downloading it from the P2P service).

That's a very basic description of how P2P networks work. Most have further features—for example, some P2P services let users search the files a host is offering, resume a download that was broken off, or switch a download in progress to a different host when the current host goes offline.

Since Napster was closed down by legal attack in 2001, P2P network developers have taken measures to protect their networks. These measures include the following:

- **Expand the categories of files shared on the network** While Napster was written to share MP3 files, other P2P networks have been developed to share other specific types of files (such as pictures, video, and other music formats) or any files at all. (Before you ask: many other types of files were shared via Napster by being disguised as MP3 files.)

- **Locate the servers in countries where the RIAA and similar U.S.-based bodies have less direct leverage than in the United States** For example, Sharman Networks Ltd., the parent company of the Kazaa P2P network, is based in Australia and incorporated in Vanuatu, a South Pacific nation.

- **Build a true peer network rather than a peer network coordinated by a server** For example, in P2P networks based on the Gnutella protocol, users join the network by attaching to a participating peer rather than to a central server.

- **Distribute the database across clients rather than storing it on central servers** Again, Gnutella is an example of this. Each computer in a Gnutella network routes search requests to and from the peers to which it's connected. Passing the search from one client to another greatly increases the traffic across any given node in the network, but it makes the network far less vulnerable to attack, because the network can easily survive the loss of any node. True P2P networks are also less vulnerable to legal attack, because there's no central server acting as a conduit for file transfers. The central server represents the focus of legal attack and also a single point of failure for the network.

> **NOTE** *Gnutella searches are inefficient, flooding the network with data that chokes performance. Applications such as Grokster and Kazaa route searches through users with fast connections for better performance. Developers are working on creating a Content-Addressable Network (CAN) with better search mechanisms. Add CAN to your P2P buzzword list, together with Chord (a scalable lookup service for P2P networks), and Tapestry (a decentralized, fault-tolerant, and scalable location and routing infrastructure).*

- **Encrypt the files placed on the hosts or redistribute the shared files so a host doesn't know which files it's sharing**   This arrangement, which is used by P2P networks such as Freenet and Mnemosyne, works only when each network user commits some space to the P2P network that the network can then use for its own purposes. (By contrast, under Napster and similar models, hosts choose exactly which folders to share and also control which files are placed in those folders.)

- **Hide the identity of the endpoints of the network by routing traffic through intermediate hosts**   This technique, used by Freenet among other networks, is intended to help P2P network users avoid identification and the possible consequences.

Darknet Users: Super-Peers and Free Riders

As P2P networks developed, their users swiftly and effortlessly gravitated into two classes, which researchers have termed super-peers and free riders. A *super-peer* is a user who offers a large number of files for download, whereas a *free rider* is a user who offers few files (or even none) but actively downloads the files others are sharing. Free riders are sometimes also called *leechers*.

Both classes of user make perfect sense. Free riders use the P2P network as a method of free consumption. Many perhaps feel that because they're not offering materials for download, they're not breaking the law, they could claim ignorance of it, or they'll simply remain under the radar while more visible users take any heat that comes down. By contrast, super-peers tend to take a higher-profile, often political position, sometimes claiming the record companies are profiteers or "pigopolists," music (or other content) "wants to be free," or that they believe in the redistribution of resources (for example, their college's or company's fast Internet connection). Some super-peers look down on free riders as freeloaders willing to benefit from others' generosity but not reciprocate; some super-peers even block downloads to users they've decided are free riders.

Efforts to Close Down the Darknet

To date, efforts to close down the darknet have concentrated, naturally enough, on those parts of it that use the Internet for transmission. (These parts represent the easiest target—imagine trying to track down the people who had purchased recordable CDs and trying to determine exactly what, if anything, they had done with them.) The following subsections briefly discuss some of the efforts made so far.

Target the Services

The first targets have been the high-profile P2P services. Napster, Inc. (the company that ran the Napster service) was closed down in 2001 after an entertaining series of high-profile court battles with enough back-and-forth to give lay observers a nasty case of whiplash.

Looking at Napster and the mind-boggling number of files being shared illegally on it, many people wondered why it wasn't shut down immediately. Certainly the RIAA and the music industry *wanted* Napster shut down as soon as possible. But because some of the files were being shared legally, the case against Napster wasn't open-and-shut. Just because the service *could* be (and was being) used to share material illegally didn't make the service itself illegal. (Remember my absurd example with contact lenses and Hummers in Chapter 2?)

Besides, Napster itself (so Napster, Inc. claimed) wasn't doing anything illegal, even if some of its users were. Napster was merely providing a service, enabling people to find the files: it wasn't hosting illegal files or allowing people to download them. This may seem like a sophism, but in the real world, it's an important point legally. If you doubt that, consider that the USPS doesn't have to open your parcels to make sure they don't contain anything wicked before conveying them to their destination, and your local friendly telco doesn't have to eavesdrop on your phone calls to see if you say anything illegal. In fact, they're expressly forbidden from doing so under most circumstances. And your ISP would allow itself to be dipped slowly in molten chocolate before agreeing to chaperone your online sessions.

Sophism or not, the law ultimately didn't buy Napster, Inc.'s arguments and closed the service down. Briefly, Napster was found to be acting as a conduit for file transfers, which made it complicit in copyright infringements perpetrated by its users.

After closing down Napster, the RIAA has targeted other P2P networks, including Madster (formerly named Aimster until AOL forced it to change its name), MusicCity, and Grokster. However, at this writing, many P2P networks are still running and huge numbers of files are still being shared, most of them apparently without permission.

Target the Super-Peers

After the services themselves, the next most obvious target is the super-peers—the users who, together, provide the bulk of the files available on particular aspects of the darknet and who provide some of the darknet's broadest connections.

Super-peers can be targeted either directly by legal action (or threats) or indirectly by convincing the user's ISP to close their account. Anecdotal evidence abounds of ISPs closing users accounts when presented with even halfway convincing evidence that the users had been sharing files illegally.

Dangers of Using the Darknet

By now, enough people have probably told you the Internet is a dangerous place for the claim to have stopped having any effect. But before you start exploring the darknet and downloading files of other people's copyrighted content from it, be clear on the dangers you might face. The following subsections detail the most obvious dangers.

Legal Retribution

The first danger is that you may expose yourself to legal retribution. Distributing other people's copyrighted content is illegal, even if you're not charging for it. In the eyes of the law, receiving anything in return for material you've shared illegally constitutes benefiting from that sharing. For example, if you offered a handful of MP3 files for download, and if you yourself downloaded a video file from someone else, the law would see you as having benefited from offering those files for download.

As mentioned a moment ago, so far, law enforcement has targeted the super-peers rather than rank-and-file users, because the super-peers give far more bang for the buck. But when ISPs can be persuaded to close the accounts of users who appear to be sharing material illegally, even users downloading illegal files become easy targets.

One of the powerful attractions of P2P is the illusion of anonymity the Internet confers to novice users. But as with almost any Internet transaction, your computer exposes its Internet Protocol (IP) address when you use most P2P networks. If your Internet connection has a static IP address (an IP address that doesn't change from one connection to the next), your computer can be identified with a minimum of effort. But even if your connection receives a different IP address from your ISP each time you connect, your ISP can easily look you up in the records they're obliged to keep for billing and security purposes. So any agency that can persuade or compel your ISP to divulge information can determine exactly what your computer has been doing.

Unwanted Fellow-Travelers

Developing complex software applications costs money—plenty of it. To finance their development, cover their other expenses, or make money, companies that produce P2P software have taken to including other applications with their products. Some of these applications are shareware and can be tolerably useful; others are adware that are useless and an irritant; others yet are spyware that report users' sharing and downloading habits.

Some packages are upfront about the software they bring with them. For example, at this writing, Kazaa installs SaveNow, DelFin, MediaLoads, and b3d projector, but it gives you a chance to prevent it from installing these applications. Morpheus supports its free version with advertising from the Gator Advertising and Information Network (GAIN) and offers the Precision Time and Date Manager utilities. Grokster barrages you with software and special offers (even for free makeup). Other packages simply install additional software without consulting you.

TIP *To detect and remove spyware from your computer, use an application such as the free Ad-aware from LavaSoft (www.lavasoft.de).*

Attacks, Viruses, and Social Engineering

Apart from adware and spyware lurking amidst the program files, P2P networks can also expose your computer to attacks and viruses. A file offered for download may not contain what its name or tag suggests. For example, a tempting picture file might prove to be a virus or other malware.

TIP *Use virus-checking software to scan all incoming files to your computer, whether they come from friends, family, coworkers, or the Internet.*

Even if the file contains what it's supposed to, it may also harbor a virus, worm, or Trojan horse. Even apparently harmless files can have a sting in the tail. For example, the tags in music files can contain URLs to which your player's browser component automatically connects. The site can then run a script on your computer, doing anything from opening some irritating advertisement windows, to harvesting any sensitive information it can locate, to deleting vital files or destroying the firmware on your computer.

P2P networks also expose users to social-engineering attacks through the chat features most P2P tools include. However friendly other users are, and however juicy the files they provide, it can be a severe mistake to divulge personal information.

Current P2P Networks

At this writing, there are a large number of P2P networks, some of which interoperate with each other. The following examples illustrate three of the longer-lasting networks:

- **Gnutella** Gnutella is a P2P protocol used by a wide variety of clients. At this writing, the leading Gnutella clients include BearShare (Windows only), Morpheus (Windows only), LimeWire (Windows, Mac, and Linux), Phex (Windows, Mac, and Linux), Gnucleus (Windows only), and Acquisition (Mac OS X only). The best place to get started with Gnutella is at the Gnutella.com web site (**www.gnutella.com**).

- **Kazaa**   (**www.kazaa.com**) is a P2P network based on the FastTrack engine and organized by Sharman Networks Ltd. Kazaa provides the Windows-only Kazaa Media Desktop application, which puts a slick graphical interface on searching the Kazaa network. Kazaa routes searches through *supernodes* (users with fast connections) to get around the inefficiency of Gnutella-like peer searching. Kazaa uses a metric called *participation level* that measures two items: the amount of data a user downloads against the amount of data they let others download from them, and the percentage of the files the user is offering that are "integrity rated" (have accurate information about them). When multiple users try to download a file from another user, Kazaa prioritizes the users with high participation levels over those with low levels.

- **Freenet**   (**freenetproject.org**) is a P2P network designed to allow "anybody to publish and read information with complete anonymity" and to prevent the network from being shut down. Freenet requires users to make space available to the network, automatically distributes files so no computer knows which files it's hosting, and encrypts the files placed on each computer for security. You can get Freenet clients for Windows, Mac OS X, and Linux. At this writing, Freenet is at its 0.5 release and, while growing in power and functionality, lags far behind the leading P2P networks for ease of use. (The Freenet interface is more user friendly than it used to be: the Freenet Node Properties dialog box now offers tabs named Normal Settings, Advanced Settings, and Serious Geeks Only.) However, should other P2P networks be suppressed, Freenet may be able to pick up the slack.

Download Music Files from Web Sites

In contrast to the darknet, where you can find just about any music file if you search hard enough, the range of legitimate music files available on the Web tends to be disappointing. This is partly because the music industry has been hesitant to make music available for download in case it gets stolen; partly because offerings are piecemeal, hard to find, and (in general) uncomfortably expensive; and at least partly because so many people are downloading so much music from the darknet that they're not really interested in struggling to find legitimate files of the same music.

Because sites often change, this section confines itself to mentioning a few of the sites that seem to have enjoyed (or seem likely to enjoy) relatively long life. To find other sites, consult your peers or put a phrase such as **online music site** into your favorite search engine.

MP3.com

MP3.com (**www.mp3.com**) claims to have 240,000 files available for download from "10,000 artists you know." Truth in advertising? The numbers are probably true enough, but if you've even heard of all 10,000 artists, you'll belong to a minute subset of the population. If you "know" (weasel word) the works of them all, you probably need your ears replacing—or surgical separation from MP3.com.

Still, MP3.com has a lot of music, and you may like some of it. Your first 150 downloads are free, once you've registered. Registration involves providing a functional e-mail address, text that approximates a first name and last name, a country (a real one, but not necessarily yours), a zip code if that country is the United States, a birth date (real or imagined), a gender, and a language preference.

Listen.com

Listen.com (**www.listen.com**) offers 20,000 albums, which Listen.com claims is the "largest legal collection of digital music in the world." Certainly, some of Listen.com's artists are big names—current offerings include Eminem, Britney Spears, and Jennifer Lopez—and you stand a fair chance of finding some music you like. You can burn tracks to CD for $0.99 a track—little enough to be attractive to some music fans.

To get even a peep out of Listen.com, you need to sign up for an account. The best way to start is with a free seven-day trial account. The trial limits you to 30-second clips of Listen.com's music library and to 20-Kbps audio streams. 20-Kbps is low enough quality to make you yearn for AM radio, so it's good only for checking out what's available; and 30 seconds is enough to practice your intro-recognition skills (with the possible exception of some of The Ramones' briefer efforts, for which you might get part of the outro as well). But even with these restrictions, you can get a fair idea of the type and range of music Listen.com has to offer and whether it appeals to you.

More of a restriction is that you have to use Listen.com's RHAPSODY application to listen to music. At this writing, RHAPSODY works only with Windows 98 and later versions, not with Mac OS. Visually, the RHAPSODY interface can charitably be described as falling into the could-be-worse category, but it's functional and easy to use.

press*play*

press*play* (**www.pressplay.com**) is a joint venture of Universal Music Group and Sony Music Entertainment. press*play* (yes, that's how it's supposed to be written) offers unlimited access to more than 200,000 songs, with subscription plans starting at $9.95 a month and a charge of $1 per song to transfer to a portable player or burn a copy to CD.

You can get a three-day free trial to press*play*, but you have to provide credit card information to do so—so remember to cancel promptly if you don't like the service. Also worth mentioning is that you can choose to exclude explicit content and apply a parental control password to your press*play* account.

Lycos Music

Lycos Music (**music.lycos.com**) provides a simple, browser-based mechanism for searching for artists, MP3 files, and lyrics. Lycos Music returns a web page of matches, through which you can navigate to the files you want to reach. Most of the files are located on servers not controlled by Lycos Music.

In the wild and woolly days around the turn of the millennium, Lycos Music turned up many results to shady web servers and FTP servers, some of which attempted to hijack your browser, cajole you into visiting porn sites, or worse. These days, the results seem mostly to be aboveboard—but there are far fewer of them.

IUMA

The Internet Underground Musical Archive (IUMA; **www.iuma.com**) is one of the longest-running Internet audio sites.

IUMA's banner—"discover unsigned artists, independent bands, local talent"—neatly summarizes what IUMA is about. Artists who use IUMA are typically looking to distribute their music as widely as possible in the hope of increasing their audience, so IUMA offers MP3 downloads as well as MP3 and RealAudio streams. That means you can download music and listen to it as often as you want, burn it to CDs, share it with friends, and so on.

This approach makes IUMA a great place for exploring new artists and different kinds of music. If you're looking for established artists, however, look elsewhere.

Find Music Files in Newsgroups

Before P2P networks became popular, many music files were shared through newsgroups as attachments. Because most newsgroups limit attachments to relatively small sizes, and music files tend to be large, most of the files had to be divided up into many parts to be posted. You would then select all the messages with the attachments that made up the file you wanted, download the messages and attachments, and recombine the attachments to reconstitute the file. Clumsy, but it worked—and still does for such files as are posted to newsgroups. Most modern newsreaders can handle dividing files and stitching them back together seamlessly (so to speak).

To find music files in newsgroups, use your newsreader's search mechanism to search for suitable words—for example, **MP3**.

Share Your Own Music on the Internet

If you have created original music of your own, and you hold the copyright to it (in other words, if you haven't granted anyone else the right to copy and distribute your music), you can use the Internet to share it with others.

As you'll have gathered from the rest of this chapter, you can share your music in any of a variety of ways. You may want to use any or all of the following means to share your music and related information:

- **Post it on your web site for download** If you have a web site, you can post your audio on it for download. Use a compressed format, such as MP3 files encoded at a rate that allows them to sound good but doesn't call for huge downloads. Some of your audience probably won't stand for huge downloads—and in any case, your ISP may allow you only a certain amount of data moved per month.

NOTE: *Another possibility is to stream your audio to listeners. But doing so will typically cost you even more bandwidth than letting them download the files, because anyone who likes the audio may well stream it multiple times. Streaming supposedly prevents people from saving your audio to disk—but as you learned in the previous chapter, this restriction is easy to circumvent.*

- **Post it on an Internet music site for download or streaming** By posting your audio to an Internet music site, you may be able to achieve far greater exposure than on your own web site—at the expense of some control over the music (typically, you grant the site some distribution rights) and the amount of material you can post. Set against this the advantage of having the Internet site pick up the tab for the bandwidth consumed by your fans voraciously streaming your tracks again and again. You may want to combine both approaches: keep most of the information on your own web site, but encourage your fans to download or stream from the Internet music site.

- **E-mail music files to people** E-mail distribution of audio is useful only for sending relatively small files (up to, say, a couple of megabytes) to relatively small numbers of people. If you're comfortable with those informal restrictions, well and good. Otherwise, use more robust means of distribution.

- **Distribute your music via P2P** P2P can be an awesome means of distributing music files—especially if you can persuade other people to distribute them for you. Unfortunately, unless you're able to generate a ferocious buzz, you're unlikely to gain wide distribution easily via P2P. This is because most P2P users are more interested in getting files by established artists than in trying out new music—which, in many cases, they can download for free from Internet music sites.

- **Post your music files to newsgroups** Another option is to post your music files to newsgroups as attachments. As mentioned earlier in this chapter, newsgroups are largely outmoded as a means of distributing music files, but if you find a suitable newsgroup that encourages posting, you may want to try doing so. (Alternatively, post a message describing your music and directing people to the web site or other site on which you're sharing it.) Before posting, set your e-mail software to divide up attachments into suitably small files so they're not rejected.

Chapter 7

Burn Audio and MP3 CDs with iTunes and MUSICMATCH Jukebox Plus

How to…

- Get up to speed with CD burning
- Understand the differences between audio CDs, data CDs, and MP3 CDs
- Configure iTunes for burning CDs
- Burn CDs with iTunes
- Configure MUSICMATCH Jukebox Plus for burning CDs
- Burn CDs with MUSICMATCH Jukebox Plus
- Troubleshoot the problems you run into when burning CDs

This chapter shows you how to burn CDs from your music library using iTunes and MUSICMATCH Jukebox Plus. I'll go through some key background to CD burning, and then show you how to configure each application for burning, how to burn CDs, and how to troubleshoot common problems you may run into.

Understand the Basics of CD Burning

Until the late 1990s, CD burning was something of a black art. After consulting the stars, the mage carefully added to a specially beefed-up computer a CD burner and burning software carefully tested to be compatible with it. After checking their mouse's entrails and defuzzing its rollers, the mage loaded an exquisitely shiny and painfully expensive blank CD, and set to work. With the right incantations, and if the moon was in Jupiter, the burn would complete, and the mage would end up with a functional CD rather than an expensive midget Frisbee.

I exaggerate, of course—but CD burning was tenuous at best. The good news is that since then, CD burning has passed from the magical to the mainstream—so much so that CD burning is built into Windows XP and Mac OS X (not to mention System 9), and most new computers include CD recorders.

Recordable CDs and Rewritable CDs

Most CD recorders are more technically *CD rewriters*—drives that can record both recordable CDs and rewritable CDs. A *recordable* CD (CD-R) is a CD that can be recorded only once, whereas a *rewritable* CD (CD-RW) is a CD that can be rewritten multiple times. Before rewriting a rewritable CD, you must erase its current contents.

CHAPTER 7: Burn Audio and MP3 CDs with iTunes and MUSICMATCH Jukebox Plus

NOTE *Packet-writing software such as Roxio Inc.'s DirectCD can write multiple sessions to recordable CDs. However, once the recordable CD is closed by having its file system committed to disc, the disc's contents can no longer be changed.*

Audio CDs, MP3 CDs, and Data CDs

An *audio CD* is a CD that conforms to the Red Book standard (see the section "Understand Ripping, Encoding, and Copying" in Chapter 2). Audio CDs contain uncompressed audio: 74 minutes for a 650MB CD, 80 minutes for a 700MB CD, and 90 minutes for an 800MB CD. You can play audio CDs on CD players (for example, a boom box or a hi-fi component) as well as on CD drives.

CAUTION *Most CD players can't play CD-RW discs, only CD-R discs.*

A *data CD* is a CD that contains data files. These data files can be anything from text files to presentations to videos, or a combination of different file types.

An *MP3 CD* is a data CD that contains only MP3 files. MP3 CDs have the advantage of being able to store far more music than an audio CD. For example, if you encode your MP3 files at 128 Kbps, you can fit about 12 hours of music on a CD. The disadvantage is that most CD players can't play MP3 CDs.

Burn CDs with iTunes

iTunes makes the process of burning CDs as simple and painless as possible. Typically, you'll want to start by choosing burning options, as described in the first subsection. You'll then be ready to burn a disc, as described in the second subsection.

Choose Burning Options

To choose burning options for iTunes, press CTRL-Y or choose iTunes | Preferences. In the Preferences dialog box, click the Burning tab to display the Burning sheet (Figure 7-1).

Choose options as follows:

- **CD Burner label or list** If you have multiple CD burners, make sure iTunes has chosen the right burner.

- **Preferred Speed drop-down list** Choose the Maximum Possible item to burn CDs at the fastest speed iTunes and the drive can manage. If you don't get good results from the maximum possible speed, reduce the speed by choosing one of the settings in the list. Test the setting and reduce the speed further if necessary.
- **Disc Format options** To create an audio CD, select the Audio CD option button (the default). Use the Gap Between Songs to specify whether to include a gap between the tracks on the CD (you can choose from 1 second to 5 seconds; the default is 2 seconds) or not (choose None). To create an MP3 CD, select the MP3 CD option button.

Click the OK button to close the Burning sheet.

NOTE *For external USB CD-RW drives, iTunes automatically sets the burn speed to 2X.*

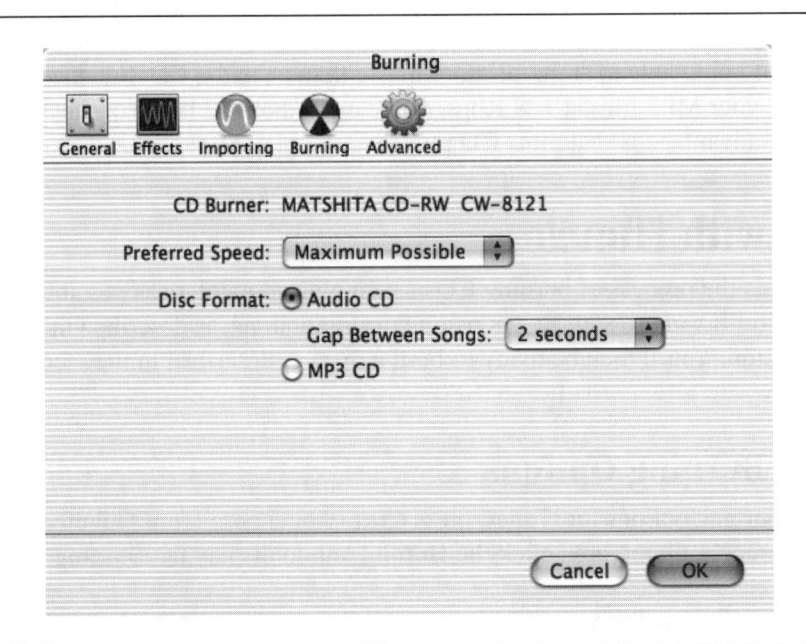

FIGURE 7-1 Choose burning options for iTunes on the Burning sheet of the Preferences dialog box.

Burn a CD

To burn a CD with iTunes, follow these steps:

1. Add to a playlist the songs that you want to have on the CD. (Alternatively, open an existing playlist.)

2. Click the Burn CD button in the upper-right corner of the iTunes window. (The Burn CD button replaces the Browse button when you select a playlist in the Source pane.) Apple has made the interface a little complicated, as explained in the following paragraphs:

   - At first, the Burn CD button is hidden behind a "trap door"—a circular icon divided into six segments by wavy lines. When you click this button, the trap door spirals away to reveal a yellow-and-black Burn CD button that pulses at you to encourage you to click it.

   - If you don't click the Burn CD button soon enough after inserting the blank CD (within about 10 seconds), your Mac ejects the CD. If this happens, reinsert the CD, and then click the Burn CD button more quickly next time.

3. When iTunes prompts you to insert a blank CD, do so.

NOTE *If you insert a blank recordable CD in your CD-recorder drive before clicking the Burn button in iTunes, Mac OS X displays a dialog box inviting you to choose what to do with the CD. Select the Open iTunes item in the Action drop-down list. Select the Make This Action the Default check box if you always want to launch iTunes when you insert a blank CD. Then click the OK button to close the dialog box.*

4. If your Burning preferences are set to create an audio CD, and the playlist you've chosen is too long, iTunes displays a dialog box to warn you of the problem and tell you your options: to create an audio CD with only the tracks that will fit or to create an MP3 CD instead. Choose MP3 CD or the Audio CD as appropriate. To fix the problem yourself, click the Cancel button, and then adjust the playlist manually.

5. Click the Burn CD button to start burning the CD. Figure 7-2 shows iTunes burning a CD.

FIGURE 7-2 iTunes lets you quickly burn a playlist to an audio CD or an MP3 CD.

Burn CDs with MUSICMATCH Jukebox Plus

Compared with iTunes, MUSICMATCH Jukebox Plus makes a meal of burning CDs—but that's at least partly because MUSICMATCH Jukebox Plus offers far more burning options than iTunes. Most notably, MUSICMATCH Jukebox Plus lets you burn data CDs as well as audio CDs and MP3 CDs, so if you don't have other CD-burning software, you can use MUSICMATCH Jukebox Plus to take care of all your burning needs. For example, you can use MUSICMATCH Jukebox Plus to back up your Word documents and Lotus 1-2-3 spreadsheets if necessary.

Choose Burning Settings for MUSICMATCH Burner Plus

The hardest part of burning CDs with MUSICMATCH Burner Plus is choosing the right settings. The following subsections discuss the options available.

To choose settings, display the Burner Plus Options dialog box, then follow these steps:

CHAPTER 7: Burn Audio and MP3 CDs with iTunes and MUSICMATCH Jukebox Plus

1. Click the Burn button in the playlist window to display the MUSICMATCH Burner Plus window.
2. Click the Options button and then choose Options | Settings.

Choose Settings for All Types of Burning

Start by choosing settings on the General tab of the Burner Plus Options dialog box (shown on the left in Figure 7-3). This tab contains the following settings:

- **Appearance group box**   Choose which skin the MUSICMATCH Burner Plus window uses, whether it always stays on top of other windows, and whether it displays a button on the taskbar.

- **Preferences group box**   In the Media Size group box, choose the type of media you're using. The default setting is 74 Minute, 650MB CD—the standard recordable CD. Choose another media type (such as 80 Minute, 700MB CD or 90 Minute, 800MB CD) as appropriate. The drop-down list includes choices for recordable DVDs and mini CDs. In the Disc Type at Startup drop-down list, choose Audio Disc, MP3 Disc, or Data Disc to specify the type of disc you'll usually want to create.

Then choose burning settings on the Burn tab of the Burner Plus Options dialog box (shown on the right in Figure 7-3). The Burn tab contains the following settings:

- **Drive group box**   Specify the CD drive to use for burning (this is an issue only if you have multiple drives) and the speed at which to record.

- **Write group box**   Make sure the Write Only (No Test) option button is selected. (This is the default.) Use the Test Only (No Write) option button if you need to troubleshoot burning problems.

- **Options group box**   Select or clear the check boxes to specify whether MUSICMATCH Burner Plus should eject the disc when it has finished burning it, whether it should beep after finishing the burn, whether it should "close" the disc, and whether it should cache data to the hard disk. Closing the disc prevents you from writing to it again. Whichever setting you choose for the Close Disc After Burn check box, MUSICMATCH Burner Plus closes audio discs so you can play them in CD players.

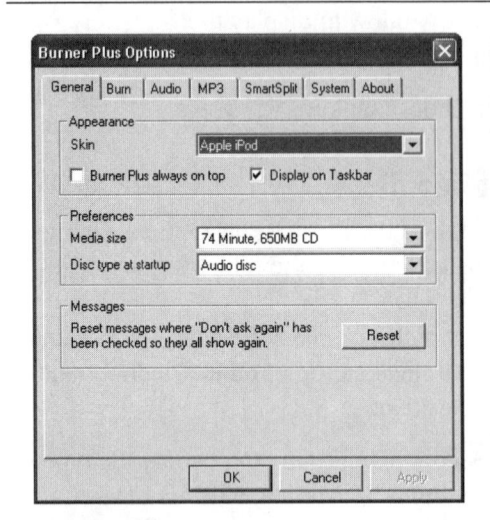

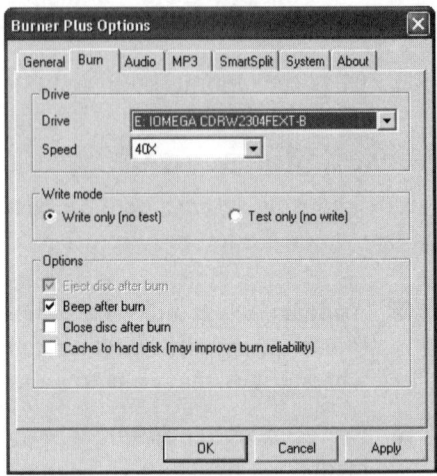

FIGURE 7-3 On the General tab (left) of the Burner Plus Options dialog box, specify the type of recordable media you're using and the default kind of disc to create. On the Burn tab (right), specify the drive, speed, writing mode, and other options.

NOTE *Caching is primarily useful when burning without caching doesn't work, but you may choose to use it all the time to ensure consistent results. Caching has two downsides: you need extra space free on the hard disk (allow 1GB for burning CDs), and it typically makes the burning process take longer because of the time required to write the data to the hard disk.*

Choose System Options

To improve burning performance, you can also change the settings on the System tab of the Burner Plus Options dialog box (Figure 7-4):

- **Memory group box** Increase the setting in the Cache Size text box to devote more memory to caching files while burning.

- **Hard Disk group box** If necessary, change the working directory for cached files and temporary files by clicking the Browse button and working in the resulting Browse for Computer dialog box. For example, you might choose to move the working directory to a faster hard drive than its default location to improve performance.

CHAPTER 7: Burn Audio and MP3 CDs with iTunes and MUSICMATCH Jukebox Plus

- **Burn Priority group box** Select the High option button, the Normal option button, or the Low option button to specify the amount of system resources Windows dedicates to burning. Selecting the High option button will improve burning performances, but other applications will run more slowly—so you might want to stop using your computer while it performs the burn.

Choose Options for Creating Audio (Red Book) CDs

If you plan to create audio CDs for use with CD players (as opposed to CD drives), check the settings on the Audio tab of the Burner Plus Options dialog box (Figure 7-5). The Audio tab contains the following settings:

- **Other Music Types group box** Select or clear the Windows Media check box and the WAV check box to specify whether MUSICMATCH Burner Plus should burn these file types to CD.

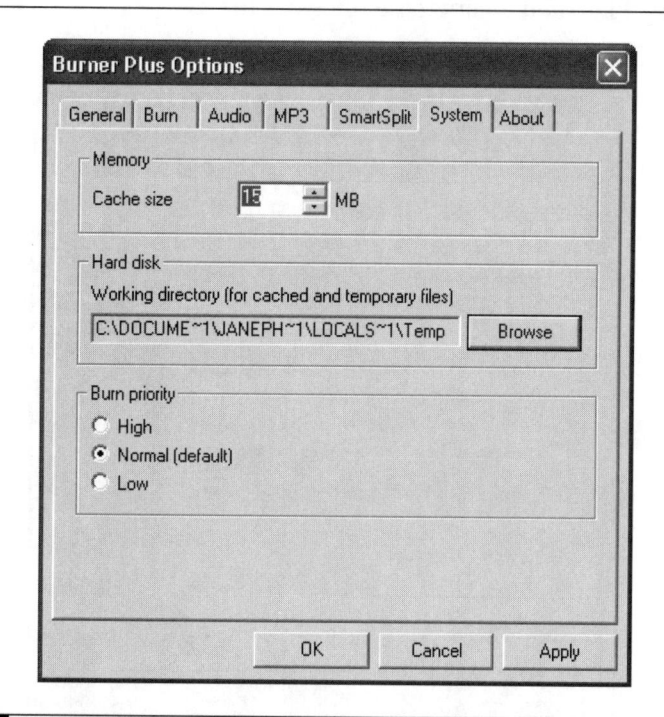

FIGURE 7-4 You can increase the cache size and burn priority on the System tab of the Burner Plus Options dialog box to improve burning performance.

- **Options group box** Choose whether to apply your current digital sound enhancements (for example, DSP settings) and volume leveling to the CD. Choose whether to insert a two-second gap between tracks instead of having one track run right into the next track. Choose whether to use track-at-once recording—writing the whole CD's track at once without breaks. (You'll seldom want to do this, but it can be useful for live recordings.)

Choose Options for Creating MP3 CDs

If you plan to create MP3 CDs, configure suitable settings on the MP3 tab of the Burner Plus dialog box (shown on the left in Figure 7-6). The MP3 tab contains the following settings:

- **Other Music Types group box** Select or clear the Windows Media check box and the WAV check box to specify whether MUSICMATCH Burner Plus should burn these file types to CD.

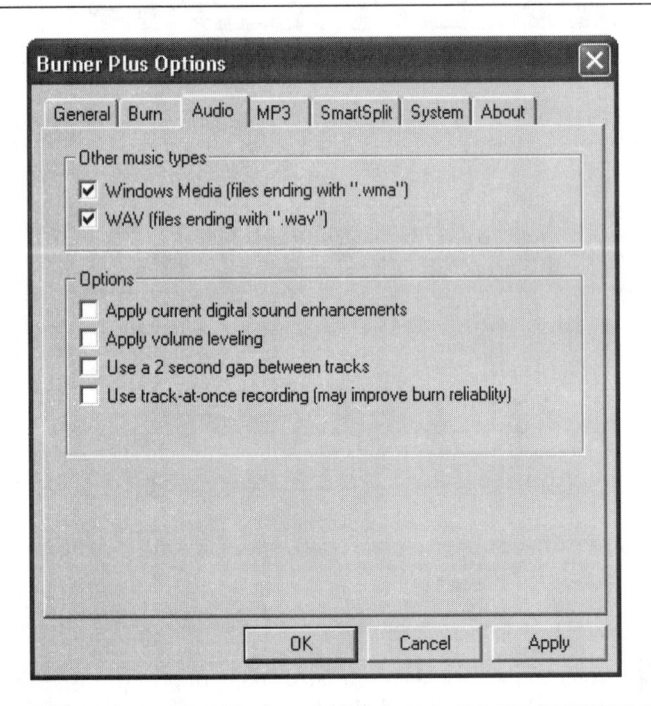

FIGURE 7-5 Choose options for burning audio CDs on the Audio tab of the Options dialog box.

CHAPTER 7: Burn Audio and MP3 CDs with iTunes and MUSICMATCH Jukebox Plus 187

NOTE *Later versions of MUSICMATCH Burner Plus include a supported Music Types group box instead of the Other Music Types group box. Again, select the check boxes for the file types you want to include on your CDs.*

- **Automatic Folder Creation (Using Tags) group box** Specify whether MUSICMATCH Burner Plus should place all the MP3 files in the root folder of the CD (the default setting) or automatically create a folder structure for them. To specify the folder structure, click the Modify button, and then use the controls in the Modify Target Disk Directory dialog box (shown on the right in Figure 7-6) to designate the data items to use and the order in which to use them. For example, you might use the artist name and album title to give the directory structure Artist Name\Album Title\.

- **Options group box** Choose whether to apply your current digital sound enhancements (for example, DSP settings) and volume leveling to the CD. Choose whether to add MultiAudio tracklists (a full set of tag information) and a playlist in the M3U format. Choose whether to include an AutoPlay file that will attempt to start the CD playing on Windows computers, and whether to include the MUSICMATCH Jukebox installer. (The installer will install the free version of MUSICMATCH Jukebox on demand.) Last, choose whether to sort the files when they're burned.

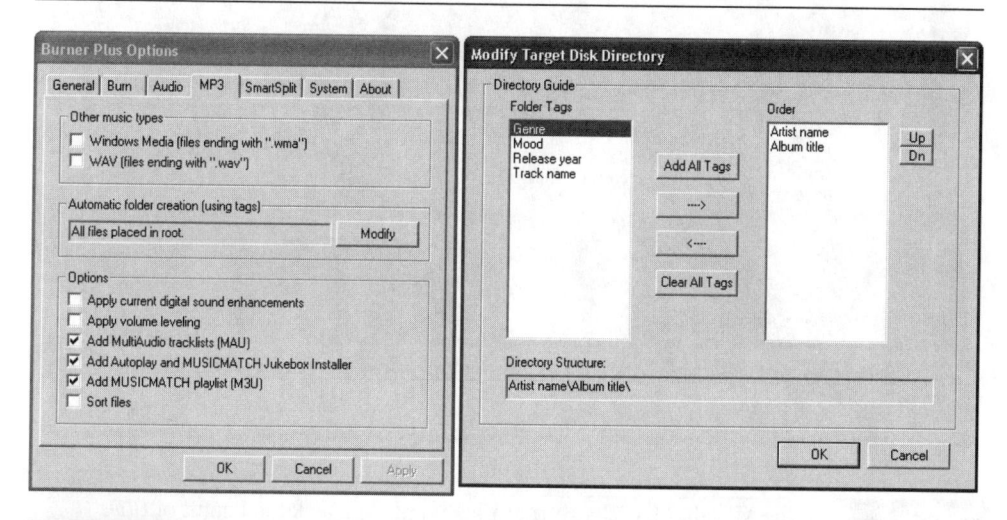

FIGURE 7-6 Choose options for burning MP3 CDs on the MP3 tab of the Burner Plus Options dialog box (left). To change the folder structure used, click the Modify button and work in the Modify Target Disk Directory dialog box (right).

Burning a CD

To burn a CD with MUSICMATCH Jukebox Plus, follow these steps:

1. Create a playlist that contains the files you want to burn to the CD. (Alternatively, open an existing playlist.)

2. Click the Burn button in the playlist window or choose File | Create CD from Playlist to display the MUSICMATCH Burner Plus window (Figure 7-7).

3. Check the type of CD MUSICMATCH Burner Plus thinks you're trying to create by seeing which of the buttons on the button bar appears pushed in.

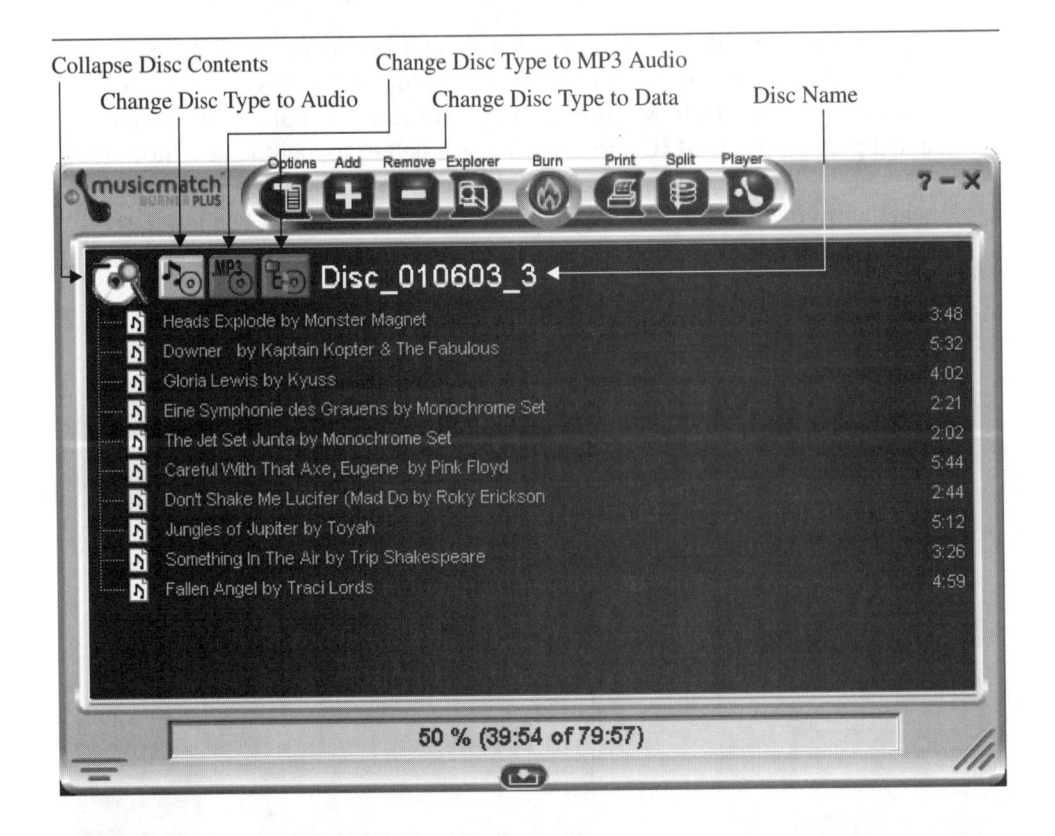

FIGURE 7-7 In the MUSICMATCH Burner Plus window, check the length of time your playlist takes up and the type of CD MUSICMATCH Jukebox Plus thinks you're trying to create.

CHAPTER 7: Burn Audio and MP3 CDs with iTunes and MUSICMATCH Jukebox Plus

To change the type of disc, click the Change Disc Type to Audio button, the Change Disc Type to MP3 Audio button, or the Change Disc Type to Data button, or issue the corresponding command from the Options | Disc | Change Type submenu.

4. Apply a name to your disc. Click the Disc Name field twice with a pause between the clicks (just like when you're renaming a file in Windows Explorer), enter the new name for the CD, and then press ENTER.

5. Check the readout at the bottom of the MUSICMATCH Burner Plus window to see how much of the CD the playlist takes up. Add or remove tracks as necessary.

- To add tracks, click the Add button, use the resulting Open Music dialog box to navigate to and select the tracks you want to add, and then click the Add button.

> **TIP** *Alternatively, drag files from a Windows Explorer window and drop them in the MUSICMATCH Burner Plus window. You can launch a Windows Explorer window by clicking the Explorer button in the MUSICMATCH Burner Plus toolbar.*

- To remove a track, select it, and then click the Remove button. Confirm the removal in the confirmation dialog box. (You can turn off the confirmation dialog box by selecting its Don't Ask Me Again check box.)

6. Once you're satisfied with the disc's contents, click the Burn button. MUSICMATCH Jukebox Plus starts the burn and displays a window illustrating its progress, as shown in the following image:

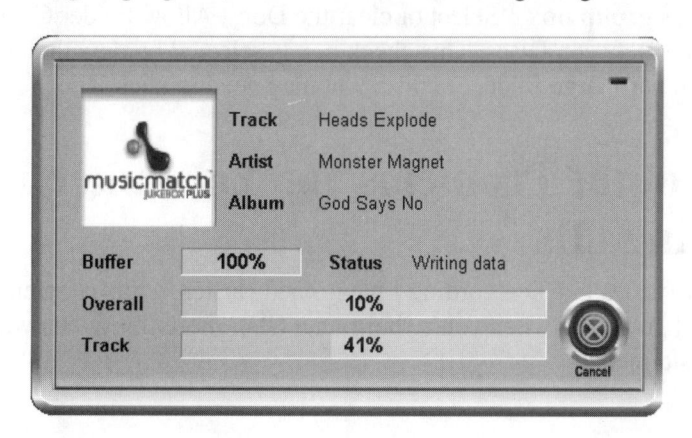

7. When the burn has finished, click the Return to Burner Plus button to return to the Burner Plus window.

Splitting a Burn List into Two or More CDs

If the total volume of files you've placed in the MUSICMATCH Burner Plus window is too great to fit on a single CD, MUSICMATCH Burner Plus changes the color of the status bar across the bottom of the window to red to warn you. You then need to take one of the following actions:

- Remove some files to make the others fit on the CD. (Use the Remove button or the Remove Files command on the shortcut menu.)

TIP *In later versions of MUSICMATCH Burner Plus, you can exclude some files from the burn without removing them from the MUSICMATCH Burner Plus window. Clear the check boxes for the files, or select the files, right-click, and choose Exclude File(s) from Burn from the shortcut menu.*

- Split the files onto two CDs by clicking the Split button on the toolbar.

You can choose these splitting settings on the SmartSplit tab of the Burner Plus Options dialog box:

- **Method group box** Select the Place Files with No Sorting (Fastest Split) option button if you want to split the files in the order you added them to the CD. Select the Place Largest Files First (Slower Split) option button if you want to try to stuff as many files as possible onto the CD.

- **Options group box** Select or clear the Don't Allow Folder Contents to Be Split Between Discs. This check box is selected by default, but if you need to burn large folders to disc, you may need to clear it.

Troubleshoot the Problems You Encounter When Burning CDs

Despite the advances in CD recording I mentioned earlier in this chapter, many things can still go wrong when you're burning a CD. These things can waste your time, effort, and media.

This section discusses how to troubleshoot the most common problems with burning CDs with iTunes and MUSICMATCH Jukebox Plus.

General: Avoid Causing Your Burner Problems

This section offers three basic tips for avoiding avoidable problems with burning CDs. These tips apply to both the PC and the Mac.

Balance Quality, Speed, and Cost

If you've worked for a demanding boss, you're probably familiar with this plaintive truism: "Here are your options for the product: quickly, cheaply, and high quality. Choose any two." (If you haven't needed to use this truism yet, file it away in your memory tickler file. Unless you have a trust fund, you'll probably need it before you're much older, given the way the economy is going—or not going, depending on how you view it.)

In the meantime, your CD recorder and burning software are probably giving you the same message. So here's what it means in the context of CD burning:

- Buy only high-quality recordable CD media. (Low-quality media isn't worth using: there's no upside to losing your data—at least, not unless the Department of Justice is on your case.) Expect to pay a market price for this media. If anyone offers you recordable CD media at bargain-basement prices, be duly suspicious. (Remember: Once badly burnt, forever shy.)

- In recording CDs, speed is worthless without accuracy. If you need to choose between recording at 48X with errors and 1X without errors, you must choose the 1X speed. Otherwise your data will be useless. This is like driving a Ferrari on icy roads: going slowly may be frustrating when you have blazing speed at your disposal, but a crash (that is, ruined data) won't benefit you at all.

- If you're buying a CD recorder, get a good one. Rather than buying the latest, fastest, and sexiest drive, consider buying a somewhat older model—you may be able to get good speed and reliability at a bargain price.

Give the CD Burner as Many Processor Cycles as Possible

Both Windows XP and Mac OS X pride themselves on being multitasking operating systems on which you can have multiple applications working actively at the same time. But because burning CDs is a processor-intensive activity, it's a good idea not to multitask actively while you're burning CDs.

To get the very best burning performance, reduce other tasks to a minimum, leave the burner as the foreground application (in other words, don't move the focus to another application window), and take your hands off the keyboard and mouse for the duration of the burn. (Because the mouse can do so much in a graphical user interface, mouse-enabled operating systems expend an inordinate amount of energy tracking exactly what the mouse is doing at any given moment.)

Get More Memory if You Don't Have Enough

Modern applications are memory hungry, modern operating systems doubly so.

Mac OS X and Windows XP will each run with 128MB RAM, but that's a bare minimum. You'll get significantly better performance with 256MB, and much better performance with 512MB or more.

Given that RAM prices are at historically low levels at this writing, now is a good time to add RAM to your computer. Unless, of course, you prefer to wait in the hope prices will go lower still…

Troubleshoot Burning CDs with iTunes

This section discusses how to troubleshoot problems in burning CDs with iTunes. The section starts with the basics and then moves on to more challenging problems.

Make Sure iTunes Supports Your CD-RW Drive

Start by making sure iTunes supports your CD-RW drive—if not, all your troubleshooting efforts will be in vain.

Choose iTunes | Preferences and then click the Burning button to display the Burning Properties dialog box (shown in Figure 7-1, earlier in this chapter). If the CD Burner readout lists your CD-RW drive by name, the drive works with iTunes.

TIP *For an up-to-date list of devices compatible with iTunes, go to www.apple.com/itunes/compatibility/.*

Prevent Screen Effects from Activating During a Burn

Configure your screen effects settings on the tabs of the Screen Effects pane of System Preferences to make sure screen effects don't kick in during a burn. On the Activation tab of the Screen Effects page, drag the Time Until Screen Effect Starts slider to a suitably long setting (for example, 40 minutes or more) or to the Never position.

Prevent Your Mac from Going to Sleep During a Burn

Configure the sleep timing settings in the Energy Saver pane of System Preferences to ensure neither your Mac nor its display goes to sleep during a burn. Even with modern CD-RW drives, your Mac's going to sleep during a burn may cause errors on the disc. Having the display go to sleep during a burn shouldn't affect the burn in many cases, but in other cases it may—particularly if you press the wrong keys or buttons when playing Prince Charming to wake your Mac. Unless you care to experiment with having your display go to sleep and checking the resulting discs, you may prefer to be safe than sorry.

To change your Mac's sleep timing settings, follow these steps:

1. Choose Apple | System Preferences to display the System Preferences window.

2. Click the Energy Saver item in the Hardware category to display the Energy Saver pane.

3. If the Energy Saver pane is in its small format, which hides the details, click the Show Details button to display the remainder of the pane. Figure 7-8 shows the full Energy Saver pane.

4. For a desktop Mac or for a PowerBook running on the power adapter (rather than the battery), the easiest option is to choose the Automatic item in the Optimize Energy Settings drop-down list. This item puts the Mac to sleep after one hour of inactivity, which should be plenty long enough for burning any recordable CD—even at 1X speed. Alternatively, you may prefer the Highest Performance item in the Optimize Energy Settings drop-down list. This item prevents the Mac from ever going to sleep without your putting it to sleep manually.

5. For a PowerBook running on battery power, you may find the Automatic item in the Optimize Energy Settings drop-down list works okay for burning if your PowerBook has a fast CD-RW drive: the Automatic item puts the display to sleep after 9 minutes and the computer to sleep after 25 minutes. On older PowerBooks, you may find these sleep settings too aggressive for comfort. In this case, you can choose the Highest Performance item if you don't care about exhausting your batteries quickly. Or you can choose the Custom item, and then choose custom settings as follows:

    - Drag the Put the Computer to Sleep When It Is Inactive For slider to a setting that will allow plenty of time for the burn to complete.

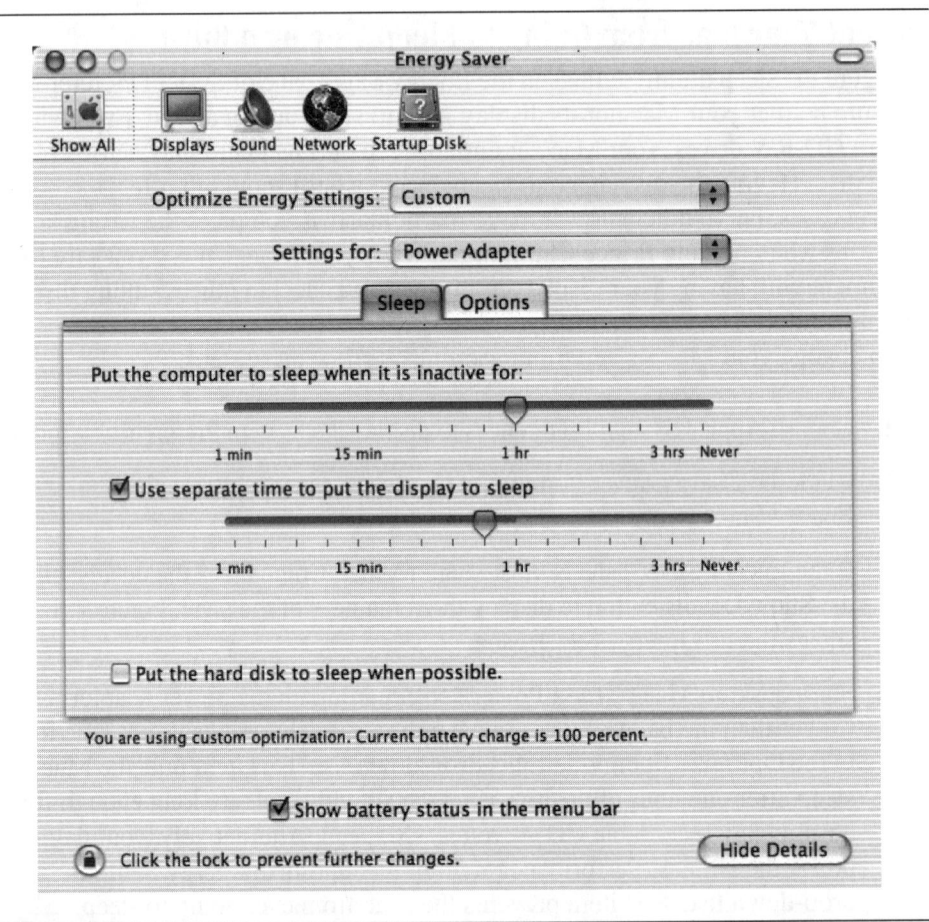

FIGURE 7-8 Configure the sleep timing settings in the Energy Saver pane of System Preferences to prevent your Mac from going to sleep during a burn.

- To configure a different sleep setting for the display than for the computer, select the Use Separate Time to Put the Display to Sleep check box and drag the slider to a setting that will allow the burn to complete. For obvious reasons, you can't set a longer sleep delay for the display than for the computer.

- Select the Put the Hard Disk to Sleep when Possible check box if you want Mac OS X to shut down the hard disk whenever possible. Because the hard disk is used extensively (though not quite continuously) during a burn, Mac OS X shouldn't try to shut the hard disk down while the burn is happening.

CHAPTER 7: Burn Audio and MP3 CDs with iTunes and MUSICMATCH Jukebox Plus

TIP *To prevent further changes to the Energy Saver configuration or other lockable preferences, click the lock icon at the lower-left corner of the Energy Saver pane. This will prevent anyone from shortening the sleep settings (or other vital settings) and throwing a monkey wrench into your burns. To unlock the locked panes, you click the lock icon again in one of the panes and enter your account name and password in the resulting Authenticate dialog box.*

6. Press COMMAND-Q or choose System Preferences | Quit System Preferences to quit System Preferences.

Reset an External CD-RW Drive

If you're using an external CD-RW drive, and you find that the drive stops responding after a burn fails, power the drive down and then back up again to reset it. If the drive uses a special eject mechanism (as LaCie drives do, among others), you may have to use that mechanism to eject the CD. Consult the drive's documentation for details.

Unable to Eject a Blank CD

Sometimes Mac OS X doesn't eject a CD the first time you issue a command to eject it. For example, if you drag the CD's icon to the Trash, Mac OS X sometimes fails to eject it. In iTunes, click the Eject button to eject the CD. You may need to click the button more than once. Allow a few seconds after each click to allow iTunes to respond.

External CD-RW Drive Stutters or Skips During Playback

Some external CD-RW drives don't play back CDs correctly, and you may hear stutters or apparent skips. To check whether the CD or the drive is the problem, try playing the CD in a CD player or in an internal CD drive (if you have one). If you don't have another CD player or CD drive, try playing another CD in the external CD-RW drive and see if that works.

Troubleshoot Burning CDs with MUSICMATCH Jukebox Plus

This section discusses three burning problems you may experience with MUSICMATCH Jukebox Plus.

"Burner Plus Cannot Write to the Media" Message

If you get the message "Burner Plus cannot write to the media currently inserted in the selected drive" when you click the Burn button in the MUSICMATCH Burner Plus window, it usually means the disc has already been closed—for example, because you've already created an audio CD on it.

If you're sure the disc is unused, check the following:

- The Media Size setting on the General tab of the Burner Plus Options dialog box is correct. Sometimes this error message indicates a mismatch between the setting and the disc.

- The burn speed is suitable for the disc. For example, if you're trying to burn at 40X a disc that's rated at 4X, you might get this error message. Some discs have their speed marked on them; others have the speed marked on the packaging. If you buy bulk discs, neither the discs nor their packaging may show the speed. In this case, if you forget the speed of the discs you bought, you'll need to experiment to establish which speed works.

If none of the preceding is the case, this disc may simply be incompatible with your CD burner—for example, because the laser in your drive doesn't like the particular type of reflective coating used by the disc manufacturer. If you've just bought a bargain spindle of discs, this could be a sharp kick in the wallet. To find out if this is why you're wasting your time, try another type of disc. Another possibility is that this disc is defective. To find out, try another.

The Songs on Your MP3 CDs Play in the Wrong Order

If the songs on MP3 CDs you create with MUSICMATCH Jukebox Plus play in alphabetical order rather than the order of the playlist you created with such care and consideration, clear the Sort Files check box on the MP3 tab of the Burner Plus Options dialog box.

Prevent Screen Savers and Powering Down During a Burn

Processor-intensive screen savers (in other words, most of the visually interesting screen savers) can cause problems with burns by diverting processor cycles from the burn at a critical moment. To avoid this happening, configure a long wait on your screen saver. To do so, follow these steps:

1. Right-click the desktop and choose Properties from the shortcut menu to show the Display Properties dialog box.

CHAPTER 7: Burn Audio and MP3 CDs with iTunes and MUSICMATCH Jukebox Plus

2. On the Screen Saver tab (shown on the left in Figure 7-9), increase the time shown in the Wait text box so it's far longer than even the slowest burn your CD recorder will ever perform.

> **TIP** *Better yet, choose None in the Screen Saver drop-down list to turn off your screen saver altogether.*

3. Click the Apply button to apply your choices.

4. To prevent your computer from going to sleep during a burn, click the Power button on the Screen Saver tab of the Display Properties dialog box. Windows displays the Power Options Properties dialog box.

5. On the Power Schemes tab (shown on the right in Figure 7-9), specify suitably lengthy times (or choose the Never item) in the Turn Off Monitor drop-down list, the Turn Off Hard Disks drop-down list, the System Standby drop-down list, and the System Hibernates drop-down list, to prevent these events from occurring during a burn.

6. Click the Apply button to implement your choices.

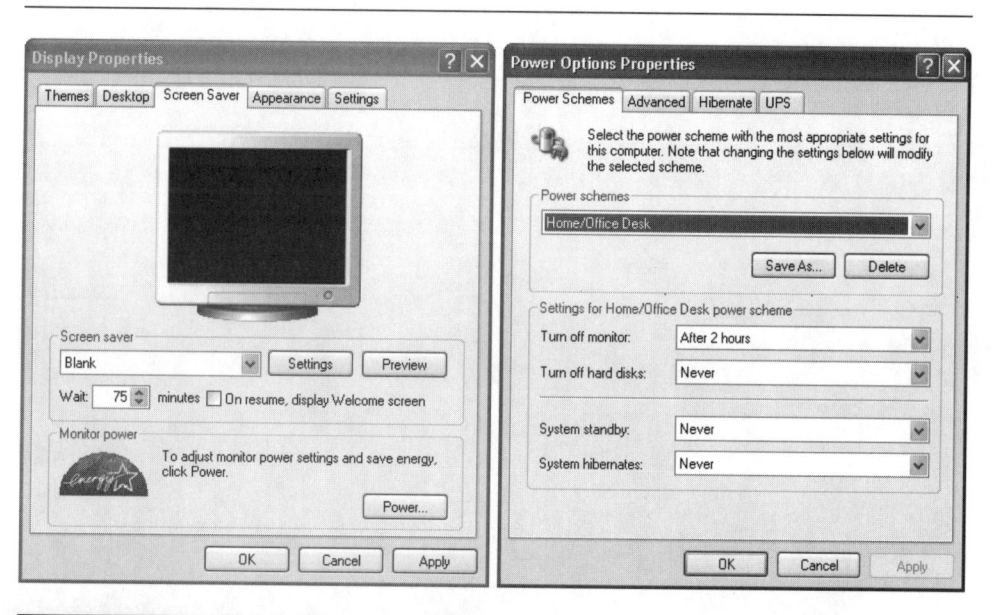

FIGURE 7-9 Configure your screen saver (left) and power schemes (right) to prevent interruptions to the burn.

Part II

Use Your iPod for Contacts, Calendar, and Other Text

Chapter 8

Use Your iPod to Take Your Contacts with You

How to...

- Understand what vCards are and what they contain
- Create vCards from your contacts
- Use iSync to put your contacts on your Mac iPod automatically
- Put your contacts on your Mac iPod manually
- Put your contacts on your Windows iPod
- View your contacts on your iPod

As you'll know from its interface, your iPod includes a Contacts category that lets you carry around your contact information and view records as necessary. You can't enter contact information directly on your iPod (because there's no means of entering it), but at least you don't have to carry your Pocket PC or Palm handheld around just to keep contact information with you. Nor do you need to type long addresses into the address book on your cell phone. (Nor do you have to do what some early adopters of the iPod did—create momentary MP3 files and insert the contact data in the tag fields. Yes, they actually did this.)

NOTE *Apple added contacts to the iPod in the iPod Software 1.1 Updater. If your iPod can't display contacts, get the latest Updater right away from www.apple.com/ipod/download/.*

This chapter shows you how to create contacts from Mac OS X and Windows XP address applications, put them on your iPod, and view them on it. The chapter also shows you how to put contacts from other sources onto your iPod. To do so, you may need to export your contact records from their existing format into a common format (such as a comma-separated values or CSV file). This isn't hard, but you may have to do a little work.

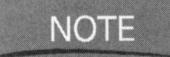

NOTE *As in the earlier chapters, the Mac parts of this chapter assume you're using Mac OS X, preferably 10.2 (Jaguar) or later. If you're still using System 9, iSync alone should give you a strong incentive to upgrade, because iSync runs only on Mac OS X 10.2.2 or later.*

Understand the Wonders of vCards

vCard is a format for storing the information that constitutes a virtual business card: a name that consists of various parts, including first, last, middle initial, title, nickname, and suffix; a company or organization; a title; one or more addresses, e-mail addresses; phone numbers; notes; and other relevant information.

As that list suggests, vCard information is mostly text, and indeed many vCards are only text. This helps keep the vCard files, which use the .vcf extension, to a tiny size, so they can be transmitted quickly across even slow dial-up connections. But vCards can also include a picture (for example, for a photo of the card's subject or for a company logo) and an audio clip (which can be used for anything from a conventional greeting to something musical, exotic, or obscene).

A Brief History of vCard

vCard was the fruit of the versit Consortium, a group set up by Apple, IBM, AT&T, and Siemens to streamline what's grandly called personal data interchange (PDI). PDI simply means one person communicating with someone else. For example, if you tell someone your name over the phone, or give someone your business card in person, you've committed—I'm sorry, *performed*—PDI. Wireless beaming capabilities in Palm and other organizers enable you to use your PDA to perform PDI PDQ. (Sorry—couldn't resist.)

vCard lets you transfer an impressive set of standardized information to someone else electronically in a format they can easily accept. So they don't have to retype your business card into their address book or contact manager, introducing errors along the way, or struggle with one of those business-card scanners that decides your company name is your name and its logo is your picture.

versit got as far as defining version 2.1 of the Electronic Business Card Specification before handing over the reins to the Internet Mail Consortium (IMC) in December 1996. Along with vCard, the IMC also took over responsibility for developing and promoting vCalendar, a format for exchanging electronic calendaring and scheduling information. The IMC subsequently released version 3.0 of the Electronic Business Card Specification, but many otherwise up-to-date applications (for example, Address Book in Windows XP) still use version 2.1.

vCards haven't generated any great excitement in non-tech circles, but most e-mail programs and address books incorporate support for vCards. So if someone using a Linux e-mail application sends you a message with a vCard attached, you can import the vCard into your address book easily whether you're using Windows, Mac OS, Linux, or another operating system.

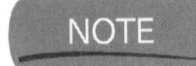

> **NOTE** There are substantial differences in formatting between version 2.1 and version 3.0, and many applications that use version 2.1 can't handle incoming vCards formatted with version 3.0. Your iPod can handle both version 2.1 and version 3.0 (which it prefers).

For the Curious Only: A Quick Look Inside a vCard

If you open a vCard that uses version 3.0 formatting in a text editor, you'll typically see text apparently formatted by someone who likes the spacebar—for example:

```
b e g i n : v c a r d
v e r s i o n : 3 . 0
f n : P h i l i p p a   J o n e s
n : J o n e s ; P h i l i p p a ; ; M r s . ;
t i t l e : M a r k e t i n g   A s s i s t a n t
o r g : N e w   A g e   P h a r m a c e u t i c a l   D e s i g n ; M a r k e t i n g
e n d : v c a r d
```

> **NOTE** Not all version 3.0 vCards use spaces between every character, but most do.

Whereas if you open a vCard that uses version 2.1 formatting in a text editor, you'll see relatively compact text, like this, apparently tagged by someone who likes capital letters:

```
BEGIN:VCARD
VERSION:2.1
N:Jones;Philippa;;Mrs.
FN:Philippa Jones
ORG:New Age Pharmaceutical Design;Marketing
TITLE:Marketing Assistant
END:VCARD
```

Each of these data-bursts contains the same information, as you can probably see if you squint a little. Each is made up of a number of fields: fn (formatted name), n (name—the various components used to constitute it), org (organization), and title (job title), in this short example. The rest of the information vCards can contain is similarly divided into fields—for example, EMAIL;PREF;INTERNET for the preferred e-mail address (in version 2.1 vCards) and "a d r ; t y p e = h o m e ; t y p e = p r e f" for a home address that's the default address (in version 3.0 vCards).

To keep itself as brief as possible, a vCard contains only those fields for which it has entries—it omits all blank fields. As long as each field included has the correct name, any combination of fields can be used in any order. The application that reads the vCard parses the data into the appropriate categories. (At least in theory. If you find your Polish contacts showing up under names such as Abstrakcja Konkretna 3. Warszawa in your address book, you'll know you've got a parsing problem.)

How Your iPod Handles vCards

Being designed by Apple to be stylishly conscious of its own limitations, your iPod handles vCards in an idiosyncratic way: it knows it can't use all the information from a vCard, so it uses only a certain number of fields. Table 8-1 explains the data your iPod displays in the order it displays them, together with examples of typical contents as you might see them and notes on other items. The bold rows in the table indicate the bold headings your iPod uses to break up the vCard information. To help you retain your sanity (and I, mine), the column showing the vCard 3.0 fields omits the maddening spaces version 3.0 vCards usually use.

NOTE *You can put up to 1,000 contacts on your iPod.*

Looking at the information in Table 8-1, you've no doubt realized there's nothing magical about the data stored in the vCard fields, so the vCard won't object if you enter the wrong type of text in a field. Therefore, you can create vCards that contain memos, shopping lists, recipes, poems, and so on, if you use the fields in the right order. For example, you could use a vCard with a BEGIN:VCARD statement, a VERSION statement, an N field, an ORG field, and an END VCARD statement to create a basic note using any text editor (for example, Notepad in Windows or TextEdit in Mac OS X). Here's an example:

```
BEGIN VCARD
VERSION:2.1
N:How to Create a vCard Note, Shopping List, or Whatever
ORG:Use the N field to name the vCard. Then type the ORG field
and enter the text you want to appear on the vCard note.
End your note with the END:VCARD statement.
END:VCARD
```

This bargain-basement vCard works fine if you copy it to the Contacts folder on your iPod. But as you'll see in Chapter 10, there are much better ways of getting text into your iPod—at least, for the Mac.

Field	vCard 2.1 Field	vCard 3.0 Field (spaces omitted)	Example or Notes
[Contact's Name]	FN	fn	Gerald Dixon
Nickname	NICKNAME	nickname	"Jerry"
Job title	TITLE	title	Family Doctor
Company	ORG (first part)	org (first part)	Four Square Physicians
Department	ORG (second part)	org (second part)	Medical
Telephone			(All the phone numbers the vCard includes. Any numbers with labels iPod doesn't recognize are lumped in with Office.)
Home	TEL;HOME	tel;type=home	510-555-1212
Work	TEL;WORK	tel;type=work	415-555-1212
Mobile	TEL;CELL	tel;type=cell	415-555-1234
E-mail			(All the e-mail addresses the vCard includes, default address first)
Default e-mail	EMAIL;PREF;INTERNET	email;type=internet;type=pref	test1@example.com
Other e-mail 1	EMAIL;INTERNET	email;type=internet	test2@example.com
Other e-mail 2	EMAIL;INTERNET	email;type=internet	test3@example.com
Web			
Home URL	URL;HOME	url;type=home	http://www.example.com/~moi
Office Address			
Office address	ADR;WORK	adr;type=work	1, Four Square Oakland, CA 94610 USA
Home Address			
Home address	ADR;HOME	adr;type=work	728 Maine Street Alameda, CA 94501 USA
Notes	NOTE	note	(Contents of the Notes field)

TABLE 8-1   vCard Fields Your iPod Can Use, in Order of Use

TIP *If you find it handy to create vCards from a text editor, create a template file—a skeleton file that contains just the BEGIN VCARD, VERSION, N, ORG, and END VCARD lines. To create a vCard, double-click this file to open it, enter the text on the N line and the ORG line, and then save the file under a different name.*

Create vCards from Your Contacts

If you're feeling energetic and punctilious, you can create your own vCards manually by typing the appropriate text (and, for version 3.0 vCards, spaces) smartly into a text editor. If you pore through the earlier part of this chapter once again, you'll find that I've just about given you enough information to create your own vCards in this way—but only just, because I'd prefer you find more creative ways of squandering your time.

On the other hand, if you're normal, you'll create vCards the easy way—by exporting them from whichever address book or contact manager you use. The first subsection discusses the main tools for creating vCards on the Mac. The second subsection discusses the most prominent Windows tools.

TIP *If you have Mac OS X, you can use iSync to put your contacts on your Mac iPod without creating vCards manually. Go straight to the section "Use iSync to Put Contacts on Your Mac iPod Automatically," later in this chapter.*

Create vCards on the Mac

On the Mac, you can create your own vCards with minimal effort from Address Book, Entourage, and Palm Desktop.

TIP *With each of these applications, you can create contacts directly on your iPod. Open a Finder window to show the Contacts folder on your iPod, and then drag the contacts to that folder to create vCards from them.*

Create a vCard from Address Book

To create a vCard from Address Book, drag an item from the Address Book to another application or location. For example, to create a vCard on the desktop, drag a vCard to the desktop. Address Book names the vCard using the contact's name, and applies the .vcf extension.

TIP *Normally, a vCard contains the data for one person or organization. But the Mac OS X Address Book can create a single vCard that contains multiple entries. To create such a vCard, select multiple cards, and then export them. Alternatively, export an entire group. You can drag any group to the desktop except for the All group. Or you can export any group (including the All group) by selecting it, issuing an Export Group vCard command from the File menu or the shortcut menu, specifying the filename and location in the Save dialog box, and then clicking the Save button.*

Create a vCard from Entourage

To create a vCard from Entourage, follow these steps:

1. Click the Address button in the upper-left pane to display your address book.
2. Select the contact or contacts from which you want to create vCards.
3. Drag the selected contact or contacts to the folder in which you want to create the vCards, or to the desktop.

CAUTION *You can export all your Entourage contacts to a tab-delimited text file by opening the Address Book, choosing File | Export Contacts, using the Save dialog box to specify the filename and location, and then clicking the Save button. But the resulting file isn't vCard compatible.*

TIP *To export all your Entourage information to your iPod, use the iPod It utility. See the section "iPod It" in Chapter 10 for details.*

Create a vCard from Palm Desktop

You can create a vCard from Palm Desktop by dragging a contact to the folder in which you want to create the vCard. But you can also create vCards by using the Export: Palm Desktop dialog box. To do so, follow these steps:

1. In the Address List window, select the contact from which you want to create a vCard.
2. Choose File | Export to display the Export: Palm Desktop dialog box (shown in Figure 8-1 with settings chosen). The Addresses item will be selected in the Modules drop-down list by default.

CHAPTER 8: Use Your iPod to Take Your Contacts with You 209

3. Use the Save As text box to specify the filename and the Where drop-down list to specify the location under which to save the file.

4. In the Items drop-down list, select the appropriate item—for example, All *NN* Addresses.

5. In the Format drop-down list, select the vCard item.

6. Click the Export button to export the contacts to the specified file.

Create vCards from Windows

This section discusses how to create vCards from the most widely used sources in Windows: Address Book, Outlook Express, and Palm Desktop.

Create a vCard from Address Book

Address Book, an applet that comes built into Windows, is the default location for storing contact information in Windows. You can launch Address Book by choosing Start | Programs | Accessories | Address Book or by clicking the Address Book button in an application such as Outlook Express, Outlook, or Microsoft Word.

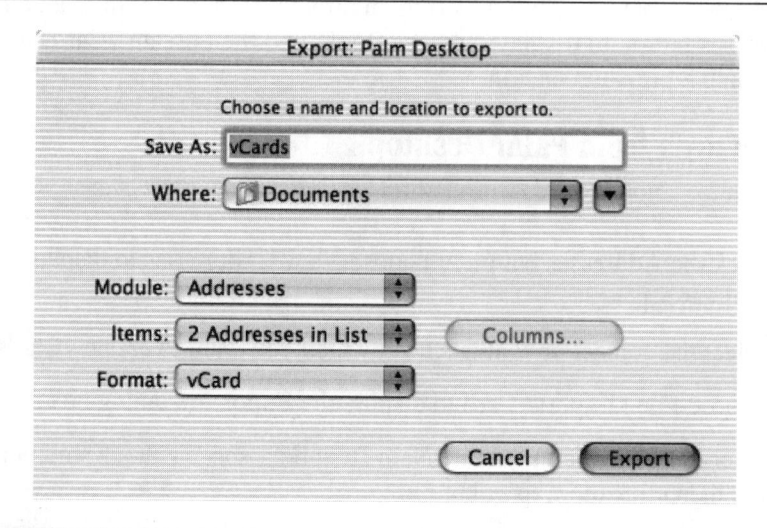

FIGURE 8-1 In the Export: Palm Desktop dialog box, specify the filename and location, choose the appropriate items, and specify the vCard format.

You can create vCards from Address Book in either of two ways. The easier and faster of the ways is to select the contacts you want to export to vCards, drag them to the desktop or the folder in which you want to create the vCards, and drop them there. This technique lets you create multiple vCards at once.

> **TIP** *For speed, open a window to display the Contacts folder on your iPod. Then drag the vCards directly into it from Address Book.*

To create a vCard from Address Book the hard way, follow these steps:

1. Select the contact from whose entry you want to create a vCard. (You can export only one contact at a time to a vCard.)

2. Choose File | Export | Business Card (vCard) to display the Export As Business Card (vCard) dialog box. This is a Save As dialog box in disguise.

3. Specify the filename and location for the file, and then click the Save button.

Create a vCard from Outlook Express

The contacts in the Windows Address Book appear in the Contacts pane in Outlook Express, but you can't export them directly from there. Instead, click the Addresses button to display Address Book, and then create vCards as described in the previous section.

Create vCards from Palm Desktop

To create one or more vCards from Palm Desktop, follow these steps:

1. Click the Addresses button or choose View | Addresses to display the Addresses pane.

2. Select the contact or contacts form which you want to create vCards.

3. Choose File | Export vCard to display the Export As dialog box.

4. Enter the filename in the File Name text box, specify the destination, and then click the Export button.

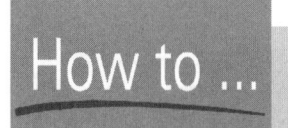

How to ... Create vCards from CSV Files

All these means of creating vCards are fine—provided your addresses are stored in one of those applications. But if the application in which your addresses are stored can't export them as vCards, you'll need to take a couple of extra steps to get the addresses onto your iPod. For example, if you use the Yahoo address book, you won't be able to create vCards directly from it.

The first step is to export the addresses from the application into a text file. Most applications can create a comma-separated values (CSV) file, so that's usually the best format to use. Other applications create tab-separated values (TSV) files, which will usually work as well.

Once you've created the CSV or TSV file, import it into an address book that can handle CSV or TSV files *and* can create vCards. On Windows XP, both Address Book and Palm Desktop can handle CSV imports, so use whichever you prefer.

On the Mac, the news isn't so good. The Address Book in Mac OS X can import only vCards and LDAP Interchange Format (LDIF) files. (Before you ask—LDAP is the abbreviation for Lightweight Directory Access Protocol, a standard protocol for accessing directory information.) And Palm Desktop can't import CSV or TSV files either. But Entourage can import just about anything in sight.

Once you've found the appropriate Import command (usually File | Import), the tricky part about importing is assigning each field in the CSV or TSV file to the corresponding field in the address book. The following illustration shows a couple of examples of the dialog boxes used for mapping data to fields. The Specify Import Fields dialog box on the left is from Palm Desktop for Windows.

The Import Contacts dialog box on the right is from Entourage, which can usually map some of the fields automatically.

The second step (you guessed it) is to export the vCards from the address application, as described in the sections "Create vCards on the Mac" and "Create vCards from Windows" both earlier in this chapter.

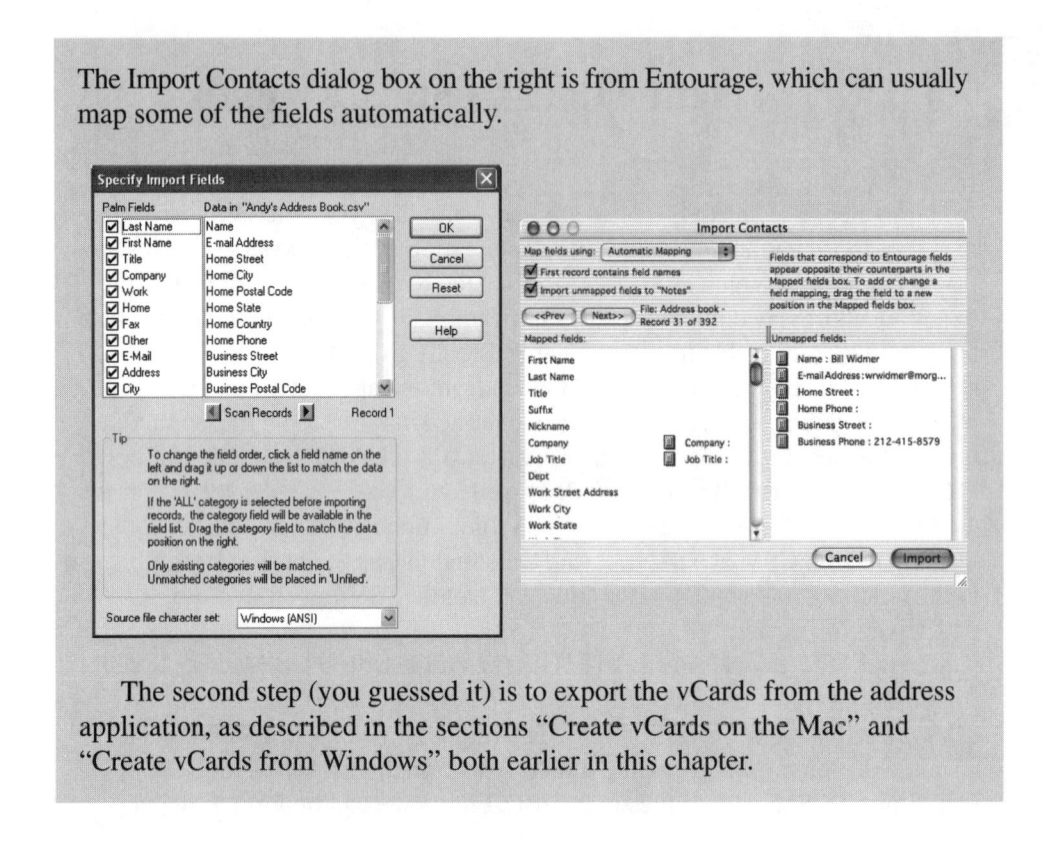

Put Contacts on Your Mac iPod

You can put your contacts on your iPod either automatically (by using iSync) or manually. As you'd imagine, doing so automatically is easier, so I'll show you how to do that first.

NOTE
If you're using System 9, you'll need to use the manual method of transferring contacts. This is because neither iSync nor Address Book works with System 9.

Use iSync to Put Contacts on Your Mac iPod Automatically

If you have Mac OS X 10.2.2 or later, the easiest and quickest way to put your contacts on your iPod is to use iSync. If you don't yet have iSync, download it from the iSync area of the Apple web site (**www.apple.com/isync**). Install iSync as usual, and then work your way through the following subsections.

> **Did you know?**
>
> ## Why Might Your iPod Show Duplicate Contacts and Calendar Information?
>
> If you use iSync to put contacts and calendar information on your iPod automatically, you can get duplicate entries for contacts and calendar information you've already copied to your iPod manually (or that you subsequently copy to your iPod manually).
>
> This happens because iSync doesn't delete any data from the iPod that iSync itself hasn't put there. So if you want to synchronize your contacts and calendar information automatically, you need to commit fully to iSync. To do so, follow these steps:
>
> 1. Connect your iPod to your Mac.
>
> 2. Enable FireWire mode if it's not currently enabled. (See the section "Put Contacts on Your Mac iPod Manually," later in this chapter, for instructions on how to do this—but if you've been putting contacts and calendar information on your iPod, you must have enabled FireWire mode at least once before now.)
>
> 3. From the Contacts folder on your iPod, import into Address Book the vCards for any contacts it doesn't yet contain. Make sure you don't add existing contacts to Address Book—it'll happily create duplicate entries that you'll then need to weed out manually.
>
> 4. From the Calendars folder on your iPod, import into iCal any calendar information it doesn't already contain.
>
> 5. Drag the Contacts folder and the Calendars folder on your iPod to the Trash. iSync will automatically create these folders if they don't exist. Alternatively, drag the contents of each folder to the Trash.
>
> 6. Run iSync and synchronize your calendars and contacts.

CAUTION *If you installed the public beta of iSync, uninstall it before installing iSync. Otherwise, you may lose data. Perform a final synchronization with the beta and back up all Contact and Calendar information. Download iSync Utilities from the Apple Support site (**www.apple.com/support**) and use it to uninstall the iSync beta. Then install iSync either by manually downloading and installing it or by using Software Update.*

Set iSync to Synchronize with Your iPod

First, you need to add your iPod to the list of devices iSync synchronizes. To do so, follow these steps:

1. Run iSync by whichever means you prefer.
2. Connect your iPod to your Mac via the FireWire cable as usual.
3. Press COMMAND-N or choose Devices | Add Device to display the Add Device dialog box (shown in the following image with a device already identified).

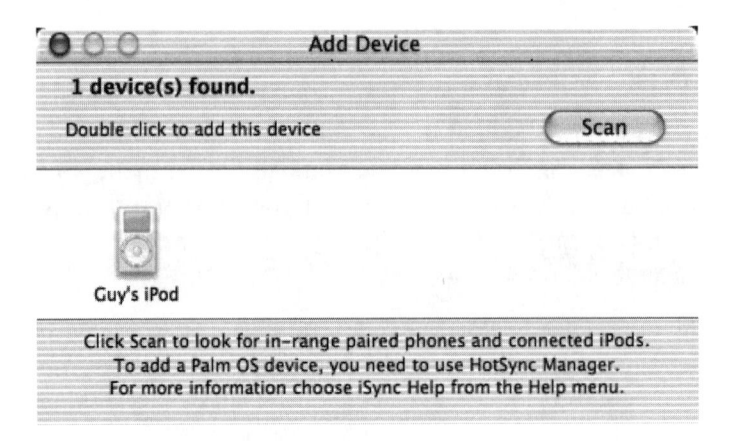

```
┌─────────────────────────────────────────────────┐
│ ⊝ ⊙ ⊙              Add Device                   │
│  1 device(s) found.                             │
│  Double click to add this device      ( Scan )  │
│                                                 │
│                    ▢                            │
│                 Guy's iPod                      │
│                                                 │
│   Click Scan to look for in-range paired phones and connected iPods.
│       To add a Palm OS device, you need to use HotSync Manager.
│       For more information choose iSync Help from the Help menu.
└─────────────────────────────────────────────────┘
```

4. If iSync doesn't scan automatically for devices, click the Scan button to force a scan.
5. Double-click the icon for your iPod to add it to the iSync window.
6. Click the close button on the Add Device window to close the window.

Figure 8-2 shows an iPod added to the iSync window.

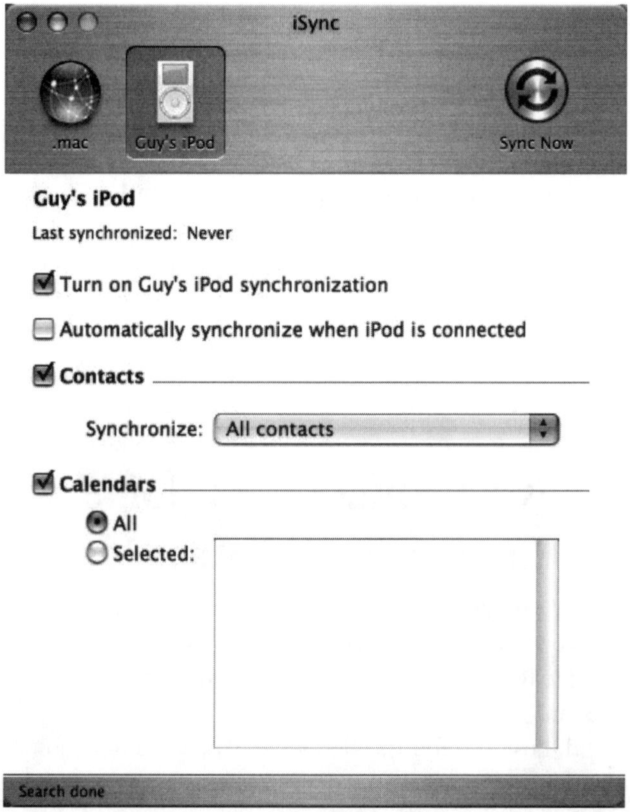

CHAPTER 8: Use Your iPod to Take Your Contacts with You 215

FIGURE 8-2 After adding your iPod to the iSync list of devices, you're ready to choose synchronization options.

Choose Synchronization Options for Your iPod

Once you've added your iPod to the list of devices iSync can synchronize with, choose the appropriate synchronization options. Your choices are as follows:

- **Turn On iPod Synchronization check box**   Controls whether or not iSync synchronizes with your iPod. Normally, you'll want to keep this check box selected, as it is by default.

- **Automatically Synchronize When iPod Is Connected check box**   Controls whether or not iSync automatically synchronizes your contacts and calendar (as appropriate) whenever you plug your iPod into your Mac. If you choose not to select this check box, you can force a synchronization by clicking the Sync Now button.

- **Contacts check box**   Controls whether or not iSync synchronizes your contacts.

- **Synchronize drop-down list**   Controls which of your contacts iSync synchronizes. The default setting for the iPod is All Contacts.

- **Calendars check box**   Controls whether or not iSync synchronizes your calendars. Select the All option button (the default) to synchronize all your calendars. To synchronize only some of your calendars (for example, just your Home calendar, not your Work calendar), select the Selected option button, and then select the check boxes for the calendars you want to synchronize.

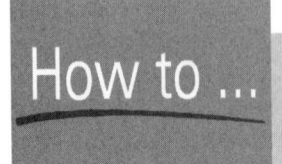

How to ... Synchronize Only Some Contacts with Your iPod

If you keep a lot of contacts in your Address Book, synchronizing them all to your iPod can take a while. It can also make the Contacts folder on your iPod difficult to navigate because you have to scroll endlessly to find the people you're interested in.

To get around these problems, you can synchronize only some of your contacts from Address Book to your iPod. To do so, follow these steps:

1. In Address Book, create a new group by clicking the Add New Group button (the + button below the Group pane), pressing CTRL-N, or choosing File | New.
2. Type the name for the group and press RETURN.
3. Select the All group (or whichever group contains the contacts you want to add to the group you'll synchronize) to display its contents.
4. Select the contacts, and then drag them to the new group you created.
5. In iSync, select the new group in the Synchronize drop-down list.
6. Synchronize your iPod as usual.

Synchronize Your Contacts and Calendar

If you chose to have iSync automatically synchronize your iPod when you connect it, all you need do to start a synchronization is to connect your iPod. If you opted for manual synchronization, connect your iPod, run iSync, and then click the Sync button.

> **TIP** *To synchronize quickly, or run iSync easily, you can add an iSync icon to the menu bar. To do so, choose iSync | Preferences, and then select the Show iSync in Menu Bar check box in the Preferences dialog box. You can then click the icon and choose Open iSync or Sync Now from the menu.*

iSync displays the Safeguard dialog box (two examples of which are shown in Figure 8-3) to make sure you understand how the synchronization will affect the data on your iPod. Click the Proceed button if you want to go ahead with the synchronization.

After synchronizing, unmount your iPod before unplugging it from your Mac. To unmount your iPod, select its icon, and then issue an Eject command from the shortcut menu or from the File menu, or press COMMAND-E. (Alternatively, drag your iPod to the Trash.)

> **TIP** *To turn off the Safeguard warnings, choose iSync | Preferences, and then clear the Show the Safeguard Panel check box in the Preferences dialog box. To change the threshold for which they appear, leave this check box selected, but choose Any, More Than 1%, More Than 5%, or More Than 10% in the drop-down list.*

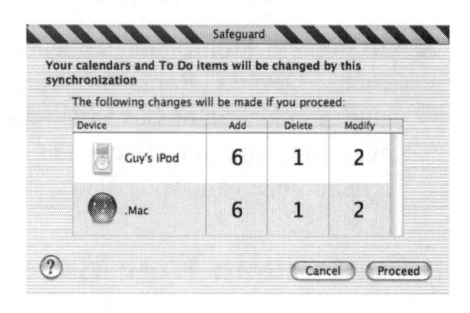

FIGURE 8-3 The Safeguard dialog box warns you of the extent of changes synchronization will cause.

Revert to Last Sync

If synchronizing your data with iSync gives you an undesirable result (for example, you lose contacts or calendar information you weren't intending to get rid of), you should be able to repair the damage by reverting to the last synchronization. To do so, choose Devices | Revert to Last Sync, and then click the Revert to Last Sync button in the confirmation dialog box (shown in the following image) that iSync displays. iSync then restores the data from a copy it made of your data at the last synchronization.

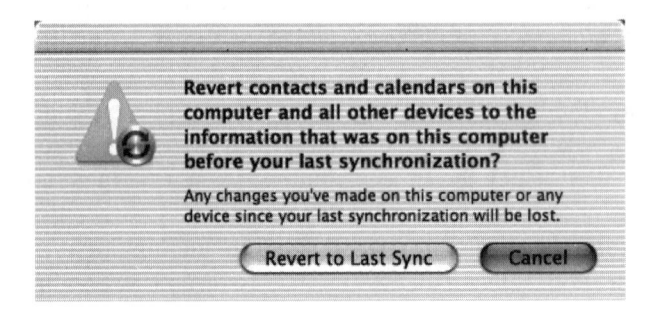

TIP *You can also force iSync to make a backup of your data at any time by choosing Devices | Backup My Data.*

Stop Synchronizing Your iPod

You can stop synchronizing your iPod either temporarily or permanently:

- To stop synchronization temporarily, select your iPod in the iSync window, and then clear the Turn On *iPod* Synchronization check box.

- To stop synchronization permanently, select your iPod in the iSync window, choose Devices | Remove Device, and then click the Remove button in the confirmation dialog box iSync displays. To make your iPod synchronize again, add your iPod once more as described in the section "Set iSync to Synchronize with Your iPod," earlier in this chapter.

Put Contacts on Your Mac iPod Manually

If you can't use iSync (for example, because you're still using System 9 or you prefer not to use Address Book) or you prefer to do things the hard way, you can

CHAPTER 8: Use Your iPod to Take Your Contacts with You

transfer your contacts to your Mac manually. To transfer contacts manually, FireWire disk use must be enabled on your iPod. If it's not enabled, follow these steps to enable it:

1. Connect your iPod to your Mac.
2. Launch iTunes if it's not configured to launch automatically.
3. In the Source pane, select the icon for your iPod.
4. Click the Display Options for Player button in the lower-right corner of the iTunes window to display the iPod Preferences dialog box.
5. Select the Enable FireWire Disk Use check box.
6. Click the OK button.

NOTE *The first time you enable FireWire disk mode, iTunes displays a dialog box warning you that using FireWire disk mode requires you to manually unmount the iPod before each disconnect, even when synchronizing songs (instead of being able to have iTunes unmount the iPod automatically). Click the OK button.*

Once you've enabled FireWire mode, you can copy the contact files directly onto your iPod by using the Finder. To do so, follow these steps:

1. Export your contacts to vCard files, as discussed in the section "Create vCards from Your Contacts," earlier in this chapter.
2. Connect your iPod to your Mac (if it's not currently connected). If iTunes is set to synchronize automatically on connection, let synchronization take place.
3. Double-click the icon for your iPod to display a Finder window of its contents.
4. Drag the vCard files to the Contacts folder and drop them there.

TIP *At the same time, you may want to remove the Instructions and Sample vCards that come preinstalled on your iPod. To do so, delete the files ipod_created_instructions.vcf and ipod_created_sample.vcf. Alternatively, you might want to store the samples in a folder on your Mac as templates in case you ever want to create vCards manually.*

5. Close the Contacts folder.

6. Eject your iPod by selecting it and pressing COMMAND-E, issuing an Eject command from the File menu or the shortcut menu, or dragging the iPod icon to the Trash.

Put Contacts on Your Windows iPod

To put contacts on your Windows iPod, you need to enable your iPod for use as a hard disk and assign a drive letter to it. (In some cases, you may find that Windows treats your iPod as a hard disk and assigns it a drive letter without your intervention.) If you've already done this, you're set to go; if not, follow these steps:

1. Display the MUSICMATCH Portables Plus window. If you don't have this window set to open automatically when you connect your iPod to your PC, open MUSICMATCH Jukebox Plus, and then choose File | Download Files to Portable Devices.

2. Right-click the item for your iPod, and then choose Options from the shortcut menu to display the Options dialog box. (Alternatively, select the item for your iPod, and then click the Options button.)

3. On the iPod tab, select the Enable FireWire Disk Use check box.

4. Click the OK button to close the Options dialog box and apply the change.

Once you've enabled FireWire mode, you can copy the contact files directly onto your iPod. To do so, follow these steps:

1. Choose Start | My Computer to open a My Computer window that lists the drives on your computer. Your iPod should now appear as a drive with its own drive letter in the Devices with Removable Storage category.

2. Double-click the icon for your iPod to open it in a Windows Explorer window. You'll see it contains the folders Calendars and Contacts. If Windows Explorer is set to display hidden files and folders, you'll see an iPod_Control folder as well.

TIP
To control whether Windows Explorer displays hidden files and folders, choose Tools | Folder Options from a Windows Explorer window. In the Folder Options dialog box, display the View tab, select the Show Hidden Files and Folders option button, and then click the OK button.

3. Open another Windows Explorer window to the folder that contains the vCard files for the contacts you want to put on your iPod.

4. Select the vCard files, drag them to the Contacts folder, and drop them there. Windows copies the vCard files to the Contacts folder.

Because you're copying the contact files directly to the iPod, you don't need to synchronize to make the files appear on your iPod.

View Your Contacts on Your iPod

To view your contacts on your iPod, follow these steps:

1. Choose Extras | Contacts from the main menu to display the Contacts submenu (shown on the left in Figure 8-4).

2. Scroll to the contact you want to view, and then press the Select button. Your iPod displays the contact's information. The right screen in Figure 8-4 shows an example. You may need to scroll down to view all the data about the contact.

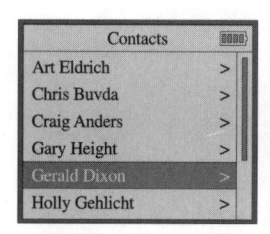

Contacts		Contacts
Art Eldrich >		**Gerald Dixon**
Chris Buvda >		Family Doctor
Craig Anders >		Four Square Physicians
Gary Height >		**Telephone**
Gerald Dixon >		mobile: 408-382-8293
Holly Gehlicht >		home: 510-555-7783
		office: 510-555-1838

FIGURE 8-4 From the Contacts submenu (left), select the contact you want to view, and then press the Select button to display the contact's information (right).

3. To display the previous contact, press the Previous button. To display the next contact, press the Next button.

4. To specify how your iPod should sort your contacts' names and display them on screen, scroll to the Contacts item on the Settings screen, and then press the Select button to display the Contacts screen.

5. To change the sort order, scroll (if necessary) to the Sort item, and then press the Select button to toggle between the First Last setting (for example, *Joe Public*) and the Last, First setting (for example, *Public, Joe*).

6. To change the display format, scroll (if necessary) to the Display item, and then press the Select button to toggle between the First Last setting and the Last, First setting.

Most people find using the same sort order and display format best, but you may prefer otherwise. For example, you might sort by Last, First but display by First Last.

Chapter 9

Put Your Calendars on Your iPod

How to...

- Understand what vCalendar and iCalendar do and what they're for
- Create iCalendar and vCalendar files from your calendars
- Use iSync to put your calendars on your Mac iPod automatically
- Put your calendars on your Mac iPod manually
- Put your calendars on your Windows iPod manually

This chapter shows you how to put your calendars on your iPod so you can keep your appointments handy along with your music.

NOTE *Apple added calendar capabilities to the iPod software in version 1.2. If your iPod doesn't have calendar capabilities, download the iPod 1.2 Updater from the Apple web site.*

If you're using Mac OS X 10.2.2 or later and iCal 1.0.2 or later, you can synchronize your calendars automatically with your iPod by using Apple's free iSync software. If you're using System 9 or Windows, you'll need to transfer calendar files to your iPod manually.

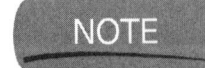

NOTE *If you've worked your way through Chapter 8 (which covers putting your contacts on your iPod), you'll be able to skip quickly through parts of this chapter, as some of the steps involved in putting your calendars on your iPod are similar to those for your contacts.*

What vCalendar and iCalendar Do and What They're For

vCalendar and iCalendar are standards for storing information about calendar events and to-do items and transferring it from one vCalendar/iCalendar-aware application to another. vCalendar and iCalendar are platform independent, so your Mac calendaring application can use the vCalendar and iCalendar formats to schedule meetings or other events with vCalendar/iCalendar-aware applications on other platforms, such as Windows, Linux, or Unix.

Typically, calendaring applications (such as iCal, Microsoft Outlook, or Microsoft Entourage) use vCalendar and iCalendar files in the background to transmit the details of events, appointments, and invitations. Under normal circumstances, you won't need to work directly with vCalendar or iCalendar files yourself. But when you need to put your calendar on an iPod, and you're not using Mac OS X 10.2.2 or later, circumstances become abnormal, and you'll need to create vCalendar files or iCalendar files by exporting them from your calendaring software.

Where vCalendar and iCalendar Came From

As you learned in the previous chapter, Apple, IBM, AT&T, and Siemens set up the versit Consortium to streamline personal data interchange (PDI). As well as vCards, versit worked on the vCalendar format for exchanging electronic calendaring and scheduling information. Then, in December 1996, the Internet Mail Consortium (IMC) took over vCard and vCalendar. The IMC kept the vCard name but changed the name of vCalendar to iCalendar (short for Internet Calendaring and Scheduling Core Object Specification) when they updated vCalendar to version 2.0.

iCalendar files contain more information than vCalendar files, so they're "better" in that sense. Sooner or later, pretty much every calendaring application will likely use iCalendar files, and vCalendar will fall by the wayside. But at this writing, vCalendar is still more widely used than iCalendar and is supported by a wider range of applications.

What's Inside a vCalendar/iCalendar File?

Like vCards, vCalendar files and iCalendar files are text files that contain information tagged to fields. A vCalendar file or iCalendar file can contain the details of one appointment or multiple appointments. vCalendar files use the .vcs extension, while iCalendar files use the .ics extension.

The following is an example of a vCalendar file created by Palm Desktop for Windows. The file contains one event.

```
BEGIN:VCALENDAR
VERSION:1.0
PRODID:PalmDesktop Generated
BEGIN:VEVENT
SUMMARY:Birthday lunch for Ulla at Charlie's
DESCRIPTION:Card, present, champagne
DTSTART:20030612T120000Z
DTEND:20030612T143000Z
```

```
DALARM:20030610T120000Z
END:VEVENT
END:VCALENDAR
```

Here's an example of an iCalendar file created by iCal on Mac OS X. The file contains two events.

```
BEGIN:VCALENDAR
CALSCALE:GREGORIAN
X-WR-TIMEZONE;VALUE=TEXT:USA/San Francisco
METHOD:PUBLISH
PRODID:-//Apple Computer\, Inc//iCal 1.0//EN
X-WR-RELCALID;VALUE=TEXT:FD2F3300-279F-11D7-8BC2-000393DB77DE
X-WR-CALNAME;VALUE=TEXT:Home
VERSION:2.0
BEGIN:VEVENT
SEQUENCE:2
DTSTART;TZID=USA/San Francisco:20030401T114500
DTSTAMP:20030110T125940Z
SUMMARY:Lunch with Peggy
UID:FD2F1A7C-279F-11D7-8BC2-000393DB77DE
DTEND;TZID=USA/San Francisco:20030401T140000
DESCRIPTION:Zza's
END:VEVENT
BEGIN:VEVENT
SEQUENCE:1
DTSTAMP:20030110T125920Z
SUMMARY:Meeting at Jake's
UID:FD2F1CA0-279F-11D7-8BC2-000393DB77DE
DTSTART;TZID=USA/San Francisco:20030401T094500
DURATION:PT1H
DESCRIPTION:Bring project reports\, laptop\, speakers\,
 iPod\n\nDiscuss:
 \n\t* New developments\n\t* Reconstitute project team?\n\t* Bill:
 progress since last meeting
END:VEVENT
END:VCALENDAR
```

Just glance through those examples, then read the following bullet points to get an executive summary of the highlights:

- Each vCalendar file and iCalendar file begins with a BEGIN:VCALENDAR statement and ends with an END:VCALENDAR statement.

- After the BEGIN:VCALENDAR statement comes a VERSION declaration of the vCalendar standard used: 1.0 for the vCalendar file, 2.0 for the iCalendar file.

- The PRODID (product ID) statement identifies the application that created the file: PalmDesktop Generated for the Palm Desktop file, -//Apple Computer\, Inc//iCal 1.0//EN for the iCal file.

- The version 2.0 file contains several other items of general calendaring information: the calendar used (Gregorian), the time zone (USA/San Francisco), the calendar name (Home), and more.

- Each event begins with a BEGIN:VEVENT statement and ends with an END:VEVENT statement.

- The SUMMARY field contains the name assigned to the event in your calendaring application—that is, the text the calendar displays for the event.

- The DESCRIPTION field contains any notes you've entered for the event.

- The DTSTART field and DTEND field give the starting date and time and ending date and time for the event in the format *YYYYMMDDTHHMMSSZ*. For example, 20030612T120000Z represents noon on June 12, 2003. In version 2.0, these fields include TZID (time zone ID) information as well.

Create iCalendar and vCalendar Files from Your Calendars

Because vCalendar files and iCalendar files are text files, in theory you could create them by typing in a text editor if you were desperate enough. But if you keep your appointments in a calendaring application, you should be able to create vCalendar files or iCalendar files much more easily by exporting either your whole calendar or particular events from it.

As you'll see in the following subsections, some calendaring applications provide better features for creating vCalendar and iCalendar files easier than other applications do. But most major calendaring applications let you create files in one format or the other.

NOTE: *If you have Mac OS X 10.2.2 or later and you're using iCal 1.0.2 or later, you don't need to create iCalendar files or vCalendar files directly. Instead, you can synchronize your calendars with your iPod by using iSync. Turn straight to the section "Use iSync to Put Your Calendars on Your iPod Automatically from Mac OS X " later in this chapter.*

Create iCalendar Files and vCalendar Files on the Mac

The following subsections show you how to create iCalendar files and vCalendar files from iCal, Microsoft Entourage, and Palm Desktop for the Mac.

Create iCalendar Files from iCal

Unlike many other applications, iCal doesn't support creating calendars by dragging to the desktop or another location. Instead, to create iCalendar files from iCal, follow these steps:

1. In the Calendars pane, select the calendar you want to export.
2. Choose File | Export to display the iCal: Export dialog box (Figure 9-1).
3. Enter the filename in the Save As text box.
4. Use the Where drop-down list to specify the folder in which to save the calendar. If your iPod is docked and mounted, you could save the file directly to your iPod's Calendars folder.
5. Click the Export button.

Create iCalendar Files from Microsoft Entourage

To create iCalendar files from Microsoft Entourage, select the appointment or event you want to export, drag it to the desktop or the folder in which you want to create the file, and then drop it there.

TIP: *To export all your Entourage information to your iPod, use iPod It. See the section "iPod It" in Chapter 10.*

Create vCalendar Files from Palm Desktop

Palm Desktop provides two ways to create vCalendar files.

To create a vCalendar file that consists of a single Date Book item, select the item, drag it to the desktop or the folder in which you want to create the file, and

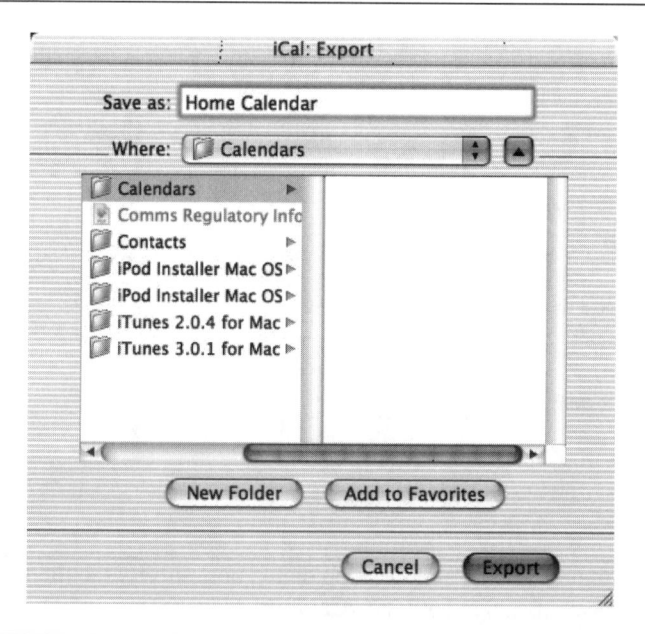

FIGURE 9-1 In the iCal: Export dialog box, specify the filename and the location in which to save it. iCal automatically creates iCalendar files.

then drop it there. If your iPod is docked and mounted as a FireWire disk, you can drag the item directly to a Finder window displaying your iPod's Calendars folder.

But usually you'll want to put more than a single Date Book item on your iPod—you'll want to put the entire contents of your Date Book on it. To do so, export your Date Book to a vCalendar file by following these steps:

1. Choose File | Export to display the Export: Palm Desktop dialog box (Figure 9-2).

2. Use the Save As text box to specify the filename and the Where drop-down list to specify the location under which to save the file. For example, if your iPod is docked and mounted, you could save the file directly to your iPod's Calendars folder.

3. Ignore the Items drop-down list. It appears to offer you the choice of exporting some Date Book items or all of them, but in fact the only choice is All Datebook Items. Similarly, ignore the Columns button, because Palm Desktop makes this unavailable when you select the vCal format.

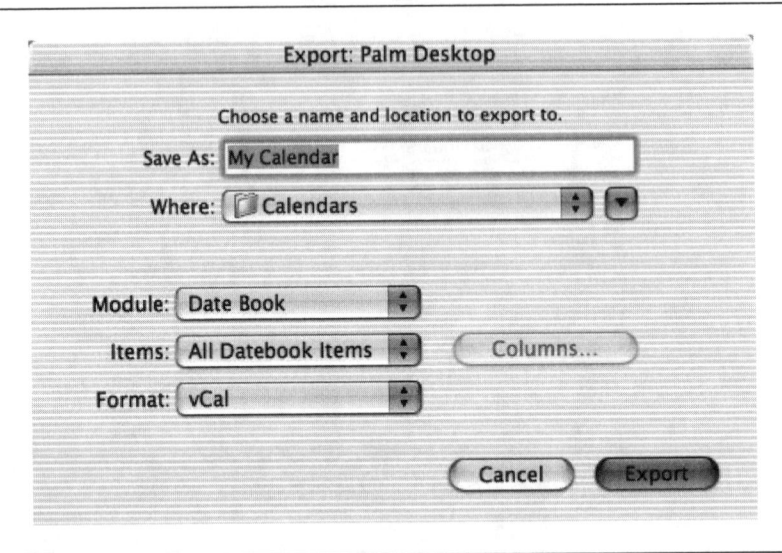

FIGURE 9-2 In the Export: Palm Desktop dialog box, specify the filename and location, and choose the vCal format.

4. In the Format drop-down list, select the vCal item.
5. Click the Export button.

Create vCalendar Files on Windows

This section shows you how to create vCalendar files from Palm Desktop for Windows and both iCalendar and vCalendar files from Microsoft Outlook.

Create vCalendar Files from Palm Desktop

To create a vCalendar file from Palm Desktop, follow these steps:

1. Click the Date button or choose View | Date Book to display your calendar.
2. If your calendar isn't already displayed in Day view or Week view, click the Day button or the Week button to display the calendar in one of those views.
3. Select the event you want to export.
4. Choose File | Export vCal to display the Export As dialog box.

5. In the File Name text box, enter the filename under which you want to save the file.

6. Specify the folder in which to save the file.

7. In the Export Type drop-down list, make sure Palm Desktop has selected the vCal File item.

8. Click the Export button to export the event.

Create vCalendar or iCalendar Files from Microsoft Outlook

To create a vCalendar or iCalendar file from Microsoft Outlook, follow these steps:

1. Click the Calendar button in the Outlook bar to display your calendar if it's not already displayed.

2. Select the appointment from which you want to create the vCalendar file or iCalendar file.

3. Choose File | Save As to display the Save As dialog box.

4. Specify the location in which to save the iCalendar file or vCalendar file.

> **TIP** *If your iPod is currently connected to your computer and has FireWire disk mode enabled, you can save the file directly into your iPod's Calendars folder. Otherwise, save your calendar files to a folder from which you can then copy them to your iPod's Calendars folder once you connect it.*

5. In the Save As type drop-down list, select the iCalendar Format item or the vCalendar Format item, as appropriate.

6. Click the Save button to save the appointment to a file.

Put Your Calendars on Your Mac iPod

As with your contacts, you can put your calendars on your iPod either automatically (by using iSync) or manually. Again, doing so automatically is easier, so I'll show you how to do that first.

> **NOTE** *If you're using System 9, you'll need to use the manual method of transferring calendars. This is because neither iSync nor iCal works with System 9.*

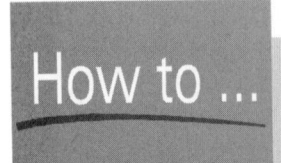

How to ... Export Multiple (or All) Appointments from Outlook

As you'll have seen if you read the previous section, Outlook lets you export only one appointment at a time to a vCalendar or iCalendar file. Unless your calendar is very sparsely populated or you have commendable reserves of patience, exporting your appointments will be a time-consuming and tedious process.

Good news: other people have run into this problem before you, and some of them decided to try to fix it. The following are three of the utilities you can use to export multiple appointments from Outlook:

- iPodSync ($6.99; **iccnet.50megs.com/Products/iPodSync/**) is a powerful shareware application that can export contacts to vCard files and appointment information to iCalendar files. You can choose a wide variety of options, such as whether to synchronize only certain fields, whether to include notes, and even whether to add birthday and anniversary dates to notes. The following illustration shows iPodSync's Calendar page, on which you can choose which appointments to synchronize. You can download a 15-day trial version of iPodSync from the preceding URL. iPodSync works with Outlook XP and Outlook 2000 on Windows XP, Windows 2000, and Windows Me.

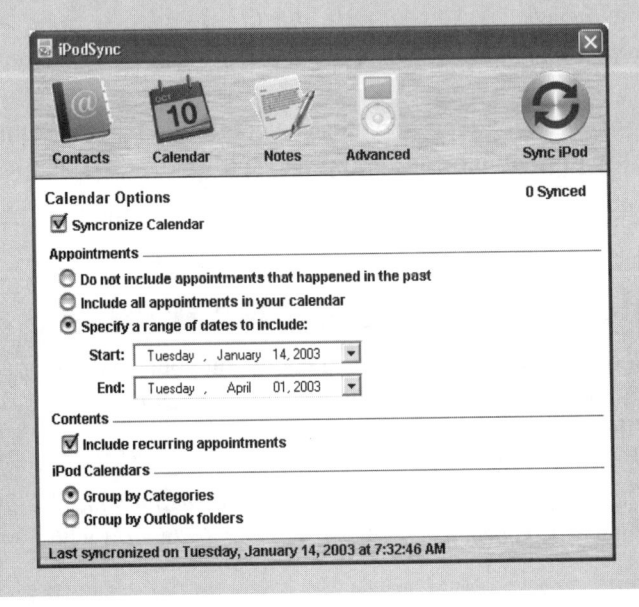

- iAppoint (freeware; **www.xs4all.nl/~hagemans/**) has a simple interface, shown in the following image, that lets you choose the calendar to work with, specify the range of dates from which you want to export appointments, and tell iAppoint where to store the file. (If your iPod is connected and mounted as a FireWire drive, you can save the file directly to the Calendars folder.) The Contacts button displays a window with controls for exporting your contacts. iAppoint is currently at version 0.5 but seems stable.

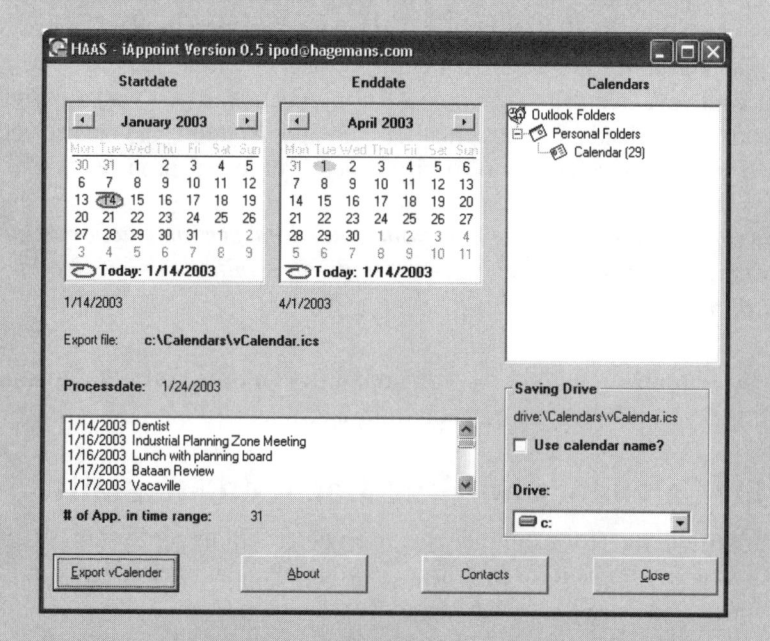

- OutPod (freeware; **www.stoer.de/ipod/ipod_en.htm**) lets you export multiple appointments into a single vCalendar or iCalendar file. OutPod, shown in the following image, also can export multiple contacts at once as well.

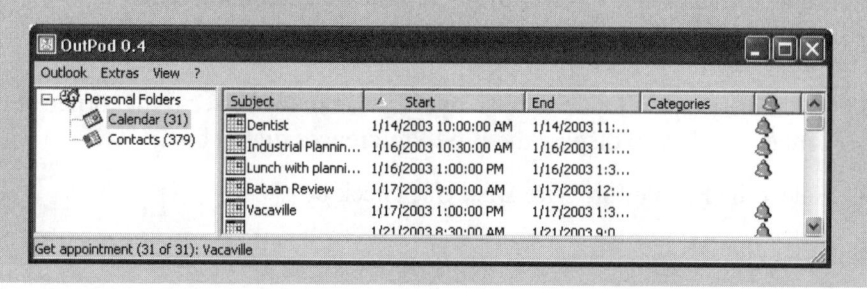

Use iSync to Put Your Calendars on Your iPod Automatically from Mac OS X

If you have Mac OS X 10.2.2 or later, the easiest and quickest way to put your calendars on your iPod is to use iSync. iSync is free, so there's no reason not to try it. If you don't have iSync yet, download it from the iSync area of the Apple web site (**www.apple.com/isync**) and install it.

Introduce your iPod to iSync by following the procedure described in the section "Set iSync to Synchronize with Your iPod" in Chapter 8. Then configure iSync to synchronize with your iPod as described in "Choose Synchronization Options for Your iPod" in Chapter 8. Make sure the Calendars check box is selected. If you want to synchronize all your calendars, select the All option button. If you want to synchronize only some of your calendars, choose the Selected option button, and then select or clear the check boxes for the calendars to specify which ones to synchronize.

> **NOTE** *If you find duplicate events in your calendars, see the sidebar "Did You Know Why Your iPod May Show Duplicate Contacts and Calendar Information?" in Chapter 8.*

After synchronizing with iSync, remember to unmount your iPod manually. (If you forget, you may lose or corrupt your data.)

Put Your Calendars on Your Mac iPod Manually

If you can't use iSync (for example, because you're still using System 9) or you prefer (for whatever reason) to synchronize your calendars manually, you can transfer your contacts to your Mac manually.

To transfer contacts manually, FireWire disk use must be enabled on your iPod. If it's not enabled, follow these steps to enable it:

1. Connect your iPod to your Mac.
2. Launch iTunes if it's not configured to launch automatically.
3. In the Source pane, select the icon for your iPod.
4. Click the Display Options for Player button in the lower-right corner of the iTunes window to display the iPod Preferences dialog box.
5. Select the Enable FireWire Disk Use check box.
6. Click the OK button.

> **NOTE** *The first time you enable FireWire disk mode, iTunes displays a dialog box warning you that using FireWire disk mode requires you to manually unmount the iPod before each disconnect, even when synchronizing songs (instead of being able to have iTunes unmount the iPod automatically). Click the OK button.*

Once you've enabled FireWire mode, you can put the calendar files directly onto your iPod. Connect your iPod to your Mac as usual, then double-click the icon for your iPod to display a Finder window of its contents.

- If you haven't yet created the calendar files, you can simply create them in your iPod's Calendars folder. For example, select the Calendars folder in the iCal: Export dialog box or the Export: Palm Desktop dialog box. Or drag an event from Microsoft Entourage or Palm Desktop directly to the Calendars folder.

- Alternatively, export your contacts to vCalendar files or iCalendar files in another folder, and then copy them from there to your iPod's Calendars folder. Using this method, you can export the contacts when your iPod isn't connected to your Mac.

After adding your calendar files to your iPod, eject your iPod in any of these ways: select it and press COMMAND-E, issue an Eject command from the File menu or the shortcut menu, or drag the iPod icon to the Trash.

Put Your Calendars on Your Windows iPod

At this writing, there's neither a version of iSync for Windows nor an equivalent that can automatically put your calendar information on your Windows iPod. So you have to do things the hard way.

First, enable your iPod for use as a hard disk. Doing so causes Windows XP to assign a letter to it. If you've already done so (for example, so you could put your contacts on your iPod, as described in the previous chapter), you're ready to load your calendar files. If not, follow these steps:

1. In the MUSICMATCH Portables Plus window, right-click the item for your iPod, and then choose Options from the shortcut menu to display the Options dialog box. (Alternatively, select the item for your iPod, and then click the Options button.)

2. On the iPod tab, select the Enable FireWire Disk Use check box.

3. Click the OK button to close the Options dialog box and apply the change.

Once you've enabled FireWire mode, and Windows has assigned a letter to your iPod's hard disk, you can copy the calendar files directly onto your iPod. To do so, follow these steps:

1. Choose Start | My Computer to open a My Computer window that lists the drives on your computer. Your iPod should now appear as a drive with its own drive letter in the Devices with Removable Storage category.

2. Double-click the icon for your iPod to open it in a Windows Explorer window. You'll see it contains the folders Calendars and Contacts. If Windows Explorer is set to display hidden files and folders, you'll see an iPod_Control folder as well.

TIP *To control whether or not Windows Explorer displays hidden files and folders, choose Tools | Folder Options from a Windows Explorer window. In the Folder Options dialog box, display the View tab, select the Show Hidden Files and Folders option button, and then click the OK button.*

3. Open another Windows Explorer window to the folder that contains the iCalendar files for the events you want to put onto your iPod.

4. Select the iCalendar files, drag them to the Calendars folder, and drop them there. Windows copies the iCalendar files to the Calendars folder.

Because you're copying the calendar files directly to the iPod, you don't need to synchronize to make the files appear on your iPod.

View Your Calendar on Your iPod

To view your calendar on your iPod, follow these steps:

1. Choose Extras | Calendar to display the Calendars screen.

CHAPTER 9: Put Your Calendars on Your iPod 237

2. If you maintain multiple calendars, the first Calendars screen contains a list of available calendars, as shown in the following image. Scroll down to the calendar you want, and then press the Select button.

```
        Calendars
All                      >
Home                     >
Other                    >
```

3. If you have only one calendar, your iPod automatically displays the calendar for the current month (the first time you access the calendar) or the last month you accessed (thereafter). The following illustration shows the calendar.

```
         May 2003
Sun Mon Tue Wed Thu Fri Sat
                 1   2   3
 4   5   6   7   8   9  10
11  12  13  14  15  16  17
18  19  20  21  22  23  24
25  26  27  28  29  30  31
```

4. Scroll backward or forward to the day you're interested in.

- To access the next month or the previous month, press the Next button or the Previous button, respectively.

- Alternatively, if you're happier scrolling, you can scroll back past the beginning of the month currently displayed to access the previous month or scroll forward past the end of the month currently displayed to access the next month.

5. Press the Select button to display your schedule for that day. The following illustration shows a sample schedule for a day.

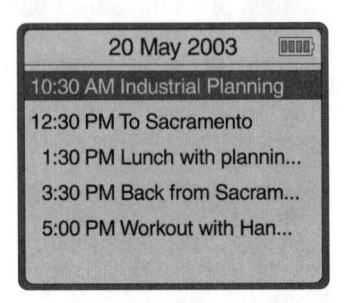

```
┌─────────────────────────────┐
│   20 May 2003      [████]   │
│ 10:30 AM Industrial Planning│
│ 12:30 PM To Sacramento      │
│  1:30 PM Lunch with plannin…│
│  3:30 PM Back from Sacram…  │
│  5:00 PM Workout with Han…  │
└─────────────────────────────┘
```

6. To view the details for an appointment, scroll to it, and then press the Select button. The following illustration shows a sample appointment. You may need to scroll down to see all the data for the appointment. From an appointment, you can press the Next button to display the next appointment or the Previous button to display the previous appointment.

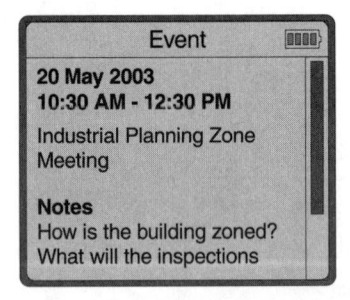

```
┌─────────────────────────────┐
│         Event      [████]   │
│ 20 May 2003                 │
│ 10:30 AM - 12:30 PM         │
│ Industrial Planning Zone    │
│ Meeting                     │
│                             │
│ Notes                       │
│ How is the building zoned?  │
│ What will the inspections   │
└─────────────────────────────┘
```

7. Once you've accessed a day, you can press the Next button to access the next day or the Previous button to access the previous day.

Chapter 10
Put Other Information on Your iPod

How to...

- Understand the limitations to putting text on your iPod
- Put text on your Mac iPod
- Put text on your Windows iPod

This chapter discusses how to store other information on your iPod so you can display it on the screen. That essentially means text information—at this writing, the iPod screen can display only text and its system graphics (such as the battery symbols and the Apple symbol).

By using your iPod as a hard drive (as discussed in Chapter 12), you can store any type of file on your iPod. But unless the file is in a text format your iPod's software can handle, you won't be able to display the file on the iPod's interface—you'll be able to work with the file only when you've connected your iPod to your computer.

NOTE *The new iPods include a Notes feature that lets you easily put text files of any size on your iPod. See "Read Notes on Your iPod" in Chapter 16 for coverage of this feature.*

Limitations to Putting Information on Your iPod

If you have an iPod and you're reading this book, you probably have a pretty favorable impression of the iPod—and so do I. But before you start putting huge chunks of text onto your iPod, it's a good idea to be clear about the limitations of the iPod as a text-display device.

The main limitation is obvious: the screen is small enough to make even the screens on low-resolution Palm devices seem spacious. Your iPod can display a heading plus seven or eight lines of text of up to about 30 characters each—enough to be useful for compact information such as recipes, memos, driving directions, or even winsome love poetry, but so small as to make reading any lengthy document more of a chore than a joy. You can see why Apple hasn't succumbed to any temptation it may have felt to incorporate an e-book reader in the iPod.

Still, if you've been reading Tolstoy on your mobile phone's display on the bus, reading text on your iPod might seem—or even be—a significant step up in the world. Besides, the iPod has enough battery power to let you read for a while in the dark;

you can play music at the same time; and putting the text on your iPod can save you from needing to tote multiple devices.

The second and less obvious limitation is that each text file you want to put on your iPod needs to go into a contact record for you to be able to display it on your iPod. Each contact record is limited to 2,000 characters—enough for about 300 average-length words. So if a file is longer than this, it needs to be divided among two or more contact records. (As you'll see later in this chapter, some applications get around this limitation.)

What Text Can You Put on Your iPod?

With the right utilities, you can put on your iPod any text file you have on your computer. That text could be anything from a parts list to a novel, from a thesis to a thesaurus.

As you'll see in the following sections, apart from text files, utility designers have concentrated on types of text that are widely useful and can be easily downloaded from sources on the Internet—for example, the following:

- **News headlines** Various iPod utilities can download news headlines from news sites; most of these utilities let you choose the sites (other utilities are limited to one site).

NOTE *Many people find news headlines more or less useless when their accompanying stories aren't available. However, you may find the headlines useful as a means of determining which sites you need to visit and which stories you want to read. But this still pales in comparison to AvantGo on Palms and Pocket PCs—AvantGo delivers both the headlines and the full stories.*

- **Weather reports** Various iPod utilities can download weather reports from online sites. You specify the city (or ZIP code) and the type of weather reports (for example, today's forecast or a five-day report), and the utility downloads the relevant information.

- **Stock quotes** Several utilities can download stock quotes. You specify the stock symbols and (in some cases) choose the frequency of updates.

- **Lyrics** Some utilities can look up the lyrics to songs you specify.

- **Horoscopes** Some utilities can download horoscopes.

All the items are created as contacts, so your Contacts folder on your iPod can get jammed. But apart from your needing to scroll further than usual, accessing the information is easy.

Mac Utilities for Putting Information on Your iPod

This section discusses some applications for putting information on your iPod from the Mac, starting with the most useful.

iSpeakIt (Mac OS X)

iSpeakIt ($8.95; **www.ispeak-it.com**) is a versatile utility that lets you load news headlines and summaries (from Google), driving directions, weather forecasts, and text files onto your iPod. No stock quotes or horoscopes, but otherwise, so far, par for the course. But whereas most file-loading utilities can load only text files and rich-text files, iSpeakIt can also load PDFs (Portable Document Format—Adobe Acrobat files), HTML files, Word documents, and AppleWorks documents. To load PDFs, you must have the full version of Acrobat installed on your Mac, not just the free Acrobat Reader application. To load Word documents, you need to have Word installed. To load AppleWorks documents—okay, you saw it coming—you have to have AppleWorks installed.

Loading Word, PDF, HTML, and AppleWorks documents is great, but what do those have to do with speaking, you ask? Little or nothing. The name comes from iSpeakIt's other capability—it lets you have your Mac's text-to-speech capability read text files to MP3 files and load them into iTunes (and thus onto your iPod). You can have iSpeakIt make MP3 files of the news, driving directions, and weather forecasts it downloads. You can also load the text of Word, AppleWorks, and PDF documents if you have the relevant applications, as mentioned earlier.

If you have severe sight problems, then Mac's text-to-speech capability can be a great boon. But for most people, the computerized delivery lies somewhere between a curiosity and a perversion. You'll know if you want to make MP3 files from text files—and if you do, iSpeakIt is the application to use to do so.

Figure 10-1 shows iSpeakIt wrangling some text.

iPod It (Mac OS X)

iPod It ($14.95; **www.ipod-it.com**) is a utility that enables you to copy contacts, notes, tasks, e-mail, and calendar information from Microsoft Entourage to your iPod. If you use Entourage, iPod It is a great way of taking the information with you.

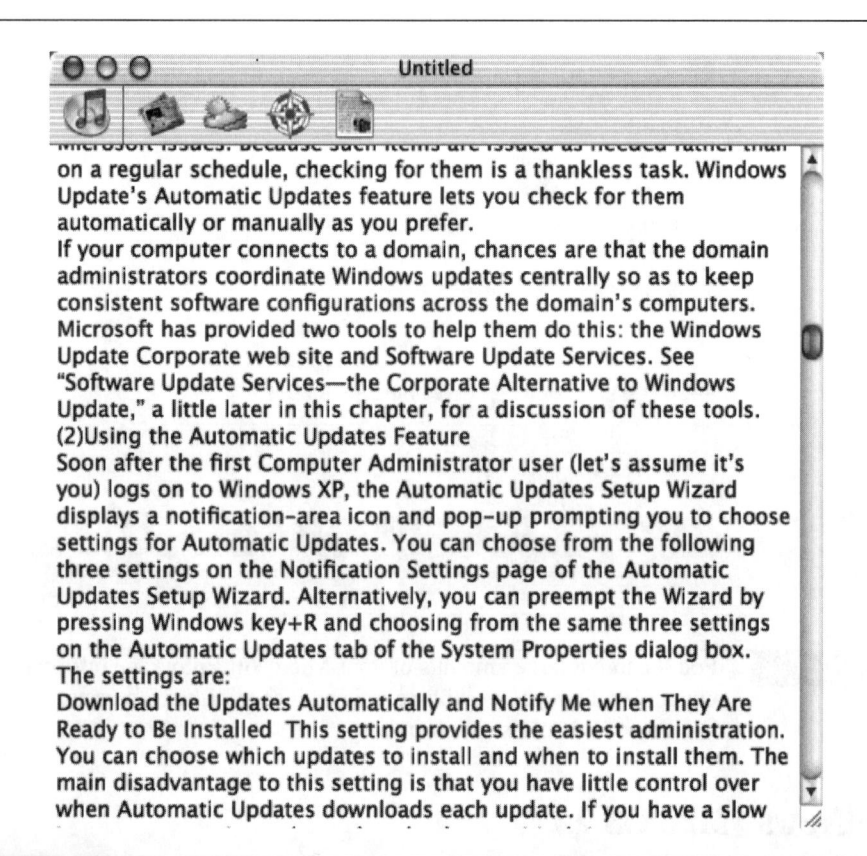

CHAPTER 10: Put Other Information on Your iPod   **243**

FIGURE 10-1   iSpeakIt can create MP3 files from document text by harnessing the text-to-speech capability built into Mac OS X.

iPod It also supports downloading news headlines from Google, weather forecasts, and directions, and even subscribing to published iCal calendars. iPod It's Clean feature lets you quickly remove specific categories of information—events, contacts, mail, notes, tasks, directions, weather, vCard files, and iCal files—from your iPod. This can save you time managing your iPod's non-music content.

iPod It (shown in Figure 10-2) requires Mac OS X 10.1 or higher and Entourage X.

FIGURE 10-2 iPod It can put large amounts of your Microsoft Entourage information on your iPod—together with news headlines, weather forecasts, directions, and published calendars.

PodNews (Mac OS X)

PodNews from Cliché Software ($9.00; **www.clichesw.com**) can put a variety of text information on your iPod: headlines from a wide range of news sites, weather information for cities of your choice, stock quotes for companies you specify, lyrics to songs, notes, and driving directions. The notes you have to create yourself; everything else is downloaded.

To use PodNews 3 (the current version), your Mac must be running Mac OS X 10.2, and your iPod must have iPod software version 1.2 or later. You also need to have enabled FireWire disk mode on your iPod. (See the section "Enable FireWire Disk Mode on the Mac" in Chapter 12 for instructions.)

PodNews uses a straightforward interface with multiple sheets you access via the button bar. The Sync sheet, shown on the left in Figure 10-3, contains options for choosing whether or not to launch PodNews when you connect your iPod, whether or not to sync automatically, and whether or not to unmount your iPod after synchronization. The Notes sheet, shown on the right in Figure 10-3, lets you create text notes.

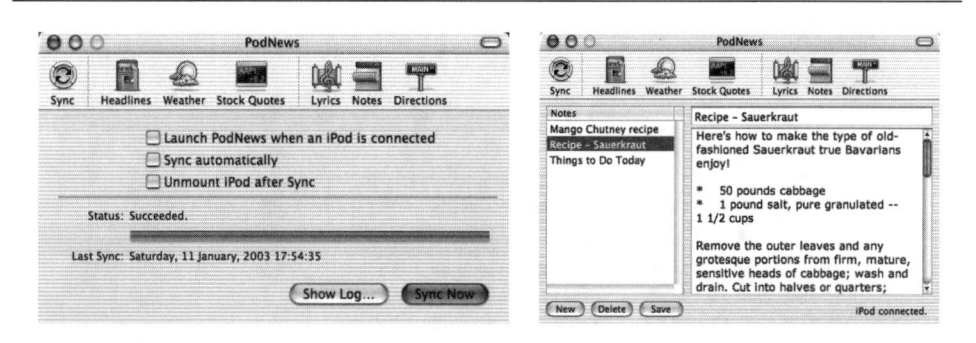

FIGURE 10-3 PodNews lets you put news, weather, stock quotes, lyrics, notes, and driving directions on your iPod.

NOTE *When choosing which items to add to your iPod with PodNews and when to synchronize them, bear in mind that synchronizing real-time information such as weather or stock quotes may take a little while over a slow connection (such as a modem connection). Your Internet connection is the limitation, not the FireWire connection to your iPod.*

Pod2Go (Mac OS X)

Pod2Go (free; **www.kainjow.com/pod2go/website**) lets you put news, weather, stock quotes, text files, and even horoscopes on your iPod. Once you've specified the news sources, cities for the weather reports, stock symbols, and sign of the zodiac, Pod2Go downloads the information automatically when you sync.

Pod2Go requires Mac OS X 10.2.2 or higher and iPod Software 1.2 or later. Figure 10-4 shows the Text tab of Pod2Go, which lets you add text files or rich-text files to your iPod via drag-and-drop or by clicking the Add button. Pod2Go neatly gets around the 2,000-character limit of contact records, so each text file appears as a single item on your iPod.

iTeXpod (System 9 and Classic)

iTeXpod (freeware; **dgeoffroy.free.fr/index.html/**) is a tiny utility for converting text files to vCard files. iTeXpod gets around the 1,000-character limitation for vCard files, so it's a great way to get longer text files onto your iPod.

The following illustration shows iTeXpod working on converting a text file to a vCard. iTeXpod puts a page number every seven lines in the resulting file to help

How to Do Everything with Your iPod

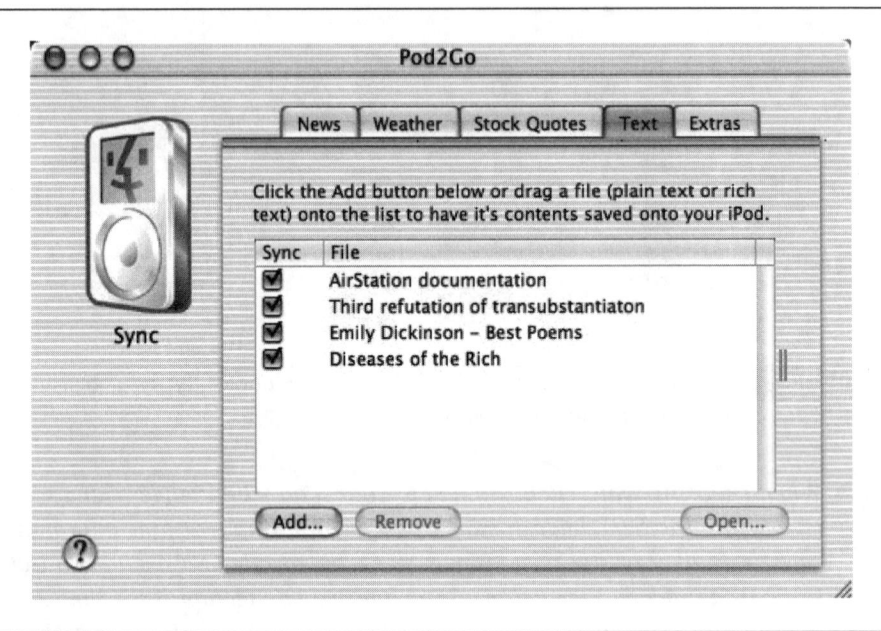

FIGURE 10-4 Pod2Go can put news, weather, stock quotes, text files, and horoscopes on your iPod.

you keep track of where you are in long texts. Some users like this feature; others find it bothersome.

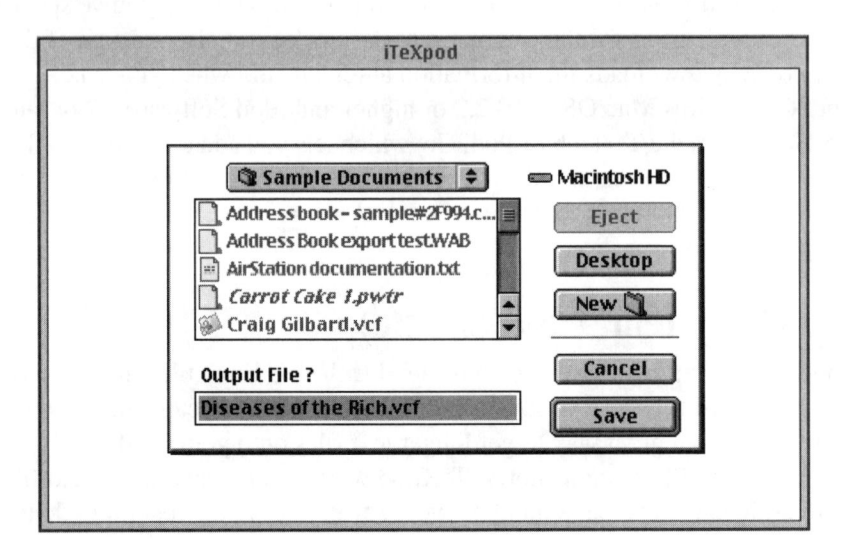

Text2iPodX (Mac OS X)

Text2iPodX (freeware; **homepage.mac.com/applelover/text2ipodx/text2ipodx .html**) is a utility that lets you put a whole text file into a single contact on the iPod.

The Text2iPodX developer has decided to go minimalist on the user interface. To use Text2iPodX, you drag a text file and drop it on the Text2iPodX icon. You'll then see a dialog box like that shown on the left in the following illustration. Choose whether to save the file on your hard disk or on your iPod. If you choose the hard disk, you then use the Choose a Folder dialog box to specify the location. If you choose your iPod (as you most likely will do), you see a dialog box such as that shown on the right in the following illustration.

iPodMemo (Mac OS X and System 9)

iPodMemo (freeware; various sites including **www.versiontracker.com**) is a text editor with which you can create memos of up to 1,000 characters. At this writing, iPodMemo is at an early stage of development, but future versions should include substantially more features.

iPodMemo works on both Mac OS X and System 9. Figure 10-5 shows iPodMemo running on Mac OS X. You need to have at least iPod Software 1.1—but if you don't have even 1.1 these days, you're doing yourself no favors.

PodWriter (Mac OS X)

PodWriter (freeware; **www.steigerworld.com/doug/podwriter.php**) is a small text-editor that you can use to put text files on your iPod. At this writing, PodWriter is limited to 1,000 characters in a file, so it pales in comparison to some of the utilities discussed so far in this chapter. But PodWriter is free, has a straightforward interface (Figure 10-6), and works well, so you may want to consider it, particularly for creating memos and other short notes.

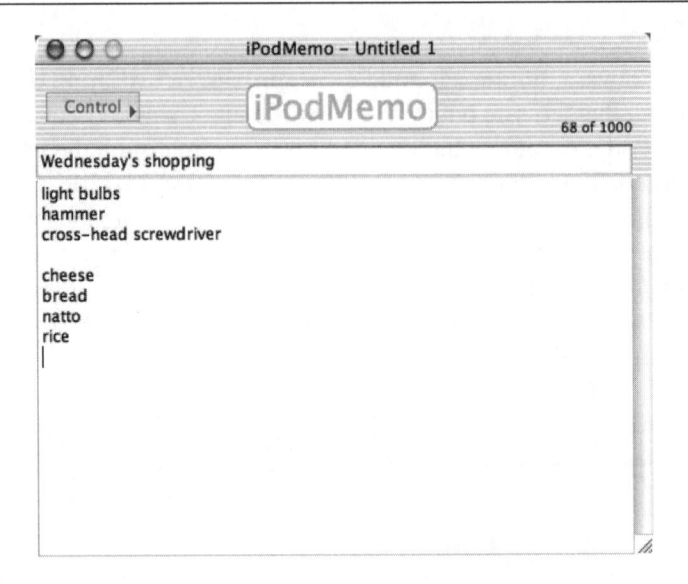

FIGURE 10-5 iPodMemo is a basic editor for creating short notes.

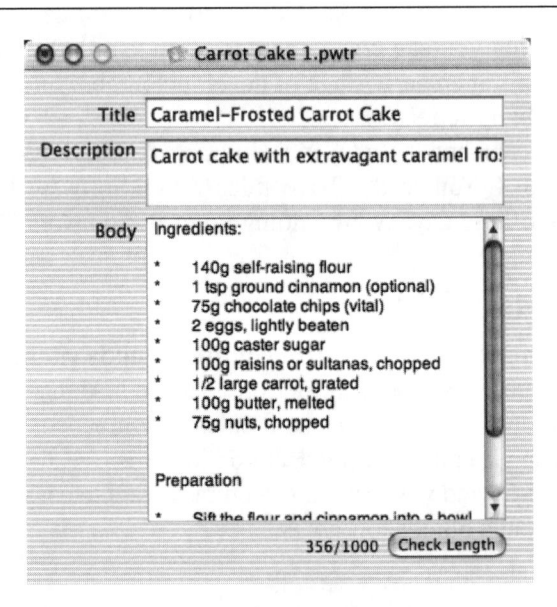

FIGURE 10-6 PodWriter provides a straightforward interface for creating short text notes on your iPod.

A Windows Utility for Putting (Some) Text on Your iPod

This section discusses a Windows utility for putting text on your iPod. Only one? Yes—because Windows iPods have been around for a far shorter time than Mac iPods, not many utilities have been developed. Another reason is that most Windows-based scripting and programming languages are much more difficult than AppleScript, the scripting language in which many Mac utilities are written.

EphPod

EphPod (freeware; **www.ephpod.com**) is a mature utility originally designed, in the days before Windows iPods were released, to enable Windows users to use Mac-formatted iPods. EphPod still performs that function (for which you need to have the non-freeware application MacOpener installed on your PC), but it also works without MacOpener for Windows-formatted iPods.

Among its other features, which I'll discuss in the section titled "EphPod" toward the end of Chapter 14, EphPod lets you download news feeds.

> **TIP** *Two great places for finding utilities such as those discussed in this chapter are VersionTracker.com (**www.versiontracker.com**) and MacUpdate (**www.macupdate.com**). You'll also find utilities at Apple's Mac OS X Downloads page (**www.apple.com/macosx/downloads**).*

Part III

iPod Care, Advanced Topics, and Troubleshooting

Chapter 11

Keep Your iPod in Good Working Shape

How to...

- Understand what your iPod consists of
- Get the maximum life possible from your iPod's battery
- Avoid doing things that make your iPod unhappy
- Keep your iPod's operating system up-to-date
- Carry and store your iPod safely
- Clean your iPod

This chapter covers how to keep your iPod in good working shape. It starts by discussing what your iPod contains, then tells you how to maximize battery life. From there, this chapter walks you through things that make your iPod unhappy; how to keep your iPod's operating system up-to-date; and how to carry, store, and clean your iPod.

What You Might Want to Know about Your iPod's Internals

Unless your background is in consumer electronics, you probably don't need to know much about what's inside your iPod to appreciate the massive amount of songs it can store and the audio quality it delivers. But you'll find it helps to have a general idea of what your iPod contains and how it's constructed, because this knowledge can help you use your iPod more effectively and either head off or troubleshoot problems. (See Chapter 15 for a full discussion of troubleshooting your iPod.)

CAUTION *Your iPod isn't user-upgradeable—in fact, it's designed to be opened only by trained technicians. If you're not such a technician, don't try to open your iPod: you're unlikely to achieve anything positive, and if your iPod is still under warranty, you'll void the warranty.*

Your iPod is based around a hard drive that takes up the bulk of the space inside the case. The hard drive is similar to those used in the smaller portable PCs. Some of the remaining space is occupied by a rechargeable battery that provides up to ten hours of playback. The length of time the battery provides depends on how you use it (more on this in the following section). Like all rechargeable batteries, the iPod's battery gradually loses its capacity—but if your music collection grows,

CHAPTER 11: Keep Your iPod in Good Working Shape

or if you find the iPod's non-music capabilities useful, you'll probably want to upgrade to a higher-capacity iPod in a couple of years anyway.

> **TIP** *Apple doesn't replace iPod batteries. In theory, if you could find a replacement battery, you might be able to replace the battery yourself. But because opening your iPod's case voids your warranty, it's probably not a good idea even to try.*

Your iPod includes a 32MB memory chip that's used for running the iPod's operating system and for caching music from the hard drive. The cache reads up to 20 minutes of data ahead from the hard drive for two purposes:

- Once the cache has read the data, your iPod plays back the music from the cache rather than from the hard disk. This lets the hard disk *spin down* (stop running) until it's needed again. Because hard disks consume relatively large amounts of power, the caching spares the battery on your iPod and prolongs battery life.

> **NOTE** *After the hard disk has spun down, it takes a second or so to spin back up—so when you suddenly change the music during a playlist, there's a small delay while your iPod spins the disk up and then accesses the song you've demanded. If you listen closely (put your ear to your iPod), you can hear the disk spin up (there's a whee sound) and search (you'll hear the heads clicking).*

- The hard disk can skip if you jiggle or shake your iPod hard enough. If your iPod was playing audio back directly from the hard disk, such skipping would interrupt audio playback, much like bumping the needle on a turntable (or bumping a CD player, if you've tried that). But because the memory chip is solid state and has no moving parts, it's immune to skipping.

The length of time for which the caching provides audio depends on the compression ratio you're using and whether you're playing a playlist (or album) or individual songs. If you're playing a list of songs, your iPod can cache as many of the upcoming songs as it has available memory. But when you switch to another song or playlist, your iPod has to start caching once again. This caching involves spinning the hard disk up again and reading from it, which consumes battery power.

Your iPod's skip protection is impressive compared to some other hard disk-based digital audio players, some of which read directly from disk the whole time (and thus run down the battery very quickly). Compared to many portable CD players, your iPod's skip protection is amazing. But compared to solid-state players, the iPod's skip protection looks more like a brave and mostly successful attempt to catch up. Of course, the iPod blows the doors off all solid-state players for capacity, so these players aren't exactly direct competition for each other.

Maximize Your iPod's Battery Life

The section "Recharge Your iPod's Battery to Keep the Songs Coming" in Chapter 1 ran you through the basics of recharging your iPod's battery. But if you're reading this chapter, you probably want to know how the battery works, what you can do to shoehorn in as much power as possible, and how you can squeeze out as much battery life as possible.

Your iPod's battery is a lithium polymer that's rated for 500 or more charging cycles. (A *charging cycle* is a full discharge—running the battery all the way down till it has no charge left—followed by a full charge.) Lithium polymer batteries have no memory effect, so you don't need to discharge them fully before recharging them. That means you can recharge your iPod at any time that's convenient.

NOTE *Memory effect, since you ask, is a phenomenon that occurs with older battery technologies. If you don't fully discharge a battery based on such a technology, when you start charging the battery, it may figure that it was fully discharged at that point after all. In other words, the battery resets its zero-charge level to the level at which you started charging it. By doing so, it squanders that part of its capacity that's below the new zero-charge level, and so reduces the amount of power it can provide.*

If you recharge your iPod's battery every other day, 500 charges should last you the best part of three years. If you recharge your iPod's battery less frequently than that, there's a good chance the battery will outlast the hard drive—or both will last until you scrape together the dough for the terabyte vidPod that Apple will probably be selling in five years' time.

Don't Let the Battery Discharge Fully

To get the most life out of your battery, don't let it discharge fully. However little you use your iPod, recharge it fully at least once every three weeks to prevent the battery from going flat. This means if you go on vacation for a month, you should take your iPod with you and recharge it during that time. (But you were going to take your iPod with you on your vacation anyway, weren't you?)

Reduce Demands on the Battery

To get the longest possible playback time from your iPod, reduce the demand on the battery as much as possible. Here are three ways to do so:

- Play your music by album or by playlist rather than hopping from one track to another. Remember that your iPod can cache ahead on an album or playlist to minimize the time the hard disk is spinning. But when you ask your iPod to produce another track it hasn't cached, it has to spin up the hard disk and access the song.

- Use MP3 files on your iPod rather than WAV files or AIFF files (on a Mac iPod). Because they're uncompressed and therefore much bigger than MP3 files, WAVs and AIFFs prevent your iPod from using its cache effectively, so the hard disk has to work much harder. This chews through battery life.

- Minimize your use of the backlight. It's anything but a searchlight, but even so, it uses up battery life you'd probably rather spend on playing songs.

Understand What Makes Your iPod Unhappy

The following three subsections discuss items that are likely to make your iPod unhappy: unexpected disconnections, fire and water (discussed together), and punishment. None of these should come exactly as a surprise, and you should be able to avoid all of them most of the time.

Disconnecting Your iPod at the Wrong Time

If you've ever performed a successful synchronization with your iPod, you'll know the drill for disconnecting your iPod from its FireWire cable: Wait until your iPod has stopped displaying the *Do not disconnect* message and is showing the *OK to disconnect* message. Then you can safely unplug the FireWire cable. But not before.

The main danger in disconnecting your iPod from the FireWire cable at the wrong time is that you may interrupt data transfer and thus corrupt one or more files. Typically, you'll know when data is being transferred, because iTunes and MUSICMATCH Jukebox Plus display status information and progress messages as they update your iPod and transfer data to it. Similarly, if you're using your iPod in FireWire disk mode, you'll know when you're copying or moving data to it, because you'll have instigated the copy or move operation.

In theory, you could scramble the data on your iPod's hard drive badly enough that you'd need to restore your iPod before you could use it. A restoration would lose any data on the iPod that you didn't have on your computer—so a badly timed disconnection could cost you valuable data.

In practice, however, disconnecting your iPod during data transfer is likely to corrupt only those files actually being transferred at the moment you break the connection. If those files are valuable, and if you're moving them to your iPod rather than copying them, corrupting them could cause you problems. But in most cases, you won't need to restore your iPod.

Disconnecting the FireWire cable without warning when no data is being transferred should do nothing worse than annoy your computer. If you disconnect your iPod from your Mac at the wrong time, your Mac displays a warning dialog box (shown in the following image) telling you that you should have ejected it properly and that data may have been lost or damaged. Bow your head in contrition, and then click the OK button.

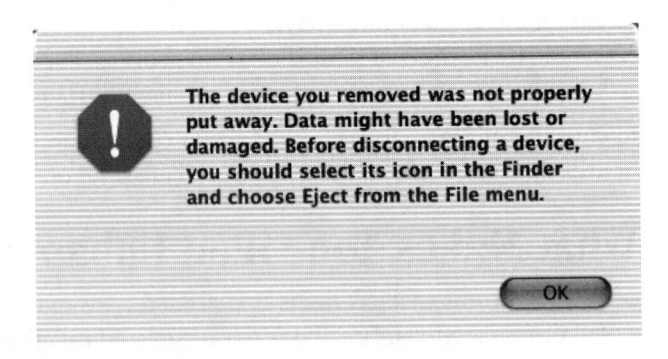

> The device you removed was not properly put away. Data might have been lost or damaged. Before disconnecting a device, you should select its icon in the Finder and choose Eject from the File menu.
>
> OK

MUSICMATCH Jukebox Plus handles unexpected disconnections with aplomb. It simply registers that the iPod has gone and removes its entry from the Attached Portable Devices list in the MUSICMATCH Portables Plus window.

Your iPod Doesn't Like Fire or Water

Apple reckons iPods work at temperatures of up to 158 degrees Fahrenheit (70 degrees Celsius). You're unlikely to voluntarily endure temperatures this high only in a sauna or steam room, so scratch any plans you may have had for using your iPod in such locations. The more likely danger is that you'll leave your iPod running in a confined space, such as the glove box of a car in the full sun, and that it might reach a temperature such as this. If you live in sunny climes, take your iPod with you when you get out of the car.

CAUTION *If your iPod gets much too hot or much too cold, don't use it. Give your iPod time to return to a more normal temperature before trying to find out if it still works.*

Your iPod isn't waterproof, so don't expect to use it for swimming or in the bath. You can get various water-resistant cases for iPods, but they're all intended to keep out rain and splashes rather than to go deep-sea diving with you.

Your iPod Isn't Indestructible

Apple has built the iPod to be tough, so it'll survive an impressive amount of rough handling. Macworld columnist Chris Breen has written about how he eventually destroyed an iPod by dropping it from a bicycle traveling at 30 mph. (This was after the iPod survived a 25-mph drop from the bicycle, a drop while jogging, and a stationary drop from waist height—each of which caused some damage to the iPod and probably weakened it.)

I haven't destroyed an iPod for your edification (or mine), but have no doubt I could do so if I needed to. Running the iPod over with a Hummer, hitting it squarely with an eight-pound sledgehammer, or playing Sinatra uninterrupted for a couple of days should do the trick. In the meantime, my two iPods have traveled the equivalent of halfway around the world and taken a few falls that would have damaged me— so I reckon they're doing pretty well.

Keep Your iPod's Operating System Up-to-Date

To get the best performance from your iPod, it's a good idea to keep its operating system up-to-date. To do so, follow the instructions in the next two sections to update your Mac iPod or your Windows iPod, respectively.

Update Your Mac iPod

To update your Mac iPod on Mac OS X, follow these steps:

1. Download the latest version of the Updater from the Apple Software Downloads web site (**www.apple.com/swupdates/**).

2. Double-click the disk-image file to mount the disk image.

3. Double-click the disk image to display its contents in a Finder window.

4. Double-click the iPod Software Updater folder to display its contents in the Finder window.

5. Double-click the iPod.pkg file to open it. The Updater displays the Authenticate dialog box (shown in the following image). Enter your password in the Password or Phrase text box, and then click the OK

button. If you entered the correct password, the Updater displays the Install iPod window.

6. Click the Continue button to navigate your way through the Introduction screen, the Read Me screen, the Software License Agreement screen and its Agree/Disagree dialog box, until you reach the Select a Destination screen, shown in the following image:

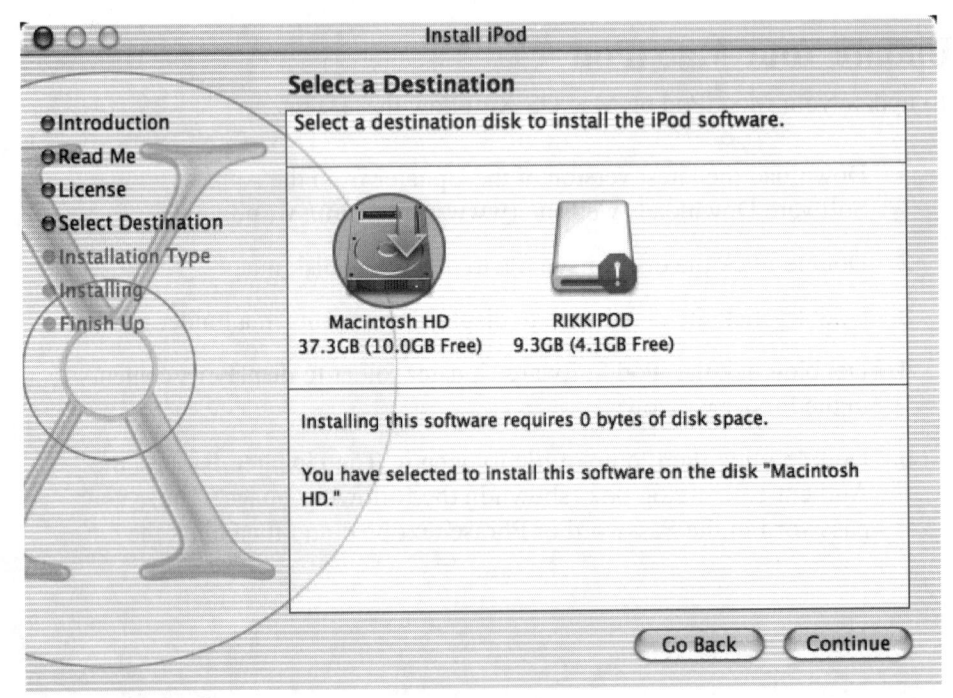

CHAPTER 11: Keep Your iPod in Good Working Shape   **261**

7. Select the disk on which you want to install the Updater software. If your iPod is connected, as in the illustration, the Select a Destination screen will show a red octagon bearing a white exclamation point on the icon for your iPod to indicate you can't install the Updater on it.

8. Click the Continue button to display the Installation Type screen. The Updater offers only an Easy Install.

9. Click the Install button or the Upgrade button to perform the installation. The iPod Software Updater displays the Install button the first time you install an iPod Software Updater package on your computer. For subsequent updates, the iPod Software Updater displays the Upgrade button.

10. When the installation is complete, click the Close button to close the Install iPod window.

11. Connect your iPod to your Mac via the FireWire cable.

12. Open a Finder window to Applications:Utilities:iPod Software, and then double-click the iPod Software Updater icon to display an iPod Software Updater window such as that shown in the following image:

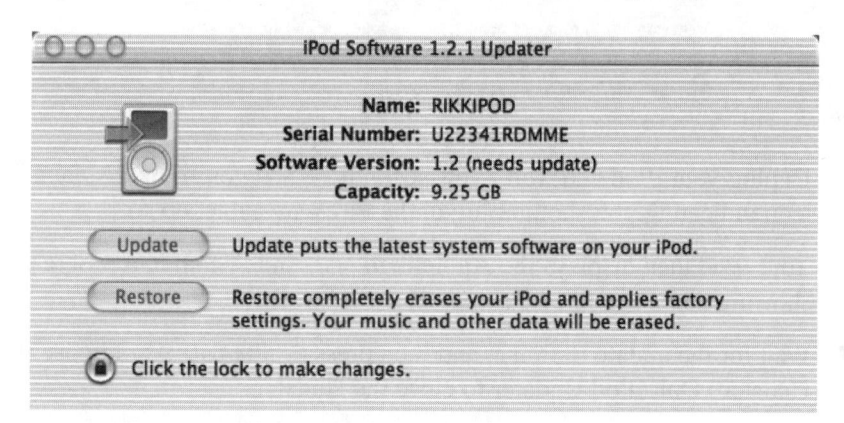

```
                   iPod Software 1.2.1 Updater
                  Name:  RIKKIPOD
          Serial Number:  U22341RDMME
       Software Version:  1.2 (needs update)
              Capacity:  9.25 GB

   ( Update )    Update puts the latest system software on your iPod.
   ( Restore )   Restore completely erases your iPod and applies factory
                 settings. Your music and other data will be erased.

   🔒  Click the lock to make changes.
```

13. If the lower-left corner of the Updater window contains a lock icon and the text "Click the lock to make changes," click the lock icon to display the Authenticate dialog box. Enter your password in the Password or Phrase text box, and then click the OK button. If you entered the correct password, the Updater returns you to the Update window and enables the Update button (if you can install an updated version of the iPod software) and the Restore button, as shown in the following image:

262 How to Do Everything with Your iPod

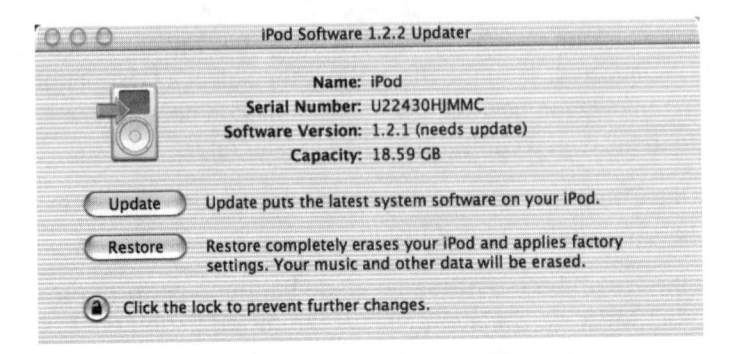

14. Click the Update button. The Updater updates your iPod's software and displays a message (shown in the following image) telling you to unplug and then replug your iPod so it can complete the update process:

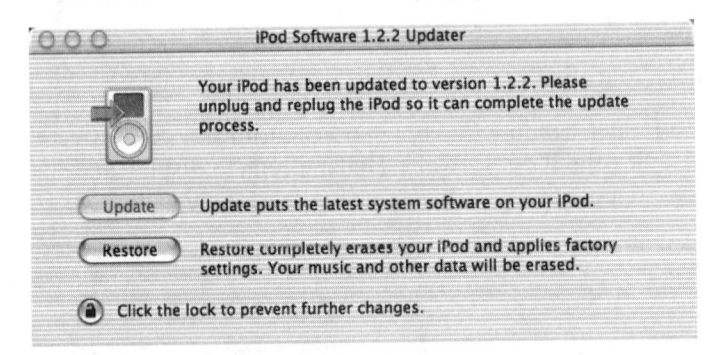

15. Unplug your iPod and wait a few seconds. When your iPod displays an icon indicating you should plug in the FireWire cable, do so.

16. Your iPod then displays the Apple logo and, underneath it, a progress bar showing the progress of the update.

17. Wait for the update to finish, and then press COMMAND-Q or choose iPod Updater | Quit iPod Updater to close the Updater.

18. Your iPod should then appear on your desktop. If it doesn't, you may need to reset it by holding down the Menu button and the Play/Pause button for several seconds.

19. iTunes displays the iTunes Setup Assistant page shown in the following illustration:

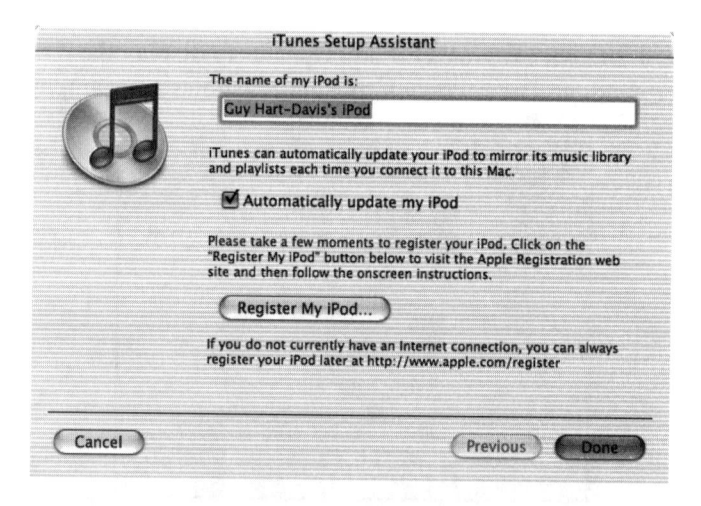

CHAPTER 11: Keep Your iPod in Good Working Shape   263

20. Enter the name for your iPod in the text box. Select or clear the Automatically Update My iPod check box as appropriate. Then click the Done button. iTunes then synchronizes your iPod with the music library if it's set for automatic synchronization.

Update Your Windows iPod

To update your Windows iPod on Windows XP, follow these steps:

1. Download the latest version of the Updater from the Apple Software Downloads web site (**www.apple.com/swupdates/**).

2. Double-click the distribution file to launch the setup routine.

3. In the Choose Setup Language dialog box, choose the language to use for the installation.

4. Navigate through the Welcome screen and the License Agreement screen. The InstallShield Wizard then installs the iPod Software Updater.

5. On the InstallShield Wizard Complete screen, choose whether to let the wizard automatically restart your computer now or to restart it yourself later. (For example, you might choose to restart manually later because you were working in another application or downloading a file.) Then click the Finish button.

6. After Windows restarts, connect your iPod to your computer. Close MUSICMATCH Jukebox Plus if it launches automatically.

264 How to Do Everything with Your iPod

7. Choose Start | All Programs | iPod | Updater to display the iPod Software Updater window. The following illustration shows an example:

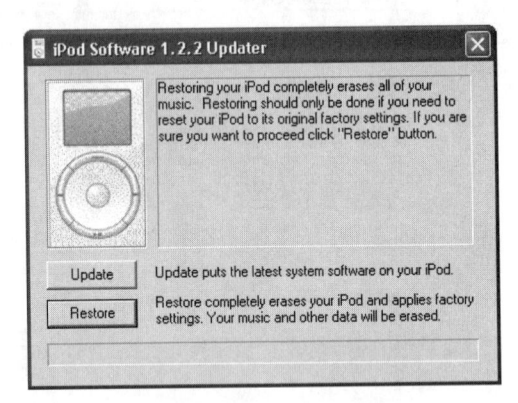

8. Click the Update button. The iPod Software Updater updates your iPod's software, and then prompts you to disconnect your iPod to allow the firmware to be reflashed, as shown in the following illustration:

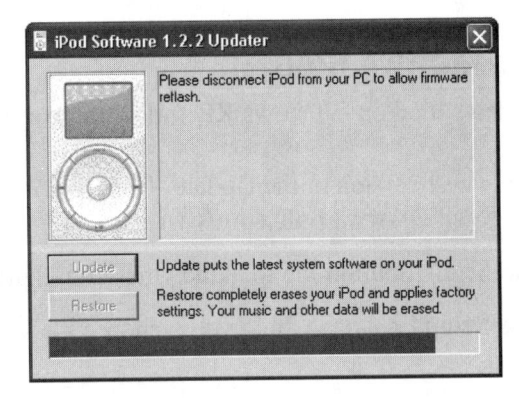

9. Unplug the FireWire cable from your iPod for a few seconds. When your iPod displays a FireWire icon, plug the cable back in.

10. Wait while the iPod Software Updater completes the update process. The iPod Software Updater displays a progress bar across the bottom of the window as it works.

11. The iPod Software Updater window then displays an Update Complete message, as shown in the following illustration:

CHAPTER 11: Keep Your iPod in Good Working Shape

12. Click the Close button (the × button) in the upper-right corner of the iPod Software Updater window to close the iPod Software Updater. MUSICMATCH Portables Plus launches automatically and activates your iPod.

How to... How to Restore Your Windows iPod to an Earlier Version of the iPod Software

If you install an update that produces an effect you don't like, you can run an earlier Updater again to restore your Windows iPod to the previous version of the iPod software—provided that you have a copy of the earlier Updater.

Each Updater you install automatically overwrites its predecessor, presumably to spare you the indignity of installing an older version of the iPod software by mistake. Similarly, Apple tends to remove older updaters from the Apple Software Downloads web site to encourage people to download the latest versions. For this reason, it's a good idea to keep copies of the Updaters you download.

Apple has designed the Mac Updaters to refuse to overwrite their successors, so you can't use this method to restore a Mac iPod to an earlier version of the software.

Carry and Store Your iPod Safely

Carrying and storing your iPod safely is largely a matter of common sense.

- Use a case to protect your iPod from scratches, dings, and falls. The 10GB and 20GB iPods include a sturdy case that offers good protection. You can buy a wide variety of other cases, from svelte-and-stretchy little numbers designed to hug your body during vigorous exercise to armored cases apparently intended to survive industrial accidents. See the section "Cases" in Chapter 13 for more information on cases.

- If your iPod spends time on your desk or another surface open to children, animals, or moving objects, consider investing in a stand to keep it in place. A stand should also make your iPod easier to control with one hand. For example, if you patch your iPod into your stereo, you might use a stand to keep it upright so you could push its buttons with one hand. Some stands can also supply power via your iPod's FireWire cable. See the section "Stands" in Chapter 13 for more information on stands.

Clean Your iPod

To keep your iPod looking its best, you'll probably need to clean it from time to time. Before cleaning your iPod, unplug it from the FireWire cable and close the cover of the FireWire port to help avoid getting liquid in the port.

Various people recommend different cleaning products for cleaning iPods. You'll find various recommendations on the Web—but unless you're sure the people know what they're talking about, proceed with great care. In particular, avoid any abrasive cleaner that may mar your iPod's acrylic faceplate or its polished back and sides.

Unless you've dipped your iPod in anything very unpleasant, you'll do best to start with Apple's recommendation: simply dampen a soft, lint-free cloth (such as an eye-glass cloth or a camera lens cloth) and wipe your iPod gently with it.

But if you've scratched your iPod, you may need to resort to heavier duty cleaners. I've read good reports of the Novus plastic polishes (**www.oldphones.com/novus.html**) and the Nu-Life polishing kit (which includes a cleaner/polish solution and a scratch remover/surface restorer solution and is available from various sources). I can't vouch for either.

Chapter 12

Use Your iPod as a Hard Drive

How to...

- Decide whether or not to use your iPod as a hard drive
- Enable FireWire disk mode on your Mac iPod
- Enable FireWire disk mode on your Windows iPod
- Transfer files to and from your iPod
- Start up your Mac from your iPod
- Back up your iPod so you don't lose your music or data
- Optimize your iPod's hard disk to improve performance

Apple sells the iPod primarily as a portable music player—and, as you know by know, it's arguably the best portable music player around. But (as you also know by now), the iPod is essentially an external FireWire hard drive with sophisticated audio features. This chapter shows you how to use your iPod as a hard drive for backup and portable storage. If your computer is a Mac, you can even boot from your iPod for security purposes or to recover from disaster.

NOTE *One hard-drive feature this chapter doesn't show you is how to transfer song files from your iPod's music database onto your computer. The section "Transfer Music Files from Your iPod to Your Computer" in Chapter 14 covers this subject.*

Why Use Your iPod as a Hard Drive?

If all you want from your iPod is huge amounts of music to go, you may never want to use your iPod as a hard drive. Even so, briefly consider why you might want to use your iPod as a hard drive:

- Your iPod provides a great combination of portability and high capacity. You can get smaller portable-storage devices (for example, CompactFlash drives, Smart Media cards, and Memory Sticks), but they're expensive and have much lower capacities.
- You can take all your documents with you. For example, you could take home that large PowerPoint presentation you need to get ready for tomorrow.

- You can use your iPod for backup. If you keep your vital documents down to a size you can easily fit on your iPod (and still have plenty of room left for music), you can quickly back up the documents and take the backup with you wherever you go.

- You can use your iPod for security. By keeping your documents on your iPod rather than on your computer, and by keeping your iPod with you, you can prevent other people from accessing your documents. If your computer is a Mac (and if it's the right kind of Mac—more on this later), you can even boot your Mac from your iPod, thus preventing anyone else from using your computer at all.

The disadvantages to using your iPod as a hard disk are straightforward:

- Whatever space you use on your iPod for storing non-music files isn't available for music.

- If you lose or break your iPod, any files stored only on it will be gone forever.

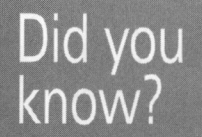

Did you know? Did You Know iPods Have Been Used to Steal Software?

iPods have even been used to steal software from stores. For example, enterprising thieves have plugged iPods into Macs in computer stores such as CompUSA and copied application software (such as Microsoft Office) from the Mac onto the iPod.

This approach usually works only on the Mac. This is because software installations on Windows not only typically place files in multiple folders (as opposed to a single folder on the Mac) but also rely on system files installed by the installation routine.

Of course, stealing software like this is horribly illegal. But you can use the same technique legally to move an application from one Mac to another if you don't have a means of connecting them. For example, if you scratch your Microsoft Office CD so it won't work in a CD drive anymore, and you need to migrate to a new Mac, you might need an alternative means of transferring Office from your old Mac to your new one. (Yes, this is a stretch. But such emergencies do occur.) More likely, you might copy your Microsoft Office installation to your iPod so you could restore it easily if the copy on your hard drive became corrupted when you were on the road without your Office CD.

Enable FireWire Disk Mode

To use your iPod as a hard drive, you need to enable FireWire disk mode. In FireWire disk mode, your computer uses your iPod as an external hard disk. You can copy to your iPod any files and folders that will fit on it.

NOTE *You can copy song files and playlists to your iPod in FireWire disk mode, but you won't be able to play them on the iPod. This is because when you copy the files, their information isn't added to the iPod's database the way it's added by iTunes, MUSICMATCH Jukebox Plus, and other applications (for example, EphPod or XPlay) designed to work with the iPod. This way your iPod's interface doesn't know the files are there, and you can't play them.*

From the point of view of the computer, a FireWire hard disk works in essentially the same way as any other disk. The differences are that the disk is external and that it may draw power along the FireWire cable rather than being powered itself.

When you use your iPod as a FireWire disk, it draws power from the computer provided by the FireWire controller and FireWire cable supply power. If the controller doesn't supply power (for example, because it's a PC Card controller and can't muster the required wattage) or if the cable can't transmit the power (for example, because it's a four-pin cable rather than a six-pin cable), your iPod has to rely on its battery power.

CAUTION *Using your iPod as a FireWire disk with a controller or cable that can't supply power may run the battery down quickly. Bear in mind that your iPod can't use its caching capabilities when you use it as a FireWire disk. (Caching works only for playlists and albums, when your iPod knows which files are needed next and so can read them into the cache.) If your iPod isn't receiving power, check the battery status periodically to make sure your iPod doesn't suddenly run out of power.*

Enable FireWire Disk Mode on the Mac

To enable FireWire disk mode on the Mac, follow these steps:

1. Connect your iPod to your Mac via the FireWire cable.
2. Launch iTunes (for example, click the iTunes icon in the dock).
3. In the Source pane, select the icon for your iPod.

CHAPTER 12: Use Your iPod as a Hard Drive 271

4. Click the Display Options for Player button in the lower-right corner of the iTunes window to display the iPod Preferences dialog box.

5. Select the Enable FireWire Disk Use check box.

6. Click the OK button. iTunes displays the warning dialog box shown in the following image, telling you that using FireWire disk mode requires you to manually unmount the iPod before each disconnect, even when synchronizing songs (instead of being able to have iTunes unmount the iPod automatically).

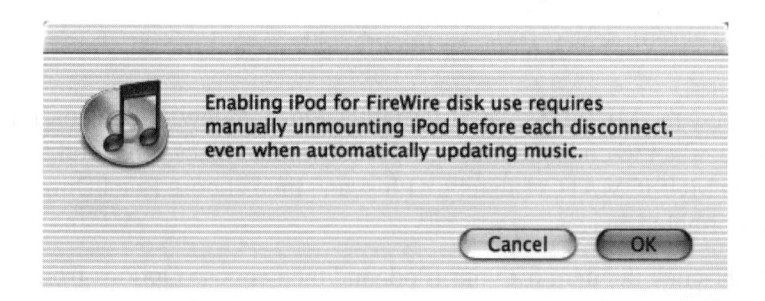

> Enabling iPod for FireWire disk use requires manually unmounting iPod before each disconnect, even when automatically updating music.
>
> Cancel   OK

7. Click the OK button if you can live with this limitation. Otherwise, click the Cancel button to cancel your use of FireWire disk mode.

8. If you clicked the OK button in the warning dialog box, click the OK button again in the iPod Preferences dialog box to close the dialog box. If you clicked the Cancel button in the warning dialog box, click the Cancel button in the iPod Preferences dialog box to dismiss the dialog box.

Once you've enabled FireWire disk mode on your Mac iPod, you'll need to unmount your iPod manually after synchronizing your music library or transferring files to or from your iPod. To unmount your iPod, take any of the following actions:

- In the Source pane in iTunes, select the icon for your iPod, and then click the Eject iPod button in the lower-right corner of the iTunes window.

- Select the icon for your iPod on the desktop, and then issue an Eject command from the File menu or the shortcut menu.

- Drag the desktop icon for your iPod to the trash.

When your iPod displays the *OK to disconnect* message, you can safely disconnect it.

Enable FireWire Disk Mode on the PC

To use your iPod as a FireWire hard disk on the PC, you need to enable FireWire disk mode—at least in theory. In practice, you may find you don't need to enable FireWire disk mode to use your iPod with your PC. On the PCs I've used (with Windows XP, Windows 2000 Professional, and Windows Me), Windows Explorer always assigns the iPod a drive letter even when it's *not* in FireWire disk mode. But you may find your iPod behaves differently with your PC—or you may choose to explicitly enable FireWire disk mode in any case. (Enabling FireWire disk mode certainly won't do any harm.)

To enable FireWire disk mode on the PC, follow these steps:

1. Display the MUSICMATCH Portables Plus window. If you don't have this window set to open automatically when you connect your iPod to your PC, open MUSICMATCH Jukebox Plus, and then choose File | Download Files to Portable Devices.

2. Right-click the item for your iPod, and then choose Options from the shortcut menu to display the Options dialog box. (Alternatively, select the item for your iPod, and then click the Options button.)

3. On the iPod tab, select the Enable FireWire Disk Use check box.

4. Click the OK button to close the Options dialog box and apply the change.

Once you've enabled FireWire disk mode, your iPod appears to Windows Explorer as a removable hard drive. Windows Explorer automatically assigns a drive letter to the drive, so you can access it as you would any other drive connected to your computer.

If you read through the Mac section on enabling FireWire disk mode, you may wonder if, when your Windows iPod is in FireWire disk mode, you need to eject it manually before disconnecting it from your computer. You do—but you usually need to eject a Windows iPod anyway even when it's not in FireWire disk mode, so there's nothing extra to worry about.

CHAPTER 12: Use Your iPod as a Hard Drive 273

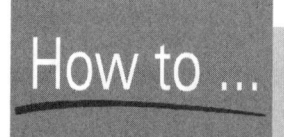

How to ... How to Force FireWire Disk Mode

If your FireWire port is unpowered (or underpowered), you may need to force your iPod to enter FireWire mode. To do so, follow these steps:

1. Connect your iPod to the FireWire cable.
2. Hold down the Menu button and the Play button on your iPod for about five seconds to reboot your iPod.
3. When your iPod displays the Apple logo, hold down the Previous button and Next button briefly. Your iPod sends the computer an electronic prod that forces the computer to recognize it.

Transfer Files to and from Your iPod

When your iPod is in FireWire disk mode, you can transfer files to it by using the Finder (on the Mac), Windows Explorer (on Windows), or another file-management application of your choice. (You can transfer files by using the command prompt if you so choose.)

CAUTION *If your iPod appears in the My Computer window named Removable Drive, and Windows Explorer claims the disk isn't formatted, chances are you've connected a Mac-formatted iPod to your PC. Windows Explorer can't read the HFS Plus disk format that Mac iPods use, so the iPod appears to be unformatted. (HFS Plus is one of the disk formats Mac OS X can use. HFS Plus is also called the Mac OS Extended format.)*

You can create and delete folders on your iPod as you would any other drive. Don't mess with the iPod's system folders, such as the Calendars folder, the Contacts folder, and the iPod_Control folder.

NOTE *As mentioned earlier, don't transfer music files to your iPod by using file-management software if you want to be able to play the files on your iPod. Unless you transfer the files by using iTunes, MUSICMATCH Portables Plus, or another application designed to access the iPod's music database, the details about the files won't be added to the iPod. You won't be able to play those files on your iPod because their data hasn't been added to its database of contents.*

The exception to transferring files from your iPod is transferring song files that you've put on your iPod by using iTunes, MUSICMATCH Jukebox Plus, or another application that can access the iPod's music database. The section "Transfer Music Files from Your iPod to Your Computer" in Chapter 14 shows you how to do this.

Start Up Your Mac from Your iPod

You can start up (*boot*) your Mac from your iPod by turning your iPod into a bootable FireWire disk. This capability can be useful for backup—you can start your Mac from your iPod even when your Mac hard disk has gone south—but you may also want to use it for security: by making your iPod the only bootable disk for your Mac, you can prevent other people from booting your Mac when your iPod isn't present. If you carry your iPod with you, you can extend that restriction to any time you're not using your Mac.

CAUTION *Apple doesn't support using your iPod as a bootable FireWire disk. So if you can't make this work, you don't get to complain to Apple.*

You can make your iPod bootable in either of two ways: by installing Mac OS X (or System 9) on it directly, or by cloning an existing installation of Mac OS X (or System 9). The following subsections discuss these options.

NOTE *You can't start up your PC from your iPod. And for this capability to work with the Mac, the Mac needs to have a built-in FireWire port. As you've read earlier in this book, most recent Macs do. But if you have (for example) a PowerBook G3 without a FireWire port, you won't be able to boot it from a bootable FireWire disk via a PC Card FireWire card.*

Install Mac OS X (or System 9) Directly on Your iPod

The most straightforward way to make your iPod bootable is to install Mac OS X (or System 9) on it directly. To do so, you run the installation routine from your

Mac OS X (or System 9) installation CD exactly as you would do to install the operating system on your Mac, except that you specify your iPod, rather than your Mac's hard disk, as the destination disk for the install.

Installing the operating system directly works fine if you have a version of the operating system that fits on a single disc—either a single CD or a single DVD. In practice, this means that you can install Mac OS X versions before 10.2 (for example, 10.1.*x*) or System 9 from a CD, because those operating systems fit on a single CD. But to install Mac OS X 10.2 or later, you need to have a DVD (and a DVD drive), because 10.2 takes up two CDs. The problem with having two CDs is that installing to the iPod tends to fail when you switch to the second CD.

To install a Mac operating system on your iPod, follow these steps:

1. Make sure your iPod has plenty of free space. You'll need between 1GB and 2GB for Mac OS X 10.2, depending on which files you choose to install. For System 9, you'll need a more modest amount of space—from 250MB to 500MB, depending on the options you choose.

2. Configure your iPod for use as a FireWire disk and connect it to your Mac.

3. Insert the Mac OS CD in your CD drive or DVD in your DVD drive.

4. Restart your Mac.

5. When you hear the system sound, hold down C to boot from the CD drive or DVD drive.

NOTE *Alternatively, if you're installing Mac OS X, double-click the Install Mac OS X application to display the Install Mac OS X window, and then click the Restart button. That way, you don't need to hold down C when your Mac restarts.*

6. Follow through the installation procedure until you reach the Select Destination screen.

7. Specify your iPod as the destination for the installation.

NOTE *The Mac OS X installation routine offers you the option of erasing your hard drive and formatting it using either Mac OS Extended (HFS Plus) or Unix File System. Don't use this option. Erasing the disk will do more harm than good.*

8. When installing Mac OS X, it's a good idea to customize the installation to reduce the amount of space it takes up. On the Installation Type screen, click the Customize button. On the resulting Custom Install screen, clear the check boxes for the items you don't want to install.

- You must install the Base System item and the Essential System Software item, so the Installer doesn't let you clear their check boxes.

- You'll know if you need the BSD Subsystem files (130MB), the Additional Printer Drivers files (nearly 500MB in all), the Fonts for Additional Languages (3MB), the Additional Asian Fonts (155MB), and the Localized Files (240MB altogether). BSD is the abbreviation for the Berkeley Software Distribution, a family of Unix versions. You need the BSD Subsystem files to use features such as sharing files via File Transfer Protocol (FTP), share your Internet connection, or use Telnet or Secure Shell (SSH). You'll probably need these features on your Mac, but you may not want them on your iPod.

- You might choose to include only some of the Additional Printer Drivers and only some of the Localized Files to keep down the amount of space needed.

9. Click the Install button to start the installation.

10. When the installation routine for Mac OS X displays the message that your system will restart in 30 seconds, unplug your iPod. Otherwise, your Mac will try to boot from it, even though it isn't configured for booting. Go to the section "Designate Your iPod as the Startup Disk," later in this chapter, and tell your Mac you want it to boot from your iPod.

Clone an Existing Operating System onto Your iPod

The second way to make your iPod bootable is to clone an existing operating system onto it. This operating system can be either Mac OS X or System 9, provided that the cloning tool you use supports cloning that operating system.

One cloning tool that supports both Mac OS X and System 9 is Carbon Copy Cloner (CCC), a $5 shareware utility that you can download from **www.bombich .com/software/ccc.html**. If your Mac is running Mac OS X, you may need to install the BSD Tools for CCC before you can install Carbon Copy Cloner. (Again, BSD is the abbreviation for the Berkeley Software Distribution, a family of Unix versions.) The Carbon Copy Cloner installation routine warns you if you need to install the BSD Tools for CCC and helps you to download them, so you won't have any difficulty with that step. Figure 12-1 shows the Cloning Console of Carbon Copy Cloner.

Before using the cloning utility, set up the operating system as you want it to be cloned. That might mean stripping down the operating system to include only the items you want on your iPod so as not to waste its precious disk space with unnecessary files. Or it might mean including a full set of troubleshooting tools and applications so you can use your iPod to troubleshoot any problems you run into.

Designate Your iPod as the Startup Disk

After installing the operating system on your iPod (or cloning the operating system onto it), you need to designate your iPod as the startup disk to make your Mac boot from it.

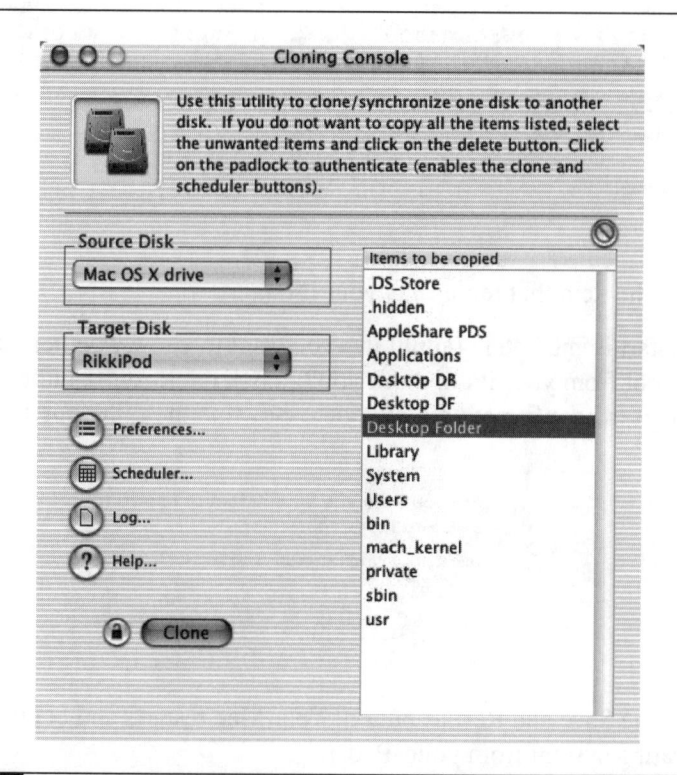

FIGURE 12-1 You can use a cloning utility such as Carbon Copy Cloner to clone an existing operating system installation onto your iPod.

How to Do Everything with Your iPod

To designate your iPod as the startup disk, follow these steps:

1. Choose Apple | System Preferences to display the System Preferences window.

2. Click the Startup Disk icon in the System area to display the Startup Disk sheet (shown in the following image):

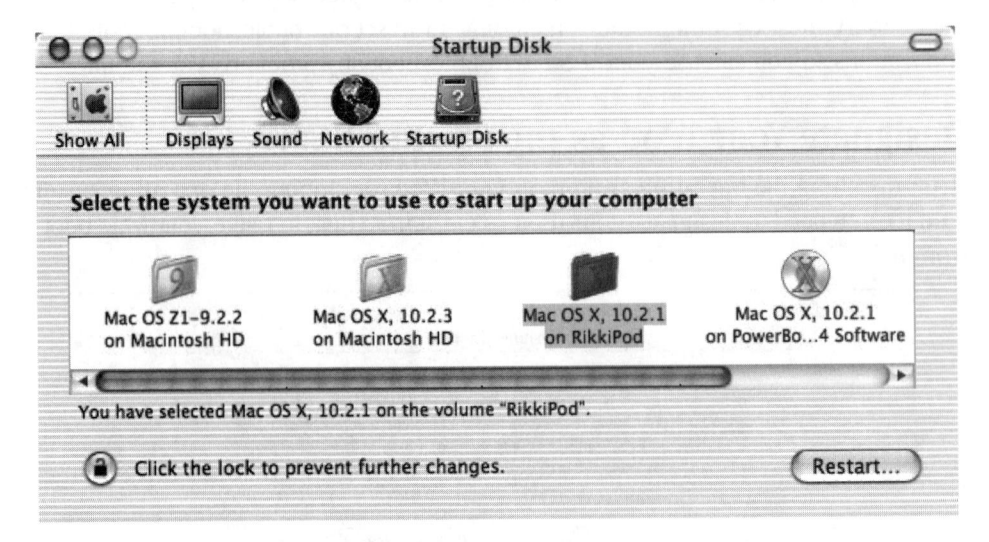

3. Select the item that represents your iPod.

4. To restart immediately (admit it—you want to know whether your Mac will boot from your iPod, don't you?), click the Restart button. Mac OS X displays the confirmation dialog box shown in the following image:

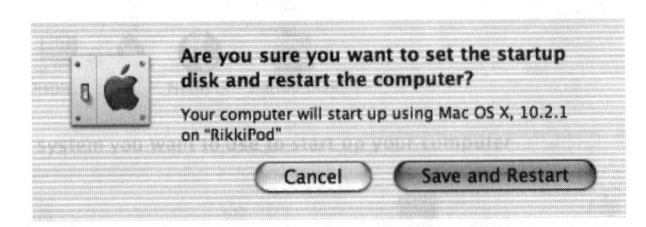

5. Click the Save and Restart button. Your Mac restarts and boots the operating system from your iPod.

If you don't want to restart your Mac immediately, close the Startup Disk sheet. Then restart your Mac as normal whenever you want to.

How to... How to Display All Available Startup Disks

If your Mac fails to boot from your iPod, you may have a nasty moment—or your Mac may give up on looking for your iPod and decide to boot from its hard disk anyway. If it *doesn't* boot at all, and you find yourself looking forlornly at a blank screen, take the following steps:

1. Press CONTROL-COMMAND-POWER to force a restart.
2. When your Mac plays the system sound, hold down OPTION to display a graphical screen of the available startup disks.
3. Click the disk from which you want to start the computer.
4. Click the → button to start your Mac using that startup disk.

To stop your Mac from booting from your iPod, use the Startup Disk sheet of System Preferences to designate the appropriate operating system on your hard disk as the startup disk.

Back Up Your iPod so You Don't Lose Your Music or Data

If you synchronize your complete music library with your iPod, and perhaps load your contacts and some calendar information on your iPod as well, you shouldn't need to worry about backing it up. That's because your computer contains all the data that's on your iPod. (Your iPod essentially represents a backup of part of your hard disk.) So if you lose your iPod, or it stops functioning, you won't lose any data you don't have on your computer.

If your computer's hard disk goes south, you might need to recover your music library, contacts, and calendar data from your iPod onto another computer or a new hard disk. You can transfer contacts and calendar data by mounting your iPod in FireWire mode and using the Finder or Windows Explorer (as appropriate) to access the contents of the Contacts folder and the Calendars folder. For instructions on recovering song files from your iPod, see the section "Transfer Music Files from Your iPod to Your Computer" in Chapter 14.

So, normally, your iPod will be the vulnerable member of the tag team. But if you store files directly on your iPod, you should back them up to your computer to make sure you don't lose them if your iPod vanishes or its hard disk gives up the ghost.

To back up files, either use a file-management utility (for example, the Finder or Windows Explorer) to simply copy the files or folders to your computer, or use custom backup software to create a more formal backup. For example, you might use the Backup Utility included with Windows XP (Start | All Programs | Accessories | System Tools | Backup) to back up your Windows iPod. On Mac OS X, you might use the Backup application to back up your files to your .Mac iDisk (which you can access via any Internet connection); you might use iDisk Utility to mount your .Mac iDisk via WebDAV (a protocol for transferring information to web servers); you might use the Finder's Go | Connect to Server command to connect to your .Mac iDisk via Apple File Protocol, which usually gives faster transfer speeds than WebDAV; or you might prefer a commercial alternative such as Dantz Retrospect (**www.dantz.com**).

Optimize Your iPod's Hard Disk to Improve Performance

If you've been using a Windows computer for a while, you'll know you need to optimize your computer's hard disk every now and again to keep it performing well. This is because each file of any size beyond the smallest files occupies multiple clusters of the sectors into which a hard disk is divided. If the clusters are close to one another, the hard disk's read head can read the clusters without needing to travel back and forth unnecessarily across the disk. But if the clusters are spread out all over the disk, the read head needs to travel further to do the reading. Traveling further makes the reading take longer.

Ideally, of course, your operating system writes each file into a nice neat series of contiguous clusters, the sun shines, and you don't get parking tickets when you overstay your welcome in a tightly patrolled area. But when your hard disk grows full, your operating system is forced to break files across whichever clusters are available on the disk rather than being able to put them all together. The disk's read head has to travel further, and so reads take longer; fog settles or snow falls; and you get parking tickets or a free Denver boot.

Breaking files across various clusters is called *fragmentation*. To reduce fragmentation and improve performance, you can *defragment* (or *defrag*) a drive. The defragmentation utility rearranges and rewrites the data so that files are written onto contiguous clusters wherever possible. As a result, your disk's read head can access any given file more quickly and with less effort, performance improves, and the sun clears the fog so you see the traffic warden coming in time to move your car.

> **NOTE** *When you're using your iPod only for music, contacts, and calendars, you won't necessarily need the ultimate performance its hard drive can deliver. Performance is more important when you're using your iPod as an external disk. However, having your song files defragmented may help you squeeze a little more playing time out of your iPod's battery.*

Apple takes a relatively robust view of fragmentation, stating "the file system used on Macintosh computers is designed to work with a certain degree of fragmentation…You should not need to frequently defragment the computer's hard disk." But even Apple concedes "If you create and delete a large number of files, your hard disk may become fragmented to the point that you may see a slight slow-down of file system performance."

Interestingly enough (or trivially enough, depending on your point of view), this line of Apple's is very close to what Microsoft used to claim in the early days of its Windows NT operating system—the file system essentially didn't get fragmented, or if it did, the fragmentation didn't really matter. Reality subsequently intruded on this vision of a maintenance-free file system to such an extent that Windows XP (which is based on Windows NT) includes a Disk Defragmenter that Microsoft recommends you run regularly to keep your disks in good shape.

This little history lesson might lead you to suspect that defragmenting Mac drives would be a good idea as well—and most people agree that it is. Apple doesn't specifically recommend any single defragmentation utility, but most people find that utilities such as Norton Utilities for the Mac's Speed Disk from Symantec Corporation (**www.norton.com**) or PlusOptimizer from Alsoft, Inc. (**www.alsoft.com**) get the job done.

Defragmenting utilities reshuffles the files on your hard disk so files are stored on contiguous clusters wherever possible. Depending on the efficiency of the defragmenter, you may need to run it twice or more to get the files arranged as well as possible.

Run the Windows XP Disk Defragmenter

To run the Disk Defragmenter included with Windows XP, choose Start | All Programs | Accessories | System Tools | Disk Defragmenter. Alternatively, follow these steps:

1. Choose Start | My Computer to open a My Computer window.

2. In the Devices with Removable Storage area, right-click the drive that represents your iPod, and then choose Properties from the shortcut menu to display the Properties dialog box.

3. Click the Tools tab to display it.

4. Click the Defragment Now button to display the Disk Defragmenter window (Figure 12-2).

The Disk Defragmenter utility is straightforward to use. You select the drive you want to defragment, and then click the Analyze button to analyze it or the Defragment button to defragment it. If you click the Analyze button, Disk Defragmenter displays a summary of the state of the drive and tells you whether or not you need to defragment it.

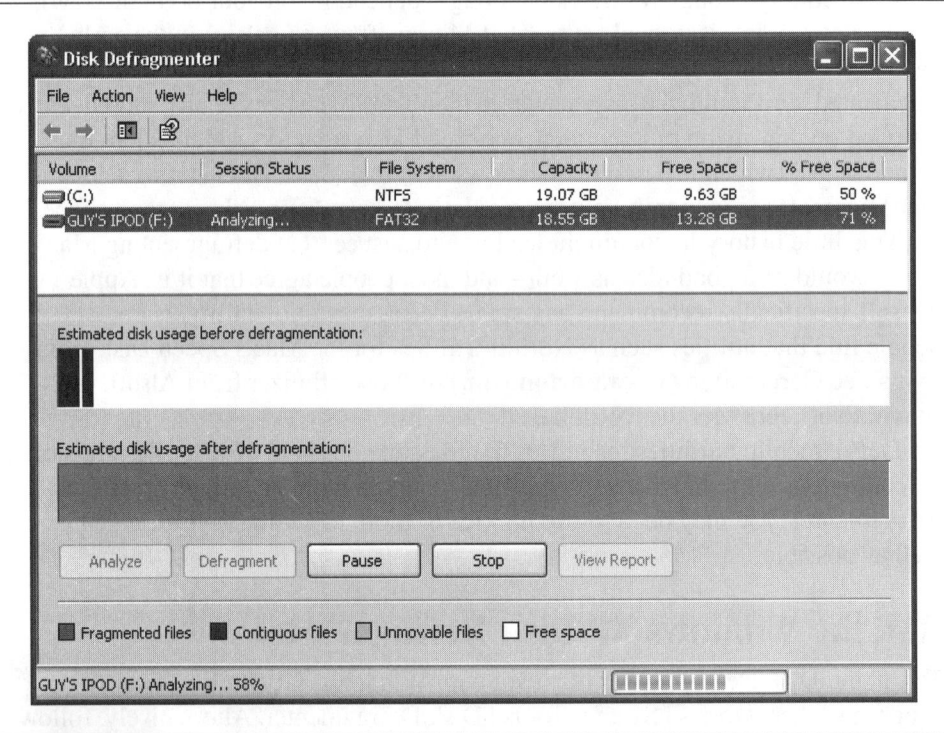

FIGURE 12-2 You can use the Disk Defragmenter utility included with Windows XP to defragment your Windows iPod.

Defragment Your Mac iPod (or Windows iPod) the Cheap and Easy Way

If you prefer not to pay for a defragmenter for your Mac, you don't need to: you can defragment your iPod easily by moving all the files off it, optionally reformatting it, and then putting the files back on it. When you put the files back on your iPod, they're written in contiguous clusters as much as possible.

NOTE *You can defragment your Windows iPod by using this technique as well. But in most cases you'll do better to use the Disk Defragmenter utility that comes with Windows.*

The cleanest way to perform defragmentation this way is to restore your iPod's operating system (as described in the section "Restore Your iPod" in Chapter 15) and then synchronize your iPod with your computer. Restoring the iPod removes all the files, leaving the disk in great shape. This synchronization will take much longer than normal synchronizations because your computer will have to transfer every file to your iPod.

Before you defragment your iPod in this way, make sure you have a copy of all the files on it.

- If your iPod contains only a copy of your iTunes music library and synchronized copies of your contacts and calendars, you shouldn't need to worry about making copies of the files—your Mac already contains copies of them.

- If your iPod contains files other than your iTunes music library, your contacts, and your calendars, you may need to copy them to (or back them up to) your Mac or another drive.

- If you've installed an operating system on your Mac iPod, don't restore your iPod unless you want to lose the operating system. Instead, move the files from your iPod to a different disk, and then move them back again.

Chapter 13

Enhance Your iPod with Accessories

How to...

- Select alternative cases for your iPod
- Learn about power adapters and car adapters for your iPod
- Investigate headphone accessories for your iPod
- Choose stands for your iPod
- Learn about strange accessories you might possibly want
- Connect your iPod to your home stereo or car stereo

Like many a consumer product that's been a runaway success, the iPod has spawned a huge market for accessories—from cases to stands, from handbags to a custom jacket. (That's a jacket for the iPod user, not for the iPod itself.)

Some of these accessories are widely useful (although you may not need any of them yourself). Others are niche products, to put it kindly. Others are—well, weird. Sure, you *could* figure out a way to use them; but would you want to buy them?

This chapter discusses the major categories of accessories (leaving you to choose the types that you need) and highlights some of the less-obvious and more innovative accessories that you might want to know about for special needs.

NOTE *For some types of accessories, such as power adapters and cassette adapters, you don't need to restrict your horizons to iPod-specific accessories—you can choose generic accessories as well. Generic accessories are often substantially less expensive than custom accessories, give you much more flexibility, or both. So I'll mention generic accessories as well as custom accessories where appropriate in this chapter.*

Cases

Your iPod is built to be carried, so it's hardly surprising a wide variety of cases has been developed for iPods—everything from bifold cases to armband cases to armored cases.

Many people find the case that comes with 10GB and 20GB iPods fine and functional for everyday use: it attaches firmly to a belt or a stiff waistband, and it keeps your iPod securely in place unless you undertake extreme activity (for example, skateboard stunts or gymnastics) or you attempt to renegotiate your relationship with gravity. The case is open at the top and so lets you access your iPod's FireWire port, headphone socket, and hold switch. It doesn't let you access your iPod's front-panel controls, but the remote control included with the 10GB and 20GB iPods duplicates the key functions of the front-panel controls for playing music, so you don't need to use the front-panel controls once you've started playing an album or playlist.

Choosing an iPod case is as fiercely personal a choice as choosing comfortable underwear or choosing a car. Different aspects of cases are important to different people, and while one size (read: the standard iPod case) may suit many, it doesn't fit all. As with underwear (or a car), you may prefer not to use a case at all—but your iPod's shiny surfaces will tend to get scratched, and you'll need to be careful not to drop your iPod onto any unforgiving surface.

But as with underwear (and, to a lesser extent, a car), one point is vital: to make sure the case you choose is the right size for the model of iPod you have. As you'll remember from Chapter 1, the 10GB iPod is a little slimmer than the 5GB iPod, and the 20GB iPod is a little less svelte than the 5GB iPod. So if you put a 10GB iPod in a 20GB case, it may rattle around a bit (depending on the design of the case). If you try to stuff a 20GB iPod in a skintight 10GB case, the iPod or the case will probably become unhappy. (You may too.)

Beyond getting the size right, the remaining choices are yours. The following paragraphs summarize the key ways in which the cases differ. You get to decide which points are important for you.

- **How the case attaches to you (if at all)** Many cases attach to your belt, others to a lanyard that goes around your neck. Others yet attach to an armband, which some people find better for performing vigorous activities. (Other people find the iPod a little heavy for wearing on an arm.) Some cases come with a variety of attachments—for example, a belt clip and an armband, or a mounting for sticking your iPod to a flat surface. Other cases are simply protective, designed to be carried in a pocket or a bag.

NOTE *Examples of armband cases include the Action Jacket from Netalogic, Inc. ($29.99; www.everythingipod.com). The Action Jacket is made of thick neoprene with holes that let you see the screen and access the front-panel controls. It attaches either to a belt clip or an armband.*

- **The amount of protection the case provides** In general, the more protection a case provides, the larger and uglier it is, the more it weighs, and the more it costs. Balance your need for style against your iPod's need for protection when gravity gets the better of your grip.

TIP *If you have a rugged lifestyle and want your iPod to share it, consider the iPod Armor case from Matias Corporation ($49.95; **halfkeyboard.com/ products/ipodarmorinfo.html**). The iPod Armor cradles your iPod in a full metal jacket made of anodized aluminum padded with open-cell EVA foam. If you land on this case, you're more likely to damage yourself than your iPod.*

- **Whether or not the case is waterproof**   If you plan to take your iPod outdoors for exercise, you may want to get a case that's water-resistant or waterproof. Alternatively, carry a sturdy plastic bag in your pocket for weather emergencies.

- **Whether or not the case lets you access your iPod's controls**   On the face of it, access to the controls might seem a compelling feature in a case—and in some cases (literally, for once, in both senses), it is. But if you have a remote control for your iPod, your need to access your iPod's controls once you've set the music playing will be much less. Generally speaking, the more waterproof the case, the less access it offers to your iPod's controls.

- **Whether or not the case can hold your iPod's headphones and remote control**   If you'll be toting your iPod in a bag or pocket, a case that can hold your iPod's ear-bud headphones and remote control as well as the player itself may be a boon. You may even want a case that can accommodate the FireWire cable and power adapter for traveling. But if you're more interested in a case that straps firmly to your body and holds your iPod secure, you probably won't want the case to devote extra space to store other objects.

TIP *If you're looking for a case that'll take your iPod's complete entourage, consider the type of case designed for portable CD players and built into a padded belt.*

- **Whether or not you need to take your iPod out of the case to recharge it**   Some cases are designed to give you access to your iPod's FireWire port and front panel controls, so you can leave your iPod in the case unless you need to admire it. With more protective cases, you usually need to remove your iPod more often.

- **What the case is made of and how much it costs**   Snug cases tend to be made of neoprene. Impressive cases tend to be made of leather. Leather and armor cost more than lesser materials.

TIP *When shopping for a case, look for special-value bundles that include other iPod accessories you need—for example, a car cassette adapter or a card adapter.*

Stands, Docks, and Mounting Kits

Cases are (or can be) great—but you won't always want to carry your iPod. Sometimes, you'll want to park it securely so you can use it without worrying about knocking it down, or so you can contemplate its lustrous beauty.

For such occasions, you need a stand, a dock (essentially a stand that connects to your stereo, your computer, or both), or a mount kit, depending on where you want to position your iPod. Again, you know your needs, and I can only guess at them (and I'd rather not do even that). The following are brief details on some of the options available to you.

- **PodStand**   The PodStand (formerly called the iStand) from Larry Nixon ($14.95; **www.the-istand.com**) is a simple acrylic stand barely wider than your iPod. The PodStand holds your iPod upright, does nothing else, and comes in white, black, and clear models.

- **DVBase**   The DVBase from DVForge Division of Sanders Tool and Mould Co., Inc. ($59.99; **www.dvforge.com/dvbase.html** and various other retailers) is a sleek stand made of polished aluminum to match the polished nickel stainless steel on your iPod's back and sides. The base holds your iPod at a jaunty angle to the universe and looks beautiful but has no other function. At this writing, DVForge is also offering a DVBaseLtd version of the DVBase, "individually machined from a solid billet of T6 aircraft grade aluminum" and laser engraved with serial numbers. Yours for $99.99.

- **iPodCradle**   The iPodCradle from BookEndz ($29.95; **www.bookendzdocks.com/bookendz/dock_cradle.htm**) is a simple white cradle that holds your iPod firmly in an almost-upright position. It has no other function.

- **iPodDock**   The iPodDock, also from BookEndz ($44.95; **www.bookendzdocks.com/bookendz/dock_cradle.htm**) is a stand that holds your iPod upside down so it connects with audio and FireWire ports built into the unit. The iPodDock connects to your stereo and computer, allowing you to charge your iPod and play back music. The problem, as you'd imagine, comes with trying to navigate your iPod's display upside down.

- **FlipStand** The FlipStand from Speck Products ($34.95; **www.speckproducts.com**) is a protective hard case for your iPod that also acts as a stand when you flip the door fully open. The FlipStand includes inserts to make it fit the 5GB, 10GB, and 20GB iPods.

- **iPod Stand** The iPod Stand from Power Support of Japan (around $59; various retailers) is a steel stand that can fit into a cup holder in a car or simply stand on your desktop. The iPod Stand seems to have been designed by committee (or possibly by congealment), but it's sturdy enough to withstand significant punishment. You may be tempted to use it as a paperweight or to defend your desk.

- **Gripmatic** The Gripmatic from Netalog, Inc. ($29.99; **www.everythingipod.com**) is a multi-angle mount designed for use in the car. You can mount the Gripmatic either with screws or with adhesive (both of which are provided).

Power Adapters

Your iPod should have come with a power adapter for recharging from the mains instead of recharging along the FireWire cable from your Mac or PC. But you may want to supplement the standard adapter with a more specialized adapter.

Basic AC Power Adapters

If you break or lose your power adapter, or simply want a second adapter so you can keep one upstairs and one downstairs, you can buy another iPod Power Adapter (that's the formal name) from the Apple Store (**store.apple.com**) or from an authorized reseller. The iPod Power Adapter costs $49.99.

You can also get equivalent power supplies from other sources. For example, Netalog, Inc. (**www.everythingipod.com**) offers the iPod AC Adapter for $39.99. This unit is more compact than the iPod Power Adapter, but its prongs aren't removable.

Powered FireWire Adapters for Unpowered FireWire Ports

If your computer has an unpowered FireWire port (for example, a four-pin port on a PC or a six-pin port on a CardBus or PC Card device), one option is to get a powered FireWire adapter to attach to your FireWire cable so you can recharge your iPod by plugging it into your computer. The adapter sits between the unpowered port and your power-capable FireWire cable and "injects" power into the cable. Examples of such adapters include the FireCable from CompuCable Manufacturing Group (**www.compucable.com**) and the FireJuice 6 and FireJuice 4 from SiK, Inc. ($25; **www.sik.com/firejuice.php**).

The disadvantage to such an adapter, as you might guess, is that you have to plug it into an AC socket for it to have any power to supply to your iPod. Most people find it easier to use their iPod's power adapter to recharge the iPod directly from the AC. But if you want to make synchronization and recharging a one-stop option, you might want to try such an adapter.

Power-Only FireWire Cable for Playing While Charging from a Computer

The HotWire from SiK, Inc. ($13; **www.sik.com/hotwire.php**) is a FireWire cable that transfers power but not data. By using this cable, you can charge your iPod from a computer while continuing to use your iPod to play music, instead of having your iPod become a slave to your computer the moment you plug it in.

Car Adapters

If you drive extensively (or live in a vehicle), you may find even your iPod's impressive battery life isn't enough for your lifestyle. To recharge your iPod in your car, you need a power adapter that'll run from your car's 12-volt accessory outlet or cigarette-lighter socket. Technically, such an adapter is an *inverter*, a device that converts DC into AC, but we'll stick with the term "adapter" here.

You can choose between a generic car adapter, a FireWire car adapter, and a custom car adapter for the iPod. The following subsections discuss these options.

Generic Car Adapter

The simplest and most versatile option is to get a generic car adapter that plugs into your car's 12-volt accessory outlet or cigarette-lighter socket. Models vary, but the most effective types give you one or more conventional AC sockets. You plug your iPod's power adapter into one of these AC sockets just as you would any other AC socket, and then plug the FireWire cable into your iPod's power adapter.

The advantage to these adapters is that you can run any electrical equipment off them that doesn't draw too heavy a load: a portable computer, your cell phone charger, a portable TV, or whatever. The disadvantage is that such adapters can be large and clumsy compared with custom adapters.

Cost usually depends on the wattage the adapter can handle: you can get 50-watt adapters from around $20 and 140-watt adapters for around $50, whereas 300-watt adapters cost more like $80. A 50-watt adapter will take care of your iPod and portable computer easily enough.

FireWire Car Adapters

Your next option is to get a car adapter that provides a FireWire port into which you can plug your iPod's cable. The adapter draws power through the 12-volt accessory socket or cigarette-lighter socket and provides power to the FireWire port.

An example of such an adapter is the FirePod charger from CompuCable Manufacturing Group (**www.compucable.com**). The FirePod provides one FireWire port and one USB port, so it's not an iPod-only product.

iPod-Specific Adapters

If the only thing you want to power from your car is your iPod, you can get a car adapter specially designed for the iPod. You'll find an impressive number of different models available, including the following:

- Griffin PowerPod ($19.99; **www.griffintechnology.com**) is an adapter with a FireWire socket into which you plug your FireWire cable.

- XtremeMac Premium iPod Car Charger ($19.99; **www.xtrememac.com/foripod/car_charger.shtml**) is an adapter with a springy coil of FireWire cable built in. You plug the other end of the FireWire cable into your iPod, and you're in business.

- The AutoPod charger from Netalog, Inc. ($19.99; **www.everythingipod.com**) is similar to the iPod Car Charger—an adapter with a built-in, coiled FireWire cable. You can choose between black and white models.

> **NOTE** *The ultimate iPod-specific power adapter is the TransPod, a power adapter built into an iPod holder wih an RF transmitter for sending your iPod's output to your car radio. See the section "Connect Your iPod to Your Car Stereo" later in this chapter.*

World Travel Adapters

If you travel abroad with your iPod, the lightest and easiest way to recharge it is from your PowerBook, iBook, or portable PC (if that PC has a six-pin FireWire port rather than a four-pin port, which can't transfer power). You have to have your computer with you, of course, and you need a way to plug in your computer to the mains so you don't deplete its battery charging your iPod. But even that tends to be better than having to plug in your iPod separately.

If you need to recharge your iPod directly from the mains, get an adapter that lets you plug your iPod's power adapter into the mains. The adapter can handle multiple voltages, so you can safely plug it in even in countries that think 240 volts is just a refreshing tingle.

As in so many things in life, you can choose between a set of cheap and ugly adapters and a set of stylish and sophisticated adapters. The cheap and ugly adapters you can get from any competent electrical supply shop; they consist of an assortment of prong-converter receptacles into which you plug your iPod's U.S. prongs. The resulting piggyback arrangement is clumsy and vaguely obscene looking, and sometimes you have to jiggle the adapters to get a good connection. But these adapters are inexpensive (usually from $5 to $10) and functional, and they work for any electrical gear that can handle the different voltages.

The stylish and sophisticated adapters are (surprise, surprise) designed by Apple and are (collectively) called the World Travel Adapter Kit. The kit costs $39.95 from the Apple Store (**store.apple.com**) or an authorized reseller. You slide the U.S. prongs off your iPod adapter and replace them with a set of prongs suited to the country you're in. The Kit includes six prongs that'll juice up your iPod in continental Europe, the United Kingdom, Australia, Hong Kong, South Korea, China, and Japan, as well as in the United States. These adapters also work with the white power adapters that come with the PowerBook G4 and the iBook, but they won't help you plug in any of your other electrical equipment.

Headphones and Enhancers

As discussed in the section "Connect Your Headphones or Speakers" in Chapter 1, you can connect pretty much any standard type of headphones to your iPod—over-the-ear (circumaural) headphones, on-the-ear (supra-aural) headphones, or in-the-ear headphones (ear buds). If the headphones have a quarter-inch jack, you'll need a miniplug converter (make sure its quality is high enough for your headphones). And if you want to enhance sound quality, you might want to try a headphone amplifier.

Choosing headphones should be a straightforward matter of balancing sound quality, comfort, cost, style, and special needs, such as excluding other noises or keeping your ears warm. I'll let you make the choice on your own; but in the next three subsections, I'll quickly mention three headphone-related products that may be of interest. Okay, the first product is actually a pair of headphones, but it's an unusual pair that you might care to know about.

Zip Cord Retractable Earbuds

Getting the headphone cord tangled is a perennial problem with ear-bud headphones, particularly when you need to stuff them into your pocket or pack quickly. The Zip Cord Retractable Earbuds from Netalog, Inc. ($26.95; **www.everythingipod.com**) feature an integrated spool onto which you can quickly retract the cord when you need to stow them.

iShare Earbud Splitter

The iShare Earbud Splitter ($9.95; **www.xtrememac.com/foripod/ishare.shtml**) is a Y-shaped cable that lets you plug two sets of headphones into the same iPod. You can daisy-chain two or more iShare Earbud Splitters to add more people if you all share the same iPod and the same taste in music. The iShare Earbud Splitter balances the sound so each set of headphones receives the same volume and quality. (With bargain-basement splitters, you may lose volume or quality.)

The Splitter is best used in static situations such as on a plane, in a car, or on the sofa reacquainting yourself with the baser parts of heavy metal after your sensitive neighbors have twitched their way to bed. On the street, Splitter users run the risk of garroting children, lassoing lampposts, and suffering unexpected sharp tugs at their ears.

Koss eq50 Three-Band Equalizer

If your iPod's graphic equalizer settings don't always suit you, or you want to be able to change the equalizer settings manually while you're playing music, try a portable graphic equalizer such as the Koss eq50 ($19.99, various retailers). You plug the eq50 into your iPod, and then plug your headphones or other listening gear into the eq50.

The eq50 is a pocket-size unit that runs on two AAA batteries. It offers three frequency sliders, giving you reasonable, but not fine, control over the equalization of your music.

Weird Stuff

This section mentions a couple oddball accessories determined not to fit into the previous categories.

Burton Amp Jacket

Burton Snowboards and Apple teamed up to produce the Burton Amp ($499.95; **www.burton.com/gear/pr_amp_jacket.asp**), a waterproof GORE-TEX snowboarding jacket designed to house an iPod. The iPod fits into a secure chest pocket from which wires run to a remote control built into a fabric data strip on the left forearm. From the remote control, wires run to the neck of the jacket, where you plug in your headset.

If you're a fanatical snowboarder, you own an iPod, you're short a waterproof jacket, and you happen to have $500 burning a hole in your upper thigh, the Burton Amp may seem an unmissable opportunity. For most of the rest of the world, though, the jacket is a fair illustration of the triumph of style over sense.

Most boarders will achieve the same effect at no cost by attaching their iPod's own remote control to their torso or sleeve, padding or reinforcing an internal pocket, and perhaps running the wires under the fabric (or taping them down) to avoid tangling in aerial maneuvers. If they have $500 in urgent need of a new home, they'll buy a new board or a second iPod for the rest of their music collection, or perhaps put down a deposit on a 17-inch PowerBook.

Groove Bag

The Groove Bag from Felicidade is a bizarre anti-fashion accessory—a soft, faux-leather bag containing amplified speakers and a pocket for your iPod. The iPod pocket is see-through, giving you access to your iPod's controls and enabling you to flash your iPod at passersby.

If you carry a Groove Bag, you *will* be stared at—but that might be the reason why you'd carry one. To protect you from yourself, the Groove Bag is available only in Japan at this writing—together with a mind-squeezing variety of electronic gadgets too sophisticated or nichey for the U.S. market. (If you go to Tokyo, go to Akihabara, the electronics paradise. But you'd be well advised to leave your wallet at home to prevent yourself from going hog-wild.)

Connect Your iPod to Your Stereo

Connecting your iPod to your stereo is easy. In most cases, all you need is a cable with a miniplug at one end for your iPod's headphone socket and two RCA plugs at the other end to go into your amplifier or boom box. (For some cassette players, you'll need a miniplug at each end of the cable.)

If you have a high-quality receiver and speakers, get a high-quality cable to connect your iPod to them. After the amount you've presumably spent on your iPod and your stereo, it'd be a mistake to degrade the signal between them by sparing a few bucks on the cable.

When you connect your iPod to your stereo, turn the volume all the way down on the iPod and on the amplifier before making the connection. Connect the RCA plugs to one of the inputs on your amplifier or boom box—for example, the AUX input. Then increase the volume on the two controls in tandem until you reach a satisfactory sound level. Too low a level of output from your iPod may produce noise on the wire as your amplifier boosts the signal. Too high a level of output from your iPod may cause distortion.

CAUTION *Don't connect your iPod to the Phono input on your amplifier. This is because the Phono input is built with a higher sensitivity to make up for the weak output of a record player. Putting a full-strength signal into the Phono input will probably blow it.*

Connect Your iPod to Your Car Stereo

You can connect your iPod to your car stereo in any of the following ways:

- Use a cassette adapter to connect your iPod to your car's cassette player.
- Use a radio-frequency device to play your iPod's output through your car's radio.
- Wire your iPod directly to your car stereo and use it as an auxiliary input device.

Each of these methods has its merits and disadvantages. The following subsections tell you what you need to know to choose the best option for your car stereo.

Use a Cassette Adapter

If your car stereo has a cassette player, your easiest option is to use a cassette adapter to play audio from your iPod through the cassette deck. You can buy such adapters for between $10 and $20 from most electronics stores.

The adapter is shaped like a cassette and uses a playback head to input analog audio via the head that normally reads the tape as it passes. A wire runs from the adapter to your iPod.

A cassette adapter can be an easy and inexpensive solution, but it has a couple of disadvantages. First, the audio quality tends to be poor, because the means of transferring the audio to the cassette player's mechanism is less than optimal. If the cassette player's playback head is dirty from playing cassettes, audio quality will be that much worse. (Clean the cassette player regularly using a cleaning cassette.)

Second, many auto-reverse cassette players can't play input from a cassette adapter for more than 30 minutes or so without deciding they need to change directions and look for more music on the other side of the adapter—which can't supply it. So if you use a cassette adapter, you may have to reset the direction of play every once in a while. This isn't difficult, but it gets tedious fast.

> **CAUTION** *If you use a cassette adapter in an extreme climate, try to make sure you don't bake it or freeze it by leaving it in your car.*

Use a Radio-Frequency Adapter

If your car stereo doesn't have a cassette deck, your easiest option for playing music from your iPod may be to get a radio-frequency adapter. This device plugs into a sound source (your iPod in this case) and broadcasts a signal on an FM frequency to which you then tune your radio to play the music. Better radio-frequency devices offer a choice of frequencies to allow you easy access to both the device and your favorite radio stations.

Radio-frequency devices can deliver reasonable audio quality. If possible, try before you buy by asking for a demonstration in the store (take a portable radio with you if necessary).

The main advantages of these devices are that they're relatively inexpensive ($25, give or take $10) and they're easy to use. They also have the advantage that you can put your iPod out of sight (for example, in the glove compartment—provided it's not too hot) without any telltale wires to help the light-fingered locate it.

On the down side, most of these devices need batteries (others can run off the 12-volt accessory outlet or cigarette lighter socket), and less expensive units tend not to deliver the highest sound quality. The range of these devices is minimal, but at close quarters, other radios nearby may be able to pick up the signal—which could be embarrassing, entertaining, or irrelevant, depending on the circumstances.

Wire Your iPod Directly to Your Car Stereo

If neither the cassette adapter nor the radio-frequency adapter provides a suitable solution, or if you simply want the best audio quality you can get, connect your iPod directly to your car stereo.

How easily you can do this depends on how the stereo is designed:

- If your car stereo is one of the few that has a miniplug input built in, get a miniplug-to-miniplug cable, and you'll be in business.

- If your stereo is built to take multiple inputs—for example, a CD player (or changer) and an auxiliary input—you may be able to simply run a wire from unused existing connectors. Plug your iPod into the other end, press the correct buttons, and you'll be ready to rock-and-roll down the freeway.

- If no unused connectors are available, you or your local friendly electronics technician may need to get busy with a soldering iron.

If you're buying a new car stereo, look for an auxiliary input that you can use with your iPod.

An Integrated Solution: the TransPod

The TransPod from Netalog, Inc. ($99.95, **www.everythingipod.com**) is a one-stop solution for using your iPod in your car. TransPod combines a cradle for holding the iPod with a power adapter and a wireless transmitter to pipe the iPod's output to your car radio.

Your iPod slides up into the cradle so the miniplug and FireWire plug in the top of the sleeve go into your iPod's headphone port and FireWire port. You then plug the charger plug into your 12-volt accessory outlet or cigarette-lighter socket, which supports the cradle and provides power to the iPod and the TransPod. You can play music back as your iPod charges, so you can keep the tunes going continuously.

The only drawback to the TransPod (apart from the price) is that it makes your iPod highly visible to the covetous—so you'd be well advised to remove it when you park.

Chapter 14

Learn Advanced iPod Skills

How to...

- Convert your iPod from Mac to Windows and back
- Change the computer to which your iPod is linked
- Synchronize several iPods with the same computer
- Load your iPod from multiple Macs or multiple PCs
- Transfer song files from your iPod's music library to your computer
- Use your computer to play songs directly from your iPod

This chapter shows you how to perform a variety of advanced maneuvers with your iPod. It starts by walking you through the processes of converting a Mac iPod to a Windows iPod and a Windows iPod to a Mac iPod. It then shows you how to change the computer to which your iPod is linked—a useful skill when you upgrade your computer. The chapter explains the nuances of synchronizing several iPods with the same computer, and shows you how to load your iPod from multiple Macs or multiple PCs (but not a mixture).

The chapter also discusses how to transfer song files from your iPod's music library to your computer, a skill that can save your music library when your computer has disk trouble. The chapter ends by showing you how to play songs from your iPod through your computer.

Convert Your iPod from Mac to Windows—and Back

From the way Apple sells iPods for Windows and iPods for the Mac as separate products, it's not immediately apparent that you can convert your iPod from Mac to Windows or from Windows to Mac. But you *can* do so, and you may want to do so if you migrate from the Mac to the PC, or from the PC to the Mac, or if you simply use both platforms and want to move your iPod to the computer with the most room for your music library.

There are two main differences between Mac iPods and Windows iPods:

- Mac iPods come formatted with the HFS Plus file system, which delivers good performance with both Mac OS X and System 9. Windows iPods use the FAT32 file system, which works with Windows Me, Windows 2000, and Windows XP, among other operating systems (for example, Linux).

- Mac iPods come with iTunes (although you'll probably have iTunes installed on your Mac already). Windows iPods come with MUSICMATCH Jukebox Plus and an iPod plug-in.

Convert Your Windows iPod to Work with the Mac

To convert your Windows iPod to work with the Mac, follow the steps in the section "Restore Your iPod on Mac OS X" in Chapter 15. The restore process does the following:

- Wipes out all the contents of your iPod's hard disk.
- Formats the hard disk with the HFS Plus file system.
- Installs a fresh copy of the iPod operating system files with default settings.
- Creates default folders (including the Contacts folder and Calendars folder) and sample contacts.

Convert Your Mac iPod to Work with Windows

To convert your Mac iPod to work with Windows, follow the steps in the section "Restore Your iPod on Windows XP" in Chapter 15. The restore process does the following:

- Wipes out all the contents of your iPod's hard disk.
- Formats the hard disk with the FAT32 file system.
- Installs a fresh copy of the iPod operating system files with default settings.
- Creates default folders (including the Contacts folder and Calendars folder) and sample contacts.

Change the Computer to Which Your iPod Is Linked

Each iPod can synchronize with only one computer at a time: a Mac iPod can synchronize with only one Mac, and a Windows iPod can synchronize with only one PC. This computer is known as the *home* computer—home to the iPod, not necessarily in your home. However, you can use two or more Macs to load files onto the same Mac iPod, or two or more PCs to load files onto the same Windows iPod. See the sections "Load Your Mac iPod from Two or More Macs" and "Load Your Windows iPod from Two or More PCs" later in this chapter for details.

You can also change the Mac to which your Mac iPod is linked, or the PC to which your Windows iPod is linked, at any time. The following subsections discuss how to do so.

> **CAUTION** *Linking your iPod to another computer replaces all the songs and playlists on your iPod with the songs and playlists on the other computer. Be sure you want to change the link before you proceed. You can restore your previous music library by linking again to the first computer, but, even with FireWire file-transfer speeds, you'll waste a good deal of time if your music library is large.*

Change Your Mac iPod's Home Mac

To change your Mac iPod's home Mac to another Mac, follow these steps:

1. Install iTunes on the other Mac if it doesn't already have it installed. Also install any relevant updates.

2. Connect your iPod via the FireWire cable to the Mac you want to make your iPod's new home Mac.

3. iTunes displays the dialog box shown in Figure 14-1, warning you your iPod is linked to another iTunes music library and asking if you want to change the link to the iTunes music library on this Mac.

4. If you're sure you want to replace your music library, click the Yes button.

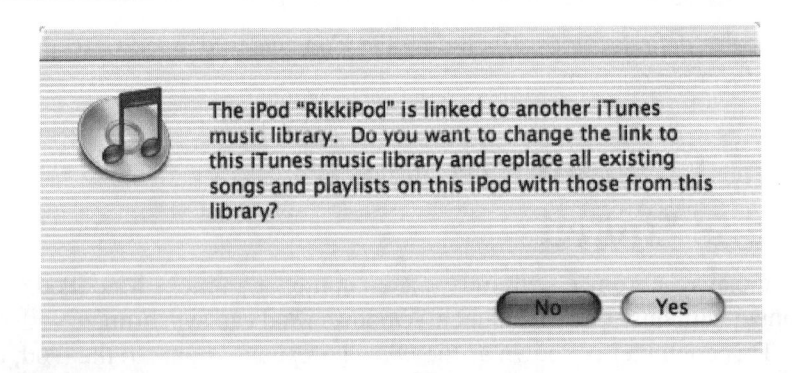

FIGURE 14-1 When you link your iPod to a different Mac, iTunes replaces all the songs and playlists on your iPod with the songs and playlists on the other Mac.

CHAPTER 14: Learn Advanced iPod Skills   303

Because changing your iPod to a different Mac replaces the entire music library, the initial synchronization may take a long time (depending on how big the music library is).

Change Your Windows iPod's Home PC

To change your Windows iPod's home PC to another PC, follow these steps:

1. Install MUSICMATCH Jukebox Plus and the iPod software on the PC you want to make your iPod's new home PC. (See the section "Install MUSICMATCH Jukebox Plus on Your PC" in Chapter 4 if you need a reminder of the installation routine.)

2. Connect your iPod via the FireWire cable to the new home PC.

3. Windows may display a Found New Hardware notification-area pop-up when it notices the iPod is connected. After installing the iPod, it may then display the System Settings Change dialog box, telling you that the new hardware is installed and you need to restart your computer. At this point, you probably don't need to restart your computer, so click the No button.

4. MUSICMATCH Jukebox Plus then launches and activates MUSICMATCH Portables Plus. MUSICMATCH Portables Plus displays a MUSICMATCH Portables dialog box such as that shown in the following image, warning you that the iPod is set up to synchronize with a different computer and that synchronizing the iPod will replace all the content on the iPod with content from this computer. The wording in the dialog box depends on whether your iPod is configured to synchronize the music library (as in the dialog box shown) or selected playlists.

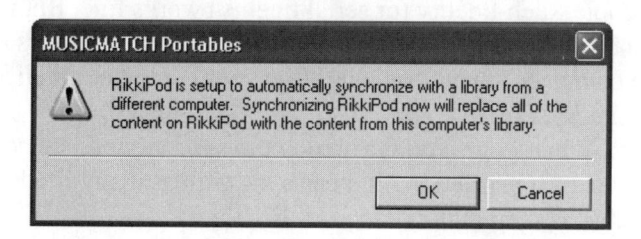

5. Click the OK button. MUSICMATCH Portables Plus displays another MUSICMATCH Portables dialog box ensuring that you want to synchronize this iPod with this computer. Again, the wording depends on whether your

iPod is configured to synchronize the music library (as in the following image) or selected playlists.

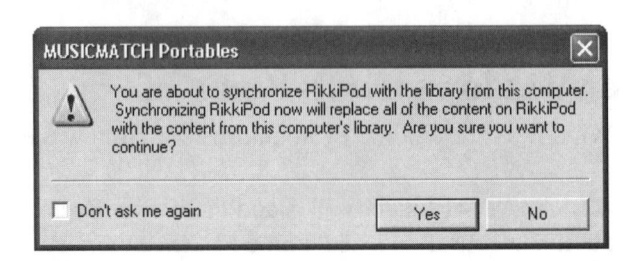

> **MUSICMATCH Portables**
>
> ⚠ You are about to synchronize RikkiPod with the library from this computer. Synchronizing RikkiPod now will replace all of the content on RikkiPod with the content from this computer's library. Are you sure you want to continue?
>
> ☐ Don't ask me again   [Yes]   [No]

6. Click the OK button. MUSICMATCH Portables Plus configures your iPod to synchronize with this computer, and then performs the synchronization.

7. Configure synchronization options for your iPod as discussed in the section "Change Synchronization Options for Your iPod" in Chapter 4.

8. Configure audio options for your iPod as discussed in the section "Choose Audio Options for Your iPod" in Chapter 4.

Synchronize Several iPods with the Same Computer

As you've seen earlier in this book, a computer and an iPod usually have a mutually faithful relationship. As discussed in the previous section, the iPod can decide to leave its home computer and set up home with another computer. It can even switch to the other platform (Mac or PC) if it wants OS-reassignment as well as a new home.

For most people, such fidelity (or serial fidelity) works fine. But if you have several iPods and one computer—for example, if several music-lovers in a household share the same computer—what happens? Can your computer practice polyPodry (or perhaps poliPodry)?

Briefly—yes. While your iPod is wired not to sync around, the computer in the partnership has no such restrictions and can sync with as many iPods as you have. Here are the points to keep in mind:

- Even if your computer has plenty of FireWire ports, it's best not to plug in more than one iPod at once. That way, you don't get confused, and synchronization can take place at full speed.

- Each iPod has a unique ID number that it communicates to your computer on connection, so your computer knows which iPod is connected to it. You can even give two or more iPods the same name if doing so amuses rather than confuses you.

- You can configure different updating for each iPod by choosing options in the iPod Preferences dialog box (in iTunes) or the Options dialog box in MUSICMATCH Portables Plus when the iPod is connected.

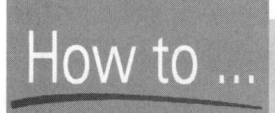

How to ... How to Synchronize Two Different iPods Using the Same Computer

Synchronizing two or more iPods with the same computer works well enough provided that each iPod user is happy using the same music library or the same set of playlists. But if you want to synchronize the full music library for each iPod, yet have a different music library on each, you need to take a different approach.

In most cases, the easiest solution is to have a separate user account for each separate user who uses an iPod with the computer. (Most computer experts and software designers recommend that each user have a separate user account anyway to prevent one user from trashing another user's work or settings. But reality frequently refuses to correspond to their edicts.)

Place the music files that users will share in a folder that each user can access. In iTunes, make sure that the Copy Files to iTunes Music Folder when Adding to Library check box on the Advanced sheet of the Preferences dialog box (iTunes | Preferences) is cleared so iTunes doesn't consolidate the files for the music library. (MUSICMATCH Jukebox Plus doesn't have a consolidation feature like this, so this problem doesn't occur on Windows.)

If you have enough free space on your hard disk, each user can set up their own music library under their own user account and store all their music files in it. But unless your hard disk is truly gigantic, sharing most of the files from a central location is almost always preferable.

Load Your iPod from Two or More Computers at Once

As you've heard several times by now in this book, you can synchronize your iPod with only one computer at a time—your iPod's home computer. You can change your iPod's home computer from one computer to another, and even from one platform (Mac or PC) to the other, but you can't actively synchronize your iPod with more than one computer at once.

But you *can* load tracks onto your iPod from computers other than the home computer. The computers must use the same platform (Mac or PC) as the home PC, and they need to have iTunes or MUSICMATCH Jukebox Plus installed (as appropriate to the platform). Beyond that, you need to configure the iPod for manual updating on each computer involved—on the home computer as well as on each other computer. Otherwise, synchronizing the iPod with the home computer after loading tracks from other computers will remove those tracks (because they're not in the home computer's music library).

The following subsections walk you through the steps to using two or more Macs (the first subsection) or two or more PCs (the second subsection) to load song files on your iPod.

Load Your Mac iPod from Two or More Macs

To load your Mac iPod from two or more Macs, follow these steps:

1. Synchronize with the home Mac as described in Chapter 3.

2. Configure the home Mac for manual updating (select the Manually Manage Songs and Playlists option button in the iPod Preferences dialog box).

3. Install iTunes on the other Mac (or Macs) if it (or they) doesn't already have it installed. Also install any relevant updates.

   NOTE *For best results, both (or all) Macs involved should be running the same version of iTunes. Connect your iPod via the FireWire cable to the second Mac.*

4. When iTunes displays the dialog box warning you that the iPod is linked to another music library and asking if you want to change the link to the music library (as shown in the following image), click the No button.

> The iPod "Guy's iPod" is linked to another iTunes music library. Do you want to change the link to this iTunes music library and replace all existing songs and playlists on this iPod with those from this library?
>
> No   Yes

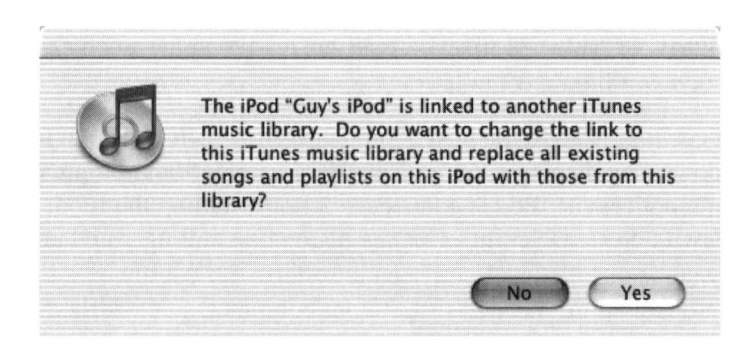

5. Select the entry for your iPod in the Source pane in iTunes to display the contents of the iPod.

6. Click the iPod Options button to display the iPod Preferences dialog box.

7. Select the Manually Manage Songs and Playlists option button, and then click the OK button in the dialog box that warns you you'll need to unmount your iPod manually before each disconnect.

8. Click the OK button to close the Preferences dialog box.

9. Drag song files or folders from your iTunes library or from a Finder window, and then drop them on your iPod or on one of its playlists.

10. Unmount your iPod by issuing an Eject command before you disconnect it.

NOTE *From this point on, to add further song files to your iPod from your home computer, add the files manually. Don't synchronize your iPod with your home computer, because synchronization will delete from the iPod all the song files your music library doesn't contain.*

Load Your Windows iPod from Two or More PCs

To load your Windows iPod from two or more PCs, follow these steps:

1. Synchronize your iPod with its home PC, as discussed in Chapter 4.

2. With your iPod still connected to its home PC, click the Options button to display the Options dialog box. On the Synchronization tab, clear the Automatically Synchronize on Device Connection check box. Then click the OK button.

3. Install MUSICMATCH Jukebox Plus and the iPod plug-in on each computer to which you'll connect your iPod.

4. Connect your iPod to the next computer from which you want to load files. Windows may display a Found New Hardware notification-area pop-up when it notices the iPod is connected. After installing the iPod, it may then display the System Settings Change dialog box, telling you that the new hardware is installed and you need to restart your computer. At this point, you probably don't need to restart your computer, so click the No button.

5. MUSICMATCH Jukebox Plus then launches and activates MUSICMATCH Portables Plus. MUSICMATCH Portables Plus displays a MUSICMATCH Portables dialog box such as that shown in the following image, warning you that the iPod is set up to synchronize with a different computer and that synchronizing the iPod will replace all the content on the iPod with content from this computer. The wording in the dialog box depends on whether your iPod is configured to synchronize the music library or selected playlists (as in the dialog box shown).

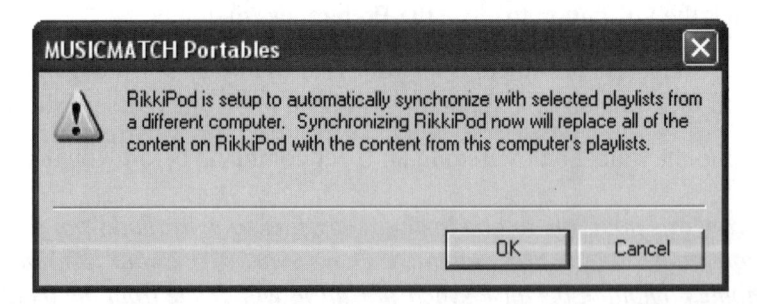

6. Click the Cancel button to close the MUSICMATCH Portables dialog box.

7. Once you've done this, you can add songs or playlists to your iPod by dragging them from your MUSICMATCH Jukebox Plus music library or from a Windows Explorer window and dropping them on the iPod or in a playlist in the MUSICMATCH Portables Plus window.

8. After you finish loading tracks, click the Eject button in the MUSICMATCH Portables Plus window to unmount your iPod before you disconnect it.

NOTE *From this point on, to add further song files to your iPod from your home computer, add the files manually. Don't synchronize your iPod with your home computer, because synchronization will delete from the iPod all the song files your music library doesn't contain.*

Transfer Music Files from Your iPod's Music Library to Your Computer

For copyright reasons, your iPod's basic configuration prevents you from copying music files (for example, MP3 files or WAV files) from your iPod's music library to your computer. This restriction prevents you from loading files onto your iPod on one computer via iTunes or MUSICMATCH Jukebox Plus, and then downloading them onto another computer. Otherwise, you could use your iPod to copy files from one Mac to another Mac, or from one PC to another PC, most likely violating copyright left, right, and in stereo by making unauthorized copies of other people's copyrighted material.

This restriction is about as effective as the "Don't steal music" admonition on the sticker you peeled off your iPod the moment you unpacked it. This is because, as you saw in Chapter 12, by turning on FireWire disk mode, you can use your iPod as a portable hard drive. In FireWire disk mode, you can copy music files onto your iPod from one computer, attach your iPod to another computer, and copy or move the files from the iPod to that computer. The only limitation is that the files you copy this way aren't added to your iPod's music database, so you can't play them on the iPod. But if you want to use your iPod for copying or moving the files, that shouldn't concern you too much.

So you can use your iPod to violate copyright easily if you want to. You can also use many other technologies and devices to violate copyright in this way—anything from a CD burner to a parallel cable to an Internet connection can make illegal copies of files.

But what concerns us here is that, once you've added song files to your iPod's music library, you can't immediately get them back. Normally, you shouldn't need to get them back, because they'll be redundant copies of the song files stored on your computer's hard drive or other drives.

But there may come a time when you need to get the song files out of your iPod's music library for legitimate reasons. For example, if you dropped your iBook, or your PC's hard disk died of natural causes, you might need to copy the music files from your iPod to a replacement computer. Otherwise, you might risk losing your entire music collection.

iPod enthusiasts have developed several utilities for transferring music files from an iPod's hidden music storage to a computer. This section discusses some of the possibilities. First, though, let's look at where the song files are stored on your iPod, how you can access them through conventional file-management utilities (such as the Finder or Windows Explorer), and why copying the files using conventional means yields unsatisfactory results.

Where—and How—Your iPod Stores Song Files

As you saw in Chapter 12, when you turn on FireWire disk mode, you can access the contents of your iPod's hard drive by using the Finder (on the Mac) or Windows Explorer (on Windows). Until you create other folders there, though, you'll find only the Calendars folder and the Contacts folder on your iPod—there's no trace of your song files.

> **NOTE** *You can also use other file-management utilities (if you have them) for manipulating files on your iPod, but in this chapter, I'll assume you're sticking with the Finder and Windows Explorer.*

This is because the folders in which the song files are stored are formatted to be hidden on Windows and to be invisible on the Mac. Before you can see the folders or the files they contain, you need to change the Hidden attribute on the Windows folders or the Visible attribute on the Mac folders.

> **TIP** *If you're comfortable with Unix commands, you can open a Terminal window on Mac OS X and use the ls command to list the folders and files, even though they're invisible to the Finder. You can also use the SetFile command to make hidden files visible in the finder.*

Make the Hidden Folders Visible on the Mac

To make hidden folders visible on your Mac running Mac OS X, download and install TinkerTool from **www.bresink.de/osx/TinkerTool2.html**. TinkerTool is a free configuration utility that lets you perform a variety of tweaks on Mac OS X, including making hidden folders visible.

After installing TinkerTool, follow these steps to make hidden folders visible:

1. Choose Apple | System Preferences to open the System Preferences window. (At this writing, the TinkerTool installation routine opens System Preferences automatically for you.)

2. In the Other group, click the TinkerTool icon to launch TinkerTool.

3. On the Finder tab (which is displayed by default and shown in the following image), select the Show Hidden and System Files check box in the Finder Options area.

CHAPTER 14: Learn Advanced iPod Skills   **311**

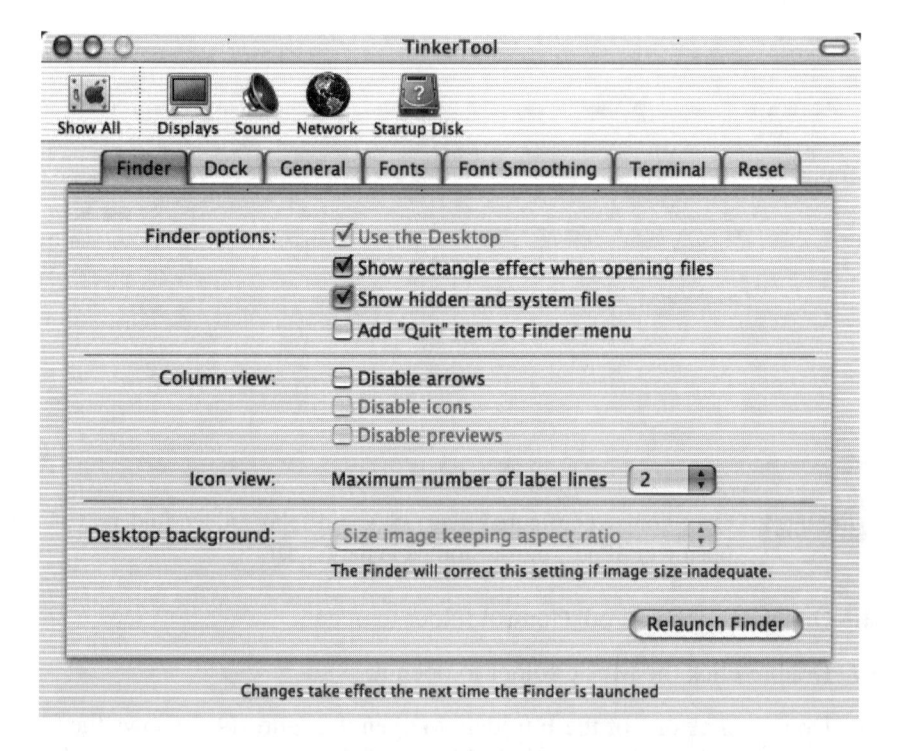

[TinkerTool window screenshot showing Finder options including "Use the Desktop", "Show rectangle effect when opening files", "Show hidden and system files", "Add 'Quit' item to Finder menu", Column view options, Icon view, and Desktop background settings, with a Relaunch Finder button.]

4. Click the Relaunch Finder button in TinkerTool to relaunch the Finder. (You need to relaunch the Finder to make it read the now-visible folders.)

5. Press COMMAND-Q or choose System Preferences | Quit System Preferences to quit System Preferences.

After the Finder relaunches, you can examine the song folders. To do so, follow these steps:

1. Connect your iPod to your Mac via the FireWire cable as usual.

2. If you haven't yet enabled FireWire disk mode, enable it.

3. Double-click your iPod's icon on the desktop to display its contents in a Finder window. The contents will include the Calendars folder and the Contacts folder, as before, but you'll also be able to see the previously hidden files and folders: the iPod_Control folder, the .Trashes folder, and the files .DS_Store, .VolumeIcon.cns, Desktop DB, Desktop DF, and Icon.

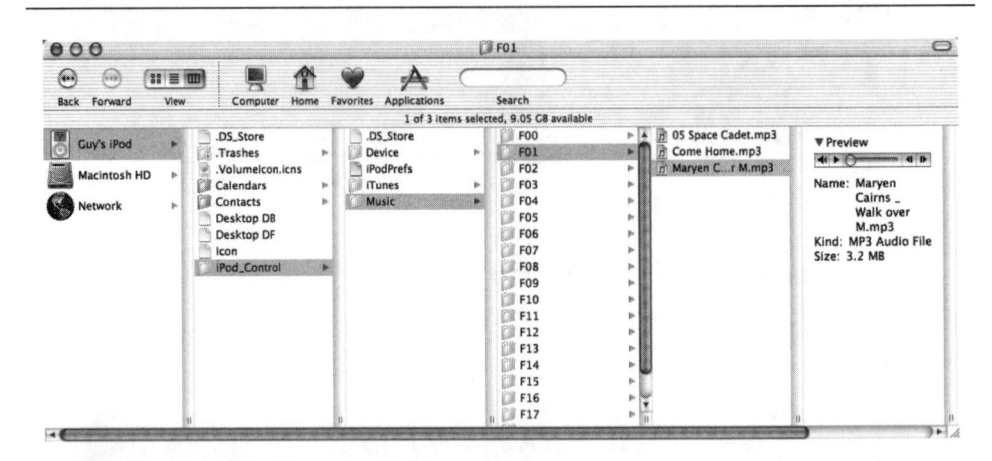

FIGURE 14-2 Once you've configured Mac OS X to display hidden folders, you can open your iPod's music storage in the Finder.

4. Double-click the iPod_Control folder to open it.

5. Double-click the Music folder to open it.

6. Double-click one of the F folders to open it. Figure 14-2 shows the structure of the iPod's music folders in Column view.

Making the Hidden Folders Visible in Windows

To display hidden files and folders in Windows XP, follow these steps:

1. Choose Start | My Computer to open a My Computer window.

2. Choose Tools | Folder Options to display the Folder Options dialog box.

3. Click the View tab to display it (Figure 14-3).

4. Select the Show Hidden Files and Folders option button.

5. Click the OK button to apply the change and to close the Folder Options dialog box. Windows Explorer now displays hidden files and folders as well as normal, unhidden files and folders.

To see the song folders on your iPod, follow these steps:

CHAPTER 14: Learn Advanced iPod Skills **313**

1. Double-click the icon for your iPod in the My Computer window. Windows Explorer displays the contents of your iPod: the Calendars folder and the Contacts folder as before, but also an iPod_Control folder that was previously hidden.

2. Double-click the iPod_Control folder to display its contents: a Device folder, an iTunes folder, and a Music folder.

3. Double-click the Music folder to display its contents: a series of folders named F*NN*, where *NN* is a two-digit number: F00, F01, F02, and so on.

4. Double-click one of these F folders to display its contents. Figure 14-4 shows an example.

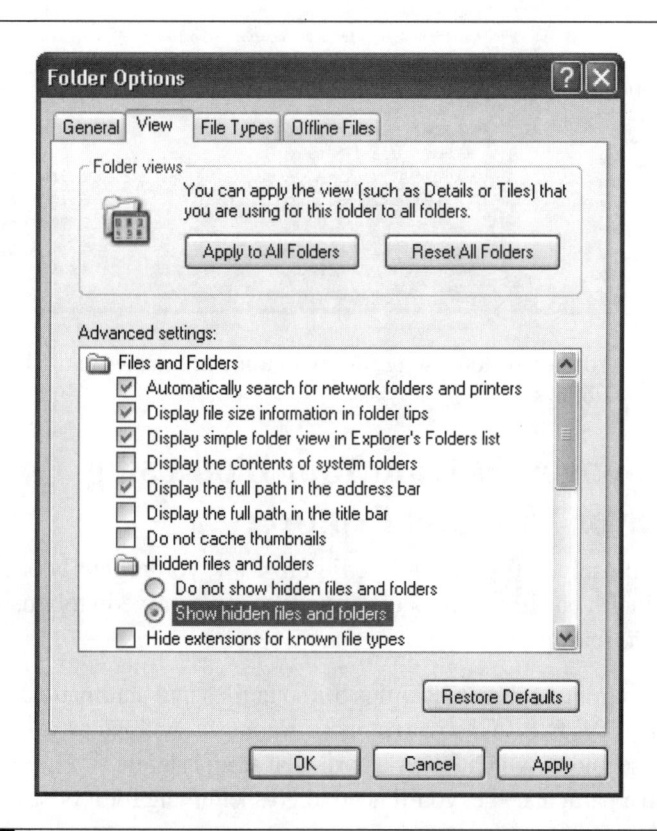

FIGURE 14-3 Select the Show Hidden Files and Folders option button on the View tab of the Folder Options dialog box in Windows Explorer to display hidden files and folders.

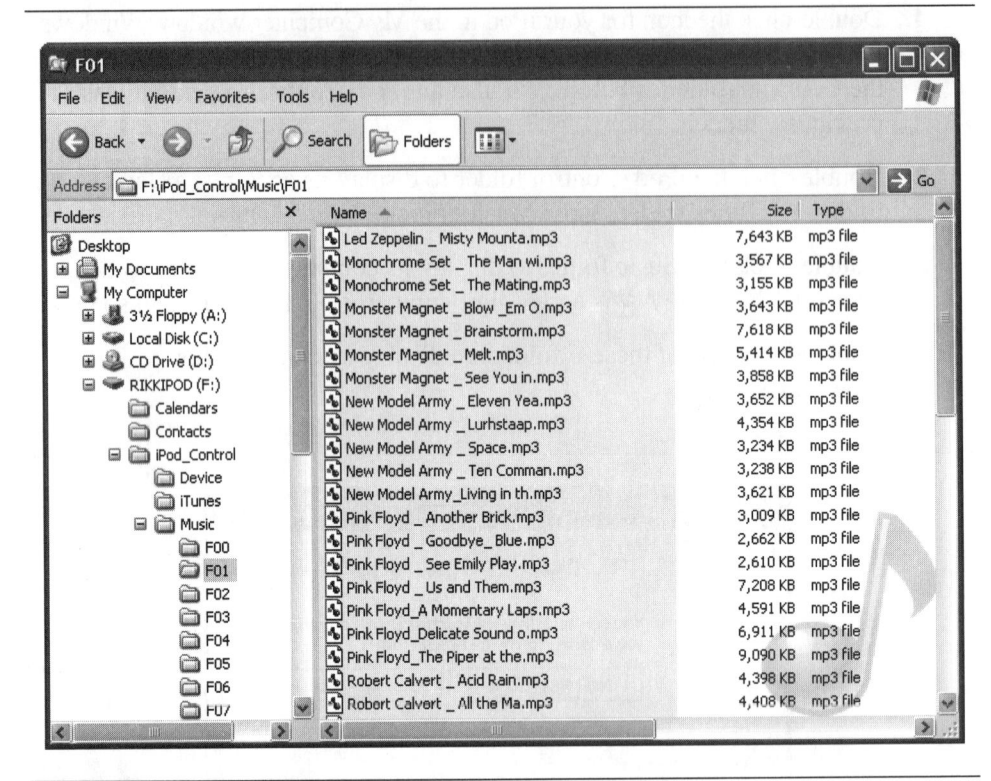

FIGURE 14-4 Your iPod stores song files with truncated names in the F01 folder and its siblings.

Transfer Song Files from Your iPod Using the Finder or Windows Explorer

If you looked closely at Figure 14-2 or Figure 14-4, you probably have noticed that the way in which your iPod stores the song files isn't immediately useful to most humans for two reasons:

- First, your iPod arbitrarily lumps the song files into automatically named folders (F01, F02, and so on) at its convenience. As long as your iPod's internal database knows which folder a particular song is in, that's fine. But if you want to find a particular file, you'll need to go spelunking for it or search for it.

- Second, your iPod truncates and mashes the names of the song files. It truncates longer filenames down to 27 characters, plus the extension. So the track "Pink Floyd – Get Your Filthy Hands Off My Desert.mp3" becomes "Pink Floyd _ Get Your Filth.mp3"—a more interesting title, perhaps, but not how you want the file represented in your file system. And it substitutes extended characters with alternative formulations. For example, "Alizée" becomes "Aliz_e". Again, such machinations confuse humans, and you'll find it tedious renaming such files.

So if you copy (or move) song files from your iPod's song folders to your computer (or another computer), you'll need to perform some heavy-duty sorting and renaming afterwards. Even this will likely be preferable to losing your entire music collection (if you've lost your music library)—but you'll probably feel there's got to be a better way.

There is. Read on.

Utilities for Transferring Song Files from Your iPod to Your Computer

This section discusses three utilities for transferring song files from your iPod to your computer. If you don't like the look (or performance) of these utilities, search sites such as VersionTracker.com (**www.versiontracker.com**), MacUpdate (**www.macupdate.com**), and Apple's Mac OS X Downloads page (**www.apple.com/macosx/downloads**) for alternatives.

> **NOTE** *Here's a quick note for choosing utilities: They work in different ways. Some utilities read the database the iPod maintains of the tracks it holds, while other utilities painstakingly plow through each MP3 file on your iPod and extract information from its ID3 tags. As you'd guess, reading the iPod's database gives much faster results than assembling what's essentially the same database from scratch by scouring the tags.*

Podestal

Podestal (free; **www.codefab.com/unsupported/**) is a basic utility for copying song files (from the Music tab) or other files (from the Files tab) from your iPod to your computer. Basic? Yes: Podestal doesn't rename files—you'll need to do that yourself after copying them. So unless your song files use short names, you may prefer a more sophisticated solution. But Podestal is fast and easy to use.

As you can see in Figure 14-5, Podestal provides a simple user interface that lists the songs by artist. When you select one or more songs, Podestal displays an icon in the lower-right corner of the window. You drag this icon to a Finder window or your desktop to copy the song files.

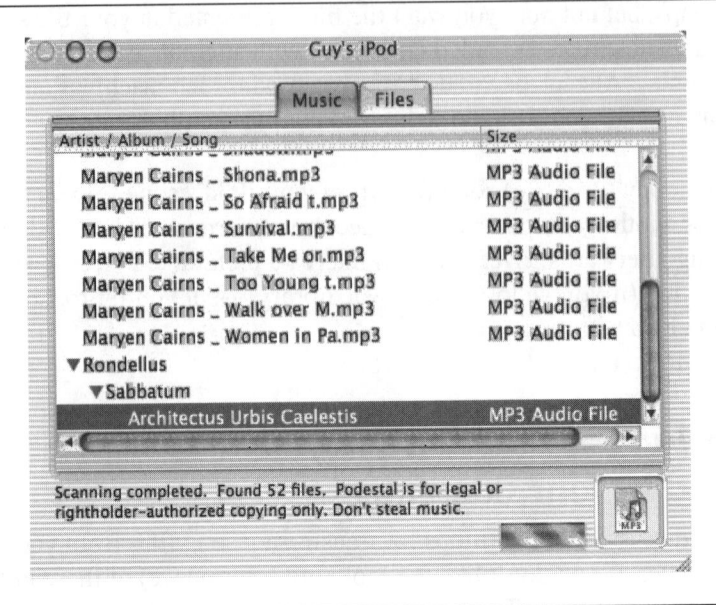

FIGURE 14-5 Podestal can quickly copy song files from your iPod, but it doesn't rename them.

PodWorks (Mac OS X 10.2 or Later)

PodWorks from Sci-Fi Hi-Fi ($5.99; **www.scifihifi.com/podworks/**) is a great utility for transferring music files from your iPod to your Mac. PodWorks requires Mac OS X 10.2 or later. You can download an evaluation version that limits you to 30 days, copying 250 songs, and copying one song at a time—enough limitations to persuade you to buy the full version. Figure 14-6 shows PodWorks.

To download song files to your Mac using PodWorks, follow these steps:

1. Click the Preferences button or choose PodWorks | Preferences to display the PodWorks Preferences dialog box, shown in the following image:

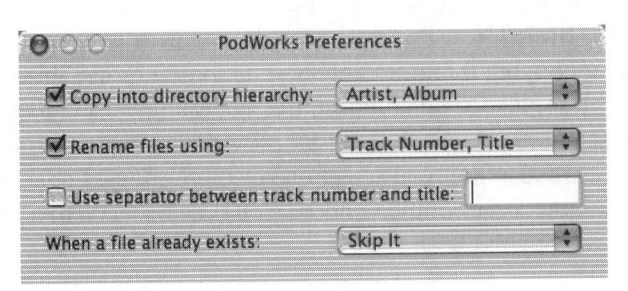

CHAPTER 14: *Learn Advanced iPod Skills* **317**

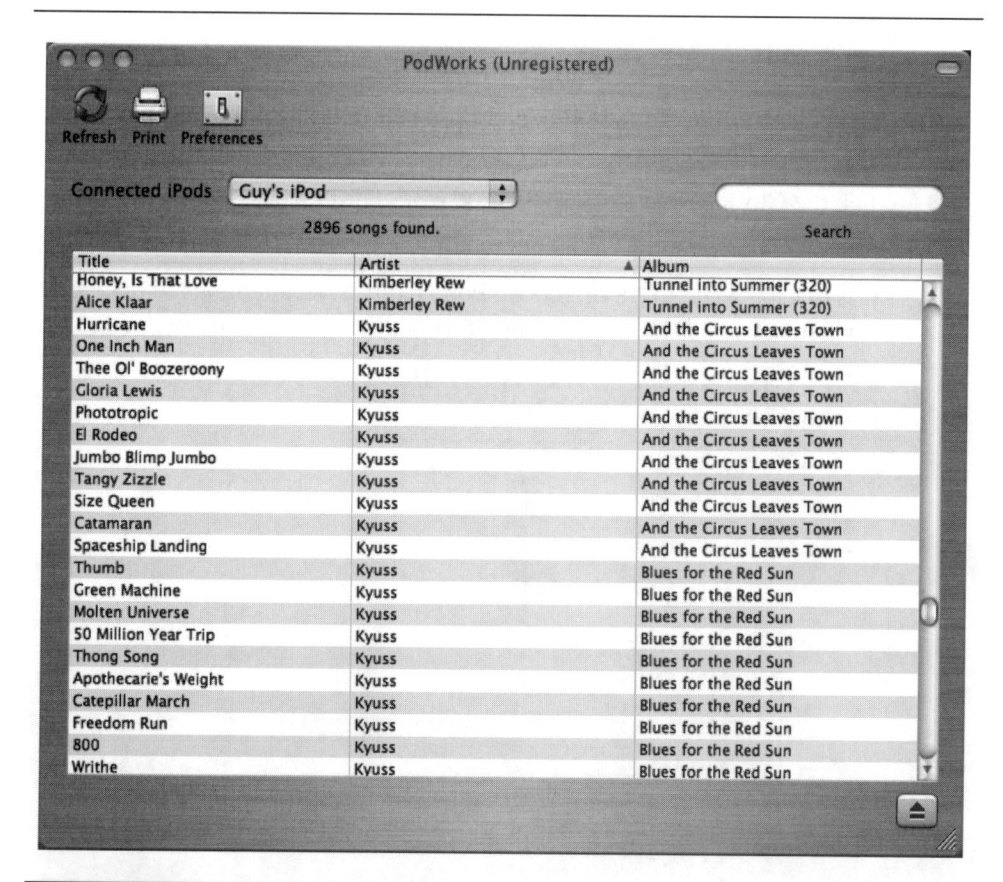

Title	Artist	Album
Honey, Is That Love	Kimberley Rew	Tunnel into Summer (320)
Alice Klaar	Kimberley Rew	Tunnel into Summer (320)
Hurricane	Kyuss	And the Circus Leaves Town
One Inch Man	Kyuss	And the Circus Leaves Town
Thee Ol' Boozeroony	Kyuss	And the Circus Leaves Town
Gloria Lewis	Kyuss	And the Circus Leaves Town
Phototropic	Kyuss	And the Circus Leaves Town
El Rodeo	Kyuss	And the Circus Leaves Town
Jumbo Blimp Jumbo	Kyuss	And the Circus Leaves Town
Tangy Zizzle	Kyuss	And the Circus Leaves Town
Size Queen	Kyuss	And the Circus Leaves Town
Catamaran	Kyuss	And the Circus Leaves Town
Spaceship Landing	Kyuss	And the Circus Leaves Town
Thumb	Kyuss	Blues for the Red Sun
Green Machine	Kyuss	Blues for the Red Sun
Molten Universe	Kyuss	Blues for the Red Sun
50 Million Year Trip	Kyuss	Blues for the Red Sun
Thong Song	Kyuss	Blues for the Red Sun
Apothecarie's Weight	Kyuss	Blues for the Red Sun
Catepillar March	Kyuss	Blues for the Red Sun
Freedom Run	Kyuss	Blues for the Red Sun
800	Kyuss	Blues for the Red Sun
Writhe	Kyuss	Blues for the Red Sun

FIGURE 14-6 PodWorks is a powerful utility for transferring music files from your iPod to your Mac.

2. To copy the song files into folders, select the Copy into Directory Hierarchy check box. Then, in the drop-down list, select the *Artist, Album* entry or the *Artist* entry, as appropriate.

3. To rename the copied files (rather than using their truncated or otherwise mangled names), select the Rename Files Using check box. Then, in the drop-down list, select the *Track Number, Title* entry or the *Title* entry, as appropriate.

4. If you select the Rename Files Using check box and choose the *Track Number, Title* entry for renaming, you can select the Use Separator Between Track Number and Title check box to make PodWorks insert a separator character in the filename. Enter the separator character or characters in the text box.

For example, you might enter a space, a hyphen, and another space to produce filenames such as 01 – Powertrip.mp3 rather than 01 Powertrip.mp3.

5. In the When a File Already Exists drop-down list, select the Skip It entry or the Overwrite It entry, as appropriate.

6. Click the Close button to close the PodWorks Preferences dialog box.

7. Select the song or songs you want to copy.

8. Press COMMAND-SHIFT-S or choose Pod | Copy Selected Songs to display the Choose Copy Destination dialog box, shown in the following image.

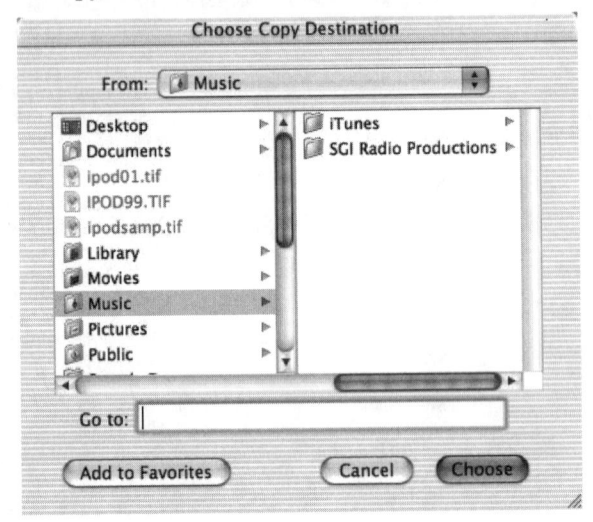

9. Specify the destination, and then click the Choose button. PodWorks creates the folders and copies the files.

TIP *Alternatively, you can drag songs from PodWorks to a Finder window to have PodWorks create the folders and files in the folder displayed.*

EphPod (Windows)

EphPod (pronounced *eefpod* rather than *effpod*, and downloadable from **www.ephpod.com**) is a free and very full-featured application for managing iPods on Windows. EphPod was originally built to enable you to use Mac iPods with Windows PCs. As you'd imagine, that was in the days before Apple teamed up with MUSICMATCH to deliver the version of MUSICMATCH Jukebox Plus that works with Windows iPods and the Updaters with which you can change Mac iPods to Windows iPods.

These days, EphPod works with Windows iPods as well. EphPod still lets you use Mac iPods with Windows, but you need to use MacOpener, a $40 product from

DataViz, Inc. (**www.dataviz.com**), to enable Windows to read a Mac iPod's HFS Plus-formatted disk. Few users want to spend good music money on MacOpener when they can convert their Mac iPod to a Windows iPod instead and manage it for free.

Unless you dislike MUSICMATCH Jukebox Plus, EphPod is primarily interesting for its extra features. For example, as discussed in the "EphPod" section in Chapter 10, you can use EphPod to put news feeds on your iPod. But for most Windows iPod users, EphPod's most compelling feature is its capability to download the song files from your iPod to your hard disk and name them according to conventions you specify. This makes EphPod great for recovering song files from your Windows iPod.

To download song files using EphPod, follow these steps:

1. Click the Configure EphPod button on the toolbar, or choose Extras | Configuration, to display the Configuration dialog box.

2. Click the Advanced Options tab to display it (see the following image):

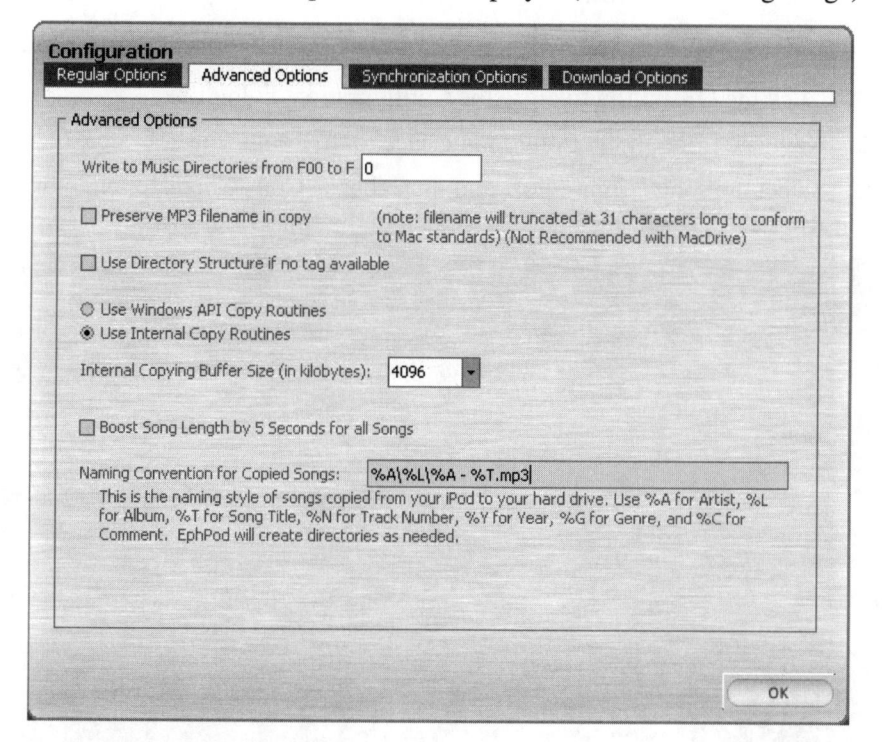

3. Make sure the Preserve MP3 Filename in Copy check box is cleared.

4. Make sure the Use Internal Copy Routines option button is selected.

5. To improve performance, increase the size of the Internal Copying Buffer Size drop-down list from its default setting of 1024KB to 4096KB.

6. In the Naming Convention for Copied Songs text box, enter the format EphPod should use for creating folders and naming the MP3 files it saves to your hard disk. You can use the variables shown in the following list to use information from the tags on the MP3 files. For example, you might use %A\%L\%A – %T.mp3 to create folders and files such as Artist\Album\Artist – Song Title.mp3.

Variable	Explanation
%A	Artist name
%L	Album title
%T	Song title
%N	Track number
%Y	Year
%G	Genre
%C	Comment

7. Click the OK button to close the Configuration dialog box.
8. Navigate through the EphPod interface to the songs you want to export.
9. Select the songs, right-click, and then choose Copy Songs to Directory from the shortcut menu, as illustrated in the following image:

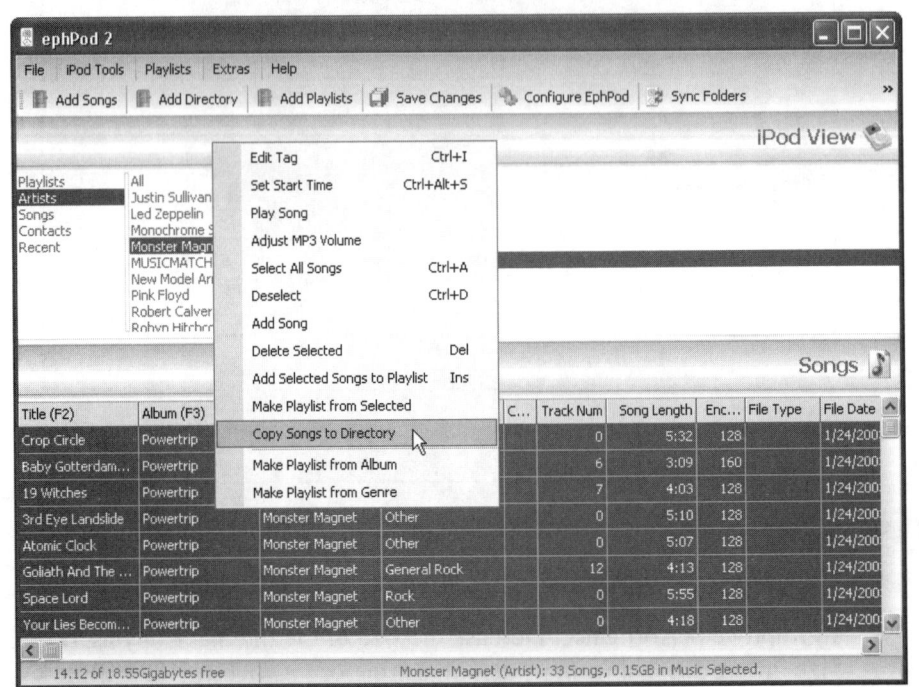

10. In the Browse for Folder dialog box, select the folder in which you want EphPod to create the folders and files.

11. Click the OK button. EphPod copies the files and folders and names them according to the convention you specified.

Play Songs from Your iPod Through Your Computer

Another capability of the iPod that's not immediately obvious is that you can play music from your iPod through your computer's speakers by setting the music playing from iTunes or MUSICMATCH Jukebox Plus. iTunes or MUSICMATCH Jukebox Plus reads the track information off the iPod via the FireWire cable and plays it through its sound system as though it were reading the data from the hard drive or another local drive. (Which it is, thanks to FireWire.)

Depending on what kind of speakers your computer has and how much you enjoy listening to them, this item may be anything from a curiosity to an indispensable part of your listening.

This capability tends to be most useful when your iPod contains tracks that the computer in question doesn't contain. (If the computer contains the tracks, it's easier to play the tracks directly from the computer.) If the computer is the one with which you use your iPod, the only reason to use this capability (beyond curiosity) is if you've configured your iPod for manual updating because it contains a music library larger than your computer can hold. More likely, you'll want to use this capability with a computer other than your own—for example, when you're visiting a friend, and you want them to hear the great music they've been missing.

To play songs from your iPod using a computer, follow these steps:

1. Connect your iPod to the computer through which you want to play the music. If this computer isn't your iPod's home computer, iTunes or MUSICMATCH Portables Plus may offer to synchronize with this computer (depending on the settings currently in effect). Click the No button.

2. Display the contents of your iPod:

    - In iTunes, select your iPod's icon in the Source pane.

    - In MUSICMATCH Portables Plus, select your iPod's icon in the left-hand pane.

3. Select the song or songs you want to play.

4. In iTunes, press SPACEBAR or click the Play button. In MUSICMATCH Portables Plus, right-click the tracks and choose Play from the context menu.

Use the iTunes controls or MUSICMATCH Jukebox Plus controls to pause play, apply equalizations, or change the volume. As usual when connected to your PC via the FireWire cable, your iPod is acting as a slave drive, so its controls won't respond.

Chapter 15

Troubleshoot Any iPod Problems You Encounter

How to...

- Avoid voiding your warranty
- Know the best approach for troubleshooting your iPod
- Learn key troubleshooting maneuvers
- Use your iPod's built-in diagnostic tools to pinpoint problems
- Troubleshoot common and less-common problems

It goes without saying that Apple has built the iPod to be as reliable as possible—after all, Apple would like to sell at least one iPod to everyone in the world who has a computer, and they'd much prefer to be thwarted in this aim by economics than by negative feedback. But even so, iPods go wrong sometimes. This chapter shows you what to do when it's your iPod that goes wrong.

This chapter pursues a two-pronged approach to troubleshooting. First, it shows you some standard troubleshooting maneuvers you may need to perform to resuscitate your iPod or rope its operating system back under control, and some diagnostics you may want to try when you think something is really wrong (or you want to see what—if anything—the diagnostic tests do). Second, it presents problems as they'll typically manifest themselves, and then walks you through troubleshooting the problems and—with any luck—solving them.

Before we get our—your—hands grubby, let's talk briefly about the warranty your iPod should have included and how you can avoid voiding it.

Your Warranty and How to Void It

Like most electronics goods, your iPod almost certainly came with a warranty. Unlike with most other electronics goods, your chances of needing to use that warranty are relatively high. This is because you're likely to use your iPod extensively and carry it with you.

Even if you don't sit on your iPod, rain or other water doesn't creep into it, and gravity doesn't dash it sharply against something unforgiving (such as the sidewalk), your iPod may suffer from other problems—anything from critters or debris jamming the FireWire port to its hard drive getting corrupted or its operating system getting scrambled. If this happens, you'll probably want to get your iPod repaired under warranty—provided you haven't voided the warranty.

CHAPTER 15: Troubleshoot Any iPod Problems You Encounter

The first iPods carried a 90-day warranty, which inspired little confidence in the iPods' durability. However, Apple then moved to a one-year warranty both for newer iPods and for those already sold. The iPod Service Page (**depot.info.apple.com/ipod/index.html**) contains details of which iPods are still under warranty.

Most of the warranty is pretty straightforward, but the following points are worth noting:

- You have to make your claim within the warranty period, so if your iPod fails a day short of a year after you bought it, you'll need to make your claim instantly.

- Apple can choose whether to repair your iPod using either new or refurbished parts, exchange it for another iPod that's at least functionally equivalent but may be either new or rebuilt (and may contain used parts), or refund you the purchase price of your iPod. Unless you have valuable data on your iPod, the refund is a great option, because you'll be able to get a new iPod—perhaps even a higher-capacity one.

- Apple takes no responsibility for getting back any data on your iPod. This isn't surprising, as Apple may need to reformat your iPod's hard drive or replace it. But this means that you must back up your iPod if it contains data you value that you don't have copies of elsewhere.

NOTE *As you'll know if you've bought electrical appliances, many retailers offer extended warranties on products. As you'll know if you've read consumer legislation, many extended warranties are essentially a waste of money. This is because the extended warranties largely duplicate your existing rights as a consumer to be sold a product that's functional and of merchantable quality. However, for a high-risk device like the iPod, some retailers' warranties are worth considering. For example, CompUSA offers a Technology Assurance Program (TAP) that provides two years of service and a one-time replacement of your iPod if you break it.*

You can void your warranty more or less effortlessly in any of the following easily avoidable ways:

- Damage your iPod deliberately.

- Open your iPod or have someone other than Apple open it for you. As discussed in the section "What You Might Want to Know about Your iPod's Internals" in Chapter 11, your iPod isn't designed to be opened by anyone except trained technicians. Unless you're highly skillful, very careful, and you have the right tools, all you'll achieve by opening your iPod is damage.

- Modify your iPod. Modifications such as installing a larger drive in the iPod would necessarily involve opening your iPod anyway, but external modifications can void your warranty, too. For example, if you choose to trepan your iPod so as to screw a holder directly onto it, you would void your warranty. (You'd also stand a great chance of drilling into something sensitive inside the case.)

How to Approach Troubleshooting Your iPod

When something goes wrong with your iPod, take three deep breaths before you do anything. Then take another three deep breaths if you need them. Then try to work out what's wrong.

Remember that a calm and rational approach will always get you further than blind panic. This is easy to say (and if you're reading this when your iPod is running smoothly, easy to nod your head at). But if you've just dropped your iPod onto a hard surface from a significant height, gotten caught with it in an unexpectedly heavy shower, or left it on the roof of your car so it fell off just in time for you to back over it, you'll probably be desperate to find out if your iPod is alive or dead.

So take those three deep breaths. You may well *not* have ruined your iPod forever—but if you take some heavy-duty troubleshooting actions without making sure they're necessary, you might lose some data that wasn't already lost or do some damage you'll have trouble repairing.

Before we start, it's worth remembering the range of things that can go wrong with your iPod:

- Your iPod's hardware—anything from the FireWire port to the battery or the hard disk
- Your iPod's software
- Your iPod's power adapter
- Your FireWire cable
- Your computer's FireWire port or FireWire controller
- The software you're using to control your iPod (iTunes or MUSICMATCH Jukebox Plus)

Given all these possibilities, be prepared to spend some time troubleshooting any problem.

Learn Troubleshooting Maneuvers

This section discusses several maneuvers you may need to use to troubleshoot your iPod: resetting your iPod, draining its battery, restoring its operating system on either Mac OS X or Windows, running a disk scan, and using its built-in diagnostic tools to pinpoint problems.

Reset Your iPod

If your iPod freezes so it doesn't respond to the controls, you can reset it by connecting it to a power source (either a computer that's not sleeping or an electrical socket), and then holding down the Menu button and the Play/Pause button for several seconds. When your iPod displays the Apple logo, release the buttons, and then give your iPod a few seconds to finish booting.

Drain Your iPod's Battery

If you can't reset your iPod, its battery might have gotten into such a low state that it needs draining. (This supposedly seldom happens—but it might happen to your iPod.) To drain the battery, disconnect your iPod from its power source and leave it for 24 hours. Then try plugging your iPod into a power source. After your iPod has received power for a few seconds, hold down the Menu button and the Play/Pause button to reset it.

If draining the battery and recharging it revives your iPod, update your iPod's software with the latest update from Apple Software Updates (**www.apple.com/swupdates**) to try to prevent the problem from occurring again. See the section "Keep Your iPod's Operating System Up-to-Date" in Chapter 11 for details on how to update your iPod's operating system.

Restore Your iPod

If your iPod is having severe difficulties, you may need to restore it. Restoring your iPod replaces its operating system with a new copy of the operating system that has Apple's factory settings.

CAUTION *Restoring your iPod deletes all the data on your iPod's hard disk— the operating system, all your music, all your contacts and calendar information—and returns your iPod to its original factory settings. So restoring your iPod is usually a last resort when troubleshooting. If possible, back up all the data you care about that's stored on your iPod before restoring it. (Only "if possible"? Yes—if your iPod is so messed up you need to restore it, you may not be able to back up the data.)*

To restore your iPod, you need the iPod Software Updater. To get the best results, it's a good idea to download the latest version of the Updater for your operating system from the Apple Software Downloads web site (**www.apple.com/swupdates/**), and then follow the instructions in the next section (for Mac OS X) or the section after that (for Windows XP).

Restore Your iPod on Mac OS X

To restore your iPod on Mac OS X, follow these steps:

1. Connect your iPod to your computer via the FireWire cable.

2. Run the iPod Software Updater. (You should find it in the Applications: Utilities:iPod Software Updater folder unless you've moved it or someone else has moved it.) Your Mac displays an iPod Software Updater window such as that shown in the following image:

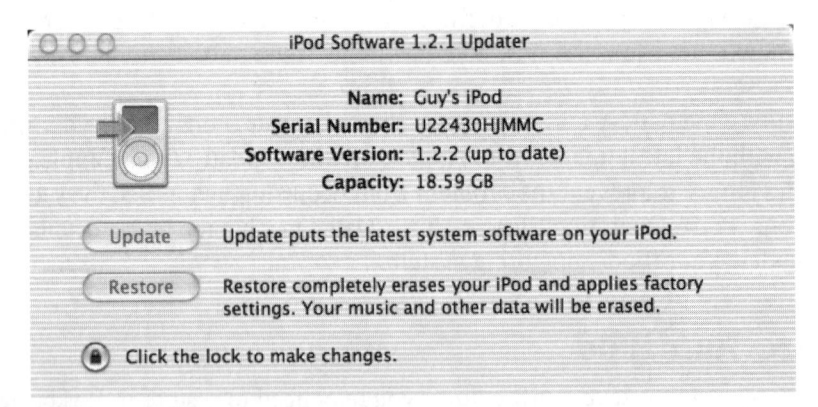

   iPod Software 1.2.1 Updater

   Name: Guy's iPod
   Serial Number: U22430HJMMC
   Software Version: 1.2.2 (up to date)
   Capacity: 18.59 GB

   Update — Update puts the latest system software on your iPod.

   Restore — Restore completely erases your iPod and applies factory settings. Your music and other data will be erased.

   🔒 Click the lock to make changes.

3. If the lower-left corner of the Updater window contains a lock icon and the text "Click the lock to make changes," click the lock icon to display the

CHAPTER 15: Troubleshoot Any iPod Problems You Encounter   **329**

Authenticate dialog box (shown in the following image). Enter your password in the Password or Phrase text box, and then click the OK button. If you entered the correct password, the Updater returns you to the Update window and enables the Update button (if you can install an updated version of the iPod software) and the Restore button.

4. Click the Restore button to start the restore process. The Updater displays a final warning, as shown in the following image, to make sure you understand you're about to lose all the data on your iPod:

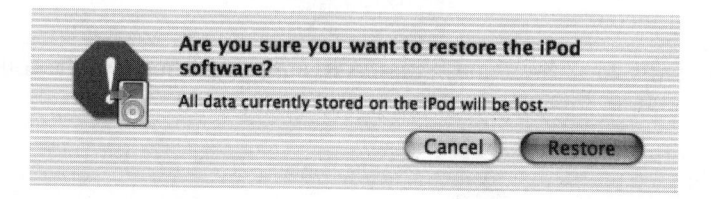

5. Click the Restore button if you're absolutely sure you want to proceed. The Updater displays the Authenticate dialog box again to make sure you're legitimate.

6. Enter your password, and then click the OK button. The Updater restores your iPod's operating system, deletes the files on it, and then displays an iPod Software Updater window, such as that shown in the following image, telling you that it has restored your iPod to factory settings and asking you to unplug and replug your iPod to complete the restore process.

330 How to Do Everything with Your iPod

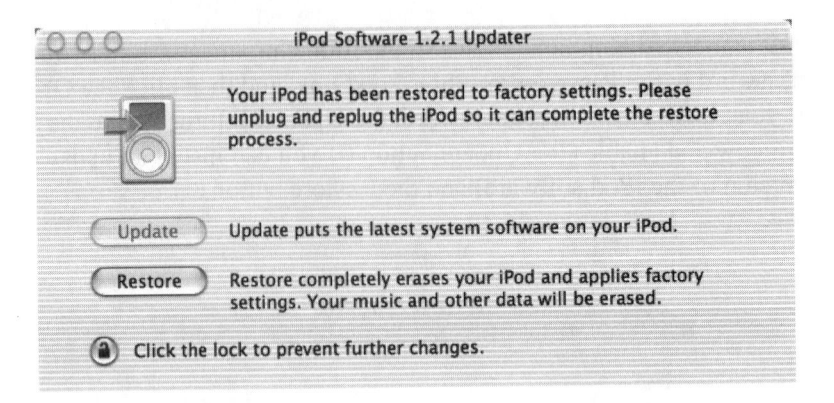

7. Unplug your iPod from the FireWire cable, and then plug it back in when it displays a FireWire cable and socket. Your iPod displays an Apple logo and a progress bar as it completes the restoration process.

8. To prevent anyone else from restoring your iPod, click the lock icon in the iPod Software Updater window.

9. Press CTRL-Q or choose iPod Updater | Quit iPod Updater to close the iPod Software Updater window.

10. Your iPod should then appear on your desktop. If it doesn't, you may need to reset it by holding down the Menu button and the Play/Pause button for several seconds.

11. iTunes displays the iTunes Setup Assistant page shown in the following illustration:

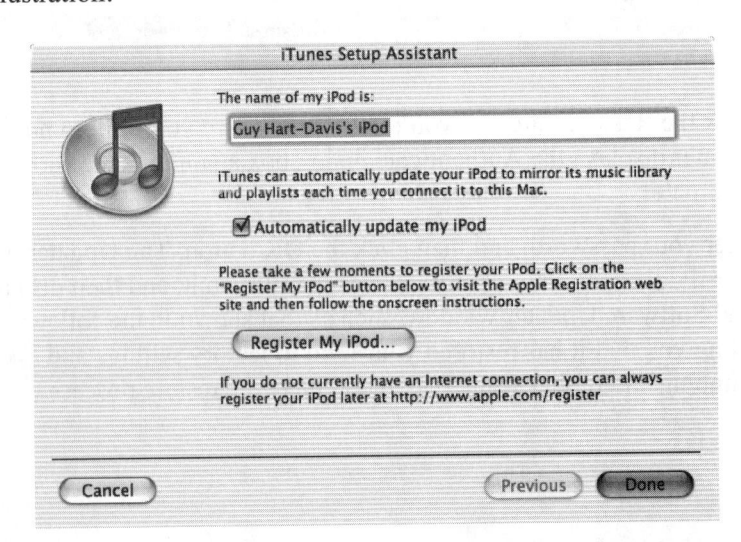

12. Enter the name for your iPod in the text box. Select or clear the Automatically Update My iPod check box as appropriate, then click the Done button. iTunes then synchronizes your iPod with the music library if it's set for automatic synchronization.

NOTE *After you next disconnect your iPod, you'll need to specify the language for it to use.*

Restore Your iPod on Windows XP

To restore your iPod on Windows XP, follow these steps:

1. Connect your iPod to your PC via the FireWire cable. If MUSICMATCH Jukebox Plus runs, let it synchronize your iPod (if it can). Then close MUSICMATCH Jukebox Plus.

2. Choose Start | All Programs | iPod | Updater to display the iPod Software Updater window (shown in the following image):

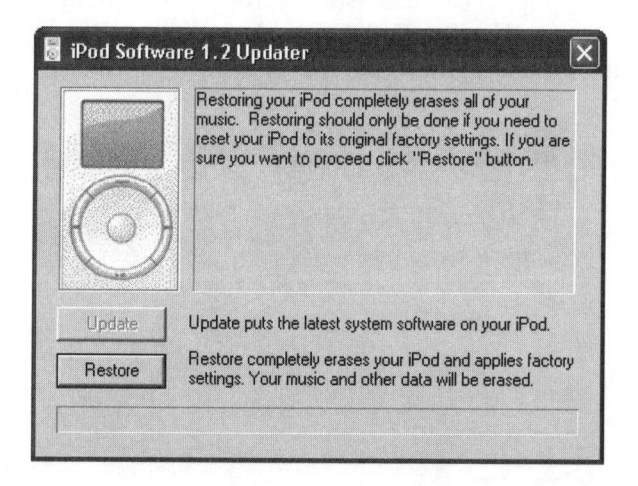

CAUTION *Unlike the iPod Software Updater for the Mac, the iPod Software Updater for Windows doesn't double-check if you're sure you know what you're doing when you click the Restore button.*

3. Click the Restore button. The Updater performs the first part of the restoration process, and then prompts you to disconnect your iPod, as shown in the following illustration, to allow its firmware to be reflashed.

332 How to Do Everything with Your iPod

> **iPod Software 1.2 Updater**
>
> Please disconnect iPod from your PC to allow firmware reflash.
>
> [Update] Update puts the latest system software on your iPod.
> [Restore] Restore completely erases your iPod and applies factory settings. Your music and other data will be erased.

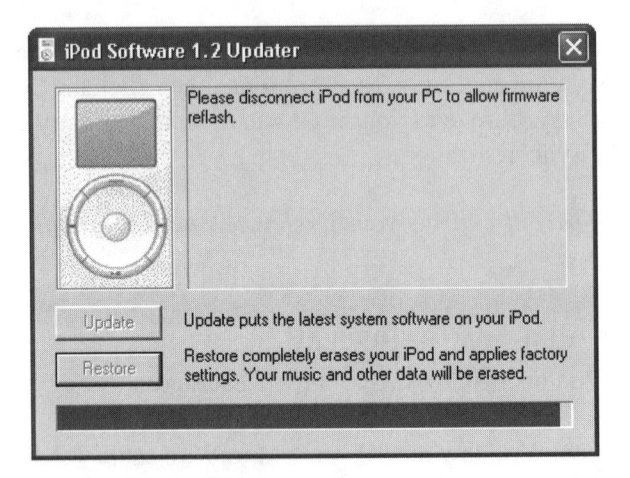

4. Unplug your iPod for a few seconds. When your iPod displays an icon indicating you should plug the FireWire cable back into your iPod, do so.

5. Wait while the iPod Software Updater completes the restoration process. You'll see a progress bar inch its way across the bottom of the iPod Software Updater window. The iPod Software Updater window then displays a Restore Complete message, as shown in the following illustration:

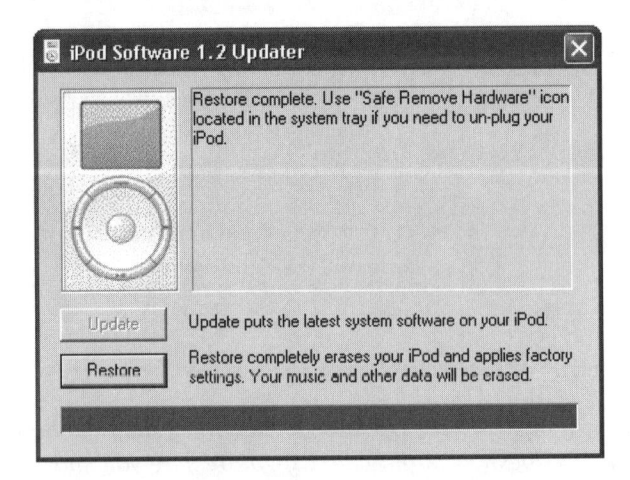

> **iPod Software 1.2 Updater**
>
> Restore complete. Use "Safe Remove Hardware" icon located in the system tray if you need to un-plug your iPod.
>
> [Update] Update puts the latest system software on your iPod.
> [Restore] Restore completely erases your iPod and applies factory settings. Your music and other data will be erased.

6. Click the Close button in the upper-right corner of the iPod Software Updater window to close the iPod Software Updater. MUSICMATCH Portables Plus launches automatically and displays the Device Setup dialog box.

CHAPTER 15: Troubleshoot Any iPod Problems You Encounter **333**

7. Configure your iPod as described in the section "First Connection: Configure Device Setup Options" in Chapter 4, and then follow through with the rest of the first-synchronization process. After you disconnect your iPod, you'll need to set the language it uses.

Run a Disk Scan

If you think there might be something wrong with your iPod's hard disk, you can make your iPod run a disk scan to find out. A scan takes roughly 15 to 30 minutes, depending on the capacity of your iPod's hard disk, so set aside plenty of time to run the scan.

To run a disk scan, follow these steps:

1. Hold down the Menu button and the Play/Pause button for a few seconds to reset your iPod.

2. When your iPod displays the Apple logo, hold down the Previous button, the Next button, the Select button, and the Menu button for a second or two. (Guitarists can usually perform this maneuver more easily than other people. If you're not a guitarist, put your iPod down on a firm surface first.)

3. Your iPod then performs a disk scan, displaying a magnifying glass poring over a hard disk and a progress bar as it does so (see the following illustration):

4. When the scan has finished, check the icon your iPod is displaying:

   - A check mark on a disk icon means the disk is fine.

   - An exclamation mark on a disk icon means the disk scan failed.

   - An arrow on a disk icon means that the scan fixed some problems it found. Restore your iPod to resume normal service. (If your iPod contains valuable files that you don't have copies of elsewhere, try to rescue those files before restoring your iPod.)

- An exclamation point in a warning triangle on a picture of an iPod with a sad face means the hard disk isn't working. Go directly to Apple Support. Do not pass Go. Collect $200 from the ATM if your iPod's out of warranty.

5. Press the Play button to exit the disk-scan mode.

NOTE *If your iPod runs a disk scan automatically when you start it, it suspects there's a problem with the hard drive. It's best to allow the scan to continue, but in extreme circumstances, you may need to cancel the scan. To cancel it, hold down the Select button for a few seconds. Your iPod then displays a disk icon with a cross mark on it, which means it'll repeat the disk scan the next time you turn it on.*

Use Your iPod's Diagnostics to Pinpoint Problems

Next along the line of troubleshooting tools are the diagnostic tools built into your iPod's operating system. To access the diagnostic tools, follow these steps:

1. Hold down the Menu button and the Play/Pause button for a few seconds to reset your iPod.

2. When your iPod displays the Apple logo, hold down the Previous button, the Next button, and the Select button together for a couple of seconds.

3. When the screen goes blank, release the buttons. Your iPod momentarily displays a screen of scattered text that details the version number of the diagnostic tools. Then it displays a list of diagnostic tests, as shown in the following illustration:

```
A . 5 IN 1
B . RESET
C . KEY
D . AUDIO
E . REMOTE
F . FIREWIRE
G . SLEEP
H . A 2 D
```

To open the diagnostic tests, use the following keys:

- Press the Next button and the Previous button to navigate through the list of tests.

CHAPTER 15: Troubleshoot Any iPod Problems You Encounter   **335**

- Press the Select button to run the highlighted test.
- Press the Play button to return from the results of a test to the diagnostic screen.
- Reset your iPod (hold down the Menu button and the Play/Pause button for a few seconds) to leave the diagnostic screen.

The following subsections discuss the diagnostic tests you'll most likely want to perform.

Check the FireWire Port

To check the FireWire port on your iPod, run the FireWire test. If your iPod displays FW PASS, your FireWire port is working. If your iPod displays FW FAIL, seek professional assistance.

Check the Audio Subsystem

To check your iPod's audio subsystem, run the Audio test. A result of 0X00000001 DONE means that your audio subsystem is okay. Any other result may mean your iPod needs help.

Check the RAM

To check your iPod's RAM (the 32MB chip used for buffering audio), run the SDRAM test. If all is well, your iPod displays SDRAM PASS. If there's a problem, your iPod displays SDRAM FAIL.

Check the iPod's Buttons

If one of the buttons on your iPod seems to stop working, you'll probably be able to tell without diagnostics. But before you call for backup, you may want to check that your iPod agrees with you that there's a problem. To do so, run the Key test. Your iPod gives you five seconds to press all the buttons on your iPod's front panel. If you do so, and all the buttons are working, your iPod displays KEY PASS. If you miss a button, or if one or more of the buttons isn't working, your iPod displays KEY FAIL.

Check the Remote Control

To check the remote control, plug in the remote control, and then run the Remote test. Press each button on the remote control: Volume Up, Volume Down, Next, Previous, and Play/Pause. (You don't need to move the Hold button on the remote control.) When you've done so, your iPod displays RMT PASS if all the buttons are working correctly. If you miss a button, or if one or more of the buttons isn't working, your iPod displays RMT FAIL.

Check the Scroll Wheel

To check the scroll wheel, run the OTPO CNT test. (OTPO is a typo—it should be OPTO.) When you do so, your iPod displays the text OPTO TEST, OPT and the value of the current position of the scroll wheel in hexadecimal (for example, 0XFFFFFFFD). To check the scroll wheel is working, scroll in either direction and watch the value change.

The OTPO CNT test is for a non-moving scroll wheel. If your iPod has a moving scroll wheel (as the earliest iPods did), use the WHEEL A2D test instead. If your iPod has a non-moving scroll wheel, the WHEEL A2D test doesn't work.

Check that Sleep Mode Is Working

To check that Sleep mode is working on your iPod, run the Sleep test. If the test works, you'll need to reset your iPod to get it working again. If your iPod doesn't go to sleep, the test has failed.

What about the Other Diagnostic Tests?

Okay—so those were the diagnostic tests that are most likely to be directly useful to you. But what are the others for?

The brief answer is that you really don't need to know. But since you're curious (or perhaps strange), Table 15-1 explains the remaining diagnostic tests briefly.

Troubleshoot Specific Problems

This section discusses how to troubleshoot specific problems with the iPod, starting with the more common problems and moving gradually toward the esoteric end of the spectrum.

Your iPod Won't Respond to Keypresses

If your iPod won't respond to keypresses, take as many of the following actions, in order, as are necessary to revive it:

1. Check that neither the Hold switch on your iPod nor the Hold switch on the remote control (if you're using it) is on.

Test	Explanation
5 in 1	Runs the following tests: LCM, RTC, SDRAM, FLASH, and WHEEL A2D.
RESET	Resets your iPod.
A2D	Tests your iPod's power system.
LCM	Checks the liquid crystal display by showing different patterns on it. (Press the Select button to display the next pattern.)
RTC	Displays the current output of your iPod's real-time clock.
FLASH	Displays a hexadecimal number identifying your iPod's current version of ROM (read-only memory).
HDD SCAN	Starts a hard-disk scan. As you saw in "Run a Disk Scan" earlier in this chapter, you can start a hard disk scan without visiting the diagnostics screen.
RUN IN	Runs a looping battery of tests: LCM, RTC, OTPO CNT, HDD, and AUDIO. Reset your iPod to escape from the loop.

TABLE 15-1 Brief Explanations of Your iPod's Other Diagnostic Tests

2. Check that the battery is charged. When the battery is too low to run the iPod (for example, for playing back music), your iPod will display a low-battery symbol—a battery icon with an exclamation point—for a few seconds when you press a key. (You may miss this icon if you're using the remote or you're pressing your iPod's buttons without looking at the screen.) Connect the iPod to a power source (either an electrical outlet or a computer that's not asleep), give it a few minutes to recharge a little, disconnect it again, and then try turning it on.

3. Reset your iPod (see the section "Reset Your iPod," earlier in this chapter).

4. Enter diagnostic mode and run the Key test. See the section "Check the iPod's Buttons" earlier in this chapter for details.

Your Remote Control Stops Working

If your iPod's remote control suddenly stops working without having suffered any obvious accident (such as you sitting on it or the dog chewing it into tinsel and confetti), check that its plug is pushed in fully. For good measure, twist the plug a little to improve the connection.

If the plug is firmly seated, enter diagnostic mode, and then run the Remote test. See the section "Check the Remote Control" earlier in this chapter for details.

Your Mac or PC Doesn't React When You Plug in Your iPod

If your computer (Mac or PC) doesn't react when you plug in your iPod, any of several things might have gone wrong. Try the actions described in the following subsections.

Unplug Any Other FireWire Devices in the FireWire Chain

If you've plugged in another FireWire device, try unplugging it. The problem may be that your FireWire controller can't supply power to another unpowered device as well as to your iPod.

Check that the FireWire Cable is Working

Check that the FireWire cable is working. Make sure the cable is firmly plugged into both the FireWire port on the computer and the port on your iPod.

NOTE *If possible, use the cable that came with your iPod rather than a third-party cable, because some third-party cables may not work with the iPod.*

If you're not sure the cable is working, you can run a partial check by plugging the FireWire cable into your iPod and its power adapter, and then plugging the power adapter into an electrical socket. If your iPod starts charging, you'll know that at least the power-carrying wires on the FireWire cable are working.

Check that the FireWire Port on the Computer Is Working

In most cases, the easiest way to check that the FireWire port on the computer is working is by plugging in another FireWire device that you know is working.

Check that the FireWire Port on Your iPod Is Working

Once you've verified that the FireWire cable and the FireWire port on the computer are both working, next check the FireWire port on your iPod. Clean out any dirt or other detritus that's worked its way into the port (this can happen if the port's cover gets loose), and make sure that the cable is securely connected.

You can run a partial check of whether this port is working by plugging your iPod into its power adapter and the adapter into an electrical socket. If your iPod starts charging, you'll know that at least the power-carrying wires in the FireWire socket are working. Chances are the other four wires are okay as well.

But if your iPod *doesn't* start charging, as is more likely, you'll have reason to believe the FireWire port on your iPod is damaged. Enter diagnostic mode and run the FireWire test as described in the section "Check the FireWire Port" earlier in this chapter.

If the FireWire port isn't working, you'll need to get your iPod repaired by an Apple technician.

Your iPod Says "Do Not Disconnect" Forever When Connected to the Computer

As you saw in Chapter 1, when you connect your iPod to your Mac or PC via the FireWire cable, your iPod displays the *Do not disconnect* message while it synchronizes with iTunes or MUSICMATCH Jukebox Plus. When synchronization is complete, your iPod should display the charging indicator for as long as it's taking on power via the FireWire cable (assuming the FireWire port is powered).

But sometimes it doesn't. If your iPod displays the *Do not disconnect* message long after synchronization should have finished, first try to remember if you've configured your iPod for use as a FireWire disk. If so, you need to unmount your iPod manually, so nothing goes wrong. Issue an Eject command (for example, click the Eject button in MUSICMATCH Portables Plus or right-click the iPod's icon on your Mac desktop and choose Eject from the shortcut menu), and your iPod should display the *OK to disconnect* message.

If you haven't configured your iPod for use as a FireWire disk, your iPod's hard drive may have gotten stuck spinning. If you pick up your iPod to scrutinize it further, you'll notice it's much warmer than usual if the drive has been spinning for a while.

When this happens, eject it in one of the following ways:

- On a Mac, from iTunes, click the Eject iPod button, press COMMAND-E, or choose Controls | Eject.

- On a Mac, from the Finder, drag the iPod to the Trash or right-click it and choose Eject from the context menu.

- On a PC, click the Eject button on the MUSICMATCH Portables Plus window to unmount the iPod. Alternatively, right-click the iPod's entry in the Attached Portable Devices list, and then choose Eject Device from the shortcut menu.

Your iPod should then display the *OK to disconnect* message, and you can disconnect it safely.

If that doesn't work, you may need to reset your iPod by holding down the Menu button and the Play/Pause button for a few seconds. After your iPod reboots, you should be able to eject it by taking one of the preceding actions.

> **TIP** *If you experience this problem frequently, try updating your iPod to the latest software version available. If there's no newer software version, or if an update doesn't help, use the AC adapter to recharge your iPod rather than recharging it from your computer.*

Your iPod Displays a Disk Icon with Magnifying Glass, Arrow, Check Mark, X, or Exclamation Point

If your iPod displays a disk icon on startup, it suspects there's a problem with its hard disk. See the section "Run a Disk Scan" earlier in this chapter for details.

Songs in Your Music Library Aren't Transferred to Your iPod

If songs you've added to your music library aren't transferred to your iPod even though you've synchronized successfully since adding the songs, there are two possibilities.

Check first that you haven't configured your iPod for partial synchronization or manual synchronization. For example, if you've chosen to synchronize only selected playlists, your iPod won't synchronize new music files not included on those playlists.

Second, check that the songs' tags include the artist's name and track name. Without these two items of information, iTunes won't transfer the songs to your iPod, because your iPod's interface won't be able to display the songs to you. (Unlike some other MP3 players, your iPod can't synthesize missing tags by breaking down the filename into artist and track name.)

Mac OS X Displays the SBOD and then Fails to Recognize Your iPod

If, when you connect your iPod to your Mac, OS X displays the Spinning Beachball of Death (SBOD) for a while (usually several minutes) and then refuses to recognize your iPod even though your iPod is displaying the *Do not disconnect* message, it may mean you've plugged a Windows iPod into your Mac.

"iTunes Has Detected a Software Update" Message

The message "iTunes has detected a software update for the iPod '*iPod*.' Would you like to install it now?" (Figure 15-1) may mean exactly what it says—that an update is available. But if iTunes gives you this message out of the blue after seemingly failing to recognize your iPod, it may mean you've plugged a Windows iPod into your Mac.

MUSICMATCH Jukebox Plus Doesn't Recognize Your iPod

When you plug your iPod into your PC, you may see this sequence of events:

1. MUSICMATCH Jukebox Plus doesn't recognize the iPod.

2. Windows displays a pop-up telling you that your new hardware was successfully configured.

3. Windows displays the System Settings Change dialog box (Figure 15-2) telling you that Windows has finished installing new devices and that you need to restart your computer to make the new settings take effect.

4. Your iPod may appear in the My Computer window as a removable disk named Removable Disk.

This sequence of events typically means you've plugged the wrong iPod (for example, a Mac iPod) into your PC.

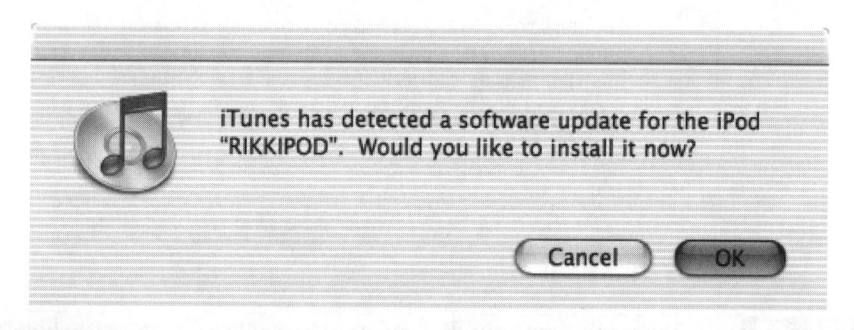

FIGURE 15-1 The "iTunes has detected a software update for the iPod" message can mean you've plugged the wrong iPod into your Mac.

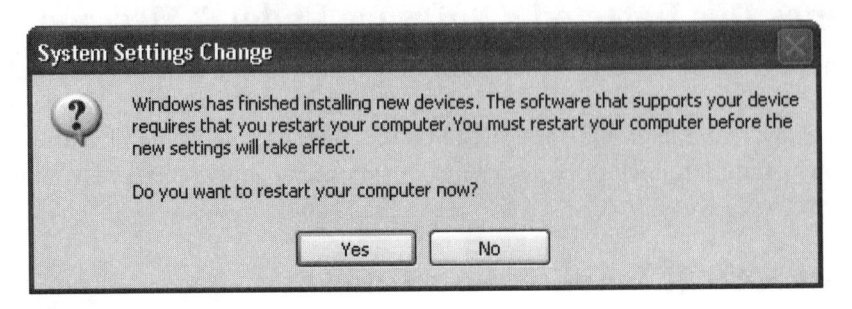

FIGURE 15-2 The System Settings Change dialog box may indicate you've plugged the wrong iPod into your PC.

"The iPod '*iPod*' Is Linked to Another iTunes Music Library"

If, when you connect your iPod to your Mac, iTunes displays the message "The iPod '*iPod*' is linked to another iTunes music library" (Figure 15-3), chances are that you've plugged the wrong iPod into your Mac. Click the No button and check which iPod this is.

NOTE *If you want to know more about moving your iPod from one Mac to another, see the section "Change the Mac to Which Your iPod Is Linked" in Chapter 14.*

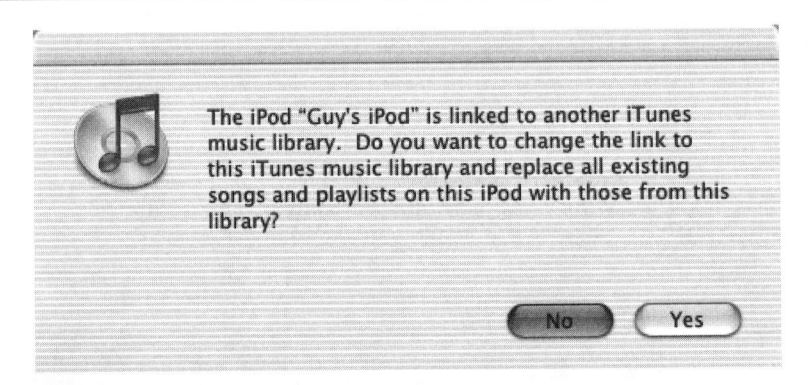

FIGURE 15-3 If iTunes tells you your iPod is linked to another iTunes music library, you've probably plugged the wrong iPod into your Mac.

Letting iTunes Copy All Song Files to Your Music Library Causes You to Run Out of Hard-Disk Space

As you saw in the section "Choose Whether to Store All Song Files in Your Music Library" in Chapter 3, iTunes can copy to your music library folder all the files you add to your music library. Adding all the files to your music library means you have all the files available in one place. This can be good when (for example) you want your PowerBook's or iBook's hard disk to contain copies of all the music files stored on network drives so you can listen to them when your 'iBook isn't connected to the network. But it can take up brutal amounts of disk space—perhaps more space than you have.

If your song files are stored on your hard drive in folders other than your music library folder, you have three choices:

- You can have iTunes copy the files to your music library, doubling the amount of space they take up. In almost all cases, this is the worst possible choice to make. (Rarely, you might want redundant copies of your song files in your music library so you could experiment with them.)

- You can have iTunes store references to the files rather than copies of them. If you also have song files in your music library folder, this is the easiest solution. To do this, clear the Copy Files to iTunes Music Folder When Adding to Library check box on the Advanced sheet of the Preferences dialog box (iTunes | Preferences).

- You can move your music library to the folder that contains your song files. This is the easiest solution if your music library is empty.

If you try to copy more files than will fit on your hard disk, Mac OS X displays the message box shown in the following illustration. But when you click the OK button to dismiss this message box, iTunes goes ahead and tries to copy all the files anyway.

Unless you're consumed by morbid curiosity to see exactly how many files iTunes can pack on your hard disk before it's stuffed to the gills, stop the copying process as soon as you can. The best way to do this is to quit iTunes by pressing COMMAND-Q or choosing iTunes | Quit iTunes. If you can't quit iTunes gently, force quit it.

Once you've done this, you may need to remove the tracks you've just copied to your music library from the folder. To do so, follow these steps:

1. Launch iTunes again.

2. Right-click or CTRL-click any displayed column heading (for example, the Song Names column heading) and select the Date Added item on the shortcut menu to display the Date Added column.

3. If necessary, scroll the iTunes window so you can see the Date Added column.

4. Click the Date Added column heading twice to produce a descending sort by the date you added the tracks to the music library. The descending sort puts the tracks added most recently at the top of the list.

5. Select the tracks you've just added.

6. Choose Edit | Clear to remove the tracks from your music library. iTunes displays the confirmation dialog box shown in the following image (unless you've already chosen to suppress its display):

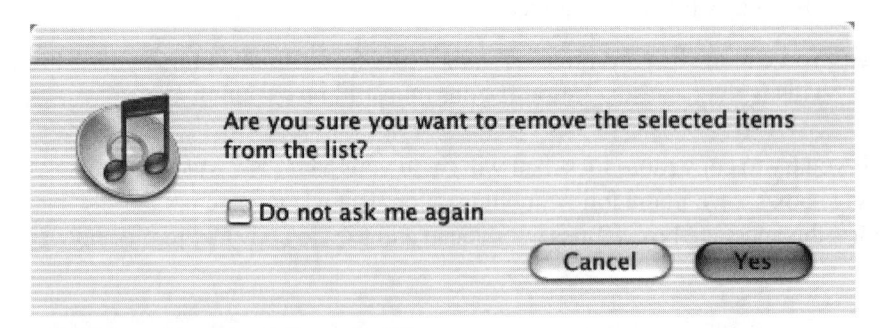

Are you sure you want to remove the selected items from the list?

☐ Do not ask me again

Cancel   Yes

7. Click the Yes button. iTunes then displays the following dialog box, telling you that some of the files are located in your iTunes music folder and asking if you want to move the files to the Trash:

8. Click the Yes button. iTunes trashes the files.

You've now gotten rid of the offending song files. Now take the following actions to prevent the problem from recurring and to restore to your music library the references to the song files in their original locations:

1. Choose iTunes | Preferences and clear the Copy Files to iTunes Music Folder when Adding to Library check box on the Advanced sheet of the Preferences dialog box. Doing this prevents the problem from recurring.

2. Add the song files to your music library again from their original folder.

"Missing theme.ini" Error Message When You First Launch MUSICMATCH Jukebox Plus

If you receive the error message "Missing theme.ini" the first time you launch MUSICMATCH Jukebox Plus, it means the Apple iPod skin hasn't installed successfully.

To download a replacement file, open Internet Explorer or another browser to **techsupp.musicmatch.com/techtools/Apple_iPod_ENU.mmz**. Windows automatically downloads the skin file, installs it, and displays a MUSICMATCH Installer dialog box like that shown in the following image. Click the Close button.

Once the skin is installed, try launching MUSICMATCH Jukebox Plus again. It should work now.

"Install Error: Reinstall iPod Plug-In"

If MUSICMATCH Jukebox Plus displays the message "Install error: Reinstall iPod plug-in," you need to remove, download, and then reinstall the plug-in. To do so, follow these steps:

1. Close MUSICMATCH Portables Plus (if it's running) and MUSICMATCH Jukebox Plus.

2. Choose Start | Control Panel to open the Control Panel.

3. Click the Add or Remove Programs link to display the Add or Remove Programs window.

4. On the Change or Remove Programs tab, select the MUSICMATCH iPod plug-in item.

5. Click the Change/Remove button. Windows displays the Confirm File Deletion dialog box, shown in the following image:

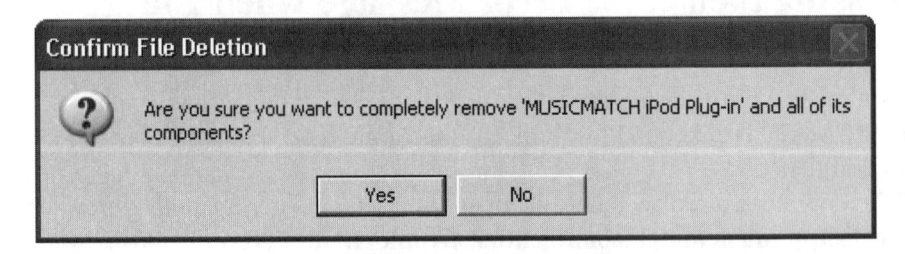

![Confirm File Deletion dialog box: Are you sure you want to completely remove 'MUSICMATCH iPod Plug-in' and all of its components? Yes / No]

6. Click the Yes button. UninstallShield launches and displays the Remove Programs from Your Computer dialog box as it works.

7. If UninstallShield displays the Remove Shared File? dialog box (an example of which is shown in the following image) to ask you whether or not to remove a shared file, click the Yes button, the Yes to All button, the No button, or the No to All button as appropriate. Normally, leaving the file on your computer is safest, in case another application is using the file unbeknownst to Windows. But in this case, you can safely choose the Yes to All button to remove all the files, because you'll replace them

CHAPTER 15: Troubleshoot Any iPod Problems You Encounter   **347**

in a moment. Click the Yes button in the confirmation dialog box that Windows displays.

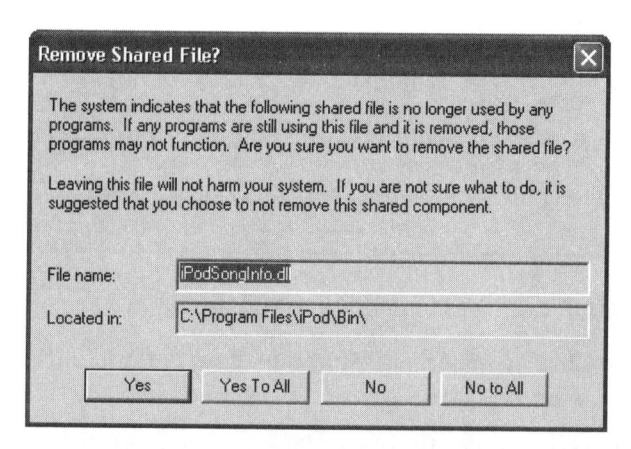

8. When UninstallShield has finished removing the iPod plug-in, it displays the Remove Programs from Your Computer dialog box. The following illustration shows an example:

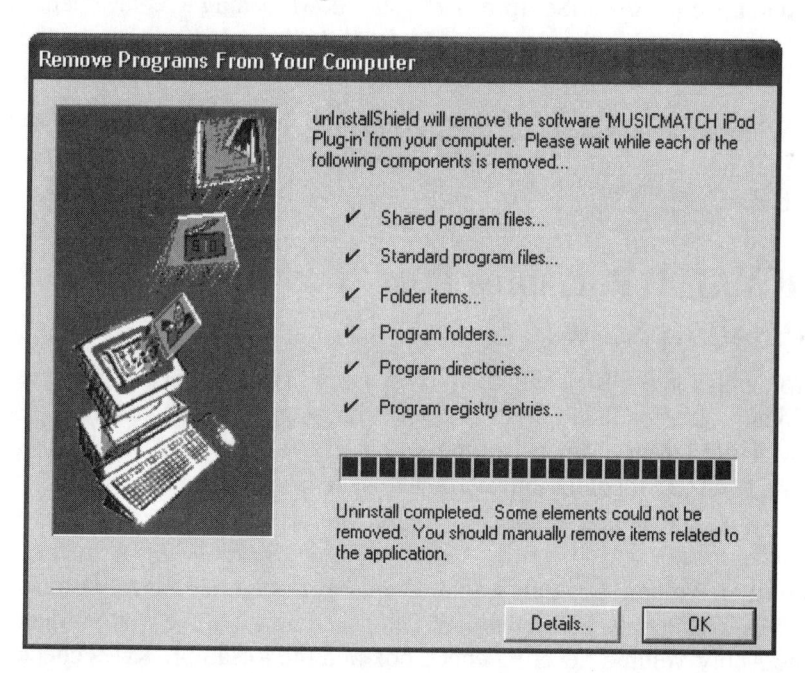

9. Click the OK button to close the Remove Programs from Your Computer dialog box. Windows displays a message box such as that shown in the following illustration:

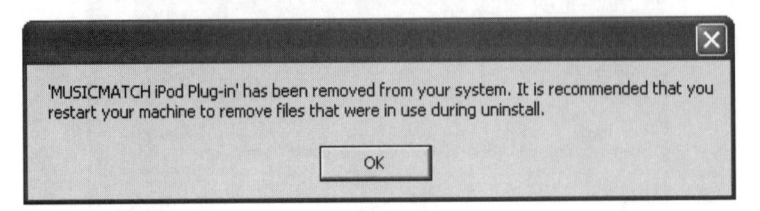

> 'MUSICMATCH iPod Plug-in' has been removed from your system. It is recommended that you restart your machine to remove files that were in use during uninstall.

10. Click the OK button to return to the Add or Remove Programs window.

11. Click the Close button (the x button) to close the Add or Remove Programs window.

12. For best effects, restart Windows. Doing so allows Windows to remove any iPod plug-in files it couldn't remove because they were in use.

13. Open Internet Explorer or another browser and go to **partners.musicmatch.com/archives/iPodSetup.mmz** to start downloading a replacement plug-in. (You need to use the capital letters on "iPodSetup" there, however much they annoy you.)

14. Windows automatically installs the plug-in. MUSICMATCH Jukebox Plus then launches and starts MUSICMATCH Portables Plus if your iPod is connected.

MUSICMATCH Portables Plus Synchronizations Are Painfully Slow

Synchronizing songs with a Windows iPod using MUSICMATCH Portables Plus tends, in any case, to take longer than synchronizing the same amount of songs with a Mac iPod using iTunes. But the Volume Leveling and resampling features in MUSICMATCH Jukebox Plus can make synchronizations take much longer. If you don't absolutely need to use these features, you can turn them off to speed up synchronization.

To turn off Volume Leveling and resampling, click the Options button in the MUSICMATCH Portables Plus window. On the Audio tab of the Options dialog box, clear the Apply Volume Leveling check box and the Resample Rates check box. Then click the OK button to close the Options dialog box.

Part IV
New iPods, iTunes 4, and the iTunes Music Store

Chapter 16

Use the New iPods

How to...

- Understand how the new iPods differ from the earlier iPods
- Decide which iPod to buy
- Set up your new iPod
- Play music through the Dock
- Use the iPod Alarm Clock feature
- Display the time in the iPod title bar
- Customize the main menu for faster use
- Use the On-the-Go playlist feature
- Apply ratings to songs on your iPod
- Read text notes on your iPod

In May 2003, Apple released three new iPod models with exciting new capabilities, a new design and a svelter waistline, and new capacities. Along with these iPods, Apple launched iTunes Music Store, an online music store from which you can effortless buy a variety of songs, download them onto your Mac, and use them on your Mac and your iPods. Apple plans to make iTunes Music Store available for PCs in the future, but at this writing, PCs can't use iTunes Music Store.

This chapter shows you how to make the most of the new features on the new iPods. Chapter 17 discusses how to use iTunes 4. Chapter 18 discusses how to use iTunes Music Store to preview and buy music.

> **NOTE** See Chapter 3 for a discussion of how to use iTunes to load music onto your Mac iPod. See Chapter 4 for a discussion of how to use MUSICMATCH Jukebox Plus to load music onto your Windows iPod.

Understand How the New iPods Differ from the Earlier iPods

The earlier iPods were such appealing and compelling products that they quickly became a huge hit with consumers. But Apple has come up with an impressive roster of changes in the new iPods to drive further sales and to encourage existing iPod owners to upgrade.

This section gives you an overview of the ways in which the new iPods differ from their predecessors, starting with the feature dearest to most iPod users' hearts—more disk space for more music.

> **NOTE** *The new iPods are for both Windows and the Mac, rather than having separate models of Windows iPods and Mac iPods.*

Capacities

The new iPods have capacities of 10GB, 15GB, and 30GB, bringing welcome increases in capacity for songs and data. As with the earlier models, these capacities are in marketing gigabytes rather than in technical, "real" gigabytes; beyond this, some space is taken up by the iPod operating system. So the 30GB iPod has a true capacity of 27.9GB rather than 30GB.

Table 16-1 shows you how many songs you can fit onto these models of iPod at widely used compression ratios for music. The table assumes a "song" to be about four minutes long and rounds the figures to the nearest sensible point.

Look, Feel, and Heft

The new iPods have a fresh case design, a slimmer profile, and a slightly lighter weight than the earlier iPods.

- **Design** On the new iPods, the four main control buttons (Previous, Menu, Play/Pause, and Next) are located in a row below the screen rather than in a ring around the Scroll wheel and the Select button. All the controls are now touch sensitive and have no moving parts.

- **Slimmer profile** Taking advantage of improvements in portable hard drives, the new iPods are slimmer than the earlier iPods. This makes the new iPods even easier on the eye, but it also means that most cases designed for earlier iPods won't work for them. The 10GB and 15GB

iPod Nominal Capacity	iPod Real Capacity	128Kbps Hours	128Kbps Songs	160Kbps Hours	160Kbps Songs	192Kbps Hours	192Kbps Songs	320Kbps Hours	320Kbps Songs
10GB	9.31GB	166	2,500	134	2,000	110	1,670	67	1,000
15GB	14.0GB	250	3,750	200	3,000	165	2,500	100	1,500
30GB	27.9GB	500	7,500	400	6,000	330	5,000	200	3,000

TABLE 16-1 New iPod Capacities at Widely Used Compression Ratios

models are the same size and weight, while the 30GB model is a shade thicker and heavier.

- **Lighter weight** The new iPods weigh a fraction less than their predecessors. The reduction in weight is welcome, but will make little difference to most users.

If you're used to the button layout and the surface feel of the earlier iPods, it may take you a little while to get used to the new button layout and surface feel of the new iPods. It's arguable whether the new buttons are easier to find by touch than the buttons on the earlier iPods. They seem designed to be tougher as well as sleeker, which is good news for those of us who use our iPods hard.

Accessories

The 15GB and 30GB new iPods come with three accessories most users will find essential: a carrying case, a remote control for easier play through headphones, and a Dock:

- **Carrying case** The case is essentially the same as that for the earlier 10GB and 20GB iPods, except that it's a bit smaller so that it fits the new iPods snugly.

- **Remote control** The remote control features a redesigned connector that uses an extra socket next to the headphone socket rather than using contacts incorporated in the headphone socket. The new connector is presumably intended to eliminate reliability problems in some of the original remote controls, which needed to be pushed home very firmly to work consistently. A side-effect is that the original remote controls won't work with the new iPods. (Nor will the new remote controls work with earlier iPods.)

- **Dock** The killer accessory for many users, the Dock is for synchronizing and charging your iPod without having to plug the FireWire cable directly into it. The Dock doubles as a stand for your iPod, providing deadly competition to some of the accessory stands discussed in Chapter 13. (In any case, most stands designed for earlier iPods won't fit the new iPods.) The Dock also includes a line-out port so that you can play music from your iPod through your stereo or through a pair of amplified speakers.

Software Improvements

The new iPods offer the following improvements to their software:

- **AAC playback** The new iPods can play back songs encoded with Advanced Audio Coding (AAC), a high-quality compression format.

See "Understand Advanced Audio Coding (AAC)" in Chapter 17 for a detailed discussion of AAC.

- **Alarm Clock**   You can set your iPod to play music (or beeps, if you prefer) at a particular time. See "Use the iPod Alarm Clock to Wake You Up," later in this chapter.

- **On-the-Go playlist**   On the new iPods, you can create a temporary playlist by using the On-the-Go playlist. This is a great improvement over having to create all your playlists on your computer. See "Queue a List of Songs on Your iPod," later in this chapter.

- **Time display**   You can set the new iPods to display the time in the title bar. See "Display the Time in the Title Bar," later in this chapter.

- **Ratings**   You can assign ratings (from one star to five stars) to songs from the iPod, whereas before you could assign ratings only from iTunes. See "Rate Songs on Your iPod," later in this chapter.

- **Redesigned and customizable menus**   The new iPods feature some menu changes designed to put the items you need closer to your fingertips. For example, the Backlight item now appears on the Main menu, so you can turn on the backlight more easily. Better yet, you can customize the Main menu by choosing which items (from a preset list) appear on it. See "Customize the Main Menu for Quick Access to Items," later in this chapter.

- **Text notes**   The new iPods can display text notes, so you no longer have to clutter up your Contacts folder with notes disguised as vCards.

- **Games**   The new iPods also offer two new games: Parachute (an action game in which you try to shoot down helicopters and parachutists before they overwhelm you) and Solitaire (a one-player card game). Parachute is easy to play, but Solitaire requires very close concentration (to distinguish the card's suits in grayscale) and determined manipulation of your iPod's controls (to move the cards). These games, which you'll find under Extras | Games, are so straightforward as not to need further explanation in this book.

Decide Which iPod to Buy

If you're in the strange position of reading this book without having an iPod, you may be wondering whether you should buy a new iPod or an earlier iPod. At this writing, it's a nice decision between the higher-capacity models of earlier iPod and the lower-capacity models of new iPod: depending on the retailer you patronize, you may be able to pick up a 20GB earlier iPod for less than a 15GB new iPod (or even a 10GB new iPod).

In this case, the decision boils down to capacity against new features. If you want to use new features such as the Alarm Clock, the On-the-Go playlist, customizable menus, or notes, you need a new iPod. If you can live with music in large quantities, an earlier iPod may offer more bang for the buck. If you want a Dock for your iPod, you need a 15GB or 30GB new iPod.

You should find these decisions easy enough to make—and in any case, they'll soon be academic, because the earlier iPods will soon disappear. The question then will change to this: Which of the new iPods should you buy?

At this writing, the 10GB new iPod isn't a good buy. It's less expensive than the 15GB iPod, but it lacks the Dock, the carrying case, and the wired remote. If you buy these items separately to add to your 10GB iPod, you'll end up spending more altogether than the 15GB iPod would have cost you in the first place—and you'll have the smaller hard disk.

Apple has set the pricing of the 15GB iPod and the 30GB iPod very delicately: at this writing, the 30GB iPod costs $100 more than the 15GB iPod, making the 15GB iPod very unattractive by comparison for anyone whose music library and essential files aren't impressively compact.

All of this goes to suggest that you'll do best to buy the highest-capacity iPod you can afford. With hard-disk technology continuing to improve, you can be sure that Apple will release iPods with capacities higher than 30GB before too long.

Set Up Your New iPod

Your new iPod is a snap to set up. You'll probably need longer to unwrap each of the components from its packaging than to put them all together. The following are the key steps:

1. Plug the 6-pin FireWire connector into a FireWire socket on your computer or on a hub attached to it.

2. If your iPod includes a Dock, connect the wide connector at the end of the FireWire cable to the Dock. The symbol side of the connector goes upward, facing the matching symbol on the dock.

3. If you have a pair of amplified speakers or a stereo input on a receiver available, connect it to the Line Out port on the back of the Dock.

4. Slide the iPod carefully onto its connector in the Dock. You'll hear it make a wriggly noise of electronic satisfaction to tell you the connection has been made. When connected, your iPod starts recharging its battery and (with default settings) automatically synchronizes its contents with the music library on the computer the Dock is connected to.

5. Install the software for your new iPod:

- If iTunes is already installed on your Mac, you'll need to download iTunes 4 via Software Update (unless you've already done so). If iTunes isn't installed on your Mac, install it from the iPod CD. See "Upgrade to iTunes 4" in Chapter 17 for a brief discussion of the process of upgrading iTunes to version 4.

- To use your iPod with a PC, install MUSICMATCH Jukebox Plus from the iPod CD. The installation for MUSICMATCH Jukebox Plus 7.5 proceeds as described in pages 102–106 except that there's an additional step of "configuring" your iPod—in other words, reformatting it and installing the Windows iPod software.

How to ... Connect a New iPod to a PC via USB

If you're using your new iPod with a PC, you can choose between using the FireWire connection that comes with the iPod or a USB 2 connection. For the USB 2 connection, you'll need to buy the iPod Dock Connector to USB 2 from the Apple Store or from a retailer. You'll also need to install a software update to tell the iPod that it's using USB.

Use USB only if you must. There are two reasons why FireWire is a better connection method than USB for the iPod:

- Unless you can't add FireWire to your PC (for example, because you have no expansion slots left on a desktop PC or no PC Card sockets free on a laptop PC), adding FireWire to your computer will probably give you better value than buying the iPod Dock Connector to USB 2.

- The USB cable doesn't charge your iPod, so you'll need to charge it manually via the power adapter. This extra step is an inconvenience rather than a showstopper, but it's well worth avoiding.

The USB connection will work with a USB 1.1 port—but it'll be horribly slow. As discussed on page 101, USB 1.1 has a maximum throughput of 12 megabits per second (Mbps) compared to USB 2's 480 Mbps and FireWire's 400 Mbps. Transferring an entire music library to your iPod via USB 1.1 will take all day, whereas FireWire or USB 2 can handle the task in less than half an hour.

Play Music Through the Dock

If your new iPod includes a Dock, you can play music from your iPod when it's docked. Plug a cable with a stereo miniplug into the Line Out connector on the Dock and connect the other end of the cable to your powered speakers or your stereo.

Use the iPod controls to navigate to the music, play it, pause it, and so on. Use the volume control on the speakers or the receiver to control the volume at which the songs play.

Use the iPod's Alarm Clock to Wake You Up

The new iPods include an Alarm Clock feature that you can use to blast yourself awake either with a beep or with one of your existing playlists. (At this writing, you can't use an artist, album, song, or composer directly—you need to create a playlist from the songs you want to wake up to.) This feature seems guaranteed to be almost as popular as the Sleep Timer feature.

To use the Alarm Clock, follow these steps:

1. Create a custom playlist for waking up if you like. (Or create several—one for each day of the week, maybe.)
2. Choose Extras | Clock | Alarm Clock to display the Alarm Clock screen.
3. Select the Alarm item and press the Select button to toggle the alarm on or off as appropriate.
4. Select the Time item and press the Select button to access the Alarm Time screen. Scroll to the appropriate time and press the Select button to return to the Alarm Clock screen.
5. Select the Sound item and press the Select button to display the Alarm Clock listing of playlists available. Select the playlist and press the Select button to return to the Alarm Clock screen.
6. Connect your iPod to your speakers or stereo (unless you sleep with headphones on).
7. Go to sleep (perchance to dream).

When the appointed hour (and minute) arrives, your iPod wakes itself (if it's sleeping) and then wakes you.

Display the Time in the Title Bar

The new iPods can display the time in the title bar in place of the name of the current screen. When you display a different screen, or when you switch on your iPod, it displays the screen's name for a few seconds, and then switches to display the time.

To make your iPod display the time, follow these steps:

1. Choose Settings | Date and Time to display the Date & Time screen.

2. Scroll to the Time in Title item, then press the Select button to turn the item On.

Customize the Main Menu for Quick Access to Items

The new iPods let you customize the main menu by controlling which items appear on it. By removing items you don't want, and adding items you do want, you can give yourself quicker access to the items you use most.

For example, the Playlists item appears by default at the top of the Main menu. If you don't use playlists, you may want to remove it so that you don't always have to scroll past it to get to the Browse item. Or you might choose to put the Artists item on the Main menu so that you don't have to go through Browse to access it.

To customize the Main menu, follow these steps:

1. Choose Settings | Main Menu to display the Main Menu screen.

2. Scroll to the item you want to affect.

3. Press the Select button to toggle the item's setting between On and Off.

4. Make further changes as necessary, then press the Menu button twice to return to the Main menu and see the effect of the changes you made.

To reset your Main menu to its default settings, choose the Reset Main Menu item at the bottom of the Main Menu screen, then choose Reset from the Reset Menus screen. (Resetting all settings also resets the Main menu, as you'd expect.)

TIP *You can display the Contrast screen quickly by holding down the Menu button for five seconds. When you do this, your iPod applies the default contrast setting. You can then scroll left or right to change the contrast as necessary. Displaying the Contrast screen in this way is especially useful when you find the current contrast setting is too light or too dark to let you see the screen enough to reset it via the menus.*

Queue a List of Songs on Your iPod

One of the features that iPod users pressed Apple for was the ability to create playlists on-the-fly on their iPods rather than having to create all playlists through iTunes or MUSICMATCH Jukebox Plus. The new iPods deliver this capability, enabling you to create one temporary playlist called On-the-Go.

To create your On-the-Go playlist, follow these steps:

1. If you've previously created an On-the-Go playlist, choose Playlists | On-the-Go | Clear Playlist to dispose of it.
2. Navigate to the first song you want to add to the playlist.
3. Press the Select button and hold it down until the song name starts flashing.

TIP *You can also queue a playlist or album by navigating to it and then pressing and holding down the Select button until the item's name starts flashing.*

4. Repeat Steps 2 and 3 to add to the On-the-Go playlist all the other songs.

To play your On-the-Go playlist, choose Playlists | On-the-Go. (Until you create your first On-the-Go playlist, selecting this item displays an explanation of what the On-the-Go playlist does.)

Rate Songs on Your iPod

As you saw in "Apply Ratings to Songs to Tell iTunes Which Music You Like" (page 79), you can use iTunes's My Rating feature to assign a rating of one star to five stars to each song in your music library. You can use your ratings to sort your music or to help Smart Playlist find suitable songs.

The new iPods let you assign ratings from your iPod as well as from iTunes. To assign a rating to the song that's currently playing, follow these steps:

1. Display the Now Playing screen if it's not currently displayed.

2. Press the Select button twice in quick succession. Your iPod displays five hollow dots under the song's name on the Now Playing screen.

3. Scroll to the right to display the appropriate number of stars in place of the five dots, and then press the Select button to apply the rating.

Read Notes on Your iPod

As you saw in Chapter 10, third-party developers quickly created tools that let you put text files (and in some cases the text from other types of files, such as rich-text format files and PDF files) onto your iPod by disguising them as contacts. In the new iPods, Apple has provided a Notes feature that lets you put text files on your iPod without clogging up your Contacts database.

At this writing, the Notes feature works effectively only with plain text files. You can put other documents, such as rich-text format documents or Word documents, into the Notes folder, but the text displayed on the iPod will include formatting codes and extended characters. These make the text nearly impossible to read.

To put notes on your iPod, create a text file and then follow these steps:

1. Enable your iPod for FireWire disk use. (See "Enable FireWire Disk Mode on the Mac" on page 270 for a Mac iPod or "Enable FireWire Disk Mode on the PC" on page 272 for a Windows iPod.)

2. Connect your iPod.

3. Copy or move the file to the Notes folder on your iPod.

NOTE *The first time you open the Notes folder on your iPod, you may want to delete the Instructions file to prevent it from continuing to appear in your listings.*

On your iPod, you can then read the file by choosing Extras | Notes, scrolling down to the file, and pressing the Select button.

Use iPod Scripts to Create and Manage Text Notes

If you use the Notes feature extensively, consider downloading the iPod Scripts collection that Apple provides for creating and managing text notes. These scripts require Mac OS X 10.2 or later.

At this writing, the iPod Scripts collection contains the following scripts:

- The List All Notes script provides an easy way of opening one of the scripts stored on your iPod for editing on your Mac. This script displays a dialog box (shown in the following illustration) that lists the notes stored on your iPod. You select the appropriate script and click the Open button to open it.

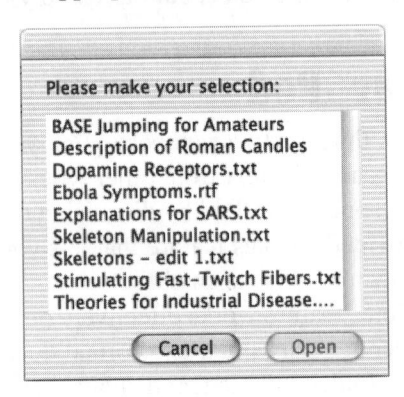

- The Clear All Notes script deletes all the notes in the Notes folder on your iPod and lets you choose whether to delete subfolders in the Notes folder as well. The following illustration shows the two dialog boxes this script displays:

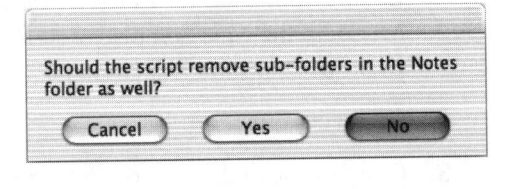

- The Eject iPod script checks that you want to eject the currently mounted iPod, and then ejects it if you click the Continue button. In normal use, you'll find it easier to eject the iPod using either iTunes or the desktop icon (if the iPod is in FireWire disk mode) rather than running this script.

- The Clipboard to Note script creates a note from the current contents of the Clipboard. This script is great for quickly grabbing part of a document or a webpage and generating a note from it. Select the text, issue a Copy command, and then run the script. Click the Continue button in the first dialog box (shown on the left in the following illustration), enter the name for the note in the dialog box shown on the right in the following illustration, and click OK. The script then displays a message box telling you that it has created the note.

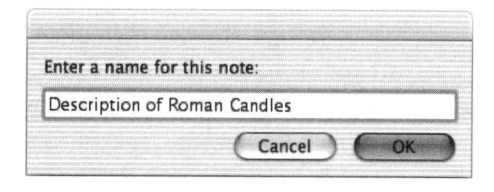

- The Note from Webpages folder contains two scripts, one called MacCentral and one called Printer Friendly. The MacCentral script is for extracting an article from the MacCentral website from the foremost browser window. The Printer Friendly script follows the same theme but is less specialized: this script extracts the contents of the foremost browser window to a note. For best effect, set the foremost window ready to print without ads and without other HTML items that will otherwise mess up the text of the note.

To use the iPod Scripts collection, follow these steps:

1. Download the iPod Scripts collection from **www.apple.com/applescript/ipod/**.

2. Move the downloaded file to the Home:Library:Scripts folder, and then expand the disk image.

NOTE *If you haven't used any scripts before, you'll need to create the Scripts folder manually under the Home:Library folder.*

3. Connect your iPod to your computer.

4. Use the Script menu to run the script. If you haven't installed the Script menu, do so as described in the following section.

Put the Script Menu on the Menu Bar

You can run the iPod scripts directly from the Scripts folder, but doing so is slower and more awkward than it needs to be. The better way to run scripts is from the Script menu that Mac OS X can display on your menu bar.

If you haven't used scripts before, you'll probably need to add the Script menu to the menu bar manually. To do so, follow these steps:

1. From the Finder, choose Go | Applications to display your Applications folder.

2. Double-click the AppleScript folder to open it in the window.

How to Do Everything with Your iPod

3. Drag the ScriptMenu.menu icon to the menu bar in the upper-right corner of your screen and drop it there. Mac OS X adds an icon that you can click to display the Script menu, shown in the following image with the iPod scripts expanded:

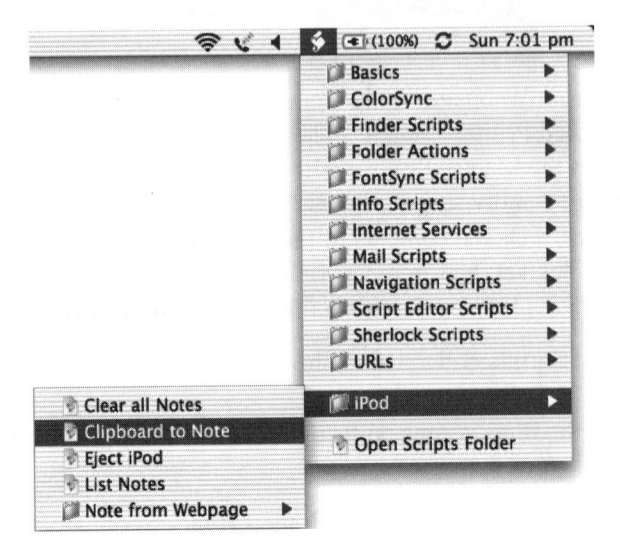

You can then run scripts easily from the desktop by using the Script menu.

Chapter 17

Use iTunes 4

How to...

- Know what the most important changes are in iTunes 4
- Understand Advanced Audio Coding (AAC)
- Understand digital rights management (DRM)
- Upgrade from iTunes 3 to iTunes 4
- Choose MP3 and AAC encoding settings
- Use the new CD- and DVD-burning features
- Share your music library with other users
- Play the music that other users are sharing
- Convert songs from AAC to MP3 (or vice versa)
- Add artwork to songs

iTunes 4 builds upon the many changes introduced in iTunes 3 by introducing a handful of major new features and a clutch of smaller tweaks and improvements.

This chapter supplements Chapter 3, which explains how to use iTunes 3, by showing you how to use the new features in iTunes 4. Use this chapter together with Chapter 3 to get fully up to speed with iTunes 4.

Summary of Changes in iTunes 4

These are the key changes in iTunes 4:

- iTunes 4 supports the Advanced Audio Coding (AAC) compression format, which offers high audio quality. iTunes can encode and decode AAC files. The new iPods and older iPods updated with iPod Software Updater 1.3 or later can play back AAC files.
- iTunes 4 enables you to share your music library or playlists with other people on your network and to use the music libraries or playlists that other people are sharing.
- iTunes 4 supports the iTunes Music Store. You can buy songs from the iTunes Music Store, or listen to previews of songs, directly through iTunes.
- iTunes 4 can burn DVDs as well as recordable CDs.

- iTunes 4 lets you add artwork to songs in your music library. When you buy a song from the iTunes Music Store, the artwork comes along with it. For songs you acquire from elsewhere or that you rip yourself, you can add artwork manually.

- iTunes 4 has some new menu commands, such as the Connect to Shared Music command and the Deauthorize Computer command, which appear on the Advanced menu. I'll show you how to use these commands later in this chapter. The Help menu offers an iTunes and Music Store Help item (alternatively, press APPLE-?) instead of the iTunes Help item that appears in iTunes 3, and a Music Store Customer Service item. The Visuals menu has changed its name to Visualizer but contains the same commands.

Understand Advanced Audio Coding (AAC)

Advanced Audio Coding (AAC) is a codec (*co*der/*dec*oder) for compressing and playing back digital audio. AAC was put together by a group of heavy hitters in the audio and digital-audio fields, including Fraunhofer IIS-A, Sony, Dolby Laboratories, AT&T, Nokia, and Lucent. AAC is newer than MP3, is generally agreed to deliver better sound than MP3, and is more tightly controlled than MP3.

AAC is one of the key components of the MPEG-4 specification, which covers digital audio and video. As you'd guess from its name, AAC covers audio components of the specification rather than video components.

Some people refer to the Advanced Audio Codec instead of Advanced Audio Coding. The same abbreviation—AAC—applies. In any case, most people stick with the abbreviation rather than using the full name.

MPEG-2 AAC and MPEG-4 AAC

At this writing, AAC comes in two flavors: MPEG-2 AAC and MPEG-4 AAC. From the names, you'd hazard that MPEG-2 AAC is part of the MPEG-2 specification for digital audio and video, whereas MPEG-4 AAC is part of the MPEG-4 specification—and you'd be right.

MPEG-2 AAC is used for several purposes. It's part of the specification for the DVD-Audio Recordable (DVD-AR) format and is used for some Internet-audio purposes, such as streaming and downloading audio.

MPEG-4 is a newer specification than MPEG-2, includes more capabilities, and delivers higher-quality sound. Among other uses (such as on your iPod), MPEG-4 AAC is used as the general audio codec for 3G wireless terminals.

QuickTime 6 includes an AAC codec. If your Mac has QuickTime 6.2 or a later version installed, iTunes uses MPEG-4 AAC as its default encoding format. (If your Mac has an earlier version of QuickTime installed, iTunes uses MP3 as its default encoding format.)

MPEG-4 AAC files use the .m4a file extension for unprotected files and the .m4p file extension for protected files. (I'll discuss protection more in a moment.)

AAC's 48 Channels

Whereas MP3 can work with only two channels (in stereo) or a single channel (in mono), AAC can work with up to 48 full-frequency channels.

If you're used to listening to music in stereo, 48 channels seems an absurd number. But typically, only a small subset of those channels would be used at the same time. For example, conventional surround-sound rigs use 5.1 or 7.1 setups, using six channels or eight channels, respectively. Other channels can be used for different languages, so that an AAC player can play a different vocal track for differently configured players. Other tracks yet can be used for synchronizing and controlling the audio.

AAC Licensing

Dolby handles the licensing end via its independent subsidiary Via Licensing Corporation (**www.vialicensing.com**). As with MP3, royalties are charged on the sale of AAC encoders and decoders (either hardware or software), but there are no fees for distributing content in AAC format. So usually the manufacturers or developers of the encoders and decoders take care of the licensing payments and pass along the costs to the end users by including them in the cost of hardware and software decoders. That means you don't need to worry about getting a license for using AAC—Apple has taken care of them for you in iTunes, QuickTime, and your iPod.

The cost of AAC licenses varies depending on the type of AAC (MPEG-4 AAC is a little more expensive than MPEG-2 AAC) and the number of channels used in the implementation. For example, stereo uses two channels (the left channel and the right channel), is widely used in consumer products, and comes at a very affordable cost. (Mono is even cheaper, but few people want to listen to mono sound when they can have stereo instead.) A high-end home-theater product using 7.1 surround sound uses eight channels and costs correspondingly more. Products classed as "professional" rather than "consumer"—for example, video-production equipment—costs even more.

Advantages of AAC

For music lovers, AAC offers higher music quality than MP3 at the same file sizes or similar music quality at smaller file sizes. Apple reckons that 128 Kbps AAC files sound as good as 160 Kbps MP3 files—so you can either save a goodly chunk of space and enjoy the same quality or enjoy even higher quality at the same bitrate.

Small file sizes are especially welcome for streaming audio over slow connections, such as modem connections. AAC streamed around 56 Kbps sounds pretty good (though not perfect), while MP3 sounds a bit flawed. Around 24 Kbps, AAC streams provide quite listenable sound, whereas MP3 streams sound quite rough.

The main advantage of AAC for the music industry is that the format supports digital rights management (DRM). AAC files can be created in a protected format with custom limitations built in. For example, the song files you can buy from the iTunes Music Store (discussed in Chapter 18) are authorized to be played on up to three different computers at the same time. If you try to play a song on a computer that's not authorized, the song won't play.

> **NOTE** *To tell if an AAC file is protected or not, check the Kind readout on the Summary tab of the Song Information dialog box. If the file is protected, the Kind readout reads Protected AAC Audio File. If not, Kind reads AAC Audio File. Alternatively, check the file extension. The .m4p extension indicates a protected file, whereas the .m4a extension indicates an unprotected file.*

Disadvantages of AAC

AAC's disadvantages are largely acceptable to most consumers, and include the following:

- At this writing, AAC files aren't widely used. One reason is that, because AAC is relatively new and hasn't been very widely implemented, few AAC encoders and decoders are available. However, in iTunes (and QuickTime), and the iPod, Apple has provided a comprehensive AAC encoding and decoding solution for the Mac.

- Encoding AAC files takes more processor cycles than encoding MP3 files. But as processors continue to increase in speed and power by the month if not by the week, this becomes less and less of a problem. For example, even relatively antiquated Macs (such as my PowerBook G3/333) have plenty of power to encode and decode AAC.

- For consumers, the largest potential disadvantage of AAC is the extent to which DRM can limit their use of the files. At this writing, Apple has delivered a relatively flexible implementation of DRM in the music sold by the iTunes Music Store. However, if Apple and the record companies tighten the licensing terms of the files in the future, consumers may have cause for concern. In this sense, AAC could act as a Trojan horse to wean customers off MP3 and onto AAC, then gradually lock them in to a format that the music industry can control.

How to ... Choose Between MP3 and AAC

Apple's current implementation of AAC in iTunes and the iPod has a lot to recommend it. AAC delivers high-quality audio, small file size, and enough flexibility for most purposes. But if you want to use the files you rip from CD on a portable player that doesn't support AAC, or you need to play them using a software player that doesn't support AAC, choose MP3 instead.

Similarly, if you want to share your music files with other people in any way other than sharing your music library via iTunes, MP3 is the way to go—but remember that you need the copyright holder's explicit authorization to copy and distribute music.

Update Your Earlier iPod to iPod Software 1.3

To be able to use AAC files on an iPod that's not of the latest generation, you need to update it to version 1.3 or later of the iPod software. Follow the instructions in "Keep Your iPod's Operating System Up-to-Date" on page 259 to update your Mac iPod or Windows iPod to the latest version. (If you're using a Mac, you can run Software Update to download the latest iPod Software Updater.)

iPod Software 1.3 enables your iPod to work with iTunes 4 and to play back AAC files. It also makes the Backlight item appear on the Main menu in place of the About item. (The About item appears on the Settings menu.) However, it doesn't add other features that the new iPods enjoy, such as Notes, extra games, or customizable menus.

Upgrade from iTunes 3 to iTunes 4

If you have one of the earlier iPods—a 5GB, original 10GB, or 20GB model—you'll need to upgrade to iTunes 4 in order to use the iTunes Music Store and AAC encoding. If you want to import music using AAC encoding as well, you need to have QuickTime 6.2 or later installed on your computer.

Use Software Update to download the latest version of iTunes automatically, and then follow through the installation routine. You may need to restart your Mac after installing the update.

When you next start iTunes, you'll need to agree to the iTunes Software License Agreement. After that, the iTunes Setup Assistant runs and walks you through the setup steps discussed in "Set Up and Configure iTunes on Your Mac" on page 60. You

CHAPTER 17: Use iTunes 4   **371**

get to choose whether to use iTunes for Internet audio content or not to modify your Internet settings, and specify whether iTunes may automatically connect to the Internet when it sees fit to download information about CDs and to receive streaming broadcasts, or whether iTunes must ask you before connecting to the Internet.

iTunes then updates your music library for iTunes 4, which may take a few minutes if your library contains a large number of songs.

As you can see in Figure 17-1, iTunes 4 has a very similar interface to iTunes 3. The following are the main differences:

- The Source pane contains a Music Store icon that connects you to the iTunes Music Store.

- The Purchased Music playlist appears after you first buy music from the iTunes Music Store.

- The Show or Hide Song Artwork button appears to the right of the Repeat button below the Source pane.

FIGURE 17-1   The iTunes 4 interface is an evolution rather than a revolution from the iTunes 3 interface.

Configure iTunes 4 to Suit Your Needs

As with iTunes 3, you configure iTunes 4 through the options on the sheets of the Preferences dialog box, which you display by pressing COMMAND-, or COMMAND-Y or by choosing iTunes | Preferences. The first time you display the Preferences dialog box in any iTunes session, it displays the General sheet. After that, it displays the sheet that was displayed when you last dismissed it.

iTunes 4 provides most of the same configuration options as iTunes 3 (see "Choose Where to Store Your Music Library" on page 62 and the sections that follow it). The new configuration settings that iTunes 4 offers are explained in this section, later in this chapter, and in the next chapter. Here's a summary of where you'll find them discussed.

- **Importing sheet** See the following subsections for details on how to choose custom MP3 encoding settings and custom AAC encoding settings.

- **Burning sheet** See "Use the New CD- and DVD-Burning Features," later in this chapter, for coverage of iTunes' new features for burning data CDs and DVDs.

- **Sharing sheet** See "Share Your Music with Other Users" and "Access and Play Another Person's Shared Music," both later in this chapter, for a discussion of iTunes' music-sharing features.

- **Store sheet** See "Configure iTunes Music Store Settings" in Chapter 18 for a discussion of the configuration options on the Store sheet.

Choose Custom MP3 Encoding Settings

The MP3 Encoder dialog box in iTunes 4 (Figure 17-2) has a different layout from the MP3 Encoder dialog box in iTunes 3. See "Choose Custom MP3 Encoding Settings" on page 66 for a discussion of these options.

The main difference is that iTunes 4 uses variable bitrate (VBR) encoding by default where iTunes 3 uses constant bitrate (CBR) encoding. As discussed in "Choose Between Constant Bitrate and Variable Bitrate" on page 43, VBR gives better results at the same file size than CBR, but it disagrees with some portable MP3 players. However, if you're using an iPod (as seems likely), you'll have nothing to worry about.

CHAPTER 17: Use iTunes 4   **373**

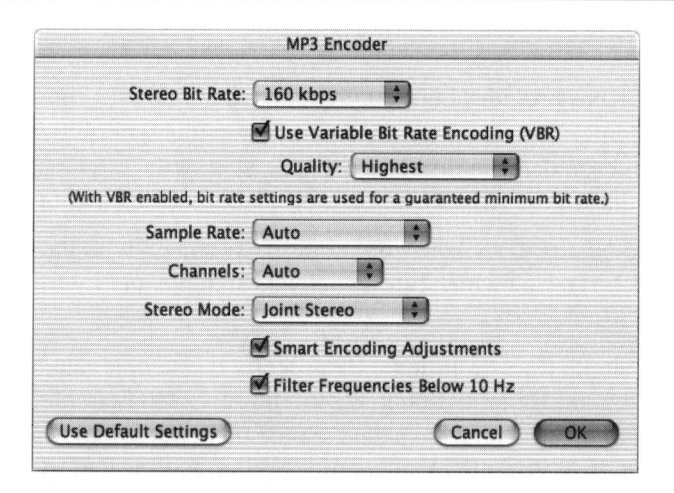

FIGURE 17-2 The MP3 Encoder dialog box in iTunes 4 offers the same options as in iTunes 3 but uses a different arrangement.

Choose Custom AAC Encoding Settings

As mentioned earlier in this chapter, iTunes uses MPEG-4 AAC as its default encoding format if your Mac has QuickTime 6.2 or a later version installed. The default setting for AAC is High Quality (128Kbps).

To configure preferences for creating AAC files, follow these steps:

1. Display the Importing sheet of the Preferences dialog box.
2. Choose AAC Encoder in the Import Using drop-down list if it's not currently selected.
3. Choose Custom in the Setting drop-down list to display the AAC Encoder dialog box (Figure 17-3).

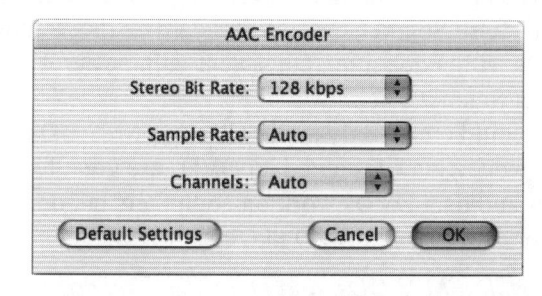

FIGURE 17-3 Configure your preferences for encoding AAC files in the AAC Encoder dialog box.

4. In the Stereo Bit Rate drop-down list, specify the bit rate. You can use from 16 Kbps to 320 Kbps; the default is 128 Kbps.

   - 128 Kbps provides high-quality audio suitable for general music listening. You may want to experiment with higher bitrates to see if you can detect a difference. If not, stick with 128 Kbps so as to get the largest possible amount of quality music on your iPod.
   - If you listen to spoken-word audio, experiment with the bitrates below 64 Kbps to see which bitrate delivers suitable quality for the material you listen to.

5. In the Sample Rate drop-down list, specify the sample rate by choosing Auto, 44.100 kHz or 48.000 kHz. 44.100 kHz is the sample rate used by CD audio; unless you have a data source that uses a 48.000 kHz sampling rate, there's no point in choosing this option. For most purposes, you'll get best results by using the Auto setting (the default setting), which makes iTunes use a sampling rate that matches the input quality. For example, for CD-quality audio, iTunes uses the 44.100 kHz sampling rate.

6. In the Channels drop-down list, select Auto, Stereo, or Mono, as appropriate. In most cases, Auto (the default setting) is the best bet, as it makes iTunes choose stereo or mono as appropriate to the sound source. However, you may occasionally need to produce mono files from stereo sources.

7. Click the OK button to close the AAC Encoder dialog box.

Use the New CD- and DVD-Burning Features

iTunes 4 contains updated features for burning CDs and for burning DVDs. You configure these features on the Burning sheet (Figure 17-4) of the Preferences dialog box.

When creating an audio CD, select the Use Sound Check check box to make iTunes use Sound Check to normalize the volume on the tracks. Using Sound Check (discussed in "Use Sound Check to Standardize the Volume" on page 25) should produce CDs with much more consistent volume across their tracks than CDs created without Sound Check.

While iTunes 3 could create only audio CDs and MP3 CDs, iTunes 4 can create data CDs as well. Data CDs and data DVDs are great for backing up your playlists. Data CDs and data DVDs work on computers but don't work on most audio CD players or conventional DVD players.

NOTE *See "Audio CDs, MP3 CDs, and Data CDs" on page 179 for an explanation of the different types of CDs.*

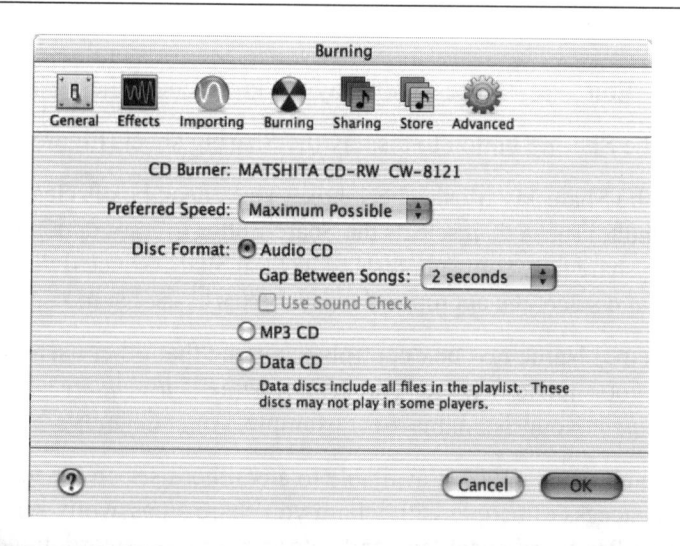

FIGURE 17-4 iTunes 4's new burning features include using Sound Check and creating data CDs.

To burn DVDs, your Mac must have a SuperDrive or a compatible DVD burner and must be running Mac OS X 10.2.4 or later. Given the right hardware, you can burn DVD-R discs and DVD-RW discs.

Share Your Music with Other Users

Running on Mac OS X 10.2.4 or a later version, iTunes 4 lets you share either your entire music library or selected playlists with other users on your network. You can share MP3 files, AAC files, AIFF files, WAV files, and links to radio stations. You can't share Audible files or QuickTime sound files.

You can share your music with up to five other users at a time, and you can be one of up to five users accessing the shared music on another computer. Each of these computers must be running Mac OS X 10.2.4 or a later version, not just the computer that's sharing the music.

Shared music remains on the computer that's sharing it, and when a participating computer goes to play a song, the song is streamed across the network. (In other words, the song isn't copied from the computer that's sharing it to the computer that's playing it.) When a computer goes offline or is shut down, any music it has been sharing stops being available to other users. Participating computers can play the shared music but can't do anything else with it: they can't burn the shared music to CD or DVD, download it to an iPod, or copy it to their own libraries.

To share some or all of your music, follow these steps:

1. Choose Edit | Preferences to display the Preferences dialog box.
2. Click the Sharing button to display the Sharing sheet (Figure 17-5).
3. Select the Share My Music check box. (This check box is cleared by default.) By default, iTunes then selects the Share Entire Library option button; if you want to share only some playlists, select the Share Selected Playlists option button and select the appropriate check boxes in the list box.
4. The Shared Name text box controls the name that other users trying to access your music will see. The default name is *username*'s music, where *username* is your username—for example, Anna Connor's Music.
5. By default, your music is available to any other user on the network. To restrict access to people with whom you share a password, select the Require Password check box and enter a strong password in the text box.
6. Click the OK button to apply your choices and close the Preferences dialog box.

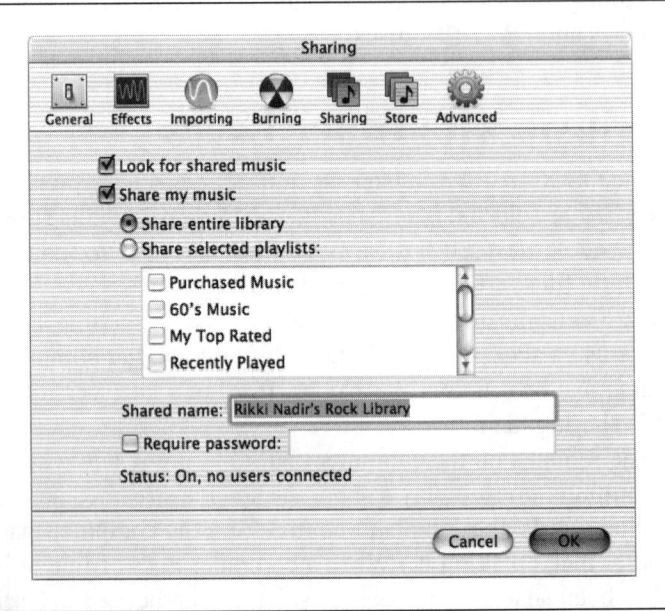

FIGURE 17-5 Use the options on the Sharing sheet to control which music (if any) you share with other users.

NOTE *When you set iTunes to share your music, iTunes displays a message reminding you that "Sharing music is for personal use only"—in other words, remember not to violate copyright law. Select the Do Not Show This Message Again check box if you want to prevent this message from appearing again.*

Access and Play Another Person's Shared Music

To access another person's shared music, your computer must have iTunes 4 running on Mac OS X 10.2.4 or a later version. You can then access shared music by following the instructions in the following three subsections.

Set Your Computer to Look for Shared Music

First, set your computer to look for shared music. Follow these steps:

1. Choose Edit | Preferences to display the Preferences dialog box.
2. Click the Sharing button to display the Sharing sheet.
3. Select the Look for Shared Music check box.
4. Click the OK button to close the Preferences dialog box.

Access Shared Music on the Same TCP/IP Subnet

Once you've selected the Look for Shared Music check box on the Sharing sheet of the Preferences dialog box, iTunes automatically detects shared music when you launch it. If iTunes finds shared music libraries or playlists, it displays them in the Source pane. Figure 17-6 shows an example of browsing the music shared by another computer.

If a shared music source has a password, iTunes displays the Music Library Password dialog box, shown in the following illustration. Enter the password and click the OK button to access the library.

FIGURE 17-6 Computers sharing music appear in the iTunes Source pane, allowing you to quickly browse the music that's being shared.

Access Shared Music on a Different TCP/IP Subnet

To make the easy sharing described in the previous section work, each of the other computers involved has to be on the same TCP/IP subnetwork as your computer. Otherwise, iTunes won't be able to see the music that's being shared by the computers.

To change the subnetwork, choose Apple | System Preferences, click the Network button, and work on the TCP/IP tab of the Network sheet. However, by changing the subnetwork, you may lose access to crucial components of your network, such as your Internet connection and your printers. Instead, you can connect to music being shared by computers on other subnets by taking the following steps:

1. Press COMMAND-K or choose Apple | Connect to Shared Music to display the Connect to Shared Music dialog box, shown in the following illustration:

2. Enter the computer's IP address or name.

3. Click the OK button. iTunes establishes the connection if possible and adds an entry for the computer's shared music to the Source pane.

Disconnect a Shared Music Library

To disconnect shared music you've connected to, follow these steps:

1. In the Source pane, select the shared music source.

2. Press COMMAND-E or choose Controls | Disconnect "Source".

Alternatively, right-click the shared music source and choose Disconnect "Library" from the shortcut menu.

Convert a Song from AAC to MP3 (or Vice Versa)

You may sometimes need to convert a song from the format in which you imported it, or (more likely) in which you bought it, to a different format. For example, you may need to convert a song in AAC format to MP3 so that you can use it on an MP3 player other than your iPod.

Don't convert a song from one compressed format to another compressed format unless you absolutely must, because such a conversion gives you the worst of both worlds. To convert a compressed file to another format, iTunes has to uncompress it first, and then compress it again. The compressed audio has already lost some information, which cannot be restored by uncompressing the audio: the uncompressed file simply contains the same audio in a less compact format. When this uncompressed file is then compressed using another compression format, further information is lost (depending on the format used, the bitrate, the processing level, and so on). So when you convert, say, an AAC file to an MP3 file, the MP3 file contains not only such defects as were present in the AAC file but also defects of its own.

So if you still have the CD from which you imported the song, import the song again using the other compressed format rather than converting the song from one compressed format to another. Doing so will give you significantly higher quality. But if you don't have the CD—for example, because you bought the song in the compressed format—converting to the other format will produce usable results.

To convert a song from one compressed format to another, follow these steps:

1. Press APPLE-, (the APPLE key and the comma key) or choose iTunes | Preferences to display the Preferences dialog box.

2. Click the Importing button to display the Importing sheet.

3. In the Import Using drop-down list, specify the encoder you want to use. For example, choose MP3 Encoder if you want to convert an existing file to an MP3 file.

4. If necessary, use the Setting drop-down list to specify the details of the format.

5. Click the OK button to close the Preferences dialog box.

6. In your music library, select the song or songs you want to convert.

7. Choose Advanced | Convert Selection to MP3 or Advanced | Convert Selection to AAC as appropriate. (The Convert Selection To item on the Advanced menu changes to reflect the encoder you chose in Step 3.)

8. iTunes converts the file or files, saves it or them in the folder that contains the original file or files, and adds it or them to your music library.

NOTE *Because iTunes automatically applies tag information to converted files, you may find it hard to tell in iTunes which file is in AAC format and which in MP3 format. The easiest way to find out is to issue a Get Info command for the song (for example, right-click the song and choose Get Info from the shortcut menu) and check the Kind readout on the Summary tab of the Song Information dialog box.*

After converting the song or songs to the other format, remember to restore your normal import setting on the Importing sheet of the Preferences dialog box before you import any more songs from CD.

Add Artwork to Songs

iTunes 4 lets you add artwork to songs and then display the artwork while the song is playing or selected in iTunes. These images aren't transferred to the iPod.

Most songs you buy from the iTunes Music Store include the appropriate artwork—for example, the cover of the single, EP, album, or CD that includes the song. For other songs, you can add your own artwork manually. For example, you might download album art or other pictures from an artist's website, and then apply those to the song files you ripped from the artist's CDs. You can use JPG, GIF, TIFF, PNG, or PhotoShop images for artwork.

iTunes provides three different ways to add artwork to songs. You can add one or more images to a single song as follows.

To add artwork to a song directly from the iTunes window, follow these steps:

1. Open a Finder window to the folder that contains the picture you want to use for the artwork. (If the picture is on your desktop, you're ready to go, but your desktop is likely to get cluttered fast.)

2. Press COMMAND-G or click the Show or Hide Song Artwork button below the Source pane to display the Artwork pane below the Source pane.

3. Drag the picture file from the Finder window to the Artwork pane and drop it there. iTunes displays the picture there and associates it with the song file.

4. Drag other picture files from the Finder window to the Artwork pane and drop them there as appropriate.

You can also add one or more images to a single song by working in the Song Information dialog box. To do so, follow these steps:

1. Right-click the song you want to affect and choose Get Info from the Shortcut menu to display the Song Information dialog box for the song. This dialog box shows the song's name in the title bar. The following illustration shows an example of the Song Information dialog box with an image added:

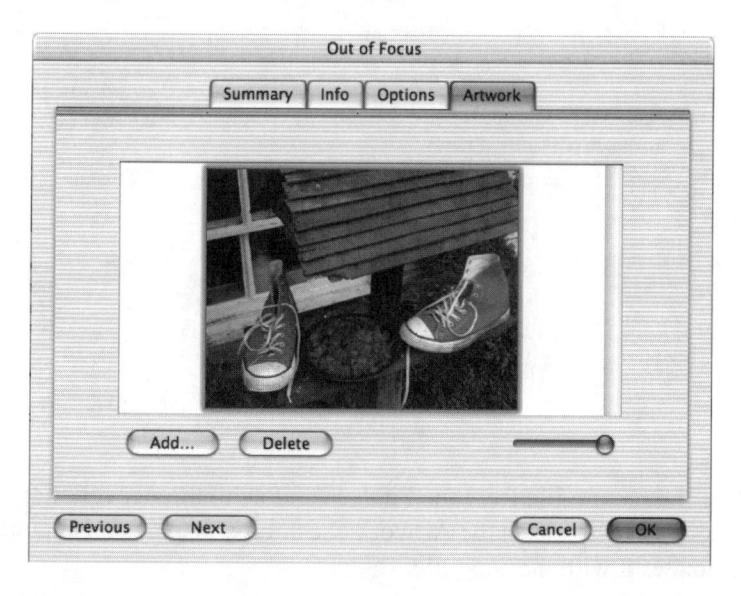

2. To add an image, click the Add button, use the Choose a File dialog box to navigate to the file and select it, and then click Choose.

3. To delete an existing image, select it in the Artwork box and click the Delete button.

4. To resize the picture or pictures to the size you want it or them, drag the slider to the left or right.

5. To work with the previous or next song in the playlist, album, or library, click the Previous button or the Next button.

6. Click the OK button to close the Song Information dialog box.

To add artwork to multiple songs at the same time, follow these steps:

1. Open a Finder window to the folder that contains the picture you want to use for the artwork.

2. Select the songs you want to affect. SHIFT-click to select multiple contiguous songs. OPTION-click to select multiple noncontiguous songs after clicking the first song.

3. Issue a Get Info command (for example, press COMMAND-I) to display the Multiple Song Information dialog box, shown in the following illustration:

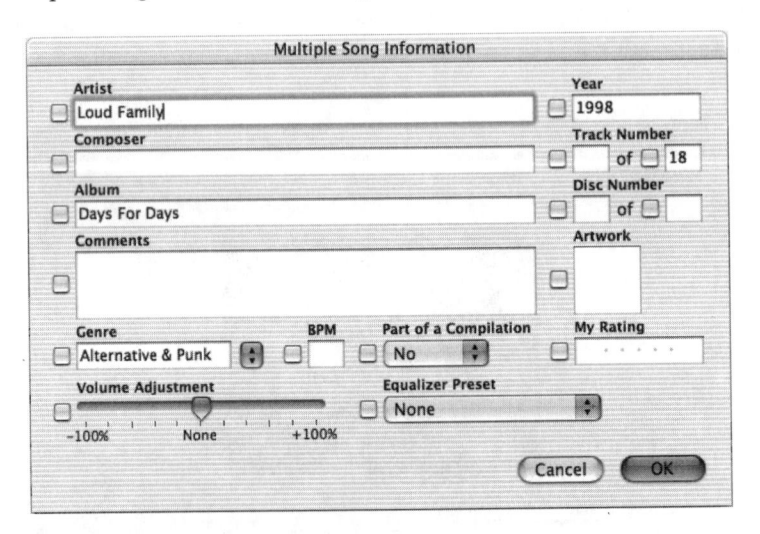

4. Drag the picture file from the Finder window to the Artwork box and drop it there. iTunes selects the Artwork check box, displays the picture, and associates it with the song file.

5. Click the OK button to close the Multiple Song Information dialog box. iTunes displays a dialog box confirming that you want to add the same art to all songs.

6. Click the Yes button.

When you've added two or more pictures to the same song, the Artwork pane displays a Previous button and a Next button for browsing from picture to picture.

You can display the current picture at full size by clicking it in the Artwork pane. Click the Close button (the × button) to close the Artwork window.

CAUTION *If you associate a graphics file that's bigger than your desktop with a song, you may not be able to reach the Close button on the Artwork window to close it. Press* COMMAND-1 *or choose Window | iTunes to display the iTunes window to regain controls of iTunes. Alternatively, press* COMMAND-Q *to quit iTunes and close the Artwork window. Restart iTunes to get the music started again.*

Chapter 18

Use the iTunes Music Store

How to...

- Understand what the iTunes Music Store is
- Understand digital rights management (DRM)
- Set up an account with the iTunes Music Store
- Configure iTunes Music Store settings
- Access the iTunes Music Store
- Buy songs from the iTunes Music Store
- Listen to songs you've purchased
- Authorize and deauthorize computers for the iTunes Music Store

If you use your iPod with a Mac running Mac OS X, you can buy music from the iTunes Music Store, Apple's online music service. This chapter discusses what the iTunes Music Store is, how it works, and how to use it.

The early part of this chapter also discusses digital rights management (DRM), because you should understand a little about DRM before using the store.

Understand What the iTunes Music Store Is

The iTunes Music Store is one of the largest and most ambitious attempts so far to sell music online. ("Download Music Files from Web Sites" on page 173 discusses other online music stores, such as MP3.com, Listen.com, and press*play*.) It's far from perfect, and its selection is limited, but it's an extremely promising start. At this writing, the iTunes Music Store is available only to the Mac, but Apple intends to make it work with Windows in the future.

These are the basic parameters of the iTunes Music Store:

- Songs cost $0.99 each. The cost of albums varies, but many cost $9.99 or so—around what you'd pay for a discounted CD in many stores.
- You can listen to a 30-second preview of any song to make sure it's what you want.

- You can burn songs to CD an unlimited number of times, although you can burn any given playlist only 10 times without changing it or re-creating it under another name.

- The songs you buy are encoded in the AAC format [discussed in "Understand Advanced Audio Coding (AAC)" in Chapter 17] and are protected with DRM (discussed in the following section).

- You can play the songs you buy on any number of iPods that you synchronize with your Mac. (You may have trouble playing the songs on other music players.)

- You can play the songs you buy on up to three computers at once.

- You can download each song you buy only once (assuming the download is successful). After that, the song is your responsibility. If you lose the song, you have to buy it again.

Understand Digital Rights Management (DRM)

As discussed at the beginning of Chapter 6 (pages 162–165), the music industry and consumers are currently engaged in a vigorous tussle over how music is sold (or stolen) and distributed:

- The record companies are aggressively rolling out copy-protection mechanisms on audio discs (see Chapter 2, pages 50–55) to prevent their customers from making unauthorized pure-digital copies of music (for example, MP3 files).

- Some consumers are trying to protect their freedom to enjoy the music they buy in the variety of ways that law and case law have established to be either definitely legal or sort-of legal. For example, time-shifting, place-shifting, and personal use suggest that it's probably legal to create MP3 files from a CD, as long as they're for your personal use.

- Other people—"consumers" in a sense other than the usual, perhaps—are deliberately infringing the record companies' copyrights by copying, distributing, and stealing music via P2P networks, recordable CDs and DVDs, and other means. We'll leave this aside for the moment.

Behind this struggle rears the specter of DRM—technologies for defining which actions a user may take with a particular work and restricting the user to those actions, preferably without preventing them from using or enjoying the work in the ways they expect to. (Yes, that's deliberately vague. Understanding and satisfying the user's expectations is a vital component of an effective implementation of DRM.)

DRM is often portrayed by consumer activists as being the quintessence of the Recording Industry Association of America's and Motion Picture Association of America's dreams and of consumers' nightmares. The publisher of a work can use DRM to impose a wide variety of restrictions on the ways in which a consumer can use the work. For example, some digital books are delivered in an encrypted format that requires a special certificate to decrypt and that effectively means the consumer can read them only on one authorized computer. DRM also prevents the consumer from printing any of the book or copying any of it directly from the reader application. As you'd imagine, these restrictions are unpopular with most consumers, and such books haven't exactly made a splash in the marketplace: consumers prefer traditional physical books that they can read wherever they want to, lend to a friend, photocopy, rip pages out of, and so on.

But how good or bad DRM is in practice depends on the implementation. When both publishers and consumers stand to gain from DRM being implemented effectively, compromise of the kind that Apple has achieved with the iTunes Music Store makes sense.

As discussed in Chapter 6, music is almost ideal for digital distribution. The record companies are sitting on colossal archives of songs that are out-of-print but still well within copyright. It's not economically viable for the record companies to sell pressed CDs of these songs, because demand for any given CD is likely to be relatively low. But demand is there, as has been demonstrated by the millions of illegal copies of such songs that have been downloaded from P2P services. If the record companies can make these songs available online with acceptable DRM, they'll almost certainly find buyers.

NOTE *In passing, it's worth mentioning that some enterprising smaller operators have managed to make an economic proposition out of selling pressed CDs or recorded CDs of out-of-print music to which they've acquired the rights. By cutting out the middleman and selling directly via websites and mail order, and in some cases by charging a premium price for a hard-to-get product, such operators have proved that making such music available isn't impossible. But doing so certainly requires a different business model than the lowest-common-denominator, pack-'em-high-and-hope-they-fly model the major record companies so doggedly pursue.*

What the iTunes Music Store DRM Means to You

At this writing, the iTunes Music Store provides a nicely weighted implementation of DRM designed to be acceptable both to customers and to the record companies that are providing the songs. The iTunes Music Store started with more than 200,000 songs—an impressive number for the record companies to agree to provide, although only a drop in the bucket compared to the millions of songs that music enthusiasts would like to be able to purchase online.

For customers, the attraction is of being able to find songs easily, acquire them almost instantly for reasonable prices, and be able to use them in enough of the ways they're used to (play the songs on their computer, play them on their iPod, or burn them to CD). For the record companies, the appeal is of a largely untapped market that can provide a revenue stream at minimal cost (no physical media are involved) and with an acceptably small potential for abuse. (For example, most people who buy songs won't burn them to CD, rip the CD to MP3, and then distribute the MP3 files.)

Being able to download music like this is pretty wonderful: you can get the songs you want, when you want them, and at a price that's more reasonable than buying a whole CD. But it's important to be aware of the following points, even if they don't bother you in the least:

- When you buy a CD, you own it. As you've seen earlier in this book, you can't necessarily do what you want with the music—not legally, anyway. But you can play it as often as you want on whichever player, lend it to a friend, and so on.

- When you buy a song from the Apple Music Store, you don't own it. Instead, you have a very limited license. If your Mac's hard disk crashes so that you lose your music library, you can't download the songs again from the Apple Music Store without paying for them again.

- The record labels that provide the music reserve the right to change the terms under which they provide the music in the future. If history tells us anything, it's that the record labels won't grant users more generous terms—instead, they'll tighten the restrictions when users have become used to the relatively loose restrictions imposed at first.

What the iTunes Music Store Means for DRM

At this writing, DRM is having a hard time gaining acceptance in the consumer market, particularly in music. For example, the copy-protection mechanisms that the record companies have been putting on audio discs have caused considerable resentment among consumers, because they're perceived as (and are) a disabling technology: they prevent many CD players from playing the audio and prevent many computers from ripping it.

By contrast, the iTunes Music Store has been greeted mostly with enthusiasm. As I see it, there are several reasons for this enthusiasm:

- Many people want to be able to buy music online and enjoy it without undue hassle.

- Apple has implemented the DRM in a slick and effective technology package: iTunes, the iTunes Music Store, and the iPod. This package is greatly facilitated by Apple's control over the hardware (the Macs and the iPods), the operating systems (Mac OS X and the iPod operating system), and the application software (iTunes).

- Generally speaking, Apple enjoys a positive image—among Mac users, among surprisingly many users of other operating systems, and in the press. Apple has carefully fostered this positive image by using public relations, advertising, and the types of hardware and software products it sells, positioning Macintosh as the best hardware and software solution for people who consider themselves nonconformists or are especially creative.

Apple is perhaps the only company that has a reasonable chance of implementing DRM effectively enough to gain it widespread acceptance. The iTunes Music Store is a very promising attempt to gain that acceptance and make online sales of music practical for both consumers and the industry.

Set Up an Account with the iTunes Music Store

To use the iTunes Music Store, you need a Mac running Mac OS X 10.1.5 or later, iTunes 4, and either a .Mac account or an Apple ID. (An Apple ID is essentially an account with the iTunes Music Store and takes the form of an e-mail address.)

To get started with the iTunes Music Store, click the Music Store item in the Source pane in iTunes. iTunes accesses the iTunes Music Store and displays its home page.

If you have a .Mac account, and it's already configured on your Mac, click the Sign In button. In the Sign Up to Buy Music on the iTunes Music Store dialog box, enter your Apple ID and password in the appropriate boxes and click the Sign In button. Remember that your Apple ID is the full e-mail address including the domain rather than just the first part of the address. For example, if your Apple ID is a .Mac address, you need to enter **yourname@mac.com** rather than just **yourname**.

The first time you sign on to the iTunes Music Store, iTunes displays a dialog box pointing out that your Apple ID hasn't been used with the iTunes Music Store and suggesting you review your account information. Click the Review button to review it. (This is a compulsory step. Clicking the Cancel button doesn't skip the review process, as you might hope—instead, it cancels the creation of your account.)

To create a new account, click the Create Account button, then click the Continue button on the Welcome to the iTunes Music Store page. The subsequent screens then walk you through the process of creating an account. As you'd imagine, you have to provide your credit card details and (at this writing) a U.S. billing address. Beyond this, you get a little homily on what you may and may not legally do with the music you download, and you have to agree to the terms of service of the iTunes Music Store. The next section discusses these terms and conditions briefly, because they're important.

Understand the Terms of Service

Almost no one ever reads the details of software licenses, which is why the software companies have been able to establish as normal the sales model in which you buy not software itself but a limited license to use it, and you have no recourse if it trashes your computer. But you'd do well to read the terms and conditions of the iTunes Music Store before you buy music from it, because you should understand what you're getting into.

> **TIP** *The iTunes window doesn't give you the greatest view of the terms of service. To get a better view, direct your browser to www.info.apple.com/usen/musicstore/terms.html.*

The following are the key points of the terms of service:

- You can use songs you download on three computers at any time. You can authorize and deauthorize computers, so you can (for example) transfer your songs from your old computer to a new computer you buy.

- You can use the songs, export them, copy them, and burn them for "personal, noncommercial use." Burning and exporting are an "accommodation" to you and don't "constitute a grant or waiver (or other limitation or implication) of any rights of the copyright owners."

- After you buy and download songs, they're your responsibility. If you lose them or destroy them, Apple won't replace them. (You have to buy new copies of the songs.)

- You agree not to violate the Usage Rules imposed by the agreement.

- You agree that Apple may disclose your registration data and account information to "law enforcement authorities, government officials, and/or a third party, as Apple believes is reasonably necessary or appropriate to enforce and/or verify compliance with any part of this Agreement." The implication is that if a copyright holder claims that you're infringing their copyright, Apple may disclose your details without your knowledge, let alone your agreement. In these days of the Patriot Act and Patriot II, you can safely assume that the government and the law enforcement authorities can easily find out anything they decide they want to know about you. But few will like the idea of (say) Sony Music or the RIAA being able to learn the details of their e-mail address, physical address, credit card, and listening habits by claiming a suspicion of copyright violation.

- Apple and its licensors can remove "products, content, or other materials" or prevent you from accessing them.

- Apple reserves the right to modify the Agreement at any time. If you continue using the iTunes Music Store, you're deemed to have accepted whatever additional terms Apple imposes.

- Apple can terminate your account for failing to "comply with any of the provisions" in the Agreement—or being suspected of failing to comply with them.

You don't have to be a rabid consumer activist to find these terms of service extremely corporate and biased against the consumer. Presumably, Apple has had to negotiate hard to persuade the record companies to make songs available through the iTunes Music Store, and the terms of service perhaps reflect the record companies' concerns about misuse and piracy and Apple's sensible desire to protect itself against redress. But the fact remains that you can use the iTunes Music Store only on Apple's terms, which are heavily biased toward Apple—and which Apple can change at any time.

Configure iTunes Music Store Settings

By default, iTunes 4 is configured to display the iTunes Music Store icon in the Source pane and to use 1-Click buying and downloading. To change your preferences, follow these steps:

1. Choose Edit | Preferences to display the Preferences dialog box.
2. Click the Store tab to display the Store sheet.
3. To prevent the iTunes Music Store item from appearing in the Source pane, clear the Show iTunes Music Store check box. Doing this disables all the other controls on the sheet, so you've nothing left to do but click the OK button.

4. If you choose to use the iTunes Music Store, select the Buy and Download Using 1-Click option button or the Buy Using a Shopping Cart option button as appropriate. 1-Click is great for impulse shopping and instant gratification, whereas the shopping cart enables you to round up a collection of songs, weigh their merits against each other, and decide which ones you feel you must have. (In other words, using the shopping cart is the more sensible approach. So Apple has made 1-Click the default setting.)

> **TIP** *If you have a slow connection, consider using the Buy Using a Shopping Cart option to queue up a stack of tracks to download overnight when the download won't compete with you for your meager bandwidth.*

5. Select or clear the Play Songs After Downloading check box as appropriate. This setting lets you hear a song the instant you've downloaded it, but if you usually listen to music while downloading, you may prefer to keep this check box cleared, as it is by default.

6. If you're using a slow Internet connection (for example, dial-up or ISDN) to download songs, you may want to select the Load Complete Preview Before Playing check box. Otherwise, the download stream may be too slow to sustain play through the preview without interruptions. (Faster Internet connections should be able to stream the previews without breaking a sweat.)

7. Click the OK button to close the Preferences dialog box and apply your choices.

Find the Songs You Want

You can find songs in the iTunes Music Store in several ways that will seem familiar if you've used other online stores:

- You can meander through the interface looking for songs by clicking links from the home page.
- You can browse by genre, artist, and album. Click the Browse button to display the Browse interface.
  - You can search for specific music by using either the Search Music Store box or by clicking the Power Search link on the home page and

using the Power Search page. You can sort the search results by a column heading by clicking it. Click the column heading again to reverse the sort order.

TIP *Be determined in your searches. Some of the artist names are incorrect at this writing. For example, if you search for the song "Talk Talk" by the group Talk Talk, you'll find it's credited to an artist named The Very Best of Talk Talk.*

Preview a Song

One of the most attractive features of the iTunes Music Store is that it lets you listen to a preview of each song before you buy it. This feature helps you ensure both that the song you're buying is the song you think you're buying and that you like it.

For some songs, the previews are of the first 30 seconds. For most songs, the previews feature one of the most distinctive parts of the song (for example, the chorus or a catchy line).

A typical download of a 30-second clip involves around 600K of data. If you have a slow Internet connection, downloading the previews will take a while (it's best to select the Load Complete Preview Before Playing check box on the Store sheet of the Preferences dialog box).

Double-click a song's listing to start the preview playing (or downloading, if you choose to load complete previews before playing).

Understand A******s and "Explicit"

The iTunes Music Store is oddly censorial in a way that most people associate with Tipper Gore rather than the Apple culture:

- Songs deemed to have potentially offensive lyrics are marked EXPLICIT in the Song Name column. Where a sanitized version of the same song is available, it's marked CLEAN in the Song Name column. Some of the supposedly explicit songs are instrumentals... you tell me how these have been cleaned.

- Strangely, other songs that contain words that are offensive to most people (such as George Carlin's "Seven Words You Can't Say on Television") aren't flagged as being explicit. So if you worry about what you and yours hear, don't trust the iTunes Music Store ratings too far.

- Any word deemed offensive is censored with asterisks (**), at least in theory. (In practice, some words sneak through.) When searching, use the real word rather than censoring it yourself.

Request Music You Can't Find

The iTunes Music Store's selection of music is deep in some areas but surprisingly shallow in others. Apple has announced its intention of greatly expanding the range of songs on offer; if and when it does so, all users of the iTunes Music Store will surely welcome the changes.

In the meantime, if you can't find a song you're looking for in the iTunes Music Store, you can submit a request for it. Click the Requests & Feedback link on the home page and use the Make a Request form to request music by song name, artist name, album, composer, or genre.

Buy a Song from the iTunes Music Store

To buy a song from the iTunes Music Store, click the Buy Song button.

If you're not currently signed in, iTunes displays the Sign In Using Your Apple Account dialog box. Enter your password and click the Buy button. (If you want iTunes to handle the password for you automatically in the future, select the Remember Password for Purchasing check box before clicking the Buy button.)

iTunes then displays a confirmation message box. Click the Buy button to make the purchase. Select the Don't Warn Me About Buying Songs Again check box if appropriate. Some people prefer to have this double-check in place to slow down the pace at which they assault their credit cards. For others, even having to confirm the purchase is an annoyance.

iTunes then downloads the song to your music library and adds an entry for it to your Purchased Music playlist.

Listen to Songs You've Purchased

When you download a song from the iTunes Music Store, iTunes adds it to the playlist named Purchased Music in the Source pane. When you display the Purchased Music playlist, iTunes automatically displays a message box to explain what the playlist is. Select the Do Not Show This Message Again check box before dismissing this message box, because otherwise it will soon endanger your sanity.

Purchased Music is there to provide a quick and easy way to get to all the music you buy. Otherwise, if you purchase songs on impulse without keeping a list, the songs might vanish in the maelstrom of music that your music library contains.

To delete the entry for a song in the Purchased Music playlist, right-click it, choose Clear from the shortcut menu, and click the Yes button in the confirmation message box. However, unlike for regular song files, iTunes doesn't offer you the opportunity to delete the song file itself—the file remains in your music library on the basis that, having paid for it, you don't actually want to delete it.

You can drag songs that you haven't purchased to the Purchased Music playlist as well.

Restart a Failed Download

If the download of a song fails, you may see an error message that invites you to try again later. If this happens, iTunes terminates the download but doesn't roll back the purchase of the song.

To restart a failed download, choose Advanced | Check for Purchased Music. Enter your password in the Enter Apple ID and Password dialog box and click the Sign In button. iTunes attempts to restart the failed download.

Review What You've Purchased from the iTunes Music Store

To see what you've purchased from the iTunes Music Store, follow these steps:

1. Click the Account button (the button that displays your account name) to display the Account Information window. (If you're not currently signed in, you'll need to enter your password.)

2. Click the Purchase History link to display details of the songs you've purchased.

3. Click the arrow to the left or an order date to display details of the purchases on that date.

4. Click Done when you've finished examining your purchases.

(Try to) Fix Problems with Your iTunes Music Store Bill

If something seems to have gone wrong with your iTunes Music Store bill—for example, you seem to have been billed for songs you didn't buy—choose Help | Music Store Customer Service and use the resulting form to try to get redress.

Authorize and Deauthorize Computers for the iTunes Music Store

When you buy a song from the iTunes Music Store, you're allowed to play it on up to three different computers at a time. iTunes implements this limitation through a form of license that Apple calls *authorization*. Essentially, iTunes tracks which computers are authorized to play songs you've purchased and stops you from playing the songs when you're out of authorizations.

If you want to play songs you've purchased on a fourth computer, you need to *deauthorize* one of the first three computers so as to free up an authorization for use on the fourth computer. You may also need to specifically deauthorize a computer to prevent it from listening to the songs you've bought. For example, if you sell or give away your Mac, you'd probably want to deauthorize it.

> **NOTE** *Your computer must be connected to the Internet for authorizing and deauthorizing computers.*

Authorize a Computer to Use iTunes Music Store

To authorize a computer, simply try to play a song purchased from the iTunes Music Store. For example, access a shared computer's Purchased Music playlist and double-click one of the songs. iTunes displays the Authorize Computer dialog box.

Enter your Apple ID and password and click the Authorize button. iTunes accesses the iTunes Music Store and (all being well) authorizes the computer. iTunes displays no notification message box, but simply starts playing the song.

Deauthorize a Computer from Using iTunes Music Store

To deauthorize a computer, follow these steps:

1. Choose Advanced | Deauthorize Computer to display the Deauthorize Computer dialog box.

2. Select the Deauthorize Computer for Apple Account option button if it's not already selected.

3. Click the OK button. iTunes displays the Deauthorize Computer dialog box.

4. Enter the appropriate Apple ID and password, and then click the OK button. iTunes accesses the iTunes Music Store, performs the deauthorization, and then displays a message box to tell you that the dirty deed is done.

Index

Symbols and Numbers

** (asterisks) in iTunes Music store, meaning of, 397
1.3, upgrading to, 370
5 in 1 diagnostic test, explanation of, 337

A

A2D diagnostic test, explanation of, 337
AAC (Advanced Audio Coding)
    48 channels of, 368
        advantages and disadvantages of, 368–369
        converting to MP3 by means of iTunes 4, 379–380
        explanation of, 44
        overview of, 367–370
AAC custom encoding settings, choosing with iTunes 4, 372–373
AAC files
    configuring preferences for, 373–374
    determining protected status of, 369
    identifying with iTunes 4, 380
AAC licensing, overview of, 368
AAC playback, improvements made to, 354–355
About item, checking, 29
AC adapters
    choosing, 290
    using, 23–24

accounts, creating for iTunes Music Store, 391–393
Action Jacket armband cases Web site, 287
Ad-aware spyware detection and removal software Web site, 171
Address Book, creating vCards from, 207–210
Advanced sheet, displaying on Mac iPods, 62
AHRA (Audio Home Recording Act), purpose of, 47
AIFF and WAV encoding settings, choosing with iTunes, 69–70
AIFF digital audio format, explanation of, 38
Alarm Clock
    improvements made to, 355
    waking up to, 358
alarms
    turning on and off, 28
    using MUSICMATCH Jukebox Plus as, 131–132
Albums category of Browse item, explanation of, 20
albums, random playing of, 25
All category of Browse item, explanation of, 19
Always On setting for Backlight Timer, explanation of, 29–30
Amadeus II audio editor for Macs
    cleaning up audio files with, 151–152
    recording audio with, 150
animal versus human hearing, 36

401

Apple Customer Privacy Statement page, displaying, 103
Apple Store Web site, 290
Apple SuperDrive Update Web site, 53
AppleCare Support Web site, 102
appointments, exporting from Outlook, 232–233
armband cases, examples of, 287
Artists category of Browse item, explanation of, 19
artwork, adding to songs using iTunes 4, 380–383
ASCII specifications for text, explanation of, 33
asterisks (**) in iTunes Music store, meaning of, 397
Audible.com Web site, 94
audio
    compression concerns, 34
    recording on Mac iPods, 145–150
    recording on Windows iPods, 145–147
    recording with iMovie, 148–149
    ripping, 41
audio cables, using with audio streams, 157
audio CDs
    creating with MUSICMATCH Burner Plus, 185–186
    explanation of, 179
audio discs, ejecting, 54
audio editors, overview of, 143–144
audio files
    compression conversion concerns, 143
    removing scratches and hiss from, 150–152
    support for, 6
audio options, choosing for MUSICMATCH Jukebox Plus, 136–137
audio quality
    determining, 35
    setting in iTunes on Mac iPods, 64–70
audio sources, connecting to create MP3 files, 145
audio streams, saving to disk, 157–160
audio subsystem, diagnostic test for, 335
Audio tab of Burner Plus Options dialog box, selecting from, 185–186
Auto Size Column command, accessing with iTunes, 70
Auto Song Detect feature in MUSICMATCH Jukebox Plus, using, 147
AutoDJ feature on Windows iPods, explanation of, 140
automatic synchronization, turning off in MUSICMATCH Jukebox Plus, 138
AutoPod charger car adapter, features of, 293

B

backing up iPods, 279–280
Backlight Timer, setting, 29–30
backup, using iPods for, 269
batteries
    advisory about discharging of, 256
    capacity of, 254–255
    charging frequency of, 23
    draining as troubleshooting maneuver, 327
    impact of memory effect on, 256
    maximizing life of, 256–257
    reducing demands on, 256–257
    running down when using FireWire, 270
battery icon, explanation of, 23
Betamax Decision of 1984, explanation of, 47
bitrates
    explanation of, 37
    specifying with iTunes, 68
    testing sound given by, 45
booting Macs from iPods, 274–278
Breakout game, playing, 24
Browse item, using, 19–20
Browser feature in iTunes, using, 81
burn lists, splitting to multiple CDs with MUSICMATCH Burner Plus, 190
Burn tab of Burner Plus Options dialog box, selecting from, 183–184

Index

"Burner Plus Cannot Write to the Media" error message, troubleshooting, 196
burning CDs
    acquiring sufficient memory for, 192
    balancing quality, speed, and cost of, 191
    with iTunes, 179–182
    with MUSICMATCH Burner Plus, 188–190
    providing ample processor cycles for, 191–192
    troubleshooting, 190–197
    troubleshooting when using iTunes, 192–195
    troubleshooting when using MUSICMATCH Burner Plus, 195–197
Burton Amp GORE-TEX snowboarding jacket, features of, 294
buttons, diagnostic test for, 335
Buy Using a Shopping Cart option in iTunes Music Store, choosing, 394

C

caching, advantages and disadvantages when burning CDs, 184–185
Cactus-200 Data Shield copy-protection
    as engineering solution, 52
    explanation of, 50
Calendar feature, accessing, 24
calendars. *See also* iCalendar; vCalendar files
    crating iCalendar and vCalendar files from, 227–231
    putting on Mac iPods, 231, 234–235
    putting on Windows iPods, 235–236
    synchronizing with Mac iPods, 217
    viewing on iPods, 236–238
car adapters, choosing, 291–293
car stereos, connecting iPods to, 297–299
cases
    armband type of, 287
    choosing, 286–289
    iPod Armor type of, 288

cassette adapters, connecting iPods to car stereos with, 297–298
CBR (constant bitrate)
    explanation of, 37
    versus VBR (variable bitrate), 43, 372
CCC (Carbon Copy Cloner) tool Web site, 276–277
CD- and DVD-burning features in iTunes 4, using, 374–375
CD burning, overview of, 178–179
CD data, downloading automatically with Mac iPods, 64
CD Extra storage format, explanation of, 39
CD Lookup options in MUSICMATCH Jukebox Plus, choosing, 115–117
CD-protection solutions, dynamics of, 52
CD-quality audio, overview of, 36
CD-R drives
    adding to Mac iPods, 60
    adding to Windows iPods, 102
CD-R (recordable CD), explanation of, 178
CD rewriters, explanation of, 178
CD-ROM drives versus DVD drives, 55
CD-RW drives, troubleshooting on Mac iPods, 195
CD-RW (rewritable CD)
    advisory about, 179
    determining iTunes support of, 192
    explanation of, 178
CDA (CD Audio) files, purpose of, 39
CDDB (CD Database)
    downloading CD information from, 115–117
    submitting CD information to using iTunes, 73–75
    submitting CD information to using MUSICMATCH Jukebox Plus, 122
    Web site, 41
CDs (compact discs)
    acceptable formats of, 52
    advisory about illegal burning of, 48
    burning with iTunes, 179–182
    burning with MUSICMATCH Burner Plus, 188–190

downloading information about using MUSICMATCH Jukebox Plus, 115–117
information sources for, 41–42
ripping and encoding audio from, 41
ripping and encoding with iTunes music library, 71–75
ripping and encoding with MUSICMATCH Jukebox Plus, 119–121
sales reductions of, 51
splitting burn lists to using MUSICMATCH Burner Plus, 190
troubleshooting burning of, 192
types of, 178–179
versatility of, 50–51
Change Music Folder Location dialog box, displaying on Macs, 63
charging cycles for batteries, explanation of, 256
Charging icon, displaying, 24
CLEAN songs in iTunes Music Store, explanation of, 397
Clear All Notes script, features of, 362
Clicker feature, turning on and off, 28
Clipboard to Note script, features of, 362
Clock feature, accessing, 24
Close button on Artwork window, accessing, 383
column displays, changing in iTunes, 70
Compact Disc Digital Audio logo, significance of, 52–53
Composers category of Browse item, explanation of, 0, 21
compressed formats, converting songs from, 379–380
compressing music, overview of, 33–34
compression rates, choosing, 42–45
Connect to Shared Music dialog box, displaying, 378
consumers versus music industry, 162–165
contact records, character limitations of, 241
contacts
  accessing, 24
  creating vCards from, 207–212

duplication in iSync, 213
maximum number of, 205
obtaining Apple Updater for, 202
putting on Mac iPods, 212–220
putting on Mac iPods manually, 218–220
putting on Windows iPods, 220–221
sorting ad displaying, 28
synchronizing with Mac iPods, 212–216, 217
viewing on iPods, 221–222
contrast on screens, changing, 27
Contrast screen, displaying quickly, 360
copy-protected discs, recognizing and using, 53
copy-protection
  advisory about circumvention of, 49
  circumventing, 55–56
  understanding implications of techniques for, 50–52
copyright law, overview of, 46–49
copyrighted material, copying legally, 47–48
copyrighted works, advisory about burning CDs of, 48
copyrights, duration of, 46
cradles, choosing, 289
Crossfade Playback check box in iTunes, using, 82
CSV (comma-separated values) files, creating vCards from, 211
Custom versus Express MUSICMATCH Jukebox Plus installations, explanation of, 105

D

darknet
  dangers associated with, 170–172
  efforts for closing down of, 169–170
  enlargement by P2P networks, 166–168
  overview of, 165–166
  super-peers and free riders of, 168–169
data CDs, explanation of, 179
data compression, overview of, 33

Date & Time screen, changing settings on, 28
Date Book, exporting to vCalendar file, 229–230
defragmentation, explanation of, 280–281
defragmenting iPods, 283
delayed Record and Delayed Recording buttons in MUSICMATCH Jukebox Plus, purpose of, 117
diagnostic tools, pinpointing problems with, 334–336
Digital Audio Extension (DAE) group box in MUSICMATCH Jukebox Plus, options in, 117
digital audio formats, WAV and AIFF as, 38–39
discs, ejecting when stuck, 54
Disk Defragmenter for Windows XP, running, 281–282
disk icon with magnifying glass, meaning of, 340
disk scans, running as troubleshooting maneuver, 333–334
disk space
  checking for Mac iPods, 59–60
  checking for Windows iPods, 101
display backlight timer, setting, 29–30
display, reading, 17
DMCA (Digital Millennium Copyright Act, Title I of, 49, 165
"Do Not Disconnect" message, troubleshooting, 339–340
Docks
  choosing, 289
  features of, 354
  playing music through, 358
driving directions, putting on Mac iPods, 242
DRM (digital-rights management)
  AAC support for, 369
  hardware and software for, 165
  understanding, 387–390
DVBase stand Web site, 289

DVD- and CD-burning features in iTunes 4, using, 374–375
DVD drives versus CD-ROM drives, 55
DVDs played back on Linux, copy-protection concerns about, 49

E

ear buds
  features of, 294
  using, 15–16
Eject iPod script, features of, 362
ejecting
  iPods, 339
  stuck audio discs, 54
Elcomsoft software company case, overview of, 49
encoding audio, explanation of, 41
End of Recording Notifications in MUSICMATCH Jukebox Plus, choosing, 114
enhancers, choosing, 294–295
Enter Upgrade Key page in MUSICMATCH Jukebox Plus, locating key for, 106
Entourage
  creating iCalendar files from, 228
  creating vCards from, 208
  using iPod It utility with, 242–244
EphPod Windows utility
  downloading song files with, 319–321
  putting information on iPods with, 249
EQ (equalization) item, explanation of, 27
equalization, improving music sound with, 26–27
equalizations
  customizing with iTunes, 85–86
  deleting and renaming presets for, 86–88
  using with MUSICMATCH Jukebox Plus, 131
Equalizer window, displaying in iTunes, 83–84
equalizers, Koss eq50 three-band type of, 294

EXPLICIT songs in iTunes Music Store, explanation of, 397
Express versus Custom MUSICMATCH Jukebox Plus installations, explanation of, 105
Extras menu, navigating, 24

F

fades and offsets in MUSICMATCH Jukebox Plus, tweaking start and end of tracks with, 115
fair use copyright provision, explanation of, 47–48
files, transferring to and from iPods, 273–274
Finder
　advisory about removing songs with, 92
　transferring song files from iPods with, 314–315
FireCable, obtaining from Web site, 291
FireJuice adapter, obtaining from Web site, 291
FireWire
　enabling for entering contacts on Windows iPods, 220
　enabling for manual entry of contacts on Mac iPods, 219
　enabling when putting calendars on Mac iPods manually, 234–235
　enabling when putting calendars on Windows iPods, 235–236
　explanation of, 12–13
　necessity of, 59
FireWire adapters, overview of, 291
FireWire cables
　obtaining from Web site, 291
　testing, 338
FireWire car adapters, features of, 292
FireWire cards, adding to Windows iPods, 100–101
FireWire disk mode
　enabling on Macs, 270–271
　enabling on PCs, 272
　forcing, 273
FireWire ports
　diagnostic test for, 335
　testing, 338–339
FLASH diagnostic test, explanation of, 337
Flat equalization, explanation of, 26
FlipStand Web site, 290
fn (formatted name) field in vCards, example of, 204
folders
　adding to MUSICMATCH Jukebox Plus music library, 124–125
　creating and deleting, 273
four-pin FireWire ports and cables, explanation of, 13
fragmentation, explanation of, 280–281
free riders in darknet, explanation of, 168–169
FreeAmp for Windows, recording MP3 streams with, 158–159
Freenet P2P network, overview of, 173

G

games, improvements made to, 355
General tab
　of Burner Plus Options dialog box, 183–184
　of Settings dialog box in MUSICMATCH Jukebox Plus, 107–109
Genre category of Browse item, explanation of, 20
Get Info command, issuing in iTunes, 79
gigabytes, explanation of, 7
Gnutella networks, explanation of, 167–168, 172
GoldWave audio editor for Windows
　eliminating unwanted sounds with, 151–152
　Web site for, 143
graphical equalizers
　improving music sound with, 26–27, 83–88

Index

using with MUSICMATCH Jukebox Plus, 131
graphics
    adding to songs using iTunes 4, 380–383
    compression concerns related to, 33
Griffin PowerPod car adapter, features of, 292
Gripmatic mount, obtaining from Web site, 290
Grokster, darknet advisory about, 171
Groove Bag accessory, features of, 295

H

handles, using with CDA files, 39–40
hard-disk space, using up when copying song files with iTunes, 343–345
hard disks
    advisory about erasure of, 275
    detecting malfunction of, 334
    optimizing, 280–283
    spinning up and down, 255
    using iPods as, 268–269
HDD SCAN diagnostic test, explanation of, 337
headphones
    choosing, 294–295
    connecting, 15–16
HFS Plus disk format, advisory about, 273
HFS Plus file system, using with Macs, 300
hidden folders
    making visible in Windows XP, 312–314
    making visible on Macs, 310–312
high-frequency sounds, explanation of, 36
high-quality MP3 files, creating with MUSICMATCH Jukebox Plus, 109–112
Hold switch, using, 22
home Mac, changing for Mac iPods, 302–303
home PC, changing for Windows iPods, 303–304
horoscopes, putting on iPods, 241, 245

HotWire FireWire cable, obtaining from Web site, 291
human versus animal hearing, 36
Hz (hertz), explanation of, 36

I

iAppoint Web site, 233
iCal
    creating iCalendar files from, 228
    sample iCalendar file created with, 226–227
iCalendar files
    creating from calendars, 227–231
    creating from Microsoft Outlook, 231
iCalendar, overview of, 224–227. *See also* calendars; vCalendar files
IEEE 1394, explanation of, 12–13
images, adding to songs using iTunes 4, 380–383
iMovie, recording audio with, 148–149
Import button in iTunes, using, 72
Import Contacts dialog box in Entourage, displaying, 212
importing settings in iTunes, changing on Mac iPods, 64–70
infrasound, explanation of, 36
"Install Error: Reinstall iPod Plug-In" error message, troubleshooting, 346–348
Instructions and Sample vCards on Mac iPods, removing, 219
Internet, sharing music files on, 176–177
intros and outros
    eliminating from MP3 files, 152–154
    skipping on iTunes, 88
iPod AC Adapter, obtaining from Web site, 290
iPod Armor cases Web site, 288
iPod boxes, contents of, 10–11
iPod buttons, diagnostic test for, 335
iPod controls
    display, 17
    explanation of, 17–18
    locking, 22
    troubleshooting, 22

iPod It Mac utility, putting information on iPods with, 242–244
iPod plug-in, downloading for use with MUSICMATCH Jukebox Plus, 102
iPod Power Adapter, obtaining from Web site, 290
iPod Service Page, Internet address for, 325
iPod Stand, obtaining from Web site, 290
iPodCradle Web site, 289
iPodDock Web site, 290
iPodMemo Mac utility, putting information on iPods with, 247–248
iPods. *See also* Mac iPods; Windows iPods
    accessories for, 354
    advisory about opening of, 254
    audio formats supported by, 6
    backing up, 279–280
    battery life of, 256–257
    booting Macs from, 274–278
    caching on, 255
    capacities at typical compression ratios, 8
    capacities of, 7, 9, 353, 355–356
    caring for, 257–259
    checking software versions of, 10
    choosing settings for, 25–28
    cleaning, 266
    cloning existing operating systems on, 276–277
    connecting headphones or speakers to, 15–16
    connecting to computers, 12–13
    connecting to PCs via USB, 357
    connecting to stereos, 296–299
    converting between Macs and Windows, 300–301
    default name for, 133
    disconnection guidelines, 257–259
    displaying contents of, 321
    displaying information about, 29
    ejecting, 339
    as hard drives, 268–269
    installing Mac OS X or System 9 on, 274–276

installing software for, 13–14
internals of, 254–256
limitations of, 5–6
limitations of putting information on, 240–241
loading from two or more computers at once, 306–308
loading with music, 14–15
look, feel, and heft of, 353–354
making bootable, 276–277
models of, 8–9
new versus earlier ones, 352–355
operating system upgrades for, 259–265
optimizing hard disks of, 280–283
overview of, 4–5
protecting, 257–259
putting text on, 241–242
recharging, 23–24
remote control features of, 354
resetting, 12, 340
resetting as troubleshooting maneuver, 327
resetting to recover from wrong languages, 11
restoring as troubleshooting maneuver, 327–333
selection criteria for, 6–8, 355–356
setting up, 11–12, 356–357
software improvements made to, 354–355
starting up Macs from, 274–278
stopping Macs from booting from, 279
storing and carrying, 266
synchronizing with different computers, 301–304
synchronizing with same computer, 304–305
temperature concerns pertaining to, 258
transferring files to and from, 273–274
turning on, 17
turning on and off, 11
updating to version 1.3, 370

Index 409

vCards used with, 205–207
viewing calendars on, 236–238
viewing contacts on, 221–222
weight and measurements of, 5
for Windows and Macs, 353
iPodSync Web site, 232
iShare Earbud Splitter, features of, 294–295
iSpeakIT Mac utility, putting information on iPods with, 242–243
iSync
    advisory about public beta of, 214
    advisory about showing duplicate contacts in, 213
    downloading, 234
    reverting to last sync with, 218
    synchronizing contacts and calendars with, 217
    using to put contacts on Mac iPods automatically, 212–214
items, accessing quickly from main menu, 359–360
iTeXpod Mac utility, putting information on iPods with, 245–246
iTunes. *See also* Mac iPods; Macs
    adding songs to, 76
    browsing music with, 81
    burning CDs with, 179–182
    changing column displays in, 70–71
    changing default synchronization settings on, 90–91
    changing importing settings for, 64–70
    choosing custom AIFF and WAV encoding settings with, 69–70
    choosing custom MP3 encoding settings with, 66–69
    connecting to Internet automatically, 64
    controlling synchronization manually with, 91–93
    creating VBR-encoded files with, 68
    customizing, 372–374
    customizing equalizations with, 85–86
    customizing playlists with, 95–98
    deleting and renaming preset equalizations with, 86–88
    devices compatible with, 192
    display of, 61
    graphical equalizer used with, 83–88
    including track numbers in song names with, 66
    joining tracks without gaps in, 75
    managing CDs with, 66–67
    playing back music with, 81–83
    rating songs with, 79–80
    removing songs from Mac iPods with, 92
    running on Mac iPods, 60
    setting sample rates with, 68
    setting up and configuring, 60–61
    setting up and configuring on Macs, 60–71
    settings for encoding MP3 files, 42
    skipping intros and outros on, 88
    specifying bitrates with, 68
    submitting CD information to CDDB with, 73–75
    system requirements for, 58
    troubleshooting burning CDs with, 192–195
    updating playlists with, 91
    updating songs with, 89
    using visualizations with, 82
    Web site for, 60
iTunes 4
    accessing and playing shared music by means of, 377–379
    adding artwork to songs by means of, 380–383
    CD- and DVD-burning features in, 374–375
    changes in, 366–367
    choosing custom AAC encoding settings with, 373–374
    choosing custom MP3 encoding settings with, 372–373
    converting songs between AAC and MP3 in, 379–380
    quitting, 383
    sharing music by means of, 375–377
    upgrading to, 370–371

"iTunes Has Detected a Software Update" error message, troubleshooting, 341
iTunes music library
    adding songs to, 76
    consolidating, 77–78
    creating, building, and managing, 71–80
    deleting songs from, 76
    ripping and encoding CDs with, 71–75
    storing on Mac iPods, 62–63
    storing song files on Mac iPods in, 63
    synchronizing part of, 92
    synchronizing with Mac iPods, 88–94
    tagging songs for correct sorting in, 78–79
iTunes music library folder, restoring to default location on Macs, 63
iTunes Music Store
    adjusting bills received from, 398
    authorizing and deauthorizing computers for, 398–399
    buying songs from, 396–399
    CLEAN songs in, 395–396
    configuring settings for, 393–394
    EXPLICIT songs in, 395–396
    finding songs in, 394–396
    listening to songs purchased from, 396–397
    overview of, 386–387
    previewing songs with, 395–396
    requesting music from, 396
    reviewing songs purchased from, 397
    setting up accounts with, 391–393
    terms of service for, 392–393
    troubleshooting song downloads from, 397–399
IUMA (Internet Underground Musical Archive) Web site, 175

J

jitter, troubleshooting with MUSICMATCH Jukebox Plus, 116–117
joint versus normal stereo, 43–45

K

Kazaa P2P network, darknet advisory about, 171–172
key2audio copy-protection, explanation of, 50, 52
keypresses, troubleshooting failure of response to, 336–337
KHz (kilohertz), explanation of, 36
Koss eq50 three-band equalizer, features of, 294

L

languages, resetting iPods for, 11
LCD display, reading, 17
LCM diagnostic test, explanation of, 337
leechers in darknet, explanation of, 168–169
List All Notes script, features of, 362
Listen.com Web site, 174
lossless compression, explanation of, 33
lossy compression, explanation of, 34
low-frequency sounds, explanation of, 36
Lycos Music Web site, 175
lyrics, putting on iPods, 241

M

Mac iPods. *See* MiPods. *See also* iPods; iTunes; Macs; Mac utilities for putting information on iPods
    adding and deleting songs from iTunes music library on, 76
    adding CD-R drives to, 60
    Amadeus II audio editor for, 150, 151–152
    browsing iTunes music on, 81
    changing column displays in iTunes for, 70–71
    changing default iTunes synchronization settings on, 90–91
    changing home Mac for, 302–303
    changing iTunes importing settings for audio quality on, 64–70

checking disk space and memory of, 59–60
checking operating system version of, 59
choosing contacts synchronization options for, 215–216
choosing custom AIFF and WAV encoding settings in iTunes for, 69–70
choosing MP3 encoding settings on, 66–69
connecting iTunes to Internet automatically with, 64
consolidating iTunes music library on, 77–78
controlling iTunes synchronization manually on, 91–93
converting to Windows iPods, 300–301
customizing playlists on, 95–98
defragmenting, 283
deleting and renaming iTunes preset equalizations on, 86–88
designating as startup disks, 277–279
equalizations used with, 27
FireWire standard for, 12–13
hard-disk advisory about, 64
joining tracks without gaps using iTunes, 75
listening to Audible.com spoken-word files on, 94
loading extra music on, 93
loading from two or more Macs, 306–307
loading music on, 14–15
mEdit freeware tool for, 154
MP3 Rage tag-editing application for, 155–156
new features of, 9
playing back iTunes music on, 81–83
preventing changes to Energy Saver configuration while burning CDs, 195

preventing sleeping while burning CDs, 193–195
putting calendars on, 231, 234–235
putting contacts on, 212–220
putting contacts on manually, 218–220
rating iTunes songs on, 79–80
recording audio on, 147–150
removing songs from, 92
ripping and encoding CDs with iTunes music library on, 71–75
running iTunes on, 60
setting sample rates in iTunes on, 68
setting up and configuring iTunes on, 60–61
Sound Studio for OS X audio editor used with, 150
SoundApp audio editor for, 143–144
specifying bitrates in iTunes for, 68
stopping synchronization on, 218
storing music libraries on, 62–63
storing song files in music library on, 63
StreamRipperX tool for, 159–160
switching between automatic and manual updating on, 93–94
synchronizing contacts and calendars on, 217
synchronizing iSync with, 214–215
synchronizing iTunes music library with, 88–94
synchronizing part of iTunes music library on, 92
tagging songs for correct sorting in iTunes music library, 78–79
turning off Safeguard warnings on, 217
unmounting, 271
unmounting after synchronization, 217
updating, 259–263
updating iTunes playlists on, 91
updating iTunes songs on, 89
using iMovie with, 148–149
using iTunes graphical equalizers with, 83–88
versus Windows iPods, 7

Mac OS X
  accessing CD-audio data with, 39, 41
  Backup application on, 280
  installing on iPods, 274–276
  putting calendars on iPods automatically from, 234
  restoring iPods on, 328–331
  troubleshooting non-ejecting CDs in, 195
  updating Mac iPods on, 259–263
Mac utilities for putting information on iPods
  iPod It, 242–244
  iPodMemo, 247–248
  iSpeakIT, 242–243
  iTeXpod, 245–246
  Pod2Go, 245
  PodNews, 244–245
  PodWriter, 247–248
  Text2iPodX, 247
MacCentral script, features of, 363
Macs. *See also* Mac iPods
  creating iCalendar and vCalendar files on, 228
  creating vCards on, 207–209
  downloading song files to, 316–318
  ejecting stuck audio discs from, 54–55
  enabling FireWire disk mode on, 270–271
  loading extra music to Mac iPods from, 93
  loading Mac iPods from, 306–307
  making hidden folders visible on, 310–312
  preparing for use with Mac iPods, 59–60
  SBOD (Spinning Beachball of Death) displayed on, 340
  setting up and configuring iTunes on, 60–71
  starting up from iPods, 274–278
  stopping from booting from iPods, 279
  transferring software between, 269
  troubleshooting connection to iPods, 338–339
  using copy-protected audio files with, 53
MacUpdate Web site, 240
Main menu, customizing for quick access to items, 359–360
mEdit for Macs, using with MP3 files, 154
megabytes, explanation of, 7
memory
  checking for Mac iPods, 59–60
  checking for Windows iPods, 101
memory effect, impact on batteries, 256
menu bar, placing Script menu on, 363–364
Menu button, using, 18
menus
  customizing for quick access to items, 359–360
  improvements made to, 355
  scrolling, 18
Microsoft Outlook
  creating iCalendar and vCalendar files from, 231
  exporting appointments from, 232–233
mid/side versus normal stereo, 44
Midbar Cactus-200 Data Shield copy-protection
  as engineering solution, 52
  explanation of, 50
MIDI (Musical Instrument Digital Interface), explanation of, 34
MiPods. *See* Mac iPods
"Missing theme.ini" error message, troubleshooting, 345–346
mono recording
  explanation of, 43
  specifying in iTunes, 68
Morpheus, darknet advisory about, 171
mounts, choosing, 290
MP3 CDs
  creating with MUSICMATCH Burner Plus, 186–187
  explanation of, 179

Index **413**

MP3 digital audio format, overview of, 37–38
MP3 encoding settings
    choosing with iTunes, 66–69, 372–373
    customizing with iTunes 4, 372–373
MP3 files
    versus AAC, 368–370
    converting to AAC by means of iTunes 4, 379–380
    copyright concerns about, 48
    creating from cassettes or vinyl records, 144–150
    creating with MUSICMATCH Jukebox Plus, 109–112
    encoding with iTunes, 42
    identifying with iTunes 4, 380
    ripping and encoding CDs to, 71–75, 120–121
    specifying quality on Mac iPods, 64–70
    tagging for sorting, 154–156
    tagging with MUSICMATCH Jukebox Plus music library, 127
    trimming to eliminate intros and outros, 152–154
MP3 Rage for Macs, tag editing with, 155–156
MP3 streams
    recording with FreeAmp for Windows, 158–159
    recording with StreamRipperX for Macs, 160
MP3 tab of Burner Plus Options dialog box, selecting from, 186–187
MP3 TrackMaker for Windows, using with MP3 files, 153
MP3 webcasting Web site, 38
MP3.com Web site, 173
mp3PRO digital audio format, explanation of, 39
MP4 digital audio format, explanation of, 39
MPEG-2 and MPEG-4 AAC, overview of, 367–368
MPEG Web site, 37

music. *See also* shared music; songs
    browsing and accessing, 19–20
    browsing with iTunes, 81
    finding with Composers category, 21
    improving with equalizations, 26–27
    loading, 14–15
    loading on Mac iPods, 93
    playing back using MUSICMATCH Jukebox Plus, 129–130
    playing back with iTunes, 81–83
    playing through Docks, 358
    sharing, 375–377
    using iTunes visualizations with, 82
music compression, overview of, 33–34
music files
    advisory about transfer of, 274
    downloading from Web sites, 173–175
    finding in newsgroups, 175–176
    posting to newsgroups, 177
    sending via e-mail, 177
    sharing on Internet, 176–177
music industry versus consumers, 162–165
music library. *See* iTunes music library and MUSICMATCH Jukebox Plus Jukebox Plus music library entries
MUSICMATCH Burner Plus
    burning CDs with, 188–190
    creating audio CDs with, 185–186
    creating MP3 CDs with, 186–187
    splitting burn lists between CDs with, 190
    troubleshooting, 195–197
MUSICMATCH Jukebox Plus Jukebox Plus, 114–115
    accessing Small Player view in, 130
    adding tracks to music library in, 121–125
    advisory about versions of, 102
    arranging windows in, 130
    changing settings for, 106
    changing skins in, 130
    changing synchronization options for, 135–136
    choosing audio options for, 136–137

choosing CD Lookup options in, 115–117
choosing end-of-recording notifications with, 114
configuring, 106–118
configuring device setup options for, 132–135
configuring music library for, 118
controlling visualizations with, 130
creating custom playlists with, 139–140
creating high-quality MP3 files with, 109–112
displaying context menus in, 130
installing on PCs, 102–106
Library window in, 107
Main window in, 107
making random selections in, 130
obtaining information about current song playing in, 130
playing back music with, 129–130
Playlist window in, 107
Recorder window in, 107
recording on Windows with, 145–147
recording with, 147
ripping and encoding CDs with, 119–121
ripping and encoding with, 112
searching for tracks with, 124
searching songs in, 130
submitting CD information to CDDB with, 122–123
troubleshooting ripping problems in, 116–117
turning off automatic synchronization in, 138
unmounting Windows iPods with, 139
updating, 118
using as alarm, 131–132
using fades and offsets in, 115
using graphical equalizer with, 131
Volume Leveling feature in, 128–129
MUSICMATCH Jukebox Plus Jukebox Plus music library
  adding specific folders or tracks to, 124–125
  configuring, 118–119
  creating, building, and managing, 118–129
  deleting songs from, 125–126
  moving, 113
  sorting alphabetically, 129
  storing and naming files in, 112–114
  synchronizing with Windows iPods, 132–139
MUSICMATCH Portables Plus synchronizations, troubleshooting slowness of, 348
My Library pane in MUSICMATCH Jukebox Plus, navigating, 129
My Music folder in MUSICMATCH Jukebox Plus, contents of, 112–113
My Rating feature in iTunes, using, 79–80

N

n (name) field in vCards, example of, 204–205
Napster, history of, 166–167, 169–170
NET Act of 1997, purpose of, 165
New Tracks Directory Options dialog box in MUSICMATCH Jukebox Plus, choices in, 113–114
news headlines
  putting on iPods, 241
  putting on Mac iPods, 242, 245
newsgroups
  finding music files in, 175–176
  posting music files to, 177
No Electronic Theft Act of 1997, purpose of, 165
normal versus joint stereo, 43–45
Norton Utilities Web site, 281
Note Power 20 solar panel, features of, 294
notes, reading, 361–364
Novus plastic polishes Web site, 266
Now Playing screen, displaying, 20–21, 22

Index **415**

O

Off setting for Backlight Timer, explanation of, 29
Offset text box in MUSICMATCH Jukebox Plus, tweaking start and end of tracks with, 115
Ogg Vorbis digital audio format, explanation of, 39
On-the-Go playlist
    creating, 360
    improvements made to, 355
operating systems
    cloning onto iPods, 276–277
    updating, 259–265
org (organization) field in vCards, example of, 204–205
Outlook
    creating iCalendar and vCalendar files from, 231
    exporting appointments from, 232–233
Outlook Express, creating vCards from, 210
OutPod Web site, 233
outros and intros
    eliminating from MP3 files, 152–154
    skipping on iTunes, 88

P

P2P (peer-to-peer) networks
    attraction of, 171
    dangers associated with, 170–172
    distributing music files by means of, 177
    enlargement of darknet by, 166–168
    Freenet, 173
    Gnutella, 172
    Kazaa, 172
P2P services, targeting to close down darknet, 169–170
packet-writing software, purpose of, 179
Palm Desktop
    creating vCalendar files from, 228–231
    creating vCards from, 208–210
    vCalendar file created by, 225–226
PCM (pulse code modulation)
    AIF and WAV files as, 38
    explanation of, 36
PCs (personal computers)
    connecting iPods to using USB, 357
    enabling FireWire disk mode on, 272
    installing MUSICMATCH Jukebox Plus Jukebox Plus on, 102–106
    loading Windows iPods from, 307–308
    troubleshooting connection to iPods, 338–339
PDI (personal data interchange), relationship to vCard development, 203
Personal Music Recommendations dialog box in MUSICMATCH Jukebox Plus, displaying, 104–105
personal use provision of AHRA, explanation of, 47, 144–145
Phone input on amplifiers, advisory about connecting iPods to, 297
place-shifting, role in Betamax Decision of 1984, 47
plain versus joint stereo, 44
Play Count column in iTunes, purpose of, 70
Play/Pause button, using, 18
playlists
    applying iTunes equalization to, 83–84
    creating automatically on Windows iPods, 140
    creating manually on Windows iPods, 139
    creating with Smart Playlists feature in iTunes, 96–98
    customizing for iTunes or Mac iPods, 95–98
    customizing with MUSICMATCH Jukebox Plus, 139–140
    playing, 19
    saving on Windows iPods, 139
    saving with MUSICMATCH Jukebox Plus, 129
    updating with iTunes, 91
PlusOptimizer defragmentation utility for Macs Web site, 281

Pod2Go Mac utility, putting information on iPods with, 245
Podestal utility, copying song files with, 315–316
PodNews Mac utility, putting information on iPods with, 244–245
PodStand, features of, 289
PodWorks utility, transferring Mac music files with, 316–318
PodWriter Mac utility, putting information on iPods with, 247–248
positional audio, explanation of, 43–44
power adapters, choosing, 290–293
PowerPod car adapter, overview of, 292
Preferences dialog box, displaying on Macs, 62
pressplay Web site, 174
Previous/Rewind button, using, 18
Printer Friendly script, features of, 363
psychoacoustics, role in MP3, 37

R

radio-frequency adapters, connecting iPods to car stereos with, 298
RAM (random access memory), diagnostic test for, 335
ratings, improvements made to, 355
Recorder tab of Settings dialog box in MUSICMATCH Jukebox Plus, options on, 110–112, 114–115
Red Book format
    explanation of, 39, 52
    using with MUSICMATCH Burner Plus, 185–186
remote control
    attaching, 23
    diagnostic test for, 335–336
    features of, 354
    troubleshooting, 337
Resample Audio Files option in MUSICMATCH Jukebox Plus, using, 137
RESET diagnostic test, explanation of, 337
resetting iPods, 340
restoring iPods, advisory about, 328, 331
RIAA (Recording Industry Association of America), purpose of, 51, 165
ripping
    explanation of, 41
    stopping with MUSICMATCH Jukebox Plus, 121
    troubleshooting in MUSICMATCH Jukebox Plus, 116–117
RTC diagnostic test, explanation of, 337
RUN IN diagnostic test, explanation of, 337

S

Safeguard warnings, turning off using Mac iPods, 217
sample rates, setting with iTunes, 68, 70
sampling, explanation of, 36
SBOD (Spinning Beachball of Death) display in Macs, displaying, 340
screen contrast, improving readability of, 27
screen effects in iTunes, preventing when burning CDs, 192
scripts, creating and managing text notes with, 361–363
scroll wheel
    diagnostic test for, 336
    using, 18–19
scrubbing through songs, 20–22
security, using iPods for, 269
Select button, using, 18
Settings dialog box in MUSICMATCH Jukebox Plus, accessing, 106
settings, selecting, 25–28
shared music, accessing and playing with iTunes 4, 377–379. See also music; songs
shuffle order, changing with iTunes, 82
shuffle settings, applying, 25
six-pin FireWire ports and cables, explanation of, 13
skins, changing in MUSICMATCH Jukebox Plus, 130
skip protection, overview of, 255–256
sleep mode, diagnostic test for, 336

Index

Sleep Timer feature, using, 28
sleeping
    preventing while burning on Mac iPods, 193–195
    preventing while burning on Windows iPods, 197
Small Speakers equalization, explanation of, 27
Smart Encoding in iTunes, purpose of, 68
Smart Playlists feature in iTunes, creating, 96–98
snowboarding, accessory for, 294–295
software
    installing for iPods, 13–14
    transferring between Macs, 269
solar panels, features of, 294
song files
    storage of, 310–314
    storing in music library on Mac iPods, 63
    tagging for correct sorting by MUSICMATCH Jukebox Plus, 126–127
    transferring from iPods to computers, 315–321
    transferring from iPods with Finder or Windows Explorer, 314–315
song folders, displaying in Windows XP, 312–313
song position, changing with Scroll wheel, 18
songs. *See also* music; shared music
    adding artwork to, 380–383
    adding to and deleting from iTunes music library, 76
    advisory about converting from compressed formats, 379
    buying from iTunes Music Store, 396–399
    changing place in, 20–21
    changing volume of, 20
    cost in iTunes Music Store, 386
    deleting from MUSICMATCH Jukebox Plus, 125–126
    finding in iTunes Music Store, 394–396
    listening to when purchased from iTunes Music Store, 396–397
    playing, 20–22
    playing from iPods through computers, 321–322
    previewing with iTunes Music Store, 395–396
    queuing, 360
    random playing of, 25
    rating, 360–361
    rating with iTunes, 79–80
    removing from Mac iPods, 92
    reviewing when purchased from iTunes Music Store, 397
    scrubbing through, 20–22
    searching with MUSICMATCH Jukebox Plus, 130
    skipping iTunes intros and outros on, 88
    specifying specific iTunes equalization for, 84–85
    starting and pausing, 20
    tagging songs for correct sorting in iTunes music library, 78–79
    tracks as, 8
    troubleshooting downloads from iTunes Music Store, 397–399
    typical size of, 395
    updating in iTunes, 89
Songs category of Browse item, explanation of, 20
Sony Decision, explanation of, 47
Sound Check feature, standardizing volume with, 25–26
Sound Enhancer check box in iTunes, using, 82
sound frequency, measuring, 36
sound quality, optimizing with uncompressed files, 45–46
Sound Studio for OS X, recording Mac audio with, 150–151
sound, testing bitrates of, 45

SoundApp audio editor Web site, 143–144
source
    recording MUSICMATCH Jukebox Plus from, 147
    specifying on Mac iPods, 147–148
Source pane in iTunes, displaying Mac iPods in, 89
speakers, connecting, 15–16
Speed Disk Web site, 281
spoken-word audio, listening to using Mac iPods, 94
spyware, detecting and removing, 171
stands, choosing, 289–290
startup disks
    designating Mac iPods as, 277–279
    displaying context menus in, 277–279
stereo
    left and right channels of, 43–44
    normal versus joint types of, 43–45
Stereo Mode in iTunes, options in, 69
stereo recording, specifying in iTunes, 68
stereos, connecting iPods to, 296–299
stock quotes, putting on iPods, 241, 245
streaming audio, saving to disk, 157–160
StreamRipperX for Macs, recording MP3 streams with, 160
super-peers in darknet, explanation of, 168–170
surround sound versus stereo, 44
Symantec Corporation Web site, 281
synchronization, preventing automation with MUSICMATCH Jukebox Plus on Windows iPods, 135
synchronizing iPods, 304–305
System 9
    accessing CD-audio data with, 39–40
    installing on iPods, 274–276
System tab of Burner Plus Options dialog box, selecting from, 184–185

T

Tag&Rename for Windows, tag editing with, 155–156

tags
    using with songs in iTunes music library, 78–79
    using with songs in MUSICMATCH Jukebox Plus music library, 126–127
TCP/IP subnets, accessing shared music on, 377–379
TCPA (Trusted Computing Platform Alliance), purpose of, 165
text
    ASCII specifications for, 33
    putting on iPods, 241–242
text editors
    iPodMemo for Mac iPods, 247–248
    PodWriter for Mac iPods, 247–248
text files
    converting to vCard files with ITeXpod utility, 245–246
    putting into contacts on Mac iPods, 247
    putting on Mac iPods, 242, 244, 247
text notes
    creating and managing with scripts, 361–363
    improvements made to, 355
Text2iPodX Mac utility, putting information on iPods with, 247
"The iPod 'iPod' is linked to another iTunes music library" error message, troubleshooting, 342
time
    changing, 28
    displaying in title bar, 359
time display, improvements made to, 355
time-shifting, role in Betamax Decision of 1984, 47
TinkerTool utility, making hidden folders on Macs visible with, 310–311
Tip of the Day dialog box in MUSICMATCH Jukebox Plus, disabling, 106
title bar, displaying time in, 359
Title I of DMCA, explanation of, 49
TotalRecorder for Windows, recording MP3 streams with, 159

Index   419

tracks
- adding and removing with MUSICMATCH Burner Plus, 189
- adding to MUSICMATCH Jukebox Plus music library, 121–125, 124–125
- adding to Windows iPods using MUSICMATCH Jukebox Plus, 137–138
- deleting from MUSICMATCH Jukebox Plus, 125–126
- dragging in playlists on Mac iPods, 95
- joining without gaps using iTunes, 75
- in normal stereo, 44
- processing for Volume Leveling in MUSICMATCH Jukebox Plus, 128
- removing from music library on Macs, 344
- repeating, 25
- searching with MUSICMATCH Jukebox Plus, 124
- as songs, 8

TransPod, using with iPods in cars, 298

troubleshooting
- disk icon displayed with magnifying glass, arrow, check mark, X, or exclamation point, 340
- "Do Not Disconnect" error message, 339–340
- failure to respond to keypresses, 336–337
- "Install Error: Reinstall iPod Plug-In" error message, 346–348
- iPod connections to Macs and PCs, 338–339
- iTunes copying song files using up hard-disk space, 343–345
- "iTunes Has Detected a Software Update" error message, 341
- Mac or PC doesn't react with iPod is plugged in, 338
- "Missing theme.ini" error message, 345–346
- MUSICMATCH Jukebox Plus doesn't recognize iPods, 341–342
- MUSICMATCH Portables Plus synchronizations, 348
- overview of, 326–327
- remote control failure, 337
- remote control stops working, 337
- SBOD (Spinning Beachball of Death), 340
- songs in music library aren't transferred to iPods, 340
- "The iPod 'iPod" is linked to another iTunes music library" error message, 342

troubleshooting maneuvers
- draining batteries, 327
- resetting iPods, 327
- restoring iPods, 327–328
- running disk scans, 333–334

U

ultrasound, explanation of, 36
uncompressed files, advantages of, 45–46
Updater
- for Mac iPods on Mac OS X, 259
- restoring to earlier versions of Windows iPod software with, 265
- for Windows iPods on Windows XP, 263

USB standard
- advisory about, 102
- connecting to PCs with, 357
- versus FireWire, 12–13, 100–101

V

VBR-encoded files, creating with iTunes, 68
VBR (variable bitrate)
- versus CBR (constant bitrate), 43, 372
- explanation of, 37
vCalendar files. *See also* calendars; iCalendar
- crating from Palm Desktop, 230–231
- creating from calendars, 227–231

creating from Microsoft Outlook, 231
creating from Palm Desktop, 228–230
creating on Windows, 230–231
exporting Date Book to, 229–230
overview of, 224–227
vCards
creating from Address Book in Windows, 209–210
creating from Address Book on Macs, 207–208
creating from contacts, 207–212
creating from CSV files, 211
creating from Entourage, 208
creating from Outlook Express, 210
creating from Palm Desktop in Windows, 210
creating from Palm Desktop on Macs, 208–209
creating from templates, 207
creating on Macs, 207–209
examining, 204–205
fields in, 206
handling with iPods, 205–207
overview of, 203–207
.vcf extension, meaning of, 207
version 1.3, upgrading to, 370
VersionTracker.com Web site, 240
Via Licensing Corporation, Web address for, 368
visualizations
controlling with MUSICMATCH Jukebox Plus, 130
using with iTunes, 82
volume
changing for songs, 18, 20–21
standardizing with Sound Check feature, 25–26
Volume Leveling feature in MUSICMATCH Jukebox Plus, using, 128–129

W

warranties, preventing voiding of, 324–326
WAV and AIFF encoding settings, choosing with iTunes, 69–70
WAV digital audio format, explanation of, 38
weather forecasts, putting on Mac iPods, 242, 245
weather reports, putting on iPods, 241
Web sites
Action Jacket armband cases, 287
Ad-aware spyware detection and removal software, 171
Amadeus II, 150
Apple, 102
Apple contacts Updater, 202
Apple Software Downloads, 259, 263
Apple Store, 290
Apple SuperDrive Update, 53
AppleCare Support, 102
Audible.com, 94
AutoPod charger car adapter, 293
Burton Amp GORE-TEX snowboarding jacket, 294–295
CCC (Carbon Copy Cloner) tool, 276–277
CDDB (CD Database), 41
downloading music files from, 173–175
DVBase stands, 289
EphPod utility, 249, 318–319
FireCable, 291
FireJuice adapters, 291
FireWire cables, 291
FlipStand, 290
FreeAmp for Windows, 158
Gnutella P2P protocol, 172
GoldWave audio editor, 143
Griffin PowerPod car adapter, 292
Gripmatic mounts, 290
HotWire FireWire cables, 291
iPod AC Adapter, 290
iPod It Mac utility, 242–244
iPod Power Adapter, 290
iPod Stand, 290
iPodCradle, 289
iPodDock, 290
iPodMemo Mac utility, 247–248
iShare Earbud Splitter, 294
iSpeakIT Mac utility, 242–243

Index

iSync, 213
iTeXpod Mac utility, 245–246
iTunes, 60
iTunes-compatible devices, 192
iTunes Music Store terms of service, 392
IUMA (Internet Underground Musical Archive), 175
Kazaa P2P network, 172
key2audio copy-protection, 50
Listen.com, 174
Lycos Music, 175
Mac OS X Downloads page, 315
MacUpdate, 240, 315
mEdit for Macs, 154
Midbar Tech Ltd. (Cactus-200 Data Shield), 50
MP3 Rage for Macs, 155–156
MP3 TrackMaker for Windows, 153
MP3 webcasting, 38
MP3.com, 173
MPEG, 37
Norton Utilities, 281
Note Power 20 solar panel, 294
Novus plastic polishes, 266
Pod2Go Mac utility, 245
Podestal utility, 315–316
PodNews Mac utility, 244–245
PodStand, 289
PodWorks utility, 316
PodWriter Mac utility, 247–248
pressplay Web site, 174
Sound Studio for OS X, 150–151
Speed Disk defragmentation utility for Macs, 281
Symantec Corporation, 281
Tag&Rename for Windows, 155–156
Text2iPodX Mac utility
TinkerTool utility, 310–311
TotalRecorder for Windows, 159
TransPod, 298
VersionTracker.com, 240, 315
Via Licensing Corporation, 368
World Travel Adapter Kit, 293
XtremeMac Premium iPod Car Charger adapter, 292
Zip Cord Retractable Earbuds, 294
Windows
 accessing CD-audio data with, 39–40
 creating vCalendar files on, 230–231
 creating vCards from, 209–210
 enabling use of Mac-formatted iPods with, 249
Windows Explorer
 hiding and displaying files and folders with, 221
 transferring song files from iPods with, 314–315
Windows iPods. *See also* MUSICMATCH Jukebox Plus Jukebox Plus entries
 adding FireWire cards to, 100–101
 adding MUSICMATCH Jukebox Plus tracks to manually, 137–138
 AutoDJ feature of, 140
 changing home PC for, 303–304
 changing MUSICMATCH Jukebox Plus synchronization options, 135–136
 checking memory and disk space on, 101
 checking operating system version of, 101
 choosing MUSICMATCH Jukebox Plus audio options for, 136–137
 choosing options for, 138–139
 configuring MUSICMATCH Jukebox Plus device setup options for, 132–135
 configuring MUSICMATCH Jukebox Plus for, 106–118
 configuring MUSICMATCH Jukebox Plus music library on, 118–119
 connecting and disconnecting for use with MUSICMATCH Jukebox Plus, 132–135
 converting to Mac iPods, 300–301
 customizing and saving playlists on, 139–140

defragmenting, 283
determining connection status of, 132
enabling for use as hard disks, 235–236
EphPod utility used with, 318–321
equalizations used with, 27
FreeAmp MP3 player for, 158
GoldWave audio editor for, 143, 151
loading from two or more PCs, 307–308
loading music on, 14–15
versus Mac iPods, 7
MP3 TrackMaker utility for, 153
preparing for MUSICMATCH Jukebox Plus Jukebox Plus, 100–102
putting calendars on, 235–236
putting contacts on, 220–221
recording audio on, 145–147
renaming, 138–139
restoring to earlier versions of iPod software, 265
synchronizing MUSICMATCH Jukebox Plus music library with, 132–139
Tag&Rename tag-editing application for, 155–156

TotalRecorder tool for, 159
unmounting, 139
updating, 102, 263–265
Windows Media Player, copying data with, 41
Windows XP
 Backup Utility in, 280
 Disk Defragmenter for, 281–282
 making hidden folders visible in, 312–314
 restoring iPods on, 331–333
 updating Windows iPods on, 263–265
WiPods. *See* Windows iPods
WMA (Windows Media Audio) digital audio format, explanation of, 38–39
World Travel Adapter Kit, features of, 293

X

XtremeMac Premium iPod Car Charger adapter, features of, 292

Z

Zip Cord Retractable Earbuds, features of, 294

INTERNATIONAL CONTACT INFORMATION

AUSTRALIA
McGraw-Hill Book Company Australia Pty. Ltd.
TEL +61-2-9900-1800
FAX +61-2-9878-8881
http://www.mcgraw-hill.com.au
books-it_sydney@mcgraw-hill.com

CANADA
McGraw-Hill Ryerson Ltd.
TEL +905-430-5000
FAX +905-430-5020
http://www.mcgraw-hill.ca

GREECE, MIDDLE EAST, & AFRICA
(Excluding South Africa)
McGraw-Hill Hellas
TEL +30-210-6560-990
TEL +30-210-6560-993
TEL +30-210-6560-994
FAX +30-210-6545-525

MEXICO (Also serving Latin America)
McGraw-Hill Interamericana Editores S.A. de C.V.
TEL +525-117-1583
FAX +525-117-1589
http://www.mcgraw-hill.com.mx
fernando_castellanos@mcgraw-hill.com

SINGAPORE (Serving Asia)
McGraw-Hill Book Company
TEL +65-6863-1580
FAX +65-6862-3354
http://www.mcgraw-hill.com.sg
mghasia@mcgraw-hill.com

SOUTH AFRICA
McGraw-Hill South Africa
TEL +27-11-622-7512
FAX +27-11-622-9045
robyn_swanepoel@mcgraw-hill.com

SPAIN
McGraw-Hill/Interamericana de España, S.A.U.
TEL +34-91-180-3000
FAX +34-91-372-8513
http://www.mcgraw-hill.es
professional@mcgraw-hill.es

UNITED KINGDOM, NORTHERN, EASTERN, & CENTRAL EUROPE
McGraw-Hill Education Europe
TEL +44-1-628-502500
FAX +44-1-628-770224
http://www.mcgraw-hill.co.uk
computing_europe@mcgraw-hill.com

ALL OTHER INQUIRIES Contact:
McGraw-Hill/Osborne
TEL +1-510-420-7700
FAX +1-510-420-7703
http://www.osborne.com
omg_international@mcgraw-hill.com

Know How

How to Do Everything with Your Digital Camera
Second Edition
ISBN: 0-07-222555-6

How to Do Everything with Photoshop Elements 2
ISBN: 0-07-222638-2

How to Do Everything with Photoshop 7
ISBN: 0-07-219554-1

How to Do Everything with Your Sony CLIÉ
ISBN: 0-07-222659-5

How to Do Everything with Macromedia Contribute
0-07-222892-X

How to Do Everything with Your eBay Business
0-07-222948-9

How to Do Everything with Your Tablet PC
ISBN: 0-07-222771-0

How to Do Everything with Your iPod
ISBN: 0-07-222700-1

How to Do Everything with Your iMac,
Third Edition
ISBN: 0-07-213172-1

How to Do Everything with Your iPAQ Pocket PC
Second Edition
ISBN: 0-07-222950-0

OSBORNE DELIVERS RESULTS!

McGraw Hill

OSBORNE
www.osborne.com